D1251665

WITHDRAWN

OXFORD MODERN LANGUAGES AND LITERATURE MONOGRAPHS

Editorial Committee

ARIADNE AUF NAXOS

by
Hugo von Hofmannsthal and Richard Strauss

ITS GENESIS AND MEANING

KAREN FORSYTH

OXFORD UNIVERSITY PRESS
1982

Oxford University Press, Walton Street, Oxford OX2 6DP

London Glasgow New York Toronto
Delhi Bombay Calcutta Madras Karachi
Kuala Lumpur Singapore Hong Kong Tokyo
Nairobi Dar es Salaam Cape Town
Melbourne Auckland

and associate companies in
Beirut Berlin Ibadan Mexico City

Published in the United States by
Oxford University Press, New York

British Library Cataloguing in Publication Data

Forsyth, Karen
Ariadne auf Naxos by Hugo von Hofmannsthal
and Richard Strauss. – (Oxford modern languages
and literature monographs)
1. Strauss, Richard. Ariadne auf Naxos
I. Title   II. Series
782.1′092′4   ML50.S/

ISBN 0–19–815536–0

Typeset by William Clowes [Beccles] Ltd.
Printed in Great Britain
at the University Press, Oxford
by Eric Buckley
Printer to the University

Preface

The Strauss–Hofmannsthal collaboration is one of the most rewarding subjects for any student of German literature and music, such was the breadth and scope of the two creative personalities at work. The correspondence, that unique and detailed record of their partnership, and other letters and primary documents, allow the student a privileged knowledge of what went into the making of each of their six operas—and, by extension, of what goes into the making of any significant work of art. In this study, because time was limited, I have looked only at *Ariadne auf Naxos.* Each or all of the operas could have been approached profitably in the same way. But the choice of *Ariadne,* with its protracted and difficult genesis, does reflect a fascination with the business of creation and of creative collaboration which I believe I share with many others.

My interest in Strauss and Hofmannsthal dates from the time when, as a student at the University of Western Australia supervised by the late Dr Maurice Benn, I wrote a short dissertation on *Elektra,* the first fruit of the collaboration. Dr Benn guided my early efforts in this field and gave me perspectives and insights for which I am still indebted to him.

This book was originally a doctoral thesis which was submitted in 1979 to the Board of Medieval and Modern Languages. I have revised the text whilst holding a Junior Research Fellowship at St. Hilda's College, Oxford. I should like to express my gratitude to the Hackett Trust of the University of Western Australia, who financed my first three years of research at St. Hilda's College and who enabled me to travel to Germany when necessary. A debt of gratitude is owed to Dr Detlev Lüders of the Freies Deutsches Hochstift in Frankfurt for answering queries about the new Hof-mannsthal edition. Permission to include some of Hof-

83-19

mannsthal's hitherto unpublished notes to *Ariadne* was kindly
granted, in the name of Hofmannsthal's heirs, by Dr Rudolf
Hirsch, also of the Freies Deutsches Hochstift. These notes
are also given in an Appendix. I further acknowledge the
permission of S. Fischer Verlag to reproduce as an Appendix
Hofmannsthal's *Szenarium* to *Ariadne*, of Boosey and Hawkes
Music Publishers Ltd. and Frau Ursula Fürstner to reproduce
the musical extracts, and of the Max–Reinhardt–Forschungs-
und Gedenkstätte to reproduce as a final Appendix the *Ariadne*
playbills.

Professor Peter Branscombe of the University of St.
Andrews, who examined my thesis, made some invaluable
suggestions and gave me some new information which I hope
I have included in my revision in a form that does them
justice. I am indebted to Miss Barbara Levick of St. Hilda's
College and Dr Derrick Puffett of Wolfson College for their
generous and sensible criticisms and corrections of the final
text. Most particularly I wish to thank Mr Gilbert McKay of
St. Peter's College, Oxford, for his sensitive and thoughtful
supervision of my thesis and for his kindness and personal
encouragement.

St. Hilda's College, Oxford   K.F.

Contents

List of Abbreviations and a Note on the Translations

Reference is made throughout to Hugo von Hofmannsthal, *Gesammelte Werke in Einzelausgabe,* edited by Herbert Steiner, 15 vols. (Frankfurt am Main, 1945 ff.)

Auf.	Aufzeichnungen, 1959
Ez.	Die Erzählungen, 1953
GuLD	Gedichte und Lyrische Dramen, 1963
DII	Dramen II, 1954
LII	Lustspiele II, 1954
LIII	Lustspiele III, 1956
PI	Prosa I, 1950
PII	Prosa II, 1951
PIII	Prosa III, 1952
PIV	Prosa IV, 1955
Bw.	Richard Strauss / Hugo von Hofmannsthal, *Briefwechsel: Gesamtausgabe,* edited by Franz and Alice Strauss, revised by Willi Schuh (Zurich, 1954)

For quotations from the Strauss–Hofmannsthal correspondence I have used the English translation by Hanns Hammelmann and Ewald Osers (see bibliography). The translations of Goethe's *Faust* are by John Shawcross (London, 1959). Otherwise the translations are my own and I assume full responsibility for any errors or infelicities of style.

Introduction

There are a number of reasons for singling out *Ariadne auf Naxos* for special study from amongst the six Strauss–Hofmannsthal progeny. First there are reasons of scholarship, and second there is the significant position of this opera within the collaboration.

The reasons of scholarship derive from the continued existence of certain critical difficulties relating to *Ariadne*. General coverage of the Strauss–Hofmannsthal œuvre is in the main most adequate. Norman Del Mar's excellent three-volume study *Richard Strauss: A Critical Commentary on his Life and Works* has invaluable chapters on each of the operas written with Hofmannsthal, although it exhibits an occasional bias in Strauss's favour.[1] William Mann's *Richard Strauss: A Critical Study of the Operas* provides alternative interpretations but is not always as reliable as Del Mar. An earlier work, Ernst Krause's *Richard Strauss: Gestalt und Werk* is lacking in the detail, both musical and literary, which makes a study definitive; incidentally it spreads the misconception that *Ariadne auf Naxos* is a serene, classical product of the 'Grecian Strauss'.[2] Other studies such as Willi Schuh's *Hugo von Hofmannsthal und Richard Strauss: Legende und Wirklichkeit* and Karl-Joachim Krüger's *Hugo von Hofmannsthal und Richard Strauss* (which although written in 1935 is still a basic text on the subject) do much to promote an accurate view of the collaboration and to redress the balance.

But there is also a place for single full-length studies on each

[1] Full publication details of works referred to in the Notes are given in the Bibliography unless the work is of a general nature or the bibliographical information is considered relevant to the text. In all other cases the work is referred to by its author and title except for those works most frequently referred to, which after the first citation are known by the author's name only or, where more than one work by the author has been cited, by the author's name and the title.

[2] Ernst Krause, *Richard Strauss: Gestalt und Werk*, pp. 367–79.

of the operas. Rudolf Schäfer has written an authoritative monograph on *Hugo von Hofmannsthals 'Arabella'*, and Eve-Maria Lenz another on *Hugo von Hofmannsthals mythologische Oper 'Die ägyptische Helena'*. Needless to say *Der Rosenkavalier* has received loving attention[3] and *Die Frau ohne Schatten* has been discussed both as an opera and as an 'Erzählung'.[4] *Elektra*, the first of the six, does not fit into quite the same category as it was originally written as an independent stage play by Hofmannsthal, yet, although there is no monograph on it, there is no shortage of penetrating analysis either.[5]

But, despite there being three full-length studies on *Ariadne auf Naxos*, two very sound unpublished theses in German by W. Stiegele[6] and Karl Dietrich Gräwe,[7] and one joint work in English by Donald G. Daviau and George J. Buelow,[8] as well as a number of articles and other sources of information, this undoubtedly remains a puzzling work. All three studies founder finally on the difficulty of resolving meaning and form in *Ariadne*. Although each presents invaluable information and individual insights, none is detached enough either from the traditional 'meaning' of the piece to recognize where this meaning is at odds with its form or from the more recent interpretation of the meaning which has swung so far in the opposite direction that form is synonymous with meaning, and received 'meaning' thus becomes superfluous.

[3] e.g. K. Pörnbacher, *Hugo von Hofmannsthal, Richard Strauss: Der Rosenkavalier: Interpretation*. Willi Schuh, *Der Rosenkavalier: Vier Studien*.

[4] e.g. Sherrill Hahn Pantle, '*Die Frau ohne Schatten' by Hugo von Hofmannsthal and Richard Strauss: An Analysis of Text, Music and their Relationship*. Jakob Knaus, *Hofmannsthals Weg zur Oper: 'Die Frau ohne Schatten'*. Belma Çakmur, *Hofmannsthals Erzählung 'Die Frau ohne Schatten'*.

[5] e.g. Elisabeth Steingruber, *Hugo von Hofmannsthals Sophokleische Dramen*. Gerhart Baumann, 'Hugo von Hofmannsthal: "Elektra"'.

[6] Waltraud Stiegele, 'Hugo von Hofmannsthals "Ariadne auf Naxos. Zu spielen nach dem Bürger als Edelmann des Molière": Entstehungsgeschichte und Metamorphosen'.

[7] Karl Dietrich Gräwe, 'Sprache, Musik und Szene in "Ariadne auf Naxos" von Hugo von Hofmannsthal und Richard Strauss'.

[8] Donald G. Daviau and George J. Buelow, *The 'Ariadne auf Naxos' of Hugo von Hofmannsthal and Richard Strauss*. Whilst Daviau and Buelow have gathered a mass of interesting information and opinion on *Ariadne* and make a valuable contribution with their thorough and sensitive musical analysis, their work suffers from not having a thesis. As a result the authors pass judgement on many separate facets of the whole without arriving at a thoroughly synthesized conclusion—a hazard of collaboration, perhaps?

Traditional *Ariadne* criticism has focused on the theme of 'Verwandlung', or what Hofmannsthal calls allomatic transformation, which might be described as the mutual transformation of two individuals, here Ariadne and Bacchus, through their love for each other. It is thus also concerned with the emotional and spiritual rebirth of the individual in love and so touches on the related Hofmannsthalian themes of fidelity and memory. These themes are best and most beautifully expressed in the so-called *Ariadne Brief* which has been ranked as one of the 'Meisterwerke deutscher Prosa',[9] and in Hofmannsthal's literary diary *Ad me ipsum*. The *Ariadne Brief*[10] is an edited version of a letter to Strauss of mid-July 1911 which was first published in the *Almanach für die musikalische Welt* (Berlin, 1912) with the express intention of enlightening the critics and preparing the ground for the October première.

This thematic constellation is treated in a symbolic, mythological manner, and given a literary form closely related to Hofmannsthal's early lyric drama in which meaning and form are happily married. The 'lyric drama' *Ariadne auf Naxos* concentrates on the heroic characters, Ariadne and Bacchus, who are part of an *opera seria* company and whose spiritual apotheosis concludes the work, and uses the other group, the *commedia dell'arte,* as light relief. Grete Schaeder is one of the few critics to notice the resemblance which *Ariadne auf Naxos* bears to the lyric drama and this she mentions only in passing.[11] But *Ariadne* is something else besides, and it is

[9] Oskar Jancke, *Kunst und Reichtum deutscher Prosa: Von Lessing bis Thomas Mann* (Munich, 1954), p. 404.

[10] PIII, pp. 138–42.

[11] 'In "Ariadne auf Naxos", mit der Hofmannsthal zum lyrischen Drama, der Stilform seiner Jugend zurückkehrt, hat der Dichter mehr versteckt, als das anmutige und geistvolle Gebilde auf den ersten Blick erraten läßt.' Grete Schaeder, *Hugo von Hofmannsthal und Goethe,* p. 55. Schaeder is referring to the hidden profundities of the transformation theme which she sees as the kernel of this lyric-dramatic libretto, and is particularly concerned with the theme's Goethean qualities of purification and elevation: 'Die reinigende, zu göttlichem Leben emporziehende Kraft der Liebe, diese wunderbare Gewißheit, von der Goethe seit jeher durchdrungen war, wird hier zum erstenmal in Hofmannsthals Werk als eine Lebensmacht offenbart. "Ariadne" bedeutet Überwindung des Todes durch die Liebe, die Musik, von der sie erfüllt ist, strömt zum Leben hin und läßt den Tod hinter sich'. Schaeder, p. 56. Karl Naef likewise claims that with *Ariadne* Hofmannsthal moved forward into 'eine gereinigte Verwandlungs- und Läuterungswelt'. Karl Naef, *Hugo von Hofmannsthal,* p. 164. In both these critics the limitations of the 'lyric-dramatic' interpretation and its bias towards an *Ariadne Brief* type appreciation of the opera are apparent.

the failure to discern a very different form beneath the 'lyric drama' which further indicts the traditional approach. A contribution of this thesis is, I believe, that it draws attention to this other, earlier, form, namely to the ironic allegory on the resolution of opposites, in this case the opposite abstract virtues of fidelity and infidelity. This allegoric form was chosen by Hofmannsthal as historically appropriate for the short, recreated Molièresque divertissement with music by Strauss, which was to be performed after his own two-act adaptation of Molière's *Le Bourgeois Gentilhomme* in over-all imitation of the *comédie-ballet* format, for his friend and colleague Max Reinhardt. The essence of this allegory is that both groups, the *opera seria* and the *opera buffa,* should come together at the end in a state of ironic, but amicable, mutual non-comprehension. These two forms, the 'lyric drama' and the allegory, are then most at odds in the final section of the opera where the work is torn apart as a result of not being either one thing or the other and is just patched up by Strauss's and Hofmannsthal's unsparing efforts. The symbolic meaning is thus threatened by a meaning inherent in a form not its own.

Recent *Ariadne* criticism has, understandably, questioned the much-quoted *Ariadne Brief's* claim to be the final word. Instead, it has emphasized and thoroughly examined form from a number of angles, not least among them the historical. Leonhard M. Fiedler's *Hugo von Hofmannsthals Molière-Bearbeitungen: Die Erneuerung der comédie-ballet auf Max Reinhardts Bühnen* (1974), with its mass of historical detail showing the authenticity of Hofmannsthal's adaptations and recreations, has made possible parts of this present study. But as Fiedler himself acknowledges, his method extends our factual knowledge about *Ariadne* without seriously interpreting it.[12] Historical background establishes beyond doubt that, in the 1912 version at least, Hofmannsthal is using the *comédie-ballet* as his model. W. Stiegele likewise recognizes Molière as the formal prototype but misses the significance of the

---

[12] 'Die folgenden Hinweise auf den Zusammenhang zwischen den einzelnen Komponenten von Hofmannsthals "Ariadne"-Oper und dem Theater der Molièr-eschen Zeit, auf Parallelen, Übereinstimmungen und offensichtliche Übernahmen, sind als notwendige Ergänzung zu den zahlreichen vorliegenden Untersuchungen des Librettos gedacht, nicht als Gesamtinterpretation des Werks.' Fiedler, p. 66.

divertissement and falls short on some points of interpretation. The extreme end of the formal school is represented by Barbara Könneker in her article 'Die Funktion des Vorspiels in Hofmannsthals *Ariadne auf Naxos*' in which she goes so far as to assert that Hofmannsthal's meaning was other than what he said it was in the *Ariadne Brief*.[13] In place of 'meaning' Könneker and those whom she represents[14] substitute form: it is proposed that *Ariadne auf Naxos* is an example of deliberate aesthetic play in which historically and stylistically disparate elements are juxtaposed in an arbitrary fashion. The audience has to make a broad synthesis of the material and so its attention is drawn to broader perspectives and insights supposedly more in keeping with our modern, complex, pluralist reality. The juxtaposition is also intended ironically, just as the synthesis, or 'truth', it arrives at is ironic; it consists in an equipoise of opposite impulses, and so I refer to this aesthetic procedure as 'formal irony'. In it, meaning *per se* is not important, although it *is* important when juxtaposed. If both the historicism and the traditional symbolism of *Ariadne*

---

[13] In order to substantiate her argument Könneker has to make Hofmannsthal write the letter for other than exegetic reasons. She suggests that Hofmannsthal deliberately brought out the theme of transformation in his letter because it was an easily comprehensible idea which he could dangle like a carrot before the obtuse Strauss whilst he got on behind the other's back with his subtle new literary experiments. Könneker, p. 126. This argument is contrived and ignores Hofmannsthal's commitment to the conventional, symbolic meaning of his libretto.

[14] Gräwe foreshadows Könneker's formal interpretation. For example, he refers to *Ariadne* as 'Hofmannsthals Montage aus Heroen-Oper und Commedia dell'arte'. Gräwe, p. 72. He further postulates juxtaposition as a 'Stilprinzip' governing the mix-up of the 'zweier a priori disparater Welten'. Gräwe, p. 102. But Gräwe is unable to sustain this interpretation and gives an orthodox reading of the transformation theme in his third Chapter 'Hofmannsthals Ariadne-Dichtung: Zur Deutung ihres Inhalts', pp. 82–105. Günther Erken proposes a technique of deliberate contrast in which styles, worlds, and characters set one another off and also form an ironic unity: 'In solchen spiegelgenau aufeinander abgestellten Kontrasten entfaltet Hofmannsthal die "abgrundtiefen Widersprüche" des Lebens (PIII 138) und bändigt sie doch zugleich in einer ironischen "Harmonie"'. Günther Erken, *Hofmannsthals dramatischer Stil: Untersuchungen zur Symbolik und Dramaturgie*, p. 115. At the end of his book Fiedler ventures to suggest a similar, but not identical, formal procedure. Fiedler argues that in his Molière adaptations Hofmannsthal uses the appearance of historical authenticity as an ironic guise for his own most personal core. Whilst this involves a juxtaposition of the modern and the historical with an ironic end in mind this suggested procedure differs from Könneker's in so far as the reason behind it is ironic disguise rather than the wish to make the audience synthesize disparate juxtaposed material. Fiedler, p. 136.

could be dismissed, then an interpretation in these terms would allow us to bypass the problems already mentioned and would bestow upon the work that unity of meaning and form otherwise felt to be lacking.

Meanwhile it has become apparent that the issue of artistic unity is the stumbling-block of *Ariadne* criticism and that in trying to resolve it many apparently contradictory approaches have been taken. A way out of this critical impasse is to adopt the relative detachment of the genetic approach. This approach has not previously been exploited to the full in connection with *Ariadne* and yet in some respects it is the most obvious for, among all the six operas, *Ariadne* was unique in its protracted and traumatic birth, and although this only lasted from 1911 to 1916, making comparison with, for example, the marathon genesis of Goethe's *Faust* out of place, yet it shares precisely those problems of unity to which all works evolving in this way are susceptible. It should be stressed here that the genetic method is not always likely to be fruitful and can even be inappropriate, as it would be with, for example, Kafka's short story *Das Urteil*. But here circumstances were such that we understand more both about the work and about its criticism if we also know its history. Understanding should not, however, be confused with aesthetic appreciation, although it may enhance it, and *Ariadne auf Naxos* must finally stand or fall in performance. The intrinsic merits which have kept it standing for the last sixty years, as well as the weaknesses, are discussed as they present themselves. Finally, the genetic approach has been supplemented by something more 'werkimmanent' in those chapters where it has seemed called for.

As may already have been guessed, the genesis of *Ariadne auf Naxos* is largely one of stratification. The 'lyric drama' and the allegory are only two of the strata laid over one another. These strata can best be observed by means of a chronology of composition and intention, realized, modified, or abandoned. The intentional fallacy, that *bête noire* of the genetic method, is hard to commit with *Ariadne* for there is scarcely one intention that did not leave its mark. In presenting the chronological development of some characters and themes a number of Hofmannsthal's unpublished notes, not previously given in an English work on *Ariadne,* have been heavily drawn upon.[15]

The genesis helps to sort out critical tangles because it draws attention to the existence and relationship of the two versions of *Ariadne.* The first version, completed in 1912, is attached to Molière's *Le Bourgeois Gentilhomme.* The second version, completed in 1916, is freed from the Molière and in its place Strauss and Hofmannsthal put their original *Vorspiel.* With the act of cutting *Ariadne* loose from Molière, historicism and symbolism are demoted to the lower ranks, making it possible to interpret the 1916 *Ariadne* in terms of formal irony. For the 1912 *Ariadne* only, more traditional methods are in order— and certain formal problems do remain. The mistake made by Könneker and those she represents is not in their actual interpretation but in the indiscriminate application of it to the two versions whose edges they have blurred.

These then are the reasons of scholarship and criticism for studying *Ariadne auf Naxos.* The second set of reasons relates to the position of this opera within the collaboration. Pivotal as this position may be, it is wrong to make too much of it. Daviau and Buelow claim, for example, that *Ariadne* was the first real fruit of the collaboration; *Elektra* and *Der Rosenkavalier* were written, according to them, as independent plays.[16] Peter Stenberg rightly points out that this is misleading, especially in regard to *Der Rosenkavalier,* which was conceived of as a libretto and was just as much a joint effort as *Ariadne,* although there is not the same intensive discussion of it in the correspondence—which means incidentally that a study of *Ariadne* reveals more about the collaboration.[17]

But *Ariadne* is important within the collaboration, not because its authors were trying to work more closely or to

[15] These notes are reproduced in Appendix A. Access to the unpublished source material to *Ariadne auf Naxos* was not granted to me. Dr Detlev Lüders Director of the Freies Deutsches Hochstift regretted that the *Ariadne* material was needed for a volume of the new critical edition, which Dr Lüders informs me is to appear in 1983 and is to be published by S. Fischer Verlag. I have therefore had to rely on Waltraud Stiegele for these notes. Dr Rudolf Hirsch, also of the Freies Deutsches Hochstift, has kindly checked Miss Stiegele's transcriptions against the Hofmannsthal originals at my request and has informed me of a number of errors and omissions, which I have duly corrected.

[16] Daviau and Buelow, p. 3.

[17] Peter A. Stenberg, 'Ariadne auf Naxos', p. 193.

produce something novel but, ironically enough, because they regarded it as a trifle, a 'Zwischenarbeit'[18] to fill in the time between major ventures. By regarding it thus, Hofmannsthal in particular gave himself, so to speak, a 'breathing-space', an opportunity to question and experiment which his exacting conscience might otherwise not have permitted him, particularly in an artistic partnership with a composer as world-famous as Richard Strauss, a man who was, furthermore, ten years his senior, and who was known to await new libretti with avid impatience. Whilst Strauss was still impatient for the *Ariadne* libretto the pressure was off to some extent (though not the pressure of time), and *both* partners, led perhaps by the analytic, introspective Hofmannsthal, were in the mood for assessing their progress to date and considering future directions.

At the centre of their deliberations was the age-old question of the relationship of word and music in opera. Hofmannsthal naturally fought for the audibility of his text. This had been a sore point with *Elektra:* in Strauss's own early estimate two thirds of the words are lost in opera. *Der Rosenkavalier* saw an improvement and Hofmannsthal wrote that as a fusion of word and music it satisfied him 'zwar *recht sehr,* aber nicht völlig' (Bw. 20 Mar. 1911, pp. 96–7). Hofmannsthal, who was in any case an anti-Wagnerian (indeed he once said that Beethoven was the last of the great masters), decided that the fault lay in the Wagnerian orchestration and mould of their previous efforts, and chose to combat this evil by returning to the older Mozartian set number opera with its clear divisions between recitative and aria which is one method of saving the word from being drowned in the music. Hofmannsthal interpreted *Der Rosenkavalier* as pointing in this direction and compared it to *Figaro.* The next major venture, already planned, was to be *Die Frau ohne Schatten,* which he compared to *Die Zauberflöte.*[19] *Ariadne* clearly was seen as a stepping-stone in this Mozartian progression.

[18] Bw. 20 Mar. 1911, p. 96. All further references to the Strauss/Hofmannsthal *Briefwechsel* are given after quotations in the text.

[19] Referring to 'Das steinerne Herz', the early name for *Die Frau ohne Schatten,* Hofmannsthal wrote 'Das Ganze . . . verhielte sich, beiläufig gesagt, zur "Zauberflöte" so wie der "Rosenkavalier" zum "Figaro", d.h. es bestände hier wie dort keine Nachahmung, aber eine gewisse Analogie.' Bw. 20 Mar. 1911, p. 96.

Strauss was ready to follow this lead. Hans Mayer, in one of his typically spiteful, but amusing, exaggerations, finds that Mozart was the only thing that Strauss and Hofmannsthal had in common.[20] Certainly there were other things, but Mozart ranked highly among them and the beginning of the period of Strauss's greatest affinity with Mozart predates *Ariadne* by a year. Willi Schuh first drew attention to the Mozart-Wagner polarity in the preface to his *Über Opern von Richard Strauss.* In an article 'Das "Mozart-Wagner-Element" im Schaffen von Richard Strauss' Hermann Fähnrich takes up this theme and divides Strauss's creative life accordingly into four distinct phases:

1. Epoche (1885–1910): Das Wagner-Element dominiert. Strauss tritt die Nachfolge Wagners im eigenen Geiste an.
2. Epoche (1910–1929): Das Mozart-Element dominiert. Strauss' Wandlung zur Tradition, als Keimkraft künftigen Schaffens.
3. Zwischenepoche (1929–1931): Vorstufe zur Synthese beider Elemente.
4. Epoche (1931–1949): Die Synthese beider Elemente in den letzten Werken des Meisters.[21]

(1. Epoch (1885–1910): The Wagner element dominates. Strauss adapts Wagner to his own intellectual needs.
2. Epoch (1910–1929): The Mozart element dominates. Strauss turns to tradition as the source of future creativity.

---

[20] The climax of Mayer's notorious attack on the collaboration is given here: 'Welche Diskrepanz! Der Augenmensch Hofmannsthal und der bayrische Musikant. Anfälligkeit und Robustheit. Ständiger Hang zum Verstummen und ständiger Hang zum Überlauten. Mißtrauen gegen künstlerische Techniken und Tendenz zur Virtuosität. Bei Hofmannsthal: unablässige Bemühung, durch Schweigen und Verschweigen das auszusagen, was gesagt werden soll . . . Bei Strauss umgekehrt: der fatale Hang, doch wieder mit blökenden Schafen, Kuhglocken, vertonten Skatgeräuschen in den Naturalismus zurückzukehren. Blieb Mozart. Hier fanden sich beide.' Hans Mayer, 'Hugo von Hofmannsthal und Richard Strauss', pp. 11–12.

[21] Hermann Fähnrich, 'Das "Mozart-Wagner-Element" im Schaffen von Richard Strauss', p. 313.

3. Intermediate epoch (1929–1931): First steps towards a synthesis of both elements.
4. Epoch (1931–1949): Synthesis of both elements in the last works of the master.)

We see then how *Der Rosenkavalier* was transitional and how *Ariadne* coincided with Strauss's own development and presaged the so-called neo-classicism of the late works. The ideal of the 'Mozartian' opera was not, however, realized by Hofmannsthal and Strauss, and *Ariadne* with its pellucid melodies, chamber orchestra and smaller dimensions is as close to it as they come, as well as being a definite forerunner of such neo-classical works as Stravinsky's ballet *Pulcinella* (after Pergolesi), produced in 1920, or his *Rake's Progress*, 1951. It was not until *Capriccio*, written with Clemens Krauss in 1942, that Strauss achieved a complete and personal synthesis of styles.

But the fault did not lie with Strauss alone. In order to write operas of Mozartian type Strauss needed a certain kind of libretto typified by simplicity, clear-cut action and characters, and attractive verse. Hofmannsthal, however, continued to provide him with libretti that tended to be too literary and that were laden with esoteric symbols and subtle psychological complexities, although the poetry was always of a high standard and invariably extremely 'composable'. It seems to have been a kind of rule with Strauss that, even in *Ariadne,* the psychological symbolism of what Peter Conrad calls Hofmannsthal's 'novelistic' libretti[22] called forth Strauss's Wagnerian strain. The neo-classical parts of *Ariadne* coincide without exception with the non-symbolic Molière and *commedia dell'arte* sections.

Thus Hofmannsthal's attempts at the time of writing *Ariadne auf Naxos* to redefine and reshape the libretto were not entirely successful. The pull in *Ariadne* between what was

[22] Conrad's thesis is that 'opera's actual literary analogue is the novel'. We need only note that by 'novelistic' Conrad means passive, internal, meditative and psychological. The antithesis to 'novelistic' is 'dramatic', namely active, external, non-reflective. Having defined his terms thus, Conrad is entitled to call Hofmannsthal's libretti 'novelistic', but this is no longer a radical assertion. Peter Conrad, *Romantic Opera and Literary Form*, p. 1.

over-literary and what was good theatre is symptomatic of a dualism in the libretti still to come.

Although *Ariadne* does not represent a coherent development or radical breakthrough in the Strauss-Hofmannsthal collaboration it shows, most clearly of all their operas, the artistic questions behind their efforts and the boundaries of the tradition within which they worked, a tradition which was beyond doubt conservative. Strauss has been called the last of the great Romantics[23] and Hofmannsthal became one of *the* conservative figures of Austrian cultural history;[24] but this 'conservatism' was kept alive and full of productive tensions by the questions and experiments that took place during the frustrating and stimulating years of the genesis of *Ariadne*.

Our investigations will be made easier if at this point dates, full titles and other details of all the works which sprang up out of the *Ariadne* idea are given. The first was the 1912 version of the opera whose full title runs *Ariadne auf Naxos: Oper in einem Aufzuge von Hugo von Hofmannsthal und Richard Strauss: Zu spielen nach dem 'Bürger als Edelmann' des Molière*. Adolph Fürstner was given the copyright to the score and the libretto.[25] The 1916 version is entitled *Ariadne auf Naxos: Oper in einem Aufzuge nebst einem Vorspiel von Hugo von Hofmannsthal: Neue Bearbeitung: Musik von Richard Strauss. Op.60*.[26] Both these versions are considered, and details of their premières are given as appendices. The 1912 and 1916 libretti can be found in the volume *Lustspiele III* of the *Gesammelte Werke*[27] and all quotations are from this edition.

---

[23] George R. Marek, *Richard Strauss: The Life of a Non-Hero*, p. 16.

[24] Central to Hofmannsthal's political and cultural ambitions for Austria was the notion of the 'konservative Revolution' with its literary analogue 'schöpferische Restauration' (PIV, p. 243). For a good discussion of Hofmannsthal's complex relation to tradition see Ralph-Rainer Wuthenow, 'Hugo von Hofmannsthal und die konservative Revolution', *Goethe-Jahrbuch*, 3 (1961), 8–26. Also, Hermann Rudolph, *Kulturkritik und konservative Revolution: Zum kulturell-politischen Denken Hofmannsthals und seinem problemgeschichtlichen Kontext* (Tübingen, 1971).

[25] *Ariadne auf Naxos: Oper in einem Aufzug von Hugo von Hofmannsthal und Richard Strauss: Zu spielen nach dem 'Bürger als Edelmann' des Molière* (Berlin, Paris, 1912).

[26] *Ariadne auf Naxos: Oper in einem Aufzuge nebst einem Vorspiel von Hugo von Hofmannsthal: Neue Bearbeitung: Musik von Richard Strauss. Op.60* (Berlin, Paris, 1916).

[27] *Ariadne auf Naxos* (1912). LIII. pp. 67–161, 35–66. *Ariadne auf Naxos* (1916). LIII, pp. 7–66. An Appendix gives those passages cut from the 1912 version of the *Oper*. LIII, pp. 373–80.

Page numbers are given in brackets immediately after the quotations. A new historical, critical edition is currently appearing but the volume containing *Ariadne auf Naxos* will not be out until 1983.[28] Musical examples are taken from the Boosey and Hawkes piano reductions[29] and numbers are given in brackets after each quotation. The first number refers to Strauss's rehearsal number printed in the score in place of bar numbers and the second, with a plus or minus sign, indicates the number of bars from the rehearsal number at which the quotation begins. The one act opera, *Ariadne auf Naxos,* which is common to the 1912 and 1916 versions is referred to throughout as the *Oper,* as it is in Strauss's score.

It is, however, beyond the scope of this study to consider either the stage play or the orchestral suite which were made as salvage attempts after the 1916 severence of the Molière left much material lying over. Hofmannsthal's stage play was an expansion of his original adaptation of *Le Bourgeois Gentil-homme.* It appeared anonymously in 1918 as an act of homage on Hofmannsthal's part but was not a success.[30] Its full title is *Der Bürger als Edelmann—Komödie mit Tänzen von Molière: Freie Bühnenbearbeitung in drei Aufzügen* and it included Strauss's original incidental music plus further music freshly composed for it.[31]

From this play Strauss drew the music which he made into his nine-movement orchestral suite, *Der Bürger als Edelmann, Op.60,* first performed on 31 January 1920 in Salzburg. This suite has enjoyed lasting success.

The number of works which originated from the *Ariadne* idea reveals both the positive and negative aspects that this material and complex of themes had for its authors: on the one

[28] See Introduction, Note 15.

[29] *Ariadne auf Naxos: Oper in einem Aufzuge von Hugo von Hofmannsthal: Musik von Richard Strauss. Op.60. Zu spielen nach dem 'Bürger als Edelmann' des Molière.* Arrangement von Otto Singer. Vollständiger Klavier-Auszug mit deutschem Text (Berlin, Paris, 1912). *Ariadne auf Naxos: Oper in einem Aufzug nebst einem Vorspiel von Hugo von Hofmannsthal: Neue Bearbeitung: Musik von Richard Strauss. Op.60.* Arrangement von Otto Singer. Vollständiger Klavier-Auszug mit deutschem Text (London, 1944).

[30] For excellent analyses of this adaptation and its lack of success see Stiegele, pp. 89–140 and Fiedler, pp. 68–88.

[31] LIII, pp 243–357. Richard Strauss, *Der Bürger als Edelmann,* Orchestersuite, Op. 60. (Leipzig, 1918).

hand it was rich and rewarding enough to go on yielding a long-term harvest but on the other it frustrated its authors and deprived them of the satisfaction of having 'said it all' in one complete work. The following chapters are confined to the 1912 and 1916 versions; nevertheless the difficulties inherent in this material are not to be overlooked.

Chapter I

Divertissement, Molière, and Historical Authenticity in the 1912 *Ariadne*

i. *The Divertissement Origins of the* Oper

The *Oper Ariadne auf Naxos* is a work which had simple beginnings, indeed simplicity was a *sine qua non* of the original plan. Many of the original intentions were realized and laid down as the first stratum, or substratum. But *Ariadne* was not one of those works which proceed from simple beginnings and surpass themselves in a more or less organic growth into complexity. Instead, further strata were laid over the original, not very strong, foundation, so that the work was built up of different, sometimes contradictory, levels. This gave rise to a number of 'faults'.

The simplicity of the original *Ariadne* plan was in fact twofold: it was to be simple at both the artistic and the technical levels. Its artistic horizons were to be no wider than a Molièresque divertissement, of which it was intended to be an historical and imaginative recreation. The *Oper* realizes these intentions and is historical in the vast amount of historically authentic detail it contains and imaginative in so far as there is no one real model on which the divertissement is based. This means that some aspects are freely found, but even where freely found, such as in the mixing up of *opera seria* and *opera buffa*, they are never improbable or historically inauthentic.

The artistic format of a divertissement during Molière's time was dictated by its function within the newly-emerged *comédie-ballet*. The divertissement was essentially a simple and undramatic vehicle, often structured as a symmetrical allegory of opposing forces finally united, which created a place for ballet, singing, music, and the slapstick of the buffoons.[1] The divertissement was an integral part of the festive *comédie-ballet*, which was the most extravagant entertainment imaginable and therefore popular at the court of Louis XIV. The *comédie-ballet* further found favour because it corresponded to the Baroque ideal of the 'Gesamtkunstwerk'; by including all the performing arts, it corresponds with the modern idea of 'total theatre' with which Hofmannsthal was concerned at the time of writing *Ariadne auf Naxos*.[2] The divertissement must therefore be rather bare of thematic interest and dramatic conflict. There is no place in it for characterization or psychological motivation. It is usually light-hearted and seldom tragic. It is a simple diversion and therefore simplicity is a *sine qua non* of its existence.

But how can we be sure that Hofmannsthal intended the *Oper* to be a recreation of a divertissement? We can judge this in part from the fact that during the early stages of work on *Ariadne* it is repeatedly referred to in the correspondence as a divertissement. In the letter of 15 May 1911 Hofmannsthal writes of their 'opernartiges Divertissement' and of the 'Divertissement "Ariadne auf Naxos"' (Bw. 15 May 1911, p. 99). In the same letter he sends a playbill which is headed 'Divertissement: ARIADNE AUF NAXOS'. The letter of 20 May 1911 refers again to 'unser Divertissement' (Bw. 20 May 1911, p. 101). In an earlier letter of 20 March 1911 the

[1] See Margarete Baur-Heinhold, *Theater des Barock: Festliches Bühnenspiel im 17. und 18. Jahrhundert*, p. 101.

[2] To put it very simply, Hofmannsthal turned to opera and the theatre after the Chandos Crisis made him despair, as Mary Gilbert says, of 'the power of words to mediate reality'. Hofmannsthal, *Selected Essays*, edited by Mary E. Gilbert, p. xxv. In the theatre language can be reinforced by music, dance, mime and stage-setting. These non-conceptual 'Künste . . . , die schweigend ausgeübt werden' (PI, p. 265) were favoured by Hofmannsthal as a way past his difficulties with language and towards a more living, vibrant, sensually appealing art form. Michael Hamburger points out a parallel between Hofmannsthal's libretti and W. B. Yeats' *Plays for Dancers*, likewise late products of the Symbolist tradition, in which mime, music, and mask are fused together. Michael Hamburger, *Hofmannsthal: Three Essays*, p. 7. Others who deal perceptively with this subject are Albin Eduard Beau, 'Hofmannsthals Wendung zur Oper' and Peter A. Stenberg, 'Silence, Ceremony and Song in Hofmannsthal's Libretti'. It is interesting to note that Hofmannsthal did not associate the 'Gesamtkunstwerk' only with Wagner, but knew that opera had always been the kind of 'total theatre' which he was now seeking to imitate: 'Die Oper ist nun einmal ein Gesamtkunstwerk, nicht etwa seit Wagner, der nur alte Welttendenzen sehr kühn und frech subjektivierte, sondern seit ihrer glorreichen Entstehung: seit dem XVII., und kraft ihrer Grundtendenz: Wiedergeburt des antiken Gesamtkunstwerkes zu sein'. Bw. 12 Feb. 1919, p. 374.

divertissement nature of the work is hinted at: ' "Ariadne"
... kann etwas sehr Reizendes werden, ein neues Genre, das
scheinbar auf ein älteres zurückgreift, wie ja alle Entwicklung
sich in der Spirale vollzieht.' (Bw. 20 Mar. 1911, p. 96.)
(*Ariadne* ... can turn into something most charming, a new
genre which to all appearance reaches back to a much earlier
one, just as all development goes in cycles.) Later, when the
full libretto had been completed and the work had become
more than just a divertissement, Hofmannsthal had occasion
to defend the connection with Molière in the 1912 version. He
did this by invoking its cultural and historical authenticity as
a divertissement:

Die ganze Sache ist ja aus den beiden theatralischen Elementen der
Molièreschen Zeit förmlich herausdestilliert, aus der mythologischen
Oper und aus den 'maschere', den tanzenden und singenden
Komödianten-figuren. Lully könnte das vertont, Callot es entworfen
haben. Auf den ersten Blick—wäre man ja nicht einmal überrascht,
dieses ganze Divertissement dem Text, dem authentischen Text,
unserer comédie-ballet 'Bürger als Edelmann' beigedruckt zu sehen.
(Bw. 26 July 1911, p. 123.)

(For the whole affair is after all actually distilled from the two
theatrical elements of Molière's age: from the mythological opera
and from the *maschere*, the dancing and singing comedians. Lully
might have set it to music, Callot might have drawn it. At first sight
indeed one would hardly be surprised to find this whole *divertissement*
printed as part of the text—the original text of our comédie-ballet
Bürger als Edelmann.)

If the nomenclature still leaves us in any doubt about the
nature of *Ariadne auf Naxos*, we need only look at the genesis
of the original idea for the 1912 version in which the *Oper* is
framed within the Molière play. This project was devised as a
thank-offering to Max Reinhardt for his last-minute help with
the Dresden première of *Der Rosenkavalier* in January 1911.
Hofmannsthal wrote to his father shortly after the première:

Ich fühle mich richtig wohl in dieser Luft des Lebens und der
Möglichkeiten, die mich hier umgibt und besonders Reinhardts
Person und Gegenwart wirkt auf mich immer und unter allen
Umständen unendlich angenehm und belebend. Auch Strauss ist
wirklich fabelhaft nett gegen mich, und geht auf alles ein, was mir

durch den Kopf geht, und da er auch sehr unter dem Charme Reinhardts ist und riesig dankbar für dessen Hilfe in Dresden, so wollen wir zusammen eine ganz kleine Oper nur für Kammermusik machen, die bei Reinhardt als Einlage in ein Schauspiel gespielt werden kann, und zwar werde ich zu diesem Zweck eine Adaptation der charmanten comtesse d'Escarbagnas von Molière machen, eine kleine Zwischenarbeit, die aber sehr wohl dem Reinhardt über eine ganze Saison weghelfen kann.[3]

(I feel very content in this environment, which gives me a sense of life and opportunity; in particular Reinhardt's personal presence has always in any circumstances an infinitely pleasant and stimulating effect on me. Strauss, too, is really fantastically nice to me and shows an interest in all the ideas which run through my head. And since he is also much captivated by Reinhardt's charm and is tremendously grateful for his help in Dresden we have decided to write a very small chamber opera, which Reinhardt could use as an intermezzo in a play and indeed to this end I shall make an adaptation of the charming comtesse d'Escarbagnas by Molière, a little interim work, which could, however, very well help Reinhardt out over a whole season.)

The scheme is a clever one for it fulfils so many functions. In a sense Hofmannsthal is able to combine in it his two major collaborations; the one with Reinhardt (and through Reinhardt with Molière) and the other with Richard Strauss. In this combination of opera and play all three are brought together; Strauss furthermore has the opportunity of expressing *his* gratitude to Reinhardt. It was a plan which gave each person something to do which he liked. Strauss could compose some attractive music, Hofmannsthal could practise libretto writing and also adapt a Molière play, and Reinhardt could produce a Molière at his *Deutsches Theater* with a crowd-drawing Strauss-Hofmannsthal opera to assure him of its success for a season.

Molière figures largely in the scheme. Some background information is needed if we are to see why this playwright was so important to Reinhardt and Hofmannsthal. In many ways there could not have been a more fitting choice, for Hofmannsthal had become interested in Molière as part of his

---

[3] Hofmannsthal's letter to his father, Berlin, January 1911. First published in Leonhard M. Fiedler, *Max Reinhardt und Molière*, pp. 9–10.

apprenticeship to the comic theatre and in conjunction with his working relationship with Reinhardt. Victor A. Oswald, Jr., reckons that Hofmannsthal's interest in Molière dates from 1909, at which time he was struggling to find an appropriate dénouement for the intricate comedy *Cristinas Heimreise* and had laid aside *Sylvia im 'Stern'* for much the same reason.[4] He was also busy turning the scenario of *Der Rosenkavalier* into a 'Komödie für Musik'. In the midst of these labours he suddenly undertook to make a literal translation of Molière's one act play *Le Mariage Forcé*. This translation was done at Reinhardt's request, for the latter was keen to attempt a Molière revival in his own theatre, and indeed Hofmannsthal's translation entitled *Die Heirat wider Willen* was performed in October 1911 in Reinhardt's Berlin *Kammerspiele*. When *Der Rosenkavalier* was again taken up, there is much evidence that Hofmannsthal had taken the opportunity of refreshing his memory of other Molière plays. *Monsieur de Pourceaugnac*, *Les Fourberies de Scapin* and *Le Bourgeois Gentilhomme* all contributed to the plot and to the characterization of Baron Ochs auf Lerchenau in particular. It is also a well-known fact that the words of the Italian tenor's aria sung during the Marschallin's levee are lifted entirely from the concluding ballet of *Le Bourgeois Gentilhomme*, thereby linking, as if by some strange premonition, the emergent Strauss-Hofmannsthal set number opera with the name of Molière. In the successful handling of the comic plot in *Der Rosenkavalier* there is further ample evidence that Hofmannsthal profited from his sudden excursion into seventeenth-century French comedy.

Apart from his desire to improve his mastery of comic techniques, Hofmannsthal was drawn to Molière with the idea of effecting a revival. In the nineteenth and early twentieth centuries Molière was very much neglected in the German-speaking world. Hofmannsthal as an accomplished Romanist was fully aware of this injustice. On 26 Dec. 1911 he wrote in connection with *Ariadne* 'Bisher existierte Molière auf der deutschen Bühne nicht—wurde ausschließlich zu Tode gespielt.' (Bw. 26 Dec. 1911, p. 135.) (Hitherto Molière has never really existed on the German stage: he has invariably been

[4] Victor A. Oswald, Jr., 'Hofmannsthal's Collaboration with Molière', p. 19.

flogged to death.) Fifteen years later Hofmannsthal could write 'Jetzt ist Molière auf den deutschen Bühnen im Aufleuchten wie eine frisch angefachte Kohle.'[5] (Now on the German stage Molière has caught fire like a freshly fanned coal.) Other than those works already mentioned, Hofmannsthal made a translation, *Die Gräfin von Escarbagnas*, never performed; a concluding ballet for this, *Die Schäferinnen*, which was used instead in Reinhardt's 1916 production of the *Eingebildeter Kranke* (not translated by Hofmannsthal, although he attended rehearsals and tried his hand at one scene);[6] and an early framework for *Ariadne auf Naxos*, also based on *La Comtesse d'Escarbagnas* and known as *Die kluge Gräfin*,[7] which remained a sketch. Then there was the constellation of works which formed the 1912 *Ariadne* and the 1917–18 *Bürger als Edelmann* adaptation; this was a not entirely successful attempt to make an independent work of the earlier two-act version, so saving Strauss's delightful incidental music. Lastly there was the free adaptation of *Les Fâcheux* entitled *Die Lästigen* (1916) which became a source for *Der Schwierige* and for which Hofmannsthal wrote a concluding ballet, *Die grüne Flöte*. All these adaptations, sketches, and translations are discussed in Fiedler's excellent book referred to in the Introduction.

Hofmannsthal could not, however, effect a Molière revival on his own. He needed a skilful and imaginative producer. Reinhardt, who was independently interested in Molière, was obviously an ideal partner in this venture. Reinhardt encouraged Hofmannsthal to make the early translations, and in fact all Hofmannsthal's works based on Molière were intended for Max Reinhardt's theatres.[8] The collaboration was a close one, author and producer cross-fertilizing each other to such an extent that Fiedler writes 'Reinhardt wird zum Mitautor—vor allem bei der Ausgestaltung besonders bühnenwirksamer und pantomimisch bestimmter Szenen—, Hofmannsthal zum

---

[5] PIV, p. 264.

[6] Molière, *Der Eingebildete Kranke* (*sic*), Akt II, Scene 6, translated by Hugo von Hofmannsthal. First published in Fiedler, pp. 157–60.

[7] Later Hofmannsthal referred to this same sketch as *Die artige Gräfin*. Bw. 8 July 1918, p. 350. This was probably a slip of memory.

[8] See Fiedler, p. 12.

Mitregisseur.'[9] (Reinhardt becomes a co-author—particularly when markedly theatrical or pantomimic scenes are being arranged—Hofmannsthal becomes a co-director.)

We can see then that Hofmannsthal's plan of a Molière play plus an opera as he described it to his father was a good one because it fulfilled so many functions. It satisfied the separate creative interests of all three collaborators and was also in harmony with the main objectives of the two different partnerships. In the case of the Hofmannsthal–Reinhardt collaboration it was an opportunity to continue work on Molière.

But was this just an artificial plan devised to suit the particular circumstances of the moment or was there some artistic naturalness and justification for it? I would suggest that the artistic justification lay in the Molièresque model, the *comédie-ballet*, of which the plan is an imitation. In this model both comedy and 'Einlage' have their rightful place. It is significant then that *La Comtesse d'Escarbagnas*, which Hofmannsthal first intended to adapt, and *Le Bourgeois Gentilhomme* are both *comédies-ballets*. It is furthermore significant that, after having dropped *La Comtesse d'Escarbagnas* for reasons which are not quite clear,[10] Hofmannsthal only ever considered Molière's 'minder bekannte . . . Stücke' (Bw. 15 May 1911, p. 99). These were the *comédies-ballets* and not the better known character comedies. If there is still any doubt that the relationship of the *Oper* to *Der Bürger als Edelmann* was that of divertissement to comedy, we need only look at the following extract from a letter to Strauss of 15 May 1911. Hofmannsthal is describing his deliberate search for a suitable

---

[9] Fiedler, p. 10. See also Hofmannsthal's three essays *Reinhardt bei der Arbeit* (Auf., pp. 333–51), *Max Reinhardt* (Auf., pp. 325–33) and *Das Reinhardtsche Theater* (PIII, pp. 429–36).

[10] See Fiedler, pp. 36–7. Performances of Hofmannsthal's adaptation *Die Gräfin von Escarbagnas* were planned by Reinhardt in 1916 and 1918, but did not take place. A short ballet *Die Schäferinnen* which filled the position previously allocated to the divertissement *Ariadne auf Naxos* was, however, performed in March 1916. Hofmannsthal may possibly have rejected *La Comtesse d'Escarbagnas* on the grounds that it is too much a 'Rahmenstück', demanding a complicated arrangement of ballets and divertissements without sufficient strength in the characterization to weld it together. It is interesting to note that the play eventually settled on, *Le Bourgeois Gentilhomme*, has many parallels with *La Comtesse d'Escarbagnas* in which there is a ridiculous countess, a female Jourdain, who mistakenly believes that an evening's entertainment is being put on for her.

Molière: 'Nun aber kommt ein anderes Lied: Ich habe den
Molière zur Hand, immer hatte ich nur an die minder
bekannten seiner Stücke gedacht; in Paris stand es auf einmal
klar vor mir, wie vortrefflich sich der "Bourgeois Gentilhomme" eigne, ein solches opernartiges Divertissement
einzulegen.' (Bw. 15 May 1911, p. 99.)[11] (But now for
something different: I *have* the Molière. I had never thought
of anything except his less well-known plays, but in Paris
suddenly it came to me how splendidly the *Bourgeois
Gentilhomme* would lend itself to the insertion of our operatic
divertissement.)

Later, in one of his increasingly rare moments of critical
understanding of the over-all intention and hence of the
individual parts of the 1912 *Ariadne*, Hofmannsthal acknowledged the importance of the Molière and so indirectly of the
Molièresque model. Strauss had just written slightingly of the
'bißchen Molière' and Hofmannsthal sprang to its defence:
'Das "bißchen Molière" bildet drei Fünftel des Theaterabends,
und ich trage meine Haut dafür zu Markte, denn nur, wenn
das Ganze herauskommt, ist meine Zusammenkoppelung ein
geistreicher Scherz, andernfalls ist sie ein Dreckzeug.' (Bw. 26
Dec. 1911, p. 135.) (This 'little bit of Molière' fills three-fifths
of the whole evening, and on it I am risking my skin—since
this dovetailing of the two works which I have devised will
prove an amusing conceit only if the overall intention comes
out; otherwise it is rubbish.)

In a letter to Princess Marie von Thurn und Taxis written
on 30 July 1912, Hofmannsthal indicates more clearly that this
combination of play and opera has historical origins: 'Ich
würde mich freilich sehr freuen, zu wissen, ob die "Ariadne"
in Ihre Hände gekommen ist und ob Sie den kleinen
Mischmasch von Comödie und Oper—der allerdings seine
historische Rechtfertigung hat—im Ganzen goutiert haben.'[12]
(I would be very glad to know if you received 'Ariadne' and if
on the whole you enjoyed the little hotchpotch of comedy and

---

[11] Stiegele informs us that the Comédie Française did not perform *Le Bourgeois
Gentilhomme* in Paris in 1911. Stiegele, Note 1, p. 19. Thus it appears that
Hofmannsthal's inspiration came from his reading rather than a visit to the theatre,
as might reasonably have been suggested.
[12] Hofmannsthal to Marie von Thurn und Taxis, 30 Juli 1912. From an unpublished
letter reproduced by Stiegele, Note 1, p. 10.

opera—which does as a matter of fact have an historical justification.)

A further source which acknowledges the debt to Molière and yet one which is scarcely ever cited in critical literature on *Ariadne auf Naxos* is Hofmannsthal's own essay *Ce que nous avons voulu en écrivant 'Ariane à Naxos'* (1912).[13] This essay was written by Hofmannsthal with the express purpose of placating the French literary and musical worlds for having tampered with those sacrosanct national institutions, Molière and Lully.[14] But even taking into account that Hofmannsthal was thus playing down the problematic Hofmannsthalian elements which later crept into the libretto, the essay is still a valid indication that Hofmannsthal was aware of the over-all form and divertissement nature of *Ariadne auf Naxos*. It is unfortunate that this awareness became more and more obscured in the middle and latter stages of the work's genesis and also in Hofmannsthal's critical writings, including letters. But perhaps he was able to refocus, as he does in this essay, when forced for the sake of a foreign audience to approach the work from a broader perspective. Whatever the case, in the essay Hofmannsthal clearly states the relation of *Ariadne*—'un divertissement musical nouveau'—to the *Bourgeois Gentilhomme*; he speaks of it as a substitute for the original divertissement, 'Le Ballet des Nations', and stresses its simplicity without deliberate irony or misrepresentation: 'A la place de ce ballet, nous avons cru pouvoir ... présenter un petit opéra dans le goût ancien, où un compositeur moderne put trouver occasion d'animer un sujet très simple par des moyens très réduits.'[15] (In place of this ballet we thought we could ... present a little opera in the early style, in which a modern composer could have an opportunity of bringing a very simple subject to life using very reduced means.)

[13] PIII, p. 135–7. First published in the *Revue musicale de la Société Internationale de Musique*, 9–10 (1912), p. 17–20. Later published in *Neue Freie Presse* on 26 May 1912 in a shortened form with the title *Ariadne auf Naxos* as an introduction accompanying the libretto. This version is also in PIII, pp. 133–4.

[14] Hofmannsthal was particularly anxious about *Ariadne*'s future reception in France 'wo gerade dieses Werk, schon wegen des sakrosankten Molière, von allen Ländern der Welt die geringsten Chancen hat'. Bw. 18 Jan 1912, p. 138. He later said that he wrote the essay 'um die französische Musikwelt zu beruhigen'. Bw. 28 June 1912, p. 162.

[15] PIII, p. 135.

So far we have established the intended relationship of the Strauss–Hofmannsthal opera to the Molière. A forerunner in Hofmannsthal's œuvre, which has never been mentioned in connection with *Ariadne*, can be found in the 1909 translation of *Les Fâcheux* bearing the title *Die Heirat wider Willen*, for which Hofmannsthal wrote a scenario for a concluding ballet.[16] We have not, however, established that Hofmannsthal intended an historical and imaginative recreation in the *Oper* itself. In the following section the *Oper* is examined from this angle, using Hofmannsthal's notes and his original scenario for the divertissement. The *Notizen* and the *Szenarium* are so crucial to our discussion that they have been reproduced as Appendices.

ii. *Historical Authenticity in the* Szenarium *to* Ariadne auf Naxos

We have suggested so far that *Ariadne auf Naxos* was intended as a recreation of a divertissement and have quoted from Hofmannsthal's letter which states that the two groups of characters, namely the *opera seria* and the *opera buffa*, are borrowed from the two theatrical elements of Molière's day: the mythological opera and the 'maschere' (Bw. 26 July 1911, p. 123). Indeed, Hofmannsthal had a precise vision of two distinct historical groups becoming entangled with each other and described *Ariadne* as 'gemischt aus heroisch-mythologischen Figuren im Kostüm des XVIII. Jahrhunderts in Reifröcken und Straußenfedern und aus Figuren der commedia dell' arte, Harlekins, Scaramouccios, welche ein mit dem heroischen Element fortwährend verwebtes Buffo-Element tragen' (Bw. 20 Mar. 1911, p. 95) (a combination of heroic mythological figures in 18th-century costume with hooped skirts and ostrich feathers and, interwoven in it, characters from the commedia dell'arte; harlequins and scaramouches representing the buffo element which is throughout interwoven with the heroic).

When sending the *Szenarium*, Hofmannsthal enclosed a letter reiterating this position and telling Strauss that he imagined it 'nicht als eine sklavische Nachahmung, sondern als eine geistreiche Paraphrase des alten heroischen Stils,

---

[16] LII, p. 94. For a description of the ballet and its relation to the play see Fiedler, pp. 33–4.

durchflochten mit dem Buffo-Stil' (Bw. 19 May 1911, p. 100) (not as a slavish imitation, but as a spirited paraphrase of the old heroic style, interspersed with buffo ingredients).

Hofmannsthal did paraphrase the heroic style. French Baroque opera preferred to take its tragic subject matter from classical mythology. In this regard Hofmannsthal was being historically authentic. The choice of 'Ariadne' is also a happy piece of historicizing, as this was a favourite operatic subject in the seventeenth and eighteenth centuries. Lilith Friedmann has counted over forty 'Ariadne' operas composed in that time.[17] Fiedler notes the performances during the reign of Louis XIV of Lully's *Les fêtes de l'Amour et de Bacchus* (1672) with inserted intermezzi from Molière's *comédies-ballets*, and of Louis Mollier's *Les Amours de Bacchus et d'Ariane* (1672) based on a play by Donneau de Visé.[18] In the following year Cambert composed an *Ariane*. Indeed, Rudolf Hirsch has even discovered that in 1772 a Weimar troupe performed Molière's *Bürger als Edelmann* together with an 'Ariadne' opera by Anton Schweitzer. It is not known, however, if Hofmannsthal was aware of this eighteenth-century example of Baroque practice.[19] Hofmannsthal himself had treated the Ariadne myth before in *Das Kind und die Gäste* (1897) and *Der Abenteurer und die Sängerin* (1898). The figure of Ariadne in Hofmannsthal's works has been well covered by Stiegele and Gräwe.[20]

In the *Szenarium* Hofmannsthal is clearly trying to give a picture of Antiquity as it appeared to French Baroque eyes. Ariadne's grotto is to be 'im Poussin'schen Stil' (Sz. 286).[21] The heroic figures are to be 'durchaus edel, im Stil der Louis XIV-Antike' (Sz. 286). An early note shows how concerned Hofmannsthal was to capture the artificial atmosphere of the

[17] Lilith Friedmann, 'Die Gestaltung des Ariadne-Stoffes von der Antike bis zur Neuzeit'.

[18] Fiedler, p. 67.

[19] Rudolf Hirsch, 'Auf dem Weg zu "Ariadne". Aus neugefundenen Briefen mitgeteilt', *Neue Zürcher Zeitung*, 15 Nov. 1970, p. 49.

[20] Stiegele, pp. 28–43. Gräwe, pp. 34–5.

[21] All quotations are from Hugo von Hofmannsthal, '*Ariadne* Szenarium und Notizen', in *Gesammelte Werke in zehn Einzelbänden, Dramen V*, pp. 286–93. Page references, given in brackets with the abbreviation 'Sz.' after the quotations, are to this publication (See Appendix B).

French Baroque: 'Arbeit: alles künstlich, abgewonnen, gezüchtet. Racine spielen, die Annäherung an Louis XIV.'[22] (Work: everything artificial, hard won, cultivated. Play Racine, approximate to Louis XIV.)

So Hofmannsthal paid attention to historical detail when choosing and treating the *opera seria*. This is no less true of the other group—represented in *Ariadne auf Naxos* by the *commedia dell'arte*. These comic characters appeared in numerous seventeenth-century works, including the intermezzi of some of Molière's *comédies-ballets*; 'Zerbinetta' in *Les Fourberies de Scapin*, 'Arlequin' in the *Ballet des Nations* from the *Bourgeois Gentilhomme* and in the second intermezzo of *L'Amour Médecin*, and 'Truffaldin' in *L'Étourdi*. Molière himself encountered the Italian comedians during his years in Southern France and also after his return to Paris, where, in 1658/9 and 1662, he shared first the Théâtre du Petit-Bourbon and then the theatre at the Palais Royal with a resident Italian troupe. The two companies appear to have enjoyed a good working relationship and in fact at the 1670 première of *Le Bourgeois Gentilhomme* the famous Harlequin Domenico Biancolelli himself played the Arlequin in the *Ballet des Nations*.

Gräwe has found other proof of the enormous care Hofmannsthal took with historical authenticity. At the time of writing *Ariadne auf Naxos*, in order to familiarize himself still more with the *commedia dell'arte*, Hofmannsthal read a book by Phillipe Monnier entitled *Venise au XVIIIe Siècle*.[23] Above the heading of Chapter 8 there is an entry in Hofmannsthal's handwriting, which is the earliest-known mention of *Ariadne*; 'Rodaun . . . 26.II.1911 (beschäftigt mit Ariadne)'.[24] In this Chapter 'Le théâtre vénitien et la comédie italienne' mention is made of most of the comic figures later named in the libretto: Mezzetin, Truffaldin, Scaramuccio, Pagliaccio, Cavicchio, Burattin, Pasquariello, Harlekin, and finally Zerbinetta.[25] These characters are also briefly de-

[22] See Appendix A, Note 1.

[23] Hofmannsthal's first written reference to Monnier is in his sketch for *Die kluge Gräfin*, reproduced in Fiedler, pp. 142–3.

[24] Michael Hamburger, 'Hofmannsthals Bibliothek', p. 48.

[25] Monnier, pp. 216–29. Willi Schuh's suggestion that the name 'Zerbinetta' came from Molière's *Les Fourberies de Scapin* is thus less probable. Willi Schuh, 'Zu

scribed. Brighella is not mentioned, but doubtless Hof-mannsthal was acquainted with the *commedia* from other sources and Brighella is one of the better known characters. Some of the names only come into the libretto during Zerbinetta's aria when she reels off a list of her former lovers. But the names of the male quartet, Harlekin, Scaramuccio, Brighella, and Truffaldin already appear in the *Szenarium*.

Under the list of *dramatis personae* in the *Szenarium* Hofmannsthal notes 'Figuren der commedia dell'arte in Callots Manier, bunt, grotesk' (Sz. 286). The reference to Callot tells us how Hofmannsthal envisaged his *commedia dell'arte*.[26] He is probably referring to a well-known set of engravings from the *Balli di Sfessania* (Neopolitan Dances) by Jacques Callot.[27] Callot's black and white drawings are executed in a very free manner with broad, flowing lines suggesting much movement. A. Nicoll argues, however, that these drawings cannot be relied upon as accurate historical records.[28] They depict the Neopolitan carnival versions of the *commedia* characters rather than the true figures of the 'comedy of skill'. It would seem, then, that at least for the *Szenarium* Hofmannsthal chose a *commedia dell'arte* that was slightly more rough-and-tumble, 'bunt, grotesk', and popular than usual. No doubt such a group would stand out well against the stylized movements and pompous classical control of the *opera seria*.

Hofmannsthal did not look only at pictures by Callot. Just as for the levee in *Der Rosenkavalier* he had drawn heavily on Hogarth's fourth 'Mariage à la Mode', from which came the little black boy, the flautist and the singer, the hairdresser and others, so did he require visual stimulus when setting the scene for *Ariadne auf Naxos*. Hofmannsthal gives the following

---

Hofmannsthals "Ariadne"-Szenarium und -Notizen', p. 89. In the earliest note to *Ariadne*, dated 26 Feb. 1911, Zerbinetta is called 'Smeraldina', as is Barak's wife in the first note to *Das steinerne Herz* written on the same day. It seems likely that after finding alternative names in Monnier Hofmannsthal decided to keep 'Smeraldina' for what became *Die Frau ohne Schatten*.

[26] It is interesting to note that Callot is mentioned twice in Chapter 8 of Monnier's book.

[27] Reproductions of several of these can be found in Allardyce Nicoll, *The World of Harlequin: A Critical Study of the Commedia dell'Arte*, pp. 156, 216. Also, Pierre-Louis Duchartre, *La Commedia dell'Arte et ses Enfants*, pp. 193, 223.

[28] Nicoll, p. 74.

directions about the stage which is to be set up in Jourdain's
house: 'Anstatt der Coulissen abwechselnd Orangenbäumchen
in Kübeln und Candelaber mit brennenden Kerzen. In der
Mitte eine künstliche Höhle / Grotte aus Pappendeckel aber
architectonisch schön, im Poussin'schen Stil.' (Sz. 286.)
(Instead of scenery little orange trees in tubs alternating with
candelabra with lighted candles. In the middle an artificial
cave/grotto out of pasteboard but architecturally beautiful, in
the style of Poussin.) Fiedler points out a similarity with stage
arrangements for improvised open-air performances at Versailles, and also informs us that this setting corresponds closely
to one of the etchings by R. Félibien which can be found in the
official description of the *Grande Fête de Versailles* at which
Molière's *George Dandin* was performed.[29] The positioning of
the *commedia* figures on the stage is also borrowed from
another of these etchings in which 'Zerbinetta, Arlekin,
Brighella, Truffaldin, Scaramuccio außerhalb der Bühne
postiert, hinter den Bäumchen . . . gleichsam zwischen den
Coulissen hervorgucken.' (Sz. 287.) (Zerbinetta, Arlekin,
Brighella, Truffaldin, Scaramuccio placed off-stage behind the
little trees . . . . look out as if from behind the scenes.) One of
these Félibien etchings was later used by the designer Ernst
Stern in his *Skizzenbuch*[30] to *Ariadne*, and as the décor was
worked out in close consultation with Hofmannsthal, who also
lent Stern some other reference books, including a *Mode au
XVIIième Siècle*,[31] it seems likely that Hofmannsthal knew
the Félibien etchings and directed Stern's attention to them.
    The two groups, who people the *Szenarium*, and the setting

[29] André Félibien, *Relation de la Feste de Versailles: Du 18. Juillet mil six cens
soixante-huit*. Fiedler, p. 70.
[30] Stern's sketch-book, which contained drawings of the sets, stage, furniture, and
props for *Ariadne*, was printed by A. Fürstner, and any group performing *Ariadne* in
the future had to apply for it along with the performing rights. See Ernst Stern,
Bühnenbildner bei Max Reinhardt, p. 96.
[31] Stern gives the following information about his sources and his method of
working: 'Ich besaß einen Neudruck des kostbaren Werks: "La mode au XVII.
Siècle" nach den zeitgenössischen Gravüren der Sammlung des Monsieur Liez, ferner
gab es hervorragende Abbildungen von Architekturen und Theateraufführungen
jener Epoche im Besitze Hofmannsthals. Ein zwingender Grund für mich, meine
Entwürfe in Paris zu zeichnen, lag also nicht vor. Außerdem wohnte Strauss nur eine
Autostunde vom Ammersee ab, und es war gewiß, daß die 'Klangfarbe' seiner Musik,
mir bei meiner Arbeit mehr helfen würde, als alle Schätze des "Musée des Arts
Décoratives"', Ernst Stern, *Bühnenbildner bei Max Reinhardt*, pp. 96–7.

are then treated with a large degree of historical detail. Reinhardt seems to have understood completely that it was a case here of an historical recreation. Accordingly he suggested that the musicians be seated on stage 'womöglich—mit dem Capellmeister am Spinett'. This was an authentic Baroque practice. Hofmannsthal noted Reinhardt's suggestion at the top of the *Szenarium* but was forced to cross it out after Strauss had raised a valid practical objection.[32]

The imaginative element in this scheme enters into it in the mixing up of the *opera seria* and the *opera buffa*. It was not uncommon in Molière's day for comedy and tragedy to share the stage on a single evening. Fiedler notes their proximity in Baroque theatre practice: 'Von den Italienern übernahm Molière auch die Praxis, nach der Aufführung eines ernsten Stückes—denn seine Schauspieler spielten auch Tragödien— das Publikum mit einem kurz, oft improvisierten heiteren Stück zu entlassen—ein Vorgehen, das auf die höfischen Aufführungen und die comédie-ballet nicht ohne Einfluß blieb.'[33] (From the Italians Molière also borrowed the practice after the performance of a serious play—for his actors also played tragedies—of sending his audience home with a short, often improvised comedy—a procedure which was not without influence on court productions and the comédie-ballet.) Still the groups appeared one after another, not together, as was also the practice at Riccoboni's Théâtre Italien in Paris, in court operas and the *Haupt- und Staatsaktionen* in Vienna during the Baroque period and in seventeenth-century Italian opera. Examples of libretti from the Roman School include S. Landi's *La Morte d'Orfeo* (1619) and D. Mazzocchi's *La Catena d'Adone* (1626). The same practice is found in Cesti's *Il Pomo d'oro* (1666) and Monteverdi's *L'Incoronazione di Poppea* (1642), both of the Venetian School.[34] In the last named, H. Holländer finds a possible literary forerunner of

---

[32] 'Orchester *auf* der Bühne unmöglich: ich brauche gerade für diese Kammer-musiksache erstklassige Leute (nur vom k. Hoforchester in Berlin), die spielen keine Komödie.' But Strauss was not intransigent: he suggested a raised stage as a compromise: 'Dagegen muß Reinhardt schon jetzt im Sommer den Orchesterraum des Deutschen Theaters so umbauen lassen, daß wir offenes, hochliegendes Orchester kriegen wie im Münchener Residenztheater'. Bw. 22 May 1911, p. 103.

[33] Fiedler, p. 68.

[34] *Harvard Dictionary of Music*, edited by Willi Apel, second revised edition (London, 1976), p. 186. See also Stiegele, p. 8.

Ariadne auf Naxos: 'Die hier vorliegende Verquickung von opera seria und opera buffa ist in der Literatur nicht ohne Vorgänger. In Monteverdis *L'Incoronazione di Poppea* erstreckt sich das burleske "Intermezzo" der Zwischenakte bis in die tragische Handlung hinein, so daß eine Vermengung von ernsten und buffa Auftritten vorliegt.'[35] (This amalgamation of opera seria and opera buffa is not without predecessors in literature. In Monteverdi's *L'Incoronazione di Poppea* the burlesque 'intermezzo' of the entr'acte stretches into the tragic action and results in a mix up of serious and buffa scenes.) However, it seems unlikely that Hofmannsthal knew the Monteverdi.

Peter Branscombe has found a more probable point of departure for Hofmannsthal, an early libretto by Bonacossi called *Ariadna abbandonata da Theseo e sponsata dal Dio Baccho* (1641).[36] In Bonacossi's comic interludes a usurer, a pedant, and a courtier appear and there are a number of jokes about food. The librettist has tried to relate the comic scenes to the main action (in which Theseus, in love with Phaedra, tries to marry Ariadne off to his son). But still the two groups do not appear simultaneously on stage. That was Hofmannsthal's own imaginative contribution—when he came to work with the historical material the temptation to mix up comic and serious elements must have been great. It was an original yet logical extension of what he had found to be the practice and must still strike an audience as a delightful and diverting cultural–historical joke.[37]

[35] Hans Holländer, 'Hugo von Hofmannsthal als Opernlibrettist, p. 553.

[36] On 15 June 1924 Hofmannsthal wrote to Max Pirker asking for Alexander von Weilen's *Die Theater Wien's*. In this volume there is a short description of Bonacossi's libretto, concluding with the significant remark 'Interessant ist an dem öden Producte nur der Versuch, die komischen Scenen mit der Haupthandlung in Verbindung zu bringen.' Alexander von Weilen, *Geschichte des Wiener Theaterwesens von den ältesten Zeiten bis zu den Anfängen der Hoftheater*, Volume I, *Die Theater Wien's* (Vienna, 1899), pp. 67–8. However, although the Weilen is a work that Hofmannsthal may very well have referred to, there is no evidence that in 1911 Hofmannsthal knew of Bonacossi's text through Weilen or any other source. I am indebted to Professor Branscombe for making this information available to me several months before the publication by the Athlone Press of his article 'Some observations on the sources of the Strauss-Hofmannsthal opera librettos', first given as a paper at the Hugo von Hofmannsthal Commemorative Symposium held at Bedford College, London, on 21–2 Mar. 1979.

[37] Cf. 'meine Zusammenkoppelung [ist] ein geistreicher Scherz', Bw. 26 Dec. 1911, p. 135.

iii. *The Structure and Plot of the* Szenarium

It would be a mistake, however, to be distracted by a too literal historicism. Let us forget the *opera seria* and *opera buffa* and look instead at the underlying structure of the *Szenarium*. Here we have a very simple allegory of two opposing forces which unite at the end. On the one side there are 'die heroischen Figuren' (Sz. 286) who represent fidelity, individual love, and 'marriage', and on the other there are 'die Figuren des Intermezzo' (Sz. 286), who represent infidelity, erotic attraction, and 'affairs'. (In the libretto the Intermezzo is entitled 'Die ungetreue Zerbinetta und ihre vier Liebhaber'.) The subject or theme of this allegory is then 'fidelity' and the two sides are perfectly matched and balanced, with Hofmannsthal at an equal critical distance from both. The allegory does not take the shape of the common formal argument or 'dispute' with both parties declaring the superiority of their point of view and their consequent enmity. Instead both state their positions, but then the one side, Zerbinetta and company, tries to win over the other—with some measure of success, as we shall see.

The divertissement opens with Ariadne lying on the ground in front of her cave in a stylized pose of grief. She has been deserted by Theseus and for her this is tragic. She sings the 'große Klage der Verlassenen, pathetisch aber ganz einfach und zum Herzen gehend' (Sz. 287) (the great lament of the abandoned woman, pathetic but quite simple and moving). Hofmannsthal envisaged both a moving emotional realism and the stylized pathos of an *opera seria* personage for Ariadne.

The comic figures make their position clear in their reaction to Ariadne's aria. They want to cheer her up and help her to take her loss less badly. Zerbinetta's dance ensemble, which follows a little later, is a statement of their view of life: 'Zerbinetta findet an jedem der 4 etwas unwiderstehliches [*sic*]. Einen sanft, einen wild, einen hoheitsvoll, einen feurig. Keinem kann sich ihr Herz ganz entziehen. Sie wundert sich über ihr eigenes Herz, das immer Vorsätze der Treue, der Enthaltsamkeit macht und sie so wenig zu halten weiß.' (Sz. 289.) (Zerbinetta finds something irresistible about each of the four. She finds one gentle, one wild, one majestic, one fiery.

From none can she quite withdraw her affections. She is amazed at her own heart, which is always making resolutions to be faithful and continent but is never able to keep them.) Zerbinetta feels no real regret at her infidelity; she is too susceptible to the charm of erotic variety.

The plot of the *Szenarium*, in so far as it has one, is built around the theme of 'trösten', a word which is used repeatedly in the text. There are four attempts, three unsuccessful and one successful, at comforting Ariadne. Each of the first three times the attempt is rebuffed. The last time Ariadne succumbs.

At the first attempt the nymphs have a short scene in which they try to reach Ariadne:

> Naiade: Sie schläft!
> Dryade: Sie weint!
> Zu dreien: Ariadne! (Sz. 287.)

Ariadne raises herself only to sing her 'große Klage'. The nymphs rightly conclude that they are unable to comfort her— 'daß sie hier zu trösten unvermögend sind'. (Sz. 287.)

The second attempt is made by the *commedia* group. They pop their heads through the scenery and express their concern about her. Arlekin tries singing a little song of which Echo repeats the refrain. But Ariadne rebuffs their good-natured attempts by ignoring them completely: 'Ariadne achtet es nicht, starrt vor sich hin. Stille' (Sz. 288). At this point Jourdain and his guests, who have been sitting watching quietly from their seats, take the opportunity of interposing some remarks.[38] They express the hope 'daß diese Verlaßne doch irgendwie werde Trost annehmen' (Sz. 288).

This second attempt is followed by the Intermezzo which is really a concerted effort by the *commedia* to cheer the heroine. They climb on to the stage and present themselves; 'Sie aufzuheitern, unternehmen sie einen Tanz' (Sz. 288). But Ariadne ignores them again. Zerbinetta then tries it alone. In an ingratiating way she tells Ariadne that she too has suffered the pain of desertion and produces a letter from her very first lover, which she proceeds to sing. Ariadne is unmoved by

---

[38] Del Mar suggests that the device of these interpolations derives from Christopher Sly in *The Taming of the Shrew*, but there is no evidence that Hofmannsthal used this rather than one of numerous other possible sources. Del Mar, p. 30.

these overtures of friendship and so the third attempt is also rebuffed.

The *commedia* figures have now tried to comfort Ariadne by diverting her and entertaining her with a dance and Zerbinetta has tried the direct approach. They grow weary of their lack of success. Each of the four male buffos now entreats Zerbinetta to join him for a 'Schäferstunde'. They sing 'Laß das undankbare Geschäft, eine Verzweifelte zu trösten. Komm mit mir!' (Sz. 288.) (Leave the thankless task of comforting a person in despair. Come with me!) There follows some comic confusion as Zerbinetta promises herself to each but slips off with Arlekin. The other three return, discover they have been tricked, and leave the stage disappointed but dancing and consoling themselves with thoughts of future success. As Gräwe points out, the language of the *Szenarium* here merges into the musicality and movement of the projected scene: 'zu dreien entdecken sie den Betrug, ärgern sich, tanzend, trösten sich, tanzend, tanzen ab, auf später sich vertröstend.' (Sz. 289.) (All three discover the deception, grow annoyed, dancing, console each other dancing, dance off, consoling themselves with thoughts of the future.) The scene itself is a demonstration of the *commedia*'s light-hearted, amorous, humorous philosophy of life. It is a philosophy better put into song than into a résumé.

After this interruption a successful attempt is made by a third party, Bacchos,[39] who belongs to the *opera seria* group and arrives on the scene somewhat in the manner of a *deus ex machina* and sweeps Ariadne off her feet, although she first goes through a short inner struggle. We are not concerned for the moment with the Bacchos depicted in the note pencilled in later by Hofmannsthal: 'Klatsch über Bacchos Herkunft und erstes Abenteuer: Knabenhaft, Sohn einer Königstochter die starb von Nymphen aufgezogen! [*sic*]' (Sz. 289.) (Gossip about Bacchos' origins and first affair. Youthful, son of a king's daughter, who died. Raised by nymphs!) This note was pencilled into the *Szenarium* on or around 28 May 1911 after Strauss had read it and returned it by post. In abbreviated form it contains the whole new dimension and direction

[39] The directly transliterated 'Bacchos' is preferred in the *Szenarium* to the latinized 'Bacchus'.

Hofmannsthal wanted to give Bacchos as he tried to make the
Szenarium into something more than a divertissement, and the
genesis of this character will be dealt with in depth later. Here
we are concerned only with the Bacchos of the *Szenarium* who
is 'ein Herrlicher, Unwiderstehlicher' (Sz. 290), altogether the
romantic hero who conquers women's hearts. He has all the
attributes of a Prince Charming; he is divinely handsome, his
voice is 'lockend werbend' (Sz. 290), he heads straight for his
love—'seines Zieles aber sicher'—although he does not know
where she is, and he has a masculine potency and vigour
which expresses itself in the manner of his arrival, which
Hofmannsthal requested be shown in the music: 'Triumphierendes Heranschreiten (nun in der Musik), Bacchos *steht da.*'
(Sz. 291.) (Triumphant striding (now in the music), Bacchos
stands there.)

Ariadne must put up some resistance to this stranger, for
after all in the allegory she is the personification of fidelity. But
she is deeply touched and softened by his voice. Ariadne's
confused emotions are portrayed on stage in a naïve, stylized,
yet not ineffective way: 'Ariadne, jedesmal, solange die
Stimme tönt, gelöst, sobald die Stimme schweigt, aufs neue
erstarrend.' (Sz. 290.) (Ariadne relaxed each time as long as
the voice sounds. As soon as the voice stops she grows stiff
again.) Ariadne explains her confusion to herself by insisting
that this must be Hermes 'der Todtenführer'. There is no need
to see in this much more than maidenly modesty and confusion
grasping at a conventional explanation of its distress. Of
course there is something ironic about Ariadne's innocent
insistence that this is Death, and the ambiguity of her emotions
is made clear in the little exchange between herself and
Zerbinetta: 'Zerbinetta, zofenhaft zudringlich, bemüht Ariadne zu schmücken, zu putzen. Ariadne läßt es geschehen, als
sei es für den Tod. Zerbinetta findet, Ariadnes Herz klopfe
höchst lebendig, ihr Auge glänze unvergleichlich.' (Sz. 290–1.)
(Zerbinetta, as fussy as a lady's maid, is busy adorning Ariadne
in her finery. Ariadne lets it happen as if it were for Death.
Zerbinetta thinks that Ariadne's heart is beating very violently,
her eyes sparkling incomparably.)

Ariadne's struggle and confusion are soon over as she and
Bacchos fall in love at first sight: 'Ariadne und Bacchos,

einander gegenüber, ganz wie ein König und eine Prinzessin'
(Sz. 291). Their relationship is that of stylized romance and
they soon move over into a proper 'Liebesduett'. The final
attempt to console Ariadne has thus been successful and the
two opposing sides can forget their differences. The Ariadne–
Bacchos relationship is a compromise between extreme views
of fidelity and infidelity. Ariadne has forgotten Theseus, but
her new love is more a marriage than an affair. There is some
truth in Zerbinetta's final comment '(ad spectatores) Wie wir
es sagten, ist es gekommen' (Sz. 291). But it is not the whole
truth.

   The *Szenarium* ends with a joyous dance in which all parties
join together. The *buffa* figures dance with the nymphs,
Zerbinetta and Arlekin dance with each other, then Ariadne
and Bacchos descend from the grotto and join them and the
whole company exits in an 'allgemeines Abgehen' (Sz. 291),
the scenic symbol of the allegoric unity.

   From this outline of the *Szenarium* we note that its basic
qualities are simplicity, stylization, and symmetry. These
qualities it has by virtue of its being a simple allegory of the
abstract quality fidelity and its opposite, infidelity. The
message and 'meaning' of this allegory is that love is an ironic
business in so far as it has both a sexual and a spiritual side
which are often at odds with each other. Hofmannsthal is
dealing here, as Borchardt rightly says, with one of those
eternally ambiguous 'ewige Verhältnisse'.[40] The type of
symmetrical allegory employed is ideally suited to such an
ironic theme: the two opposing forces of the first part are
equally matched and irony means no more than an equipoise
of conflicting impulses—the unity achieved at the end of the
allegory being a state of ironic equipoise.

   The inner structure of this divertissement has the same
quality of simplicity. As we have seen, within the over-all
pattern of the two opposite poles coming together, there are
the four smaller attempts at rapprochement. Division into
sub-units, and repetition of these, are then the main formal
principles of the divertissement; the same principle operates
in Ariadne's vacillation during Bacchos' arrival. This sort of
form has a clockwork, choreographed simplicity, even a

[40] Hugo von Hofmannsthal/Rudolf Borchardt, *Briefwechsel*, p. 84.

naïveté, which is entirely suited to the essentially undramatic divertissement.

Even the one moment of dramatic tension and climax surrounding Bacchos' arrival and entry onto the stage follows such a conventional pattern that much of its potential effect is undercut. The stereotyped nature of Bacchos' and Ariadne's interaction has been mentioned, as well as those attributes which make him the archetypal romantic figure. Their relationship is in fact the archetypal romance. Not only are we at such a primitive level that the hero knows instinctively where his beloved is although he himself is 'auf Schlangen-pfaden' (Sz. 290); but the climax of the scene is simply his physical arrival on stage. In this there are overtones of the theatre as ritual and there is clearly something ritualistic about the ensuing love-scene. So, real dramatic tension is lessened by wooden conventions and archetypal patterns. Furthermore Hofmannsthal is at pains to control the dramatic crescendo and introduces a 'Spiel und Singscene' (Sz. 290) between Ariadne and Zerbinetta, although it is true he does not want all sense of climax to be lost and observes that the scene should be performed 'ohne daß die schon anbegonnene Steigerung in der Hauptlinie dadurch verloren geht' (Sz. 290).

This exposition of the *Szenarium* has departed from a strictly historical account of the mixing of *opera seria* and *opera buffa* in favour of a view of the whole in terms of allegory. In fact Hofmannsthal's divertissement is not any the less historically authentic, for the allegory was one of the most common forms of the Baroque epoch and of Molière's time. Fiedler comments: 'Den Höhepunkt aller Aufführungen am Hof bildete jeweils die allegorische Vereinigung zweier oder mehrerer vorher als gegensätzlich gezeigter Elemente (Künste, Nationen, Gottheiten) in einer alles verklärenden Harmonie und Apotheose.'[41] (The highlight of all performances at court was always the allegoric union of two or more previously opposed elements (art forms, nations, divinities) in a radiant harmony and apotheosis.) Fiedler gives some good examples which are repeated here. In the prologue to Molière's *comédie-ballet*, *L'Amour médecin* (1665) the three arts appearing in the work, comedy, music, and ballet, announce an end to their

---

[41] Fiedler, p. 68.

rivalry. At the conclusion of the *comédie-ballet* they reappear
and sing harmoniously of their roles as 'médecins' of mankind.

In Lully's *Ballet de la Raillerie* (1659) there is an allegory of
the rivalry between the French and Italian musical styles
which raged during the period of Lully's musical dictatorship
in France. In this ballet Lully allegorizes what he considers to
be his own successful unification of the styles. The conclusion
to the dispute is quoted here:

La Musique italienne :	Si mon amour a plus de violence, Je dois chanter d'un ton plus fort. Quand on se voit prest de la mort, Le plus haut que l'on peut on demande assistance.
La Musique françoise :	Mon chant fait voir par sa langueur Que ma peine est vive et pressante. Quand le mal attaque le coeur, On n'a pas la voix éclatante.
Toutes deux :	Cessons donc de nous contredire, Puisque dans l'amoureux empire, Où se confond incessamment, Le plaisir avec le tourment, Le coeur qui chante, et celuy, qui soupire Peuvent s'accorder aysément.[42]
(Italian music :	If my love is more violent I may sing more loudly. When one sees oneself at death's door One cries for help as loudly as one can.
French music :	My song makes it plain by its languor That my suffering is sharp and insistent. When distress touches the heart One does not have a strident voice.
Both :	Let us stop disagreeing then Since in love's realm Where pleasure is often Confused with torment The heart that sings and the one that sighs Can easily agree.)

[42] Quoted in Romain Rolland, *Histoire de L'Opéra en Europe avant Lully et Scarlatti*
p. 251.

Here, as Fiedler points out, the opposition of aloof suffering in love (French music) and extravagant expressiveness (Italian music) also corresponds to the contrasting characters Ariadne and Zerbinetta. The two women further personify French morality and Italian immorality.

These two examples are not taken from divertissements, but the allegory was frequently used in divertissements,[43] as Hofmannsthal must have known from his intensive study of this genre at this time.[44]

The final example concerns the culminating dance in the *Szenarium*. This dance receives historical authentication from several quarters. Firstly there was the Baroque predilection for apotheoses of any kind and secondly the ensemble finale was typical in Italian comic opera.[45] Now whilst the divertissement is of course not an Italian *opera buffa* the presence of the buffa figures and the over-all comic atmosphere which is lent to it because it is part of a *comédie-ballet* do make this a legitimate touch. Thirdly, and this is Fiedler's final example, there is a precedent in Molière's *George Dandin ou le Mari confondu* (1668) of a final dance in which comic and tragic troupes join together. *George Dandin* is also a *comédie-ballet*, although it contains some serious passages. In the divertissement shepherds and shepherdesses try to cheer up the melancholy George Dandin. Fiedler comments on the finale: 'Den Abschluß bildet ein Disput zwischen den Anhängern Amors und Bacchus', der mit der glanzvollen Vereinigung der beiden Truppen in Tanz und Musik endet.'[46] (The conclusion is in the form of a dispute between the followers of Amor and Bacchus which ends with the

---

[43] See *French Baroque Music: from Beaujoyeulx to Rameau*, revised edition by James R. Anthony (London, 1974), p. 27 and pp. 74–8. For a short chapter on the evolution of the divertissement and its characteristics see Irène Mamczarz, *Les Intermèdes comiques Italiens au XVIIIe Siècle* (Paris, 1972), pp. 21–5.

[44] Cf. Fiedler, p. 64. 'Hofmannsthal dürfte zu diesem Zeitpunkt vor allem die tänzerischen, musikalischen und pantomimischen Einlagen der höfischen Molière-Aufführungen, die ihn bereits beim "Rosenkavalier" angeregt hatten, eingehender studiert haben.'

[45] For example, in A. Abbatini's *Dal male il bene* (1653), J. Melani's *La Tancia* (1656) or Pergolesi's *La Serva padrona* (1733). For a further comment on the traditional apotheosis ending and the use of *dei ex machinis* with particular reference to Quinault's libretti see Patrick J. Smith, *The Tenth Muse: A Historical Study of the Opera Libretto*, p. 57.

[46] Fiedler, p. 69.

magnificent union of the two troupes in dance and music.) This is a clear parallel with the ending of the *Szenarium*.

Another example of a dance finale, which Fiedler does not mention, is the closing scene of Quinault's *Les fêtes de l'Amour et de Bacchus, Pastorale de Quinault; Musique de Lully*. This scene is also a glorious Baroque apotheosis with the stage opening up to reveal a massed chorus of singers and dancers:

La perspective s'ouvre et laisse paroître dans le fond du Théatre une autre voûte de treille, sous laquelle une multitude de suivans de Bacchus sont placés, les uns sur des tonneaux, les autres sur une espèce d'amphithéatre couvert de pampres de vigne, et qui tous jouent de différens instrumens; tandis que plusieurs autres Satyres et Sylvains s'avancent au milieu du Théatre pour interrompre la fête de l'Amour et pour en célébrer une plus solomnelle à la gloire de Bacchus.[47]

(The scene opens and reveals at the back of the stage an archway of climbing vines under which there is a crowd of Bacchus' followers, some on barrels, some in a kind of amphitheatre covered with vine branches, and all are playing different instruments; meanwhile several other satyrs and wood sprites come to the middle of the stage in order to interrupt the feast to Love and to celebrate the more solemn one to the glory of Bacchus.)

We are immediately reminded of how Hofmannsthal envisaged the staging of the final moments of transformation in *Ariadne* in which the stage widens into a larger one—'Hier muß ein Wunder an Beleuchtung ... die puppenhafte Bühne in eine traumhafte *große* Bühne verwandeln—vielleicht die Kulissen ganz verschwinden.' (Bw. 30 Jan. 1912, p. 141.)[48] (Here we want a miracle of lighting ... to transform the miniature stage into a dream-like big stage—perhaps the wings must disappear altogether.)

From the *Szenarium* it is apparent that Hofmannsthal intended the divertissement *Ariadne auf Naxos* to be simple, historical, authentic, and impersonal. It was to have an

---

[47] P. Quinault, *Les fêtes de l'Amour et de Bacchus: Pastorale de Quinault, Musique de Lully* (Paris, 1784), p. 43.
[48] Cf. the *Ariadne Brief*: 'hier muß die kleine Bühne ins Unbegrenzte wachsen, mit dem Eintritt des Bacchus müssen die puppenhaften Kulissen verschwunden sein' (PIII, p. 142). In the event Hofmannsthal let the lights be dimmed and a starry sky appear: 'Alles versinkt, ein Sternenhimmel spannt sich über den zweien' (63).

imaginative dimension, but the imagination at work here was to be primarily the historical imagination. Hofmannsthal's own phrase 'eine geistreiche Paraphrase' (Bw. 19 May 1911, p. 100) is a good description of this activity. The work was therefore necessarily to be an impersonal one; the pleasure it offered its author was to be foremost that of successful 'stilistische Angleichung'.[49] An imaginative, historical recreation of a Molièresque divertissement is almost by definition an impersonal and even anonymous undertaking.

iv. *The Historical Origins of the* Zwischenspiel

This section concentrates on historical authenticity in the *Zwischenspiel*. As all the dialogue of the transitional scene was later transposed into the *Vorspiel* an interpretation is given in Chapter V. A good outline of the *Zwischenspiel* is included in Hofmannsthal's first letter on the subject of it. Hofmannsthal had the inspiration of making the Young Composer, a pupil of the Music Teacher in *Der Bürger als Edelmann*, the author of *Ariadne*. The Composer and the Music Teacher then together stand for the *opera seria* world and the Dancing Master and Zerbinetta represent the opposition. The action, such as it is, revolves round the reaction of the two groups in their real-life, backstage settings to the different instructions issued by Jourdain:

In dieser [Prosaszene] wird die Bühne aufgebaut, die Sänger sind im Begriffe, sich zu schminken, im Orchester wird gestimmt. Auf der Bühne befinden sich der Komponist und der Tanzmeister. Es soll unter Leitung des Komponisten zunächst eine kurze heroische Oper aufgeführt werden: 'Ariadne auf Naxos'. Ariadne soll klagen und den Tod herbeisehnen, dann kommt Bacchus und holt sie. Nach der Oper sollen die italienischen Masken (Zerbinetta und die ihrigen) als heiteres Nachspiel auftreten, tanzen und singen. Der Tanzmeister ist Regisseur dieses Nachspiels. So ist es auf dem Programm. Nun läßt Jourdain plötzlich durch den Lakaien sagen, er wünsche die beiden Sachen *gleichzeitig*; er wolle keine Ariadne auf einer *wüsten* Insel, sondern die italienischen Masken sollten diese wüste Insel bevölkern und ihre Späße vor Ariadne treiben. Kurz, man solle es arrangieren, aus den zwei Opern eine zu machen. Bestürzung. Wut des Komponisten, der Tanzmeister begütigt. Endlich wird die kluge

[49] Hugo von Hofmannsthal/Rudolf Borchart, *Briefwechsel*, p. 68.

Soubrette vorgerufen (Zerbinetta), ihr wird die Handlung der
heroischen Oper erzählt, der Charakter der Ariadne erklärt; sie
wird beauftragt, mit ihren Gesellen so gut als möglich ohne Störung
sich als Intermezzo in diese Oper einzumischen. Zerbinetta sieht
sogleich den springenden Punkt; eine Figur wie die Ariadne ist ihr
eine Heuchlerin oder eine Närrin, sie verspricht, nach Kräften, aber
diskret, in die Handlung einzugreifen. (Bw. 23 July 1911, p. 121.)

(In this scene the stage is being set, the singers are about to make up,
the orchestra tunes its instruments. Composer and Dancing Master
are on the stage. The Composer, we are told, is to conduct a short
heroic opera: *Ariadne auf Naxos*; Ariadne is to bewail her lot and to
long for death until Bacchus appears and carries her off. After the
opera, a lighthearted afterpiece is planned for the Italian comedians
(Zerbinetta and her companions) who are to dance and sing under
the direction of the Dancing Master. That is how the programme
reads. And now Jourdain suddenly sends his footman with the
message that he wishes the two pieces to be performed *simultaneously*,
that he has no desire to see Ariadne on a deserted island; the island
is on the contrary to be peopled by the Italian players who are to
entertain Ariadne with their capers. In short Jourdain asks them to
arrange one show out of the two operas. Consternation. The
Composer is furious, the Dancing Master tries to soothe him. Finally
they summon the clever soubrette (Zerbinetta); they tell her the plot
of the heroic opera, explain to her the character of Ariadne, and set
her the task of working herself and her companions as best she may
into this opera as an intermezzo, without causing undue disturbance.
Zerbinetta at once grasps the salient point: to her way of thinking a
character like Ariadne must be either a hypocrite or a fool, and she
promises to intervene in the action to the best of her ability, but with
discretion.)

Hofmannsthal ensures that the Molière play, the *Zwischenspiel* and the *Oper* hold together by having characters from one
part appear in another. By means of these interlocking scenes
Hofmannsthal conveys a sense of dramatic unity and continuity. In the *Zwischenspiel* the original Molière figures, the
Maître de Musique and the Maître à Danser, who appear in
the first act of *Der Bürger als Edelmann*, have quite large roles
to play. In the *Zwischenspiel* they are fundamentally extensions
of Molière's characters improvising in an imaginary situation.
The Composer is Hofmannsthal's own creation, but the idea
for him came from Molière's Élève du Maître de Musique.

Apart from this connection with Molière through original characters, the *Zwischenspiel* has an authentic position equal to the numerous *intermèdes* which are to be found in the Molièresque *comédies-ballets*. As Fiedler remarks, in the *Zwischenspiel*, as in the *intermède*,

wird die Handlung der Komödie auf eine andere Ebene verlagert, die Hinzufügung des neuen (Schauspieler-) Rahmens, der ein drittes (oder, wenn man 'Ariadne' und 'Zerbinetta' als zwei nimmt, viertes) Spiel ist, bedeutet ihrerseits eine Annäherung an die Tradition der comédie-ballet und der höfischen Aufführungen. Auf diese Tradition wird direkt angespielt, vor allem damit, daß das aufzuführende Werk das Fest eines 'großen Herren' zu schmücken hat—zwischen Dîner und Feuerwerk. Die Ungeduld des Auftraggebers Jourdain entspricht dem, was wir von der Entstehung fast aller comédies-ballets wissen—dem Willen Louis XIV, der Molière Stücke für seine Feste brauchte und dem Künstler meist nur wenig Zeit für die Ausführung der Idee ließ, die er oft genug als Auftraggeber selbst noch beeinflußte.[50]

(the action of the comedy is shifted onto another plane. The addition of the new (actor) frame, which is a third play (or a fourth if one regards 'Ariadne' and 'Zerbinetta' as two plays), approximates in turn to the tradition of the comédie-ballet and the court performances. There is a direct and particular allusion to this tradition in that the work to be performed is to embellish a festivity given by an 'illustrious gentleman'—between dinner and the firework display. The impatience of Jourdain, who commissioned the work, corresponds to what we know of the genesis of nearly all comédies-ballets: Louis XIV needed Molière plays for his festivities and often left the playwright only a little time to realize the idea, which as patron he himself often influenced.)

An excellent illustration of some of the above points is Molière's *Impromptu de Versailles* (1663), in which Molière appears *in propria persona* directing his actors in a last-minute rehearsal of a play he has been commissioned to write by Louis XIV at only a week's notice.[51] Here we have the capricious demands of the patron causing panic and rush in the preparation of an entertainment intended mostly as display of the patron's wealth. This glance behind the scenes does not,

[50] Fiedler, p. 60.
[51] Gräwe suggests that the *Impromptu de Versailles* was a source of the *Zwischenspiel*. This is quite possible although there are no obvious borrowings. Gräwe, p. 36.

however, put the *Impromptu de Versailles* on to another level; it stands on its own and is not part of a *comédie-ballet*, but it does bear witness to a tradition of backstage scenes in the French theatre in which the theatre itself becomes thematic and that fascinating question of the actor and his role, their coincidence or conflict, is exploited and is an entertainment in itself. Quinault's *Les fêtes' de l'Amour et de Bacchus*, which draws freely on Molière, has a Prologue which stands within this tradition. The scene is a magnificent room arranged for a spectacular entertainment. The actors have not yet received their scripts and are wandering about the room in a state of great agitation. In turn they beg to be informed about the coming divertissement and to be given their scripts. The person in charge finally heeds their pleas and the Prologue ends with the distribution of the scripts.[52]

The *Zwischenspiel* is thus in places an authentic imitation of a *comédie-ballet* intermezzo. Reinhardt took extra steps to reinforce the impression of stylistic and formal continuity from *Der Bürger als Edelman* to the *Zwischenspiel*: in the *Regiebuch* there is no change of scene or break between the two scenes as there was at the Stuttgart première.[53] Reinhardt also had Jourdain and not his lackey appear to give the commands. Finally the Molière adaptation itself was made with an eye to dramatic continuity and historical authenticity and Hofmannsthal worked accordingly.

v. *The 1911–12* Bürger als Edelmann

When making his own version of *Le Bourgeois Gentilhomme* (1670) Hofmannsthal relied heavily on an old translation by F. S. Bierling.[54] This translation, made in 1750,[55] has a definite archaic ring to it, although it is not so remote linguistically as to pose problems of understanding. Hofmannsthal chose it deliberately as a means of historicizing, as a way of giving a German audience the same historical perspective on Molière

---

[52] Quinault, p. 15.

[53] Stiegele, p. 68. Max Reinhardt's *Regiebuch* to *Ariadne auf Naxos* was brought out by Strauss's publisher Adolph Fürstner, Berlin and Paris, 1912. The original *Regiebuch* is now in the Theatersammlung of the Österreichische Nationalbibliothek.

[54] *Molière's ausgewählte Werke in drei Bänden*, translated by F. S. Bierling, Volume iii, *Der adelige Bürger* (Berlin, 1750), pp. 57–132.

[55] Not in 1751 as Hofmannsthal wrote. Bw. 15 May 1911, p. 99.

that a French audience would naturally have, and as Fiedler says in connection with all the Molière adaptations, to avoid distracting the audience by confronting it with a linguistic modernization.

Die Sprache der Bearbeitungen hält sich von moderner oder gar modern-lokaler oder individuell Hofmannsthalscher Diktion möglichst entfernt . . . Die der 'Heirat wider Willen' archaisiert bewußt, ebenso die der beiden 'Bürger als Edelmann'—Fassungen . . . für die zu diesem Zwecke eine Übersetzung aus dem 18. Jahrhundert zuhilfe genommen wird. Dieses Archaisieren geht jedoch so behutsam vor, daß es vom Publikum nicht als ausgesprochen fremd oder störend empfunden werden kann, und so nicht seinerseits die Aufmerksamkeit von Molière weg auf das Verfahren der sprachlichen Umwandlung lenkt.[56]

(The language of the adaptations keeps well away from modern and even modern regional or individual Hofmannsthalian diction . . . the language of the 'Heirat wider Willen' is intentionally archaic, as it is in the two 'Bürger als Edelmann' versions . . . for which an 18th century translation was used. This archaizing is, however, done so carefully that the audience cannot find it positively strange or disturbing and so for its own part it does not distract attention from Molière to the procedure of linguistic transformation.)

A detailed analysis of Hofmannsthal's adaptation of *Le Bourgeois Gentilhomme* will not be given here. The reader is directed to studies already available.[57] Broadly speaking, Molière's five acts were drastically reduced to two. Hofmannsthal ends with the banquet scene which is the opening scene of Molière's Act IV. The secondary plot, the love intrigue centring on Jourdain's daughter Lucile, her sweetheart Cleonte, and his servant Covielle, is cut altogether. The Turkish Ceremony in which Jourdain thinks he has been made a Mamamouchi disappears entirely, as does the *Ballet des Nations*, in place of which Hofmannsthal put the divertissement *Ariadne auf Naxos*. What we are left with are the components of the comedy of character, for Molière's play is in fact a mixture of *comédie-ballet* and *caractère* which can be

[56] Fiedler, p. 132.

[57] Hilde Burger, 'French Influences on Hugo von Hofmannsthal', p. 695. Fiedler, pp. 48–59 and 68–89. Wolfram Mauser, 'Hofmannsthal und Molière', pp. 8–9. Victor A. Oswald, Jr., 'Hofmannsthal's Collaboration with Molière', pp. 22–5. Stiegele, pp. 22–5 and 89–95.

divided up in this way. Thus Jourdain and all those characters who serve to show up his folly may remain. The plot now turns on Jourdain's infatuation with Dorimene, a widow who does not suspect his attentions. Neither does Dorimene suspect that her suitor Dorantes,[58] who is in debt, has manipulated Jourdain into giving Dorimene the banquet and entertainment, but simply believes they are doing him the honour of using his house.

This motif, present in the Molière, was further exploited as a thematic link between the play and the *Oper*. *Ariadne auf Naxos* is after all about a 'widow' who allows herself to be wooed and won again. Both Dorantes and Jourdain are thus presenting their suits to Dorimene by means of it. This is underlined in a number of speeches that Hofmannsthal added. Here Jourdain is enquiring about the content of the *Oper*: 'Haben Sie darauf Bedacht genommen, daß das ganze Ding für eine Witwe paßt? Es muß ganz und gar auf eine Witwe von vornehmem Stand abgesehen sein, welche zwar darauf beharrt, eine Witwe zu bleiben, welcher es aber doch am Ende schwer gemacht wird, darauf zu beharren.' (83) (Have you made sure that the whole thing is suitable for a widow? It must be aimed directly at a widow of high standing who insists on remaining a widow but who finds it difficult to do so in the end.) The Music Teacher replies 'Die Prinzessin Ariadne ist ... als eine trauende Witwe anzusehen' (83). When the Dancing Master then mentions the Intermezzo 'Die ungetreue Zerbinetta und ihre vier Liebhaber' Jourdain instantly pipes up with his question 'Ist es darin auch auf eine Witwe abgesehen? und wird sie auf eine recht spitzbübische Weise dazu gebracht, ihrer Witwenschaft untreu zu werden?' (84). In the closing lines of the *Zwischenspiel* just before the overture to *Ariadne* begins, Dorantes whispers to Dorimene to make sure the point is not lost: 'Ich habe alles, was man spielen wird, angegeben. Mein einziger Gedanke war, daß in der Musik und in der Handlung einiges enthalten sei, was Sie zu rühren vermöchte. Es handelt sich um eine Frau, die man ihrer Lage nach mit einer Witwe vergleichen darf.' (160) (I

---

[58] For the sake of clarity I have kept to Hofmannsthal's spelling of French names throughout. Hence 'Dorantes' and 'Dorimene' and not Molière's 'Dorante' and 'Dorimène'.

have indicated everything that is to be acted. My only thought was that there should be something in the music and the action which might touch you closely. It is about a woman whose situation may be compared with that of a widow.) It is ironic that at the end Dorimene, duped in her own way as badly as Jourdain, steals off with Dorantes, thus to all appearances making her choice between the two suitors whilst only intending to escape Jourdain's tedious thanks.

vi. *The 1912* Ariadne auf Naxos

The 1912 combination of play plus opera is then a carefully reconstructed imitation of the *comédie-ballet* in which historical authenticity figures largely. Continuity and unity are preserved by a number of dramatic and stylistic devices already discussed.[59] The most persuasive feature of the 1912 version is that the whole work stems from a single source, namely Jourdain's bourgeois, philistine character which gives rise to the comedy in the first half and the extraordinary mixup in the second.[60] This mix-up is not only a light-hearted cultural and historical private joke but is also, because the divertissement comes off, the happy victory of Art against the Philistines. The divertissement, by succeeding, makes a fool of Jourdain and outwits him in the same way as the Turkish

[59] Just how much care Hofmannsthal had taken with the Molière is apparent from the following extract written after Hofmannsthal had learnt that the London production was not going to use his adaptation: 'Herr Beerbohm Tree spielt mit meiner Ariadne eine andere Übersetzung des Bourgeois. Als ob das möglich wäre! als ob es sich um Übersetzung handelte! Als ob nicht meine Adaptierung und Bearbeitung ganz als Piedestal für die "Ariadne" gemodelt, mit vorbereitenden Anspielungen durchsetzt wäre! als ob es überhaupt möglich wäre, einen anderen Bourgeois zu diesem Abend zu spielen! als ob nicht das Ganze eben als ein Theaterabend gedichtet wäre.—Er spielt eine andere Übersetzung! also womöglich den ganzen drei Stunden dauernden Originalbourgeois mit der Liebesintrige und der Cérémonie turque. Und kein Wort darin, daß es sich auf die Ariadne bezieht'. This letter of 9 May 1913 is one of the nine new letters given in the fourth, revised edition of the Strauss/Hofmannsthal *Briefwechsel*, p. 709. (See Bibliography.)

[60] Hofmannsthal seized the opportunity for comic embellishment with which this character provided him and invented two hilarious reasons why Jourdain should want both groups to perform together. First, a fireworks display has been ordered for nine o'clock, leaving not enough time for other entertainments (11), and second, the *nouveau riche* Jourdain feels that a desert island reflects poorly on his house and so has come up with the idea 'diese wüste Insel durch das Personal aus dem andern Stück einigermaßen anständig staffieren zu lassen' (152). These reasons are worthy of Molière and might have been by him except for the slightly Viennese delivery of the lackey.

Ceremony does. It thus functions within the plot, although on a different level of reality to the *caractère*.

The other elements binding the parts together are, as one would expect in a *comédie-ballet*, music and dancing. The incidental music is written in Strauss's most crystalline pastiche style and certainly whets the appetite for the *Oper*.[61] This music is discussed at some length in Chapter III. The separate numbers include the overture; a pastorale scene for three singers (who later sing Najade, Dryade, and Echo), which includes the sicilienne to the words 'Du Venus' Sohn'; the minuet from Jourdain's dancing lesson (taken from Strauss's incomplete ballet *Kythere*); musical accompaniment for the fencing lesson; the entry of the journeymen tailors; the polonaise to which the first tailor dances; the entry of Dorantes and Dorimene and the elaborate dinner music in which each course is illustrated by appropriate music, the fish course, for example, by a quotation from the Rhine motif from Wagner's *Ring*, and the leg of lamb by the sheep music from Strauss's *Don Quixote*.[62] The final course is an *Omelette Surprise*. The surprise is a scullion who leaps out of a gigantic dish and performs an intoxicated, erotic dance which is intended to symbolize Dorantes's feelings for Dorimene. This dance was created by Hofmannsthal specifically for his friend the ballerina Grete Wiesenthal who did dance the part to perfection at the Stuttgart première.[63] The scenario for the dance was enclosed in a letter to Strauss of 26 April 1912. An identical undated scenario was found amongst Grete Wiesenthal's papers and is reproduced by Fiedler.[64] The shyly narcissistic movements in the dance and its bisexual undertones, emphasized by having a woman execute the role, place this kitchen-hand in the company of Hofmannsthal's other hermaphroditic youths who are discussed later.[65] The scenario reads as follows:

[61] For an intelligent discussion of pastiche in the incidental music see Alfred Rosenzweig, 'Les adaptations de Lulli et de Couperin par Richard Strauss'. Also Del Mar, pp. 11–24.

[62] Del Mar, p. 22.

[63] See the playbill of the 1912 production, Appendix C.

[64] It is not clear whether the letter to Strauss or the scenario for Grete Wiesenthal was written first.

[65] See Chapter II, pp. 88–9.

Tanzszene des Küchenjungen (2 bis 3 Minuten Musik)

Zuerst, nach dem Herabsteigen von dem Wägelchen, Schüchtern-
heit, sich in einem solchen Kreis zu finden. Bemächtigt sich mit
verstohlener Lüsternheit eines Glases mit süßem Wein, nippt daran.
Nun wird er mutiger, besieht sich die Herrschaft. Sieht bald alles
durch den goldenen Schleier leichter Trunkenheit. Die Schönheit
der Marquise berauscht ihn: er drückt durch Gebärden aus, daß sie
ihn von Sinnen bringe, ihn fliegen mache. Nun trinkt er noch einmal
ganz frech und herzhaft. Er küßt seine eigene Hand: das Ganze wird
für ihn immer spaßiger, Jourdains Gegenwart immer drolliger, das
Fluidum des Liebespaares scheint für ihn ein wirklich verstandenes
Element, an dem er sich stärker berauscht als an dem Wein—endlich
wirbelt er wie ein Toller ein paarmal um den Tisch herum und
hinaus. (Bw. 26 Apr. 1912, pp. 155–6.)

(Dancing scene of the scullion (two or three minutes of music):

At first, having got down from the little cart, he is timid at finding
himself in such company. Snatches with furtive avidity a glass of
sweet wine and sips it. Now he grows bolder and scrutinizes the
noble company. Soon he sees everything through the golden haze of
slight drunkenness. He is intoxicated by the beauty of the Marquise:
he expresses in his gestures that she is driving him out of his senses,
that she makes him fly. Now he takes another bold and lusty drink.
He kisses his own hand; the whole situation strikes him as amusing,
Jourdain's presence as increasingly droll; the atmosphere between
the two lovers is an element which he seems perfectly capable of
understanding, which intoxicates him more than the wine—finally
he spins several times round the table like a madman and off.)

Although inventive, this episode is a superfluous conceit
which does not advance a lagging and dramatically weak
second act. This act closes without further full numbers on a
lame final curtain as Dorimene, offended by Mme Jourdain,
exits rapidly. The incidental music makes the transition to the
opera of the second half less abrupt and unexpected, and
fulfils in the *Bürger als Edelmann* adaptation the same function
as Lully's pieces had for Molière.

Thus the 1912 *Ariadne auf Naxos*, although an elaborate
compound form involving many arts, or, in short, a 'Gesamtkunstwerk', may be seen primarily as an imitation of a
theatre-oriented, intellectually undemanding historical form,
the *comédie-ballet*. This compound form dictates a certain
ingenuous simplicity of the component parts in matters

aesthetic, psychological, and metaphysical or the whole would
become a conceptual hippopotamus in the theatre. Hence it is
reasonable to conclude that the literary simplicity of Hofmannsthal's divertissement *Ariadne auf Naxos* is dictated and
guaranteed by the frame into which it is put.

vii. *The Set Number Libretto*

Technical simplicity was part of the original Strauss–Hofmannsthal plan to write a small, interim work. The thank-
offering to Reinhardt was not envisaged on a grand scale.
Reinhardt's help at Dresden had not been of that order, and
the original idea outlined in Hofmannsthal's letter to his father
was an appropriately scaled gesture. Furthermore at the time
of devising it Strauss and Hofmannsthal had barely finished
seeing *Der Rosenkavalier* safely launched and were probably
not yet ready to contemplate the next major joint work.[66]
   In the letter to his father, quoted above, Hofmannsthal calls
the divertissement a small chamber opera—'eine ganz kleine
Oper nur für Kammermusik'. He speaks of the over-all plan of
the Molière plus the opera as an interim work; 'eine kleine
Zwischenarbeit, die aber sehr wohl dem Reinhardt über eine
ganze Saison weghelfen kann'. K. J. Krüger rightly draws
attention to this by referring to *Ariadne auf Naxos* as a
'Gelegenheitsarbeit'.[67]
   In the correspondence there are a number of other passages
which show how clearly Hofmannsthal was set on technical
simplicity, and his ulterior motives within the collaboration
for wanting this. An example is his letter of 20 March 1911
with its oblique reference to *Ariadne*: 'Wenn man wieder
einmal zusammen etwas machen wollte (ich meine etwas
Großes, ganz abgesehen von der 30-Minuten-Oper für ein
kleines Kammerorchester, die in meinem Kopf so gut wie
fertig ist,) . . . also: Wenn man wieder einmal etwas Großes
zusammen machen wollte, so müßte es eine bunte und starke
Handlung sein und das Detail des Textbuchs minder wichtig.'
(Bw. 20 Mar. 1911, pp. 95–6.) (If we were to work together

---

[66] *Der Rosenkavalier* was completed in June 1910 but the following months until the
première in January 1911 were devoted to polishing the work and arranging details
of the production, as the correspondence shows.
[67] Krüger, p. 132.

once more on something (and by this I mean something
important, not the thirty minute opera for small chamber
orchestra which is as good as complete in my head . . .) well
now, if we were to work together once more on something big,
it would have to possess colourful and clear-cut action, and the
detail for the libretto would be less important.) Further down
in the same letter he refers to *Ariadne* as a 'Zwischenarbeit'
and in a letter of 15 June 1911 he refers retrospectively to the
original plan as a 'Spielerei'.

Hofmannsthal's ulterior motives in writing *Ariadne* were
that this interim work, being technically and artistically so
slight, might afford him the opportunity of practising and
exploring certain aspects of libretto writing. *Ariadne* was thus
in some respects an experimental exercise in the libretto,
aimed at helping Hofmannsthal solve some of the problems
that had arisen in previous operas and intended to crystallize
the new directions the collaboration seemed to be taking.

It was particularly important for Hofmannsthal to practise
libretto writing as he was not a musician. He had received no
formal musical training and although he was deeply appreciative of much music, his was a fundamentally conservative
taste which if left to itself would have preferred Beethoven to
Strauss.[68] Hofmannsthal was aware of his limitations and the
significance of these limitations in a librettist, particularly in
one who, as he did, saw the librettist engaged in a joint task of
fusing word and music.

In the letter of 20 March 1911 Hofmannsthal wrote about
Ariadne in conjunction with these problems: 'Auch glaube ich,
es bedarf dieser Zwischenarbeit, mindestens *für mich*, um
mich mit der Musik, speziell mit Ihrer Musik, noch mehr
auskennen zu lernen, um etwas zu machen, worin wir noch
viel vollständiger zusammenkommen als im "Rosenkavalier",
der mich als ein Ganzes von Text und Musik zwar *recht sehr*,
aber nicht völlig befriedigt.' (Bw. 20 Mar. 1911, pp. 95–6.) (I
am also inclined to think that this interim work is necessary,
at least *for me*, to make myself still more familiar with music,
especially with your music, and to achieve something which
brings us even closer together than in *Rosenkavalier*—which

---

[68] For a good short introduction to Hofmannsthal's musical tastes and opinions see
Egon Wellesz, 'Hofmannsthal und die Musik'. See also Daviau and Buelow, p. 33.

as a fusion of word and music satisfies me *greatly*, but not
wholly.) Hofmannsthal's other motive in writing this interim
piece, namely the desire to experiment and at the same time
to crystallize new ideas, is also mentioned by him in this letter
and centres on the set numbers: 'Durch die kleine Zwischenarbeit wird mir vielleicht noch völlig klar werden, wie es
möglich sein wird, ein dramatisches Ganzes aufzubauen, in
welchem die *Nummern* die größte Bedeutung mehr und mehr
gewinnen müssen und wie dabei das zwischen den Nummern
Liegende stilistisch richtig zu behandeln ist.' (Bw. 20 Mar.
1911, p. 96.) (This slight interim work will perhaps make it
still clearer to me how to construct a dramatic piece as a whole
so that the *set numbers* regain more and more their paramount
importance, and help me to find the right treatment for that
which lies between the numbers.) Here is one of those turning
points in the Strauss–Hofmannsthal collaboration that justifies
calling *Ariadne* 'pivotal'.[69] With the issue of the set numbers
Hofmannsthal touches on the whole question of the 'durch-
komponierte' opera versus the number opera. Within this
collaboration the former instantly spelled 'Wagner' and the
latter 'Mozart'. Viewed very crudely, the course of the Strauss–
Hofmannsthal collaboration over the six operas can be seen as
a turning away from the Wagnerian towards the Mozartian
model. This obviously implies changes in orchestration,
thematic material, characterization, and musical and dramatic
structure. It is equally true to state that Hofmannsthal
championed the Mozartian opera and that Strauss had more
natural affinity with the Wagnerian—but it does little justice
to Strauss to argue that he was seduced by Hofmannsthal into
composing Mozartian number operas against his will or
natural inclination.[70] Hofmannsthal liked to draw compari-
sons between their works and Mozart's: *Die Frau ohne*

[69] Daviau and Buelow, p. 1.

[70] Del Mar does not go so far but suggests that Hofmannsthal's say in the subject
matter of the operas was too large. Del Mar, p. 5. On the other side, Egon Vietta, in
an extraordinary article, claims that Strauss's conservatism crushed Hofmannsthal's
avant garde spirit. Hofmannsthal would have done better, Vietta implies, to have
collaborated with Schönberg, Stravinsky or Berg. Egon Vietta, 'Die Entstehung der
"Ariadne"'. There is no point, however, in discussing what ought to or might have
been in this collaboration; we must look at what it was, and not dwell too long on the
inevitable differences between the partners.

Schatten, he predicts in this same letter of 20 March 1911, will stand in the same relation to *Die Zauberflöte* as *Der Rosenkavalier* does to *Figaro. Der Rosenkavalier* had been a half-way house towards the number opera. As Hofmannsthal wrote to Strauss, numbers such as the trio between the Marschallin, Octavian, and Sophie in the third act, had been repeatedly suggested, but the fully differentiated number with recitative or prose between had not been used. (The Italian tenor's aria is a deliberate parody of the bel canto form and cannot be counted as a number as such.) In the following letter of 19 May 1911 which accompanied the *Szenarium* it becomes quite clear that part of Hofmannsthal's intentions in writing *Ariadne auf Naxos* was to practise the set numbers and that at the same time he regarded *Ariadne* as a not very serious enterprise which was precisely why he could allow himself the luxury of experimenting:

Lesen Sie bitte das durch und sagen mir, wie weit es Ihnen entspricht ... Zu Nummern, Duetten, Terzetten, Quintetten, Sextetten ist reichlich Gelegenheit.—Sie werden gut tun, mir anzudeuten, an welchen Stellen Sie präzise Nummern legen wollen, so wie dies im 'Rosenkavalier' mehrmals geschehen ist. Diese kleine Unterlage für Ihre Musik hätte ihren Zweck erfüllt, wenn sie Ihnen Gelegenheit gäbe, sich in einer absichtlich verengten Form halb scherzhaft und doch von Herzen zu manifestieren. (Bw. 19 May 1911, pp. 100–1.)

(Please read through the enclosed and tell me how it appeals to you ... There is ample opportunity here for set numbers: duets, trios, quintets, sextets. It would be good if you were to indicate to me where you mean to place definite *numbers,* and where you intend merely to suggest them as you did repeatedly in *Rosenkavalier.* This slight scaffolding for your music will have served its purpose if it gives you an opportunity of expressing yourself on a deliberately reduced scale, half playfully and yet *from the heart.*)

We shall see later what were the consequences of Strauss's marking in the set numbers into the *Szenarium* at this very early stage. (Strauss's indications for set numbers are the italicized marginalia in the *Szenarium.*) Here we are concerned only to show that initially *Ariadne auf Naxos* was conceived partly in terms of an exercise in collaboration, focusing on the shift towards the set number. This is confirmed by Hofmannsthal's reply to Strauss's letter of 22 May 1911, giving a detailed plan of the musical numbers:

Der Überblick über die geschlossenen Nummern, die Sie wünschen, ist mir fördernd und *suggestiv*, desgleichen alles, was Sie mir noch an speziell musikalischen Wünschen und Absichten mitteilen werden. Nur so ist Zusammenarbeiten möglich. Ich werde gelegentlich Ihr Entgegenkommen fordern, wo eine Dichtung ein mehr dienendes Verhältnis der Musik in gewissen Szenen erheischt—so war es schon bei der Szene der Marschallin—umgekehrt hier soll alles nur wie ein Drahtgestell sein, um Musik gut und hübsch daran aufzuhängen. (Bw. 25 May 1911, p. 103.)

(Your list of the set numbers you would like is helpful and stimulating, and the same will certainly be true of all other specific musical wishes and intentions you may communicate to me. This is the only way to collaborate. There will be other occasions when I shall ask you to comply with requests of mine: where, in certain episodes, a given text requires a more subordinate attitude from the music, as was the case in the Marschallin's scene. Here, on the contrary, the whole thing is to be simply a framework on which to hang the music, well and prettily.)

Hofmannsthal could not have adopted such a flexible, accommodating and even self-subordinating attitude if *Ariadne* had not been regarded as an interim work. The only way Hofmannsthal with his complete artistic integrity could give himself room for experimentation was to do it in a work which, in a sense, did not count. So the scheme of adapting a Molière play and adding an opera was also fortunate because it favoured experimentation within the collaboration.

The frequent mention of experimentation should not, however, mislead us into thinking that any daring or complicated innovations were taking place. The set number is in itself a simple form and Hofmannsthal turned to it in a spirit of conservatism. In *Ariadne auf Naxos* Hofmannsthal wished to practise one basic operatic technique and sought to do so initially in isolation from other operatic problems. This simplifying conservatism, which Hofmannsthal might have preferred to call development 'in der Spirale' (Bw. 20 Mar. 1911, p. 96), is reflected in the choice of the chamber orchestra which Hofmannsthal may privately have rejoiced in as security against Strauss's Wagnerian orchestra. Possibly even in the actual idea of a Molièresque divertissement there is a nostalgia for the simpler forms of the past.

Whatever the case, it is clear that the *Oper* was to be an historical and imaginative recreation of a divertissement, constructed along the lines of a simple allegory, essentially impersonal, in the form of a thirty-minute chamber opera, an interim work and based on set numbers.

Chapter II

The Genesis of the Libretto from the
Notes and the *Szenarium*

Ariadne auf Naxos has the foundations of a simple work but matters were soon complicated. First, the *Oper* was complicated by Hofmannsthal at the literary level. When he came to write out the *Szenarium* it seems that he was strongly tempted to produce a lyric drama instead and that this was then superimposed on the earlier plan. Second, *Ariadne* was complicated during its genesis by a collaboration which was, ironically, too close. Because of pressure of time Strauss was composing material almost as it was written and as each instalment was sent to him. Strauss did not have an over-all perspective of the work (and kept calling for dramatic tension and climaxes to help him get his bearings),[1] Hofmannsthal could not be sure if he approved of the composition, and yet *Ariadne* was more or less a musical *fait accompli* before Hofmannsthal could turn round.

Not only was there a temporal closeness in the instalment method of working but there was also a great deal of closeness in defining the original *Ariadne auf Naxos* in both its artistic and technical aims. This had been necessary because of the unique circumstances which had given rise to the scheme and which we have already discussed. The result was that Hofmannsthal was pledged to certain things in the 1912 version which he really could not leave unfulfilled without being guilty of 'breach of contract', for once Reinhardt had agreed to produce *Ariadne* the arrangements and plans did amount to an artistic contract.

It was therefore difficult for Hofmannsthal to change the foundations, although inwardly he seems to have found them

---

[1] For example, Bw. 20 July 1911, p. 101; Bw. 27 July 1911, p. 106; Bw. 14 July 1911, p. 113; Bw. 19 July 1911, pp. 116–17.

burdensome and restrictive, because the contract was too closely defined.

i. 'Lyric Drama' versus Divertissement

It may seem extravagant and unfounded to claim that Hofmannsthal wished to turn the *Szenarium* into a lyric drama. No critic has made such a claim or comments to that effect except in passing.[2] Yet there is both external and internal evidence that this was so. The most telling piece of external evidence is that Hofmannsthal himself classified *Ariadne* as a lyric drama for the 1922 edition of his works.[3] The internal evidence is that it has the formal characteristics of a verse drama: poetic monologues and dialogues abound, the tone is predominantly lyrical and musical, it deals in psychological and spiritual values and it makes use of poetic symbolism, it is anti-naturalistic and uses character and action which are not dramatic.[4] The *Ariadne* libretto will be examined more closely for these features.

Why, however, was Hofmannsthal not content to turn the *Szenarium* into a Molièresque divertissement as planned and agreed in the contract? Very possibly when Hofmannsthal actually came to write the libretto in late May or early June 1911 he found the whole idea *too* slight and impersonal. There was nothing there for him to get his teeth into. No doubt he wanted to give the libretto a complex, personal touch, in short to make it his own and not just one of his anonymous Molière adaptations.[5]

Accordingly Hofmannsthal began to develop 'die seelischen Motive der Sache' (BW. 28 May 1911, p. 107) and to work out symbolic and spiritual detail. He concentrated on the figures of Ariadne and Bacchus and their relationship and referred to them as 'das Eigentliche' (Bw. 28 May 1911, p. 107). This shift towards the personal can be dated from 28 May 1911. On this

[2] See Introduction, Note 11.

[3] Werner Volke, *Hugo von Hofmannsthal in Selbstzeugnissen und Bilddokumenten*, p. 125–6.

[4] Gero von Wilpert, *Sachwörterbuch der Literatur* (Stuttgart, 1969), p. 825. See also Ronald Peacock, *The Poet in the Theatre* (London, 1946).

[5] Such as *Die Heirat wider Willen* (LII, pp. 49–94). Herbert Steiner comments 'Die Übersetzung des "Mariage forcé", "begonnen in Aussee Juli 1909", in Berlin und später in Wien aufgeführt, in Maschinenschrift vervielfältigt, blieb ungedruckt' (LII, p. 395).

day Hofmannsthal went for a walk with Max Mell and seems to have clarified points about *Ariadne* in conversation with his friend. Under the heading 'Spaziergang mit Max Mell' he noted some major Ariadne-Bacchus motifs.[6] A letter to Strauss also written on this day outlines the new ideas and shift in position (Bw. 28 May 1911, pp. 106–8). On a separate sheet he pencilled the full title of the 1912 Ariadne and the essential points of the Bacchus-Circe relationship (see Appendix B, Note 2). These new motifs and ideas satisfied Hofmannsthal's wish for a personal touch in the opera and he later wrote '*Ariadne* ist eine meiner persönlichsten und mir wertesten Arbeiten' (Bw. 18 Dec. 1911, p. 129). But in balking at slightness and impersonality Hofmannsthal was of course rejecting part of the original nature of the work which, as a divertissement, had to be slight and free of psychological motifs.

Another possible reason for Hofmannsthal's dissatisfaction may have been his largely unspoken doubts as to whether the whole plan, on which three such eminent artists as Reinhardt, Strauss, and himself were after all going to expend considerable time and creative energy, was not too insignificant and excogitated. The responsibility rested with him and he had perhaps pitched the tone too low for his partners. These qualms, which could have sprung entirely from Hofmannsthal's self-critical and exacting nature, were increased no doubt by Strauss's very cool reception of the *Szenarium* and parts of the libretto.[7] Amongst other things Strauss complained that the dramatic framework was 'an sich ja dünn' and told Hofmannsthal to get his Pegasus saddled (Bw. 22 May 1911, p. 102)—not the sorts of comments that would endear him to this librettist. In a way Hofmannsthal wanted both to have his cake and eat it with *Ariadne auf Naxos*; he wanted both an enjoyable interim work with the chance to experiment on one or two points, and yet he also wanted to make a significant, profound, and personal contribution to the operatic repertoire. This double wish may be inferred from a letter to Strauss written after Hofmannsthal had introduced the Ariadne-

[6] See Stiegele, p. 44. Also Appendix A, Note 2.
[7] For example, Bw. 20 July 1911, p. 101; Bw. 22 July 1911, p. 102; Bw. 27 July 1911, pp. 105–6; Bw. 14 July 1911, p. 113; Bw. 19 July 1911, pp. 116–18.

Bacchus motifs into the libretto: 'Überhaupt, wenn zwei Menschen wie wir eine solche "Spielerei" machen, so muß es eben eine sehr ernsthafte Spielerei werden, wir müssen nach Kräften von unserem *Besten* hineinstecken, irgendwann, irgendwo, irgendwie wird's uns schon gelohnt werden. (Bw. 15 June 1911, p. 110.) (Altogether, when two men like us set out to produce a 'trifle' like this, it has to become a very serious trifle: we must strive to put our *best* into it; some time, somewhere, somehow we are sure to receive our reward.) No doubt the same letter could have been written to Reinhardt as well.

Finally, an historical and imaginative recreation of a Molièresque divertissement was not going to provide its author with any scope for his lyric vein and Hofmannsthal was, above all else, one of the most gifted lyricists in the German language with a fully developed poetic style. It is true that since the so-called 'Chandoskrise' he had not been able to write lyric poems or lyric dramas but he had neither forgotten what he had been able to do nor ceased to hope that he would one day write lyric verse again.[8] Privately he seems to have regarded *Ariadne* as a step in this direction. On 15 July 1912 he wrote to Borchardt 'Mir ist als würde ich wieder im Lyrischen produktiver werden und als sei "Ariadne" ein Zwischenglied hiezu, eine unbewußt mir hergestellte Brücke.'[9] (It seems to me that I might be becoming more productive in a lyric vein again and as if 'Ariadne' were a link, a bridge that I had unconsciously built.) Elsewhere in the Borchardt correspondence he referred to the

---

[8] *Hofmannsthalforschung* now recognizes that the 'Chandoskrise' does not mark a complete rupture with earlier styles. Kenkel has found evidence of continuity in his careful stylistic analysis of Hofmannsthal's language. Konrad Kenkel, 'Die Funktion der Sprache bei Hofmannsthal vor und nach der Chandos-Krise', pp. 89–101. Günther Erken points out that whilst other arts became more important to Hofmannsthal than they had previously been, poetry remained important to him. Erken, pp. 47–8. The 'Chandoskrise' is then not a true watershed but a convenient term for marking phases in Hofmannsthal's life. As with most terms of this nature, there is the danger that it may be used too glibly or be made to stand for too much. This is the case with Michael Hamburger's account of Hofmannsthal the librettist. Michael Hamburger, *Hofmannsthal: Three Essays*, pp. 65–84. A more reasoned account is given by Albin Eduard Beau in his previously cited article 'Hofmannsthals Wendung zur Oper'. See Chapter I, Note 2.

[9] Hugo von Hofmannsthal/Rudolf Borchardt, 'Unbekannte Briefe', edited by Werner Volke, p. 24.

Ariadne libretto as his 'Gedicht'.[10] Judgements of this libretto made to other friends seem to have concentrated on the lyric aspects. For example, in his correspondence with R. Pannwitz Hofmannsthal later saw *Ariadne* as the first link in a series parallel to the lyric drama to be continued with the *Ägyptische Helena* and *Danae*.[11] In a letter to Dora von Bodenhausen, wife of his lifelong friend Eduard von Bodenhausen, Hofmannsthal is especially delighted at how well the three little songs have turned out and exclaims 'es sind doch richtige kleine Gedichte von mir'.[12] In a letter to Strauss about these same songs he tells Strauss he would have to look far to find three songs of comparable merit: 'Auch glaub' ich, daß sich nicht leicht in einem einaktigen Operntextbuch drei Lieder finden werden, die sich an Zartheit und zugleich an charakteristischer Bestimmtheit mit dem Lied des Harlekin, dem Rondeau der Zerbinetta und dem Circelied des Bacchus messen können. (Bw. mid-July 1911, p. 115.) (I doubt, moreover, if one could easily find in any other libretto for a one-act opera three songs of comparable delicacy, and at the same time equally characteristic in tone, as Harlekin's song, the rondo for Zerbinetta and the Circe song of Bacchus.) It does not concern us here that Hofmannsthal was making rather exaggerated claims for the songs; we only want to note how very conscious he was of every manifestation of his lyricism in the libretto and how keen he was to foster it. From this we may infer that at the time of turning the *Szenarium* into a libretto Hofmannsthal had taken a decision, either conscious or unconscious, to make it into a lyric drama.

This decision did not conflict with the wish to make *Ariadne* a more personal work. Exactly those qualities which go to make one of his works personal also make it lyric and these

---

[10] Hugo von Hofmannsthal/Rudolf Borchardt, *Briefwechsel*, p. 87. Cf. Willy Haas' account: '1911 traf ich ihn zum erstenmal. Damals hatte er noch Hoffnung, er würde neue Gedichte schaffen, und für diesen Fall versprach er mir, einige für meine *Herderblätter* auszuwählen. Aber sie kamen nicht wieder, und so bekam ich auch keine. Erst von 1912 und 1920 gibt es wieder zwei kurze, gewichtige poetische Stücke. Man könnte vielleicht noch das Lied des Harlekin und die große Arie des Bacchus in der Oper *Ariadne auf Naxos* als poetische Glücksfälle anführen.' Willy Haas, *Hugo von Hofmannsthal*, p. 18.

[11] Hugo von Hofmannsthal, 'Aus Briefen an Rudolf Pannwitz', p. 26.

[12] Hugo von Hofmannsthal/Eberhard von Bodenhausen, *Briefe der Freundschaft*, p. 128.

qualities are a gentle, muted spirituality, symbolism, a sensitive and serious ethical idealism, and overtones of the mystical. To say that Hofmannsthal wished to turn the *Szenarium* into something more personal is therefore synonymous with saying he wished to turn it into something more lyrical, and vice versa.

There is room to speculate on the development from the *Szenarium* from a different angle. It is possible that when Hofmannsthal sat down at his desk with his *Notizen* and the *Szenarium* in front of him—we know that he worked closely from these because numerous phrases and single words have been transposed into the libretto—he was faced with the too difficult task of writing the historically and stylistically authentic *words* for his divertissement, for which he had no single model. Visual detail and plot are perhaps easier to recreate than dialogue; and where he was faced with this difficult or at any rate tiresome task Hofmannsthal found his highly developed poetic style ready to assert itself and at some points even to take over.

A final factor which may figure amongst the causes of the shift was the synchronous work in 1911 on *Die Frau ohne Schatten* and the novel *Andreas*.[13] Both these works contain in much more satisfactory form the thematic material which is used in the lyric climax of *Ariadne*. In brief, this theme concerns 'das Allomatische' or the mutual transformation of two people through their love for one another. The allomatic is dealt with later; here it can only be suggested that Hofmannsthal's preoccupation with the theme flowed over into the work under way, particularly as there was a possible, though narrow, opening for it. In other words Hofmannsthal had a theme or germinal idea on hand and this theme which was more than a little adaptable was produced to pad out the 'thinness' of the *Szenarium*.

It is clear, then, that the intrusion of the lyric and personal

---

[13] As has already been noted, *Ariadne auf Naxos* and *Die Frau ohne Schatten* were both first mentioned on 26 February 1911. Hofmannsthal was busy with *Die Frau* during the next few months and on 15 May 1911 Strauss inquired after it. But Hofmannsthal, who had always regarded it as a major work, was not ready and so was relieved when in May 1911 he interrupted it in favour of *Ariadne*. The first chapter of *Andreas* was written in September 1912 but Hofmannsthal had been gathering material and ideas for it over the previous two years.

aspects prevented a simple and faithful realization of the *Szenarium* and we have speculated in a general way as to why the lyric did intrude at this point. We shall continue with an attempt at tracing the emergence of the 'lyric drama' *Ariadne auf Naxos* by means of a close study of the genesis of the libretto from the *Szenarium* and the early *Notizen* which is in effect the genesis of the literary complication.[14] Our original contention, that the foundations were not changed and that this resulted in some odd faults must be kept in mind.

ii. *The Notes and the* Szenarium *compared with the Libretto*

Hofmannsthal's notes to *Ariadne* are mostly unpublished and undated. It is not possible to give a definitive chronological order for them and the order given here is based on content, changes of names of characters, and stylistic and orthographic detail.

This first note does bear a date and place-name—'Paris Anfang Mai 1911'.[15] We know that it was in Paris that Hofmannsthal first had the idea of using *Le Bourgeois Gentilhomme* as a frame.[16] We also know from some loose jottings on the notes pertaining to *Die kluge Gräfin* (the original frame for *Ariadne*) that Hofmannsthal returned from Paris on 10 May 1911 and that work on *Ariadne* commenced in earnest after this date:

> Ariadne auf Naxos
> (als Divertissement für
> der Bürger als Edelmann.)
> entstanden seit der Rückkehr von
> Paris, 10 Mai 1911.[17]
>
> (Ariadne auf Naxos
> (as divertissement for

[14] A similar genetic study is made by Stiegele, who is furthermore the only critic to deal with the *Notizen* in depth. My findings differ from hers however because, for reasons given in this Chapter, I have dated the *Notizen* differently, and because Stiegele is not concerned with the music at all and uses her material as preparation for a full analysis of the 1918 *Bürger als Edelmann*.

[15] Stiegele, p. 43.

[16] 'In Paris stand es auf einmal klar vor mir, wie vortrefflich sich der "Bourgeois gentilhomme" eigne, ein solches opernartiges Divertissement einzulegen.' Bw. 15 May 1911, p. 99.

[17] In Fiedler, p. 142.

the Bürger als Edelmann.)
begun after the return from
Paris 10 May 1911.)

Hofmannsthal does not count the first note written in Paris. Unfortunately this note is not reproduced by Stiegele but it is adequately summarized:

Dieser Entwurf zeichnet in großen Linien die Bewegung des Ganzen, die Stationen der Handlung bis zum Auftritt von Bacchus, wie sie dann erweitert ins Szenarium eingegangen sind: Die verlassene Ariadne, das Erstarren ihrer Klagen im Schmerz, das Teilnahmslose der Nymphen ('Echo gibt ihr matte Antworten'), den trivialen Versuch der italienischen Masken, Ariadne zu trösten ('Die Zeit wird trösten. Auf dieser wüsten Insel mit Freundinnen ists gut zu plaudern'), schließlich die Ankündigung der Nymphen: 'Ein Schiff kommt gefahren.'[18]

(This sketch broadly outlines the movement of the whole, the stages of the action up to Bacchus' entry, as they then went into the *Szenarium* in an expanded form: the abandoned Ariadne, the growing numbness of agonized lament, the indifference of the nymphs ('Echo gives her faint answers'), the commonplace attempt of the Italian masques to comfort Ariadne ('Time will comfort. On this desert island it's nice to chat with friends'), finally the announcement of the nymphs: 'A ship is arriving.')

As Stiegele indicates, most of this note went into the *Szenarium*. The theme of 'trösten' is indicated in the line 'Die Zeit wird trösten' as is the healing effect of time which is taken up in the Buffo Quartet in the libretto in the line 'Die Zeit geht hin und tilgt die Spur' (41). Nothing in this note suggests that the author was thinking of more than a historically authentic divertissement. Emotions and reactions are stylized and conventional. There is great attention to the authenticity of the stage setting. This can be seen from the continuation of this note which we have already quoted in part:

Arbeit: alles künstlich, abgewonnen, gezüchtet.
Racine, die Annäherung an Louis XIV . . .
Decoration kleine Felsen wie Modelle für
Nymphenburger Porzellan, verbunden durch
Guirlanden und dazwischen Candelaber.[19]

---

[18] Stiegele, p. 43.   [19] Appendix A, Note 1.

(Work: everything artificial, worked for, cultivated.
Racine, the approximation to Louis XIV . . .
Décor little cliffs like models for
Nymphenburger porcelain joined by
garlands and candelabra between.)

It is significant that the note breaks off before Bacchus' entry.
This fact may help to date other notes and may also tell us
something about the continuity of Hofmannsthal's thought
where this character is concerned.

Another note which must have been written before 15 May
1911 is the first of the two notes to *Ariadne* (see Appendix B).
It definitely antedates the *Szenarium*, for, as Willi Schuh points
out, Zerbinetta is still going by the earlier name 'Smeraldina'.
This particular note is much abbreviated and is not very
helpful. The other notes in this group which Schuh has
inaccurately dated as belonging together will be dealt with
later.

W. Stiegele claims that apart from the above two notes none
antedates the *Szenarium*.[20] In making this claim she has not
given enough attention to the following note:

Nymphe: meldet von Bacchos. Chor jubelnd.
Ariadne: ablehnend.
Ein Schiff liegt in der Bucht, ein Einzelner ist gelandet.
Er ist herrlich, ist unwiderstehlich.
Ariadne: in dumpfem Hinbrüten.
Bacchos Stimme: Wo ich nahe, wo ich lande—
Mannes Stimme, Raubtierstimme.
Ariadne: Es ist in mir. Es greift durch alle Schmerzen. Es ist
Auflösung aller Qual.
Es ist der Götterbote, der mich zu den Schatten holt.
Die Stimme weiter. Ariadne gelöst. Zu den Nymphen.
Chor leisest: Oh daß die Stimme weiter tönte.
Stimme schweigt, Ariadne erstarrt. Chor betrübt.
Stimme ertönt wieder. Ariadne gelöst, zu den Nymphen.
Töne töne schöne Stimme,
schöne Stimme töne wieder! Bacchos:
Deine Klagen sie beleben, uns entzücken solche Lieder!
darauf entsetzt: Wer bin ich, wenn ich nochmals liebe?
O weh, er kommt hierher! o käm er nie!
O daß er käme!

[20] Stiegele, p. 43.

Zerbinetta schmückt sie. Ariadnes Erwägungen für uns gegen Schmuck. Bacchos *heftig* zieht die sich wehrende mit sich: um Deiner Schmerzen willen.[21]

(Nymphs: announce Bacchos. Chorus jubilant. Ariadne: rejecting.
A ship lies in the bay, a lone man has landed.
He is splendid, is irresistible.
Ariadne: gloomily brooding.
Bacchus' voice: Where I draw near, where I land—man's voice, predator's voice.
Ariadne: It is in me. It passes through all pain.
It dissolves all anguish. It is the messenger of the gods, who fetches me to the shades. The voice continues.
Ariadne relaxed. To the nymphs.
Chorus very quietly: Oh if only the voice would go on singing.
Voice is silent, Ariadne grows stiff. Chorus troubled.
Voice sounds again. Ariadne relaxed, to the nymphs.
Sing, sing beautiful voice,
beautiful voice sing again! Bacchos:
Your laments enliven,
Such songs delight us!
then indignant: Who am I if I love again?
O alas, he is coming this way! O if only he'd never come!
O if only he'd come!
Zerbinetta adorns her. Ariadne's considerations for us against finery. Bacchos *violently* drags the resisting girl with him: for the sake of your suffering.)

    This note continues from where the first note broke off. The nymphs announce Bacchus' arrival. The device of teichoscopy is sustained over the two notes. In the first the nymphs cry out 'Ein Schiff kommt gefahren'.[22] Here they announce 'Ein Schiff liegt in der Bucht'. Clearly Hofmannsthal wanted continuity in the report of an off-stage happening. The note closes with Bacchus dragging Ariadne away with him. Again the basic action is that of the *Szenarium*. Given the continuity of this note from the first and also the fact that this third note is a skeletal version of the relevant section in the *Szenarium*, it would seem absurd to suggest that Hofmannsthal wrote it *after* having finished the sketch.

    Furthermore, mention is made in this note of a 'Chor'.

---

[21] Appendix A, Note 3.
[22] Stiegele, p. 43.

There is, however, no chorus in the *Szenarium* or anywhere else. It is much more likely that Hofmannsthal dropped the idea of a chorus from his notes when writing the *Szenarium* than the other way round. If we compare the *Szenarium* and the note we find in fact that the role of the chorus is taken over by the nymphs. This can be seen, for example, in a comparison of the lines dealing with the effect of Bacchus' voice on Ariadne. In the note we read 'Stimme schweigt, Ariadne erstarrt, Chor betrübt'. In the *Szenarium*, 'Die Stimme schweigt. Naiade, Dryade, Echo, leisest, äußern ihre Betrübnis'.

There are also a number of similar and nearly identical phrases in both the note and the *Szenarium*. In the one there is 'Ariadne: in dumpfem Hinbrüten'. In the other, 'Ariadne tritt aus der Grotte, steht in dumpfem Hinbrüten'. In this example the phrase is kept intact. In the following two examples there are minor alterations in style:

Note:	Ein Einzelner ist gelandet
Szenarium:	Nur einer sei gelandet
Note:	Er ist herrlich, ist unwiderstehlich.
Szenarium:	ein Herrlicher, Unwiderstehlicher

The greater linguistic sophistication of the *Szenarium* versions, the use of the subjunctive in the one and the adjectival noun in the other, indicates that the note must have come before the *Szenarium* and that it was later refined and expanded. The reverse chronological order is not impossible but on this evidence much less probable. We can state definitely, however, that this work was written after the first of W. Schuh's *Notizen 1* as the name 'Smeraldina' has now been dropped in favour of 'Zerbinetta'.

Yet there are still some puzzling features. There are, for example, the lines 'Töne töne schöne Stimme / schöne Stimme töne wieder' which are identical to the first line of the nymphs' trio in the libretto and are almost identical to the second line of their second refrain (59). Surely if these lines are not in the *Szenarium*, but are in the note and the libretto, then the note came after the *Szenarium*? But we must remember that Hofmannsthal used all his notes *and* the sketch when writing the libretto and the more likely hypothesis is that he temporarily omitted parts of the notes in the *Szenarium* but picked them up again in the libretto. The trio 'Töne töne süße Stimme' is a case in point.

A final feature of Hofmannsthal's method of working from his notes is the way he summarizes or condenses some of the material. We have already mentioned the stylized, almost clockwork way in which Ariadne reacts to Bacchus' voice. In the note her reactions are spelt out one by one:

> Die Stimme weiter. Ariadne gelöst. Zu den Nymphen.
> Chor leisest: Oh daß die Stimme weiter tönte.
> Stimme schweigt, Ariadne erstarrt. Chor betrübt.
> Stimme ertönt wieder. Ariadne gelöst, zu den Nymphen.

In the *Szenarium* Hofmannsthal simply summarizes: 'Ariadne, jedesmal, solange die Stimme tönt, gelöst, sobald die Stimme schweigt, aufs neue erstarrend.' Summary, a more sophisticated procedure, also allows us to conclude that the note is earlier than the sketch. The *Szenarium* gives furthermore a more sophisticated account of Ariadne's vacillating and ambiguous emotions by showing them obliquely in the form of an ironic observation from a third person. Ariadne in the note is enthralled by the voice and then says:

> darauf entsetzt: Wer bin ich, wenn ich nochmals liebe?
> O weh, er kommt hierher! o käm er nie!
> O daß er käme!

This naïve speech is not used in the *Szenarium*, instead it is transformed into the interaction between Ariadne and Zerbinetta and Zerbinetta's ironic observation:

Zerbinetta, zofenhaft zudringlich, bemüht Ariadne zu schmücken, zu putzen, Ariadne läßt es geschehen, als sei es für den Tod. Zerbinetta findet, Ariadnes Herz klopfe höchst lebendig, ihr Auge glänze unvergleichlich.

On the basis of these notes and the *Szenarium*, which belong so much together, we shall now pause and build up a composite picture of the characters Ariadne and Bacchus as Hofmannsthal must have seen them before 28 May 1911.

Bacchus is portrayed as a splendid, irresistible, virile man. In the note he is 'herrlich' and 'unwiderstehlich'. His voice may be sweet and beautiful but it is also a 'Mannes Stimme'. In case we are left in any doubt about his masculine potency and vigour Hofmannsthal adds the word 'Raubtierstimme'. Bacchus is further characterized by the title line of one of Hofmannsthal's early poems *Wo ich nahe, wo ich lande*.[23] The hero of this poem is a mixture of the magician, poet, and adventurer, a powerful, exotic figure who conjures up in other people spiritual depths and experiences of which they had never dreamed. This figure, like Bacchus, is a full-grown man and not a boy. The poem is not inappropriately cited, for both Bacchus and this composite figure seem to be able to bring about a release of intense 'dionysian' feeling in those they touch. The exoticism of this Bacchus suggested by the reference to the poem is taken up in the *Szenarium* by the request for 'fremdartige Musik'.

In the *Szenarium* Bacchus is also splendid and irresistible— 'Ein Herrlicher, Unwiderstehlicher!'. He is compared with a god possessing strange enchanting powers over animals. His voice, not specifically referred to as a 'Mannes Stimme', is nevertheless powerful and seductive: 'Bacchos' Stimme unsichtbar, lockend, werbend'. This voice causes Ariadne to be 'erschreckt und doch beglückt'.

It is one of his masculine attributes that this divine, handsome stranger is sure of his goal and heads straight for it.

148	[23] Wo ich nahe, wo ich lande,
149	Da im Schatten, dort im Sande
150	Werden sie sich zu mir setzen,
151	Und ich werde sie ergetzen,
152	Binden mit dem Schattenbande!
153	An den Dingen, die sie kennen,
154	Lehr ich sie Geheimes nennen,
155	Auf und Nieder ihrer Glieder
156	Und den Lauf der Sterne wieder,
157	Kaum vermögen sie's zu trennen!
158	Denn ich spreche: 'Große Macht
159	Lenkt den Tag, versenkt die Nacht,
160	Doch in Euch versenkt sich gleiche
161	Sehr geheimnisvolle Reiche
162	Ruhig wie in einen Schacht.'
163	Daß sie mit verhaltnem Grauen
164	An sich selber niederschauen,
165	Von Geheimnis ganz durchwoben
166	Fühlen sich emporgehoben
167	Und den Himmel dunkler blauen! GuLD, p. 196.

As previously mentioned, he is the archetypal romantic hero who believes in a direct conquest, and his triumphant entry is crowned by the bald 'Bacchos *steht da*'. The importance of the event is underlined by Zerbinetta, Naiade, and Dryade withdrawing at this moment under elaborate bows. Echo hides. A little later Bacchus is compared with a king.

The salient feature about Ariadne in both the notes and the *Szenarium* is that although she is a mythological *opera seria* personage and hence given to grand gestures and stereotyped feelings, she is also a warm human being invested with a certain amount of psychological realism. This can be seen from the lines 'Ariadne (richtet sich auf) Große Klage der Verlassenen, pathetisch aber ganz einfach und zum Herzen gehend. Nicht leben—nicht sterben—jammervoll.' (Sz. 287.) Here Hofmannsthal successfully recreated the impression of a Baroque 'Affekt' with its mixture of rhetorical pathos and sincere emotion. Perhaps he had Handel in mind or even the earlier 'Lamento d'Arianna' by Monteverdi. In this context we can understand the sentence in Hofmannsthal's letter to Strauss which accompanied the *Szenarium*: 'Die Figur der Ariadne denke ich mir zart umrissen, aber ganz *wirklich*, so wirklich wie die Feldmarschallin.' (Bw. 19 May 1911, p. 100). (I imagine the character of Ariadne gently outlined, but altogether *real*, as real as the Marschallin.) Hofmannsthal is merely saying that in addition to hauteur and pathos Ariadne should radiate human warmth. This Ariadne is certainly also humanly fallible. She is not only the personification of abstract fidelity—if she was the allegory would not have a happy end. In the note it is true that Ariadne thinks Bacchus may be Hermes: 'Es ist der Götterbote, der mich zu den Schatten holt.'[24] But a few lines later this thought is exposed as a transparent self-deception. Ariadne asks 'Wer bin ich, wenn ich nochmals liebe?' From this line it is quite plain that she knows she is falling in love—and surely we are not meant to believe it is with the 'Götterbote'? Part of the delight we derive from this projected divertissement is the sight of Ariadne's 'Seelenschwankungen'. There would be no irony in the Ariadne–Bacchus relationship if the sexual side of love were not present and seen to be in conflict with the spiritual.

[24] Appendix A, Note 3.

The Ariadne of the *Szenarium* is no different, although, as we have seen, her ambiguous feelings are conveyed in the little scene with Zerbinetta and not through direct statement.

A fragment of the first note dated 'Paris Anfang Mai 1911' further shows the extent of the psychological realism, albeit stylized and stereotyped, which Hofmannsthal envisaged for Ariadne: 'Hineinwühlen in den Schmerz. Fingiertes Gespräch mit dem Abwesenden. Sag doch, du hast mich verachtet. Sind Männer so anders als Frauen—nein, du bist tot! gewiß.'[25] (Wallowing in pain. Imaginary conversation with the absent person. Say it, you despised me. Are men so different from women—no, you are dead! Without a doubt!) She is trying to rationalize Theseus' behaviour and finally excuses him by claiming he is dead. But in the meanwhile some quite human doubts pass through her mind.

The relationship of Ariadne and Bacchus in the *Notizen* and the *Szenarium* is also kept at a very simple level, as befits a divertissement. Within the relationship Ariadne's falling in love is the more important; Bacchus' is taken more or less for granted. Before their 'eigentliches Liebesduett' they hold a 'zartes Liebesgespräch' which, Hofmannsthal has noted in the margin, is to be 'entfernt im Stil Marschallin–Quinquin'. Again Hofmannsthal is simply drawing Strauss's attention to that realism and warmth which he wished to be conveyed in the musical style, rather than drawing any parallel between the situation and characters of Ariadne–Bacchus and the Marschallin–Quinquin. So it is apparent then that in the *Szenarium* the characterization of Ariadne and Bacchus and their relationship is appropriate to the allegoric form.

On or just before 28 May 1911 as part of the lyric shift Hofmannsthal suddenly felt compelled to give the Ariadne–Bacchus relationship a delicate new shading. Strauss had just written asking him for a second time to spur his Pegasus, and Hofmannsthal replied in the following vein:

Nun habe ich in den letzten Tagen (bevor Ihr Brief kam, der mich eher aus der Stimmung als in sie hineingebracht hätte), die schwerste und reizvollste Arbeit hinter mich gebracht, nämlich die seelischen Motive der Sache übereinzubringen, mir innerlich den Bezug zwischen den Figuren sowie zwischen den Teilen des Ganzen

[25] Appendix A, Note 4.

herzustellen, kurz, das genaue Schema der inneren Motiven zu entwerfen, das dem Dichter, ähnlich wie Ihnen ein symphonisches Gebilde, vorschweben muß, damit ihn die Arbeit anziehen, beleben und festhalten kann. Dieses seelische Gewebe ist das Eigentliche und das andere (was Sie mit dem treffenden Wort Architekturgarten bezeichnen) ist nur drum herum, so wie im 'Rosenkavalier' das Zeitkolorit, das Zeremoniell, der Dialekt usw. um das Eigentliche herum ist. Dieses Eigentliche zwischen Ariadne und Bacchus nun schwebt mir so abgestuft, so zart bewegt, so psychologisch und so lyrisch zugleich vor der Seele, daß ich es schon miserabel ausführen müßte, wenn es Sie nicht schließlich in der gleichen Weise interessieren sollte. (Bw. 28 May 1911, pp. 106–8.)

(During the past few days (before your letter arrived, the effect of which would have been to put me off rather than to encourage me) I have got through the hardest and most attractive part of the work; namely, to settle the psychological motives of the action, to establish, in my own mind, the relations between the various characters and between the different parts of the whole thing—in short, to sketch a detailed outline of the underlying motives which the poet must have before him (rather as you must have to picture your symphony) if he is to be attracted, roused and held by the work. The essence lies in this tracery of ideas, and all the rest (what you so strikingly call the formal garden) is mere trimmings, just as in *Rosenkavalier* the period flavour, the ceremonial, dialect and so on lie merely at the fringe of the essential meaning. Now, this essence of the relationship between Ariadne and Bacchus stands before my mind's eye so finely graded, so delicately animated, psychologically so convincing and at the same time so lyrical, that my execution would have to be wretched indeed if in the end it failed to arouse your interest.)

Hofmannsthal is in character when he names the lyrical in the same breath as the psychological aspects which rouse his personal interest.

Other features of this letter are the divisions into 'essential meaning' and 'trimmings', and the adjectives describing that essential part. In the following paragraph it is called 'das Zentrale' and 'die Hauptsache'. The adjectives used are words such as 'zart', 'abgestuft', and 'psychologisch'; qualities which are more or less superfluous in a divertissement. Everything points to the fact that Hofmannsthal was trying to pull the *Szenarium* inside out and that he was possibly even manœuvring to get the *commedia dell'arte*, a vital, rumbustious, unsentimental and sometimes vulgar group who had no place in a lyric drama, quietly out of the way.

In the above letter Hofmannsthal is slightly mysterious about the Ariadne-Bacchus relationship. It was obviously very dear to him and evolved gradually in his imagination. In the *Oper* their relationship is, briefly summarized, that of spiritual love and mutual transformation through love. The semi-divine Bacchus has been sexually but not spiritually aroused in a short encounter with Circe who takes pleasure in quite literally bringing out the animal in men. Now he meets Ariadne and, moved by her suffering and pain, learns to love spiritually as well. He thereby attains his full divinity.

Ariadne who is 'eine unter Millionen' (29) is eternally faithful to Theseus. Yet she too is transformed by love and can enjoy new life. This is possible because all along she takes Bacchus to be Hermes the Messenger of Death and she gives herself to Bacchus in the sincere belief that she is about to die. In fact she goes on believing this all through their final love scene and even by the end of the *Oper* has not realized her 'mistake'.

This mutual transformation Hofmannsthal elsewhere termed the 'allomatic': 'Die gegenseitige Verwandlung. Das allomatische Element.'[26] The word 'allomatic' is a neologism which, as D. Miles points out, is analogous to 'automatic', and is probably intended to mean 'occurring because of another's influence'.[27] Ariadne and Bacchus are then transformed by one another.

The symbolism in this story is rather heavy-handed and the tracery of ideas is artificial. Most unsatisfactory is Ariadne's ignorance of her own state and Hofmannsthal's symbolic and poetic contrivances which allow her to be both faithful and faithless.

Yet Hofmannsthal did have many sensitive insights into the problem of fidelity, which is the theme of this plot as it was of the *Szenarium*. These are, however, far better expressed in a letter to Strauss dated mid-July 1911 and also in the *Ariadne Brief* which is an expanded, public version of the earlier

---

[26] *Ad me ipsum*, Auf., p. 218.
[27] David H. Miles, *Hofmannsthal's Novel 'Andreas': Memory and Self*, p. 64.

letter.[28] Hofmannsthal was always convinced that he had
expressed his ideas perfectly well in the libretto.[29] For him,
then, the *Ariadne Brief* was descriptive criticism. Many other
people, including the ever-honest and straightforward Strauss,
have not found the libretto so accessible and to them the
Ariadne Brief is interpretative criticism. Whether regarded as
descriptive or interpretative, the *Ariadne Brief* has formed the
basis of all traditional *Ariadne* studies.[30] For this reason alone
it is worth quoting:

Es handelt sich um ein simples und ungeheueres Lebensproblem:
das der Treue. An dem Verlorenen festhalten, ewig beharren, bis an
den Tod—oder aber leben, weiterleben, hinwegkommen, sich
verwandeln, die Einheit der Seele preisgeben, und dennoch in der
Verwandlung sich bewahren, ein Mensch bleiben, nicht zum
gedächtnislosen Tier herabsinken. Es ist das Grundthema der
'Elektra', die Stimme der Elektra gegen die Stimme der Chrysothemis, die heroische Stimme gegen die menschliche. Es steht hier die
Gruppe der Heroen, Halbgötter, Götter—Ariadne—Bacchus—
(Theseus)—gegen die menschliche, nichts als menschliche Gruppe
der leichtfertigen Zerbinetta und ihrer Begleiter, dieser gemeinen
Lebensmasken. Zerbinetta ist in ihrem Element, wenn sie von einem
zum andern taumelt, Ariadne konnte nur *eines* Mannes Gattin oder
Geliebte, sie kann nur *eines* Mannes Hinterbliebene, Verlassene
sein. Eines freilich bleibt übrig, auch für sie: das Wunder, der Gott.
Sie gibt sich ihm, denn sie nimmt ihn für den Tod: er ist Tod und
Leben zugleich, die ungeheueren Tiefen der eigenen Natur enthüllt
er ihr, macht sie selber zur Zauberin, zur Magierin, die die arme
kleine Ariadne verwandelt hat, zaubert ihr in dieser Welt das
Jenseits hervor, bewahrt sie uns, verwandelt sie zugleich. Was aber
ein wirkliches Wunder ist für göttliche Seelen, für die irdische Seele

[28] See Introduction, p. 3.
[29] To 'prove' this Hofmannsthal read the libretto aloud to a small circle of intimate
friends, including his wife and Grete Wiesenthal, and was delighted to find that the
result was 'eine solche Freude, ein solches Mitgehen (das man für geübte Vorleser
niemals heucheln kann) und ein so erstaunliches Verstehen!' Bw. 26 July 1911, pp.
123–4. But the circumstances of this experiment were obviously in his favour,
although he sincerely thought otherwise.
[30] There is more than adequate critical coverage of this area. e.g. Grete Schaeder,
Hugo von Hofmannsthal, Volume 1, *Die Gestalten*, p. 115. Krüger, pp. 134–5. Walter
Jens, *Hofmannsthal und die Griechen*, pp. 100–9. Naef, pp. 148–54. Walter Brecht,
'Hugo von Hofmannsthals "Ad me ipsum" und seine Bedeutung', pp. 342–3. Ewald
Rösch, *Die Komödien Hofmannsthals: Die Entfaltung ihrer Sinnstruktur aus dem Thema
der Daseinsstufen*, pp. 47–9. David H. Miles, *Hofmannsthal's Novel 'Andreas': Memory
and Self*, pp. 60–71.

der Zerbinetta ist es das alltägliche. Sie sieht in dem Erlebnis der Ariadne das, was sie eben darin zu sehen vermag: den Tausch eines neuen Liebhabers für einen alten. So sind die beiden Seelenwelten in dem Schluß ironisch verbunden, wie sie eben verbunden sein können: durch das Nichtverstehen. Bacchus aber ist in dies monologische Abenteuer der einsamen Seele Ariadne nicht als ein deus ex machina eingestellt—sondern auch er erlebt das bedeutsame Erlebnis: unberührt, jung, ahnungslos der eigenen Gottheit, fährt er, wie ihn der Wind treibt, von Insel zu Insel. Sein erstes Abenteuer war typisch: nennen Sie es die Kokette, nennen Sie es die Circe. Der Chok für eine junge, unberührte unendlicher Kräfte volle Seele ist ungeheuer: wäre er Harlekin, so wäre es nichts als der Anfang einer langen Kette: aber es ist Bacchus, das Ungeheuerliche des erotischen Erlebnisses tritt an ihn heran, alles entschleiert sich ihm, das Tierwerden, die Verwandlung, die eigene Göttlichkeit, alles in einem Blitze. So entzieht er sich Circes Armen, unverwandelt, aber nicht ohne eine Wunde, eine Sehnsucht, ein Wissen. Wie es ihn nun treffen muß, das Wesen zu finden, das er lieben kann, das ihn verkennt, aber in diesem Verkennen sich gerade ganz ihm hinzugeben, die ganze Lieblichkeit ihm zu enthüllen weiß, das sich ihm ganz anvertraut, wie man sich eben nur dem Tod anvertraut, das brauche ich einem Künstler, wie Sie es sind, nicht weiter mit Worten auszuführen. (Bw. mid-July 1911, pp. 115–16.)

(What it is about is one of the straightforward and stupendous problems of life: fidelity; whether to hold fast to that which is lost, to cling to it even unto death—or to live on, to get over it, to transform oneself, to sacrifice the integrity of the soul and yet in this transmutation to preserve one's essence, to remain a human being and not to sink to the level of the beast, which is without recollection. It is the fundamental theme of *Elektra*, the voice of Electra opposed to the voice of Chrysothemis, the heroic voice against the human. In the present case we have the group of heroes, demi-gods, gods— Ariadne, Bacchus, (Theseus)—facing the human, the merely human group consisting of the frivolous Zerbinetta and her companions, all of them base figures in life's masquerade. Zerbinetta is in her element drifting out of the arms of one man into the arms of another; Ariadne could be the wife or mistress of *one* man only, just as she can be only *one* man's widow, can be forsaken by only *one* man. One thing, however, is still left even for her: the miracle, the God. To him she gives herself, for she believes him to be Death: he is both Death and Life at once; he it is who reveals to her the immeasurable depths in her own nature, who makes of her an enchantress, the sorceress who herself transforms the poor little Ariadne; he it is who conjures up for her in this world another world beyond, who preserves her for us and at the same time transforms her. But what to divine souls is a real miracle, is to the earth-bound nature of Zerbinetta just an everyday love-affair. She sees in Ariadne's experience the only thing she *can* see: the exchange of an old lover for a new one. And so these two spiritual worlds are in the end ironically brought together in the only way in which they can be brought together: in non-comprehension. In this experience of Ariadne's, which is really the monologue of her lonely soul, Bacchus represents no mere *deus ex machina*; for him, too, the experience is vital. Innocent, young and unaware of his own divinity he travels where the wind takes him, from island to island. His first affair was typical, with a woman of easy virtue, you may say or may call her Circe. To his youth and innocence with its infinite potentialities the shock has been tremendous: were he Harlekin, this would be merely the beginning of one long round of love affairs. But he is Bacchus; confronted with the enormity of erotic experience all is laid bare to him in a flash—the assimilation with the animal, the transformation, his own divinity. So he escapes from Circe's embraces still unchanged, but not without a wound, a longing, not without knowledge. The impact on him now of this meeting with a being whom he can love, who is mistaken about him but is enabled by this very mistake to give herself to him wholly and to reveal herself to him in all her loveliness, who entrusts herself to him completely, exactly as one entrusts oneself to Death, this impact I need not expound further to an artist such as you.)

Clearly the tracery of ideas in this letter complicates the *Szenarium* beyond recognition. These ideas can be seen in the libretto, but only once they have been pointed out. Regardless of how well or badly they have been realized in the libretto, the fact remains that they are often in direct contradiction to aspects of theme, characterization, and structure. These complications which resulted in some contradictory faults can best be illustrated by isolating single strands and following them through. Bacchus is a good beginning.

In the earliest notes Bacchus has no 'character' to speak of. Later, on about 28 May 1911, during that period of intensive work on *Ariadne*, it seems that many of Hofmannsthal's new thoughts sprang up around Bacchus, who seems to have made a personal and richly associative appeal to Hofmannsthal's imagination. Certainly we learn about Bacchus' psychological motives first and in more detail than we do about Ariadne's. It is even possible that the new Ariadne–Bacchus relationship stemmed from the revised character of Bacchus and not from any abstract desire to demonstrate the 'allomatic' or similar.

There is abundant information on Bacchus, dated 28 May 1911. The most detailed is in a pencilled note (the second in Appendix B):

Es ist Bacchus erste Ausreise. Noch wird seine Gottheit bezweifelt. Sein erstes Abenteuer war Circe, deren Macht an ihm versagte. Ein Grauen vor dem Verwandeltwerden hat ihm das Herz versengt. Daß er die Macht habe, zu verwandeln, zu erwecken ist eine ihm noch ungethane Erfahrung.

Sein Lied, ehe er auftritt ist Furcht vor Circe. Neue Insel, neues Leben—

Najade berichtet: von Circes Insel. Die Befreiten seine Gefährten: er entzaubert sie zum Theil. Echo weiß noch mehr zu erzählen: er ist es an dem Circes Kunst zu schanden geworden. Er ist sicherlich ein Gott. Schluß: abgehen aufs Schiff. Die 4 (Arlekin etc) jubelnd voraustanzend: Auf nach *Cythere*. (Sz. 293.)

(It is Bacchus's first voyage into the world. His divinity is still in doubt. His first affair was Circe, whose power failed with him. A terror of being transformed has singed his heart. That he has the power to transform, to awaken, is an experience he has yet to make.

His song before he appears on stage is fear of Circe. New island, new life—

Najade reports: about Circe's island. The men he released are his companions; he partially releases them from the spell. Echo has more to tell: Circe's arts came to naught with him. He must be a god. Finale: departure by ship. The 4 (Arlekin etc) dancing ahead jubilantly: heading for *Cythera*.)

The motifs of Bacchus freeing his companions from Circe's spell and of the jubilant embarkation for Cythera were not included in the libretto.

With the Circe motif Hofmannsthal is, as Norman Del Mar points out, creating 'psychological symmetry'[31] for Bacchus so that he will be as ready for transformation as Ariadne. Del Mar also indicates that Milton had already supposed such a liaison for Bacchus and that Comus was the son of Bacchus and Circe. We know that Hofmannsthal was reading *Comus*

---

[31] Del Mar, p. 27.

at this time and that he copied out a section in German translation to help him with the tone of the Ariadne–Bacchus scene (see Appendix B). It is therefore likely that Hofmannsthal drew on Milton for his Circe motif.[32] In *Ad me ipsum* there are two notes which further show how important in Bacchus' spiritual development are the erotic encounter with Circe and his resistance. The first stresses the symmetry of this motif, which is referred to as a 'verstärkendes Gegenmotif'.[33] In the second Hofmannsthal pleads on these grounds for the episode: 'es ist selten etwas weniger verstanden worden, als daß in dem Liedchen des Bacchus nicht nur eine Lebenssituation sondern eine ganze Lebensgeschichte darin steckt—daß er durch dieses Erlebnis gleichwertig neben Ariadne tritt'[34] (never has something been so little understood as that Bacchus' little song contains not only an event in his life but his whole life story—that through this experience he is on an equal footing with Ariadne).

This Bacchus is clearly a youthful figure. His experiences are those of adolescence. This is substantiated by the word 'knabenhaft' in the note pencilled into the *Szenarium*: 'Klatsch über Bacchos Herkunft und erstes Abenteuer: Knabenhaft, Sohn einer Königstochter die starb von Nymphen aufgezogen! (zu dreien wie hübsch)' (Sz.289). This is expanded in the postscript of a letter to Strauss of 28 May 1911:

P. S. Recht wichtig, damit Ihre Phantasie nicht im vornherein einen Irrweg in bezug auf die Figur des Bacchus geht. Dieser lyrische Tenor wird ganz zart zu halten sein, fast knabenhaft. (Aber es ist ganz richtig, die Rolle für einen Mann zu komponieren, nicht wieder für einen Sopran.) Es ist ein kaum aus dem Ei geschlüpfter Bacchus, der erst ein einziges Abenteuer mit Circe gehabt hat und schüchtern ist. Ich glaub', es kann ein reizender Einakter werden! (Bw. 28 May 1911, p. 108.)

(P.S. The following is most important so that your imagination should not go astray from the very outset over the character of Bacchus: this lyric tenor will have to be interpreted in the most delicate manner, almost boyish. (But it is quite correct to compose the part for a man, not this time for a soprano.) This Bacchus is but lately fledged, he has had only his one affair with Circe and is shy. I think this could make a charming one-act piece!)

[32] See also Stiegele, pp. 25–7.   [33] Auf., p. 222.   [34] Auf., p. 226.

Here is a Bacchus who is delicate, boyish, lately-fledged, and shy. In the libretto the following adjectives and phrases are used in the stage directions: 'schwermütig lieblich' (59), 'fröhlich, mit etwas graziösem Spott', 'ganz jung, zartest im Ton' (60), 'sanft', 'verträumt' (62), and 'mehr ergriffen als laut' (63). This character is the absolute antithesis of the Bacchus presented in the *Szenarium*. He is neither manly nor decisive; he is an hermaphroditic figure with rather feminine features who roams delightedly about. Instead of singing a seductive, wooing song in a 'Mannes Stimme' a 'schön halbtraurig Lied' (375) escapes his sweet bold lips. All this we may glean from Zerbinetta's description of the arriving Bacchus which was included in the 1912 *Ariadne auf Naxos* but cut from the 1916 version because it was regarded as a lengthy interruption which unnecessarily postponed the approaching climax. No other reason is given for its removal, but it is such a bad piece of writing that one wonders if Hofmannsthal was not glad to cut it anyhow. The picture presented of Bacchus is mawkish, precious and rococo:

> Zerbinetta
> (tritt eilig auf, mit einem tiefen Knicks vor Ariadne)
> Prinzessin! welchen Botenlohn hab ich verdient?
> Auf dieser Insel weilt ein Mann, ein Gott!
> Es weilt ein Wunder, ohnegleichen!
> Weilt hier und wandelt! wird den Hügel da—
> Und diese Höhle bald erreichen!
>
> Und dann—es ist ein Mann und welch ein Mann!
> Und dennoch nichts von ihrer Derbheit, ihrer Härte—
> Wangen wie eine Frau, von einem Reh das Aug,
> Ihm nachzuspähen, nachzuschleichen nur,
> Ich habe nie was Holderes erlebt!
> Verstohlen ihm zu folgen auf der Spur:
> Er geht, er gehet nicht! er schreitet, schwebt,
> Unschlüssig schweift er hin, die Arme aufgeworfen,
> Lacht auf: ein Knabe, nein, ein Kind!
> Man denkt: ein junges Reh,
> Das sich erstrickt, und stutzt im Morgenwind.
>
> Ist es derselbe, der auf einmal lauscht,
> Wenn etwas in den Zweigen rauscht,
> Sich anspannt und in einem Sprunge
> Mit unbegreiflich wildem Schwunge

Sich panthergleich hinschleudert auf ein Tier?
Ach, alles duckt sich, alles hängt und drängt,
Gefangen auch zu sein von diesen Händen,
Und wärs in ihrem Druck das Leben zu beenden! . . .

Doch er—als ging es ihm um völlig andere Dinge
Als seine Hände schaffen—ach—
Er läßt das kaum Gefangene entspringen,
Sieht ihm nicht einmal nach—
Ein Schatten wie von einem dunklen Kranz,
Den eine unsichtbare Hand ihm flieht,
Fliegt über sein Gesicht,
Es wechselt unter hell und dunklem Glanz.
Indes sein Auge in die Ferne sieht,
Entströmt den süßen kühnen Lippen
Ein schön halbtraurig Lied,
Das ihm, ich weiß nicht wie, zu Sinn gekommen! (374–5.)

        (Zerbinetta
    (enters quickly, with a deep curtsy to Ariadne)
Princess! what reward has your messenger earned?
On this island there tarries a man, a god!
There tarries a wonder, unparalleled!
Tarries here and wanders! soon will reach the hill there—
And this cave!

And then—it is a man and what a man!
And yet nothing of their roughness, of their hardness—
Cheeks like a woman, eyes of a deer,
Only to spy after him, to steal after him,
I have never experienced anything more lovely!
Secretly to follow in his tracks:
He walks, he does not walk! he strides, hovers,
Irresolutely he roams about, his arms outstretched,
Gives a laugh: a lad, no, a child!
One thinks: a young deer
That stretches itself, and is startled in the morning breeze.

Is it the same creature that straightway pricks its ears
If something rustles in the twigs,
Tenses and in one leap
With incredible wild verve
Hurls itself upon an animal?
Ah, everything crouches, everything pushes and shoves
To be caught by these hands,
Even if it means dying in their pressure! . . .

But he—as if he were concerned about quite other things
Than what he was doing—ah—
He lets his recent capture escape,
Does not even glance after him—
A shadow as from a dark wreath,
Which an invisible hand binds for him,
Flits across his face,
It changes under bright and dark light.
Whilst his eye gazes into the distance
A beautiful half-melancholy song
Escapes his sweet bold lips,
A song, which came to him I know not how!'

Not only is Zerbinetta's speech precious but it is also full of
contradictions. It is contradictory because Hofmannsthal had
two pictures of Bacchus: firstly the manly, romantic hero of
the *Szenarium* and secondly the gentle, dreamy adolescent. In
the libretto the second picture is superimposed on to the first
so that Bacchus himself has a double or split character. The
reactions of those about him are sometimes to the first and
sometimes to the second Bacchus. His character is then one of
the faults or mutations which were mentioned in the
Introduction.

Hofmannsthal did not deliberately superimpose a contradictory picture on to the earlier Bacchus. Circumstances were
such that he was obliged to keep quite closely to the *Szenarium*
whilst also trying to work out his 'lyric drama', and he was
probable unaware of how much the earlier character intruded.
But in Zerbinetta's speech the contradictions were sometimes
so glaring that even he could not fail to notice them and he
tries to make a virtue of necessity by attempting to pass them
off as signs of a quixotic, 'contradictory' personality. The
speech can be divided into four parts. These divisions are
shown in the above quotation. In each division it appears that
Hofmannsthal has used different notes.

The first part is full of breathless excitement and wonder.
Almost every sentence is punctuated with an exclamation
mark. Zerbinetta says Bacchus is 'ein Mann', 'ein Gott', and
'ein Wunder'. True to character, she makes insinuations about
the new arrival's behaviour on the grounds of his sex: 'Und
dann—es ist ein Mann und welch ein Mann.' When writing
these lines Hofmannsthal probably worked from the note

beginning 'Nymphe: meldet von Bacchos. Chor jubelnd'.[35] This note has the same ecstatic, triumphant tone, as does the paragraph in the *Szenarium* which Strauss marked 'Beginn des Finales' (Sz. 289). In this paragraph the nymph reports that he who has landed is 'sicherlich ein Gott'.

In the next part Hofmannsthal was working from those notes which dealt with Bacchus the youthful innocent. Now he is 'ein Knabe, nein, ein Kind!' (374). In the libretto the nymphs repeat that he is 'ein Knabe' (56–7). Furthermore, he has eyes like a deer.

In the third part Bacchus is again likened to a young deer but he is also 'panthergleich'. These contradictory images become too much and the feigned wonder of Hofmannsthal's rhetorical 'Ist es derselbe' does not make the character more credible to us. In fact it seems fair to hazard a guess that Hofmannsthal has gone back to working from the *Szenarium*. The image of the panther in particular is strongly reminiscent of the 'Raubtier' in the earlier note.[36]

But obviously such masculine vigour and cruelty will not do for the second, easily shockable Bacchus, and in part four Bacchus, in a fit of dreamy vagueness, lets the animals go and sings a melancholy little ditty which we may take to be the 'Circe Lied'. This dreamy Bacchus is the one of the letters and the notes of 28 May 1911.

Clearly the Bacchus in this speech is highly contradictory and no number of 'dochs' or 'dennochs' is going to convince the reader otherwise.

The dual Bacchus appears in other places. In the letter of mid-July 1911, for example, Bacchus at first corresponds to the figure in *Wo ich nahe, wo ich lande*. Particularly the line 'die ungeheueren Tiefen der eigenen Natur enthüllt er ihr' puts the reader in mind of the poet-magician's powers. Yet in the third paragraph there appears the second innocent, young, and unaware Bacchus for whom this experience of falling in love is so vital. He is both active and passive, transformer and transformed, enchanter and enchanted. This, far from striking the reader as an intensely revealing spiritual paradox, seems in this instance at least psychologically improbable, the more

[35] Appendix A, Note 3.
[36] Appendix A, Note 3.

so since the genesis of this character points to outright contradiction rather than intentional paradox. If Hofmannsthal is only talking about the process of falling in love as an example of each partner being both active and passive, transformer and transformed then Hofmannsthal's 'paradox' is true. But his ponderous symbolism and arcane terminology do not show this human truth in any fresh light. The same split in Bacchus' character can be found in the *Ariadne Brief*.

These contradictions are not limited to characterization. In the third part of the *Oper*, from Bacchus' entry onwards, structure is often in conflict with character and content. When writing the libretto Hofmannsthal adhered very closely to the *Szenarium* as regards structure, as we have seen. Bacchus' entry and movements are structured in the *Szenarium* in a rectilinear fashion. He is announced, heralded with elation, the heroine is excited and agitated, he arrives, they fall in love, sing a duet, and live happily ever after. The structural dynamics are simply climax and release. As the hero *is* a mere *deus ex machina*[37] we are not interested in his individual feelings and it does not matter that he arrives so late in the piece. In the libretto Hofmannsthal retained this structure exactly, but tried to squeeze the hero of his new 'lyric drama' into it.

The first problem was that the revised Bacchus is now a major character with a personal history which must be made known to the audience for the sake of the 'psychological symmetry' of the plot. It is doubtful whether it is dramatically ever very convincing when a major character enters two thirds of the way through a play in the manner of a *deus ex machina*. Hofmannsthal makes some attempt at ameliorating this weakness by giving a detailed account of Bacchus' past before he appears on stage. A narrative account of his childhood, youth and affair with Circe is given by the three nymphs who sing 'somewhat in the manner of the three Norns'.[38] Zerbinetta then delivers her description of his person and approach.[39] R.

---

[37] Hofmannsthal denies this in his long letter to Strauss: 'Bacchus aber ist in dies monologische Abenteuer der einsamen Seele Ariadne nicht als ein deus ex machina eingestellt'. Bw. Mitte Juli 1911, p. 116.

[38] Del Mar, p. 43.

[39] See Chapter II, pp. 77–9.

Borchardt has rightly criticized this lengthy and tedious narrative exposition of a character who is already very late in arriving:

Wenn ich einen Einwand habe, so betrifft er das Motiv der Circe, das mir, wenigstens in der Breite, die es einnimmt,—in den Erzählungen der Mädchen—nicht ganz glücklich scheint. Welchen Zwecken es dient—wie es Ihnen dazu dient a contrario die knabenhafte Reinheit des Dionysos zu malen und die Vereinigung der Beiden gegen Zerbinettas Lebensweisheiten sicherzustellen, ist mir wohl klar, dennoch aber scheint mir der Aufwand ein wenig unverhältnismäßig, vor allem in Anbetracht des schleppenden das durch so spät auftretende reine Expositionsmomente—Hineinziehen nicht auftretender Personen—in die schon in Bewegung befindliche Handlung kommt [sic]. Muß denn Dionysos, als junger Gott durchaus eine Vorgeschichte haben wie Ariadne, um vor einem schönen unglücklichen Mädchen zugleich zu wissen und nicht zu wissen wie ihm wird? Verzeihen Sie diese Bemerkung, die fast ins Genre Zerbinettas einschlägt, die ich aber doch nicht unterdrücken kann. Im Grunde liegt nichts daran, und die Musik wird keine Müh haben, mit ihren Mitteln die dramatische Retardation auszugleichen.[40]

(If I have an objection it is to do with the Circe motif, which does not seem quite happy to me, at least not in the time that it occupies—in the girls' stories. I am quite clear about what purpose it serves—how it enables you to portray a *contrario* the youthful purity of Dionysos and to secure the alliance of the two against Zerbinetta's worldly wisdom—nevertheless the expenditure seems a little excessive to me—particularly in view of the retarding effect upon an action already in progress—of introducing purely expositional material so late and of mentioning characters who do not appear. As a young god must Dionysos really have a prehistory like Ariadne in order to know, and yet not to know, how he feels when he stands in front of a beautiful, unhappy girl? Pardon this remark which is almost in Zerbinetta's genre but which I cannot suppress. Basically it is not important and the music will easily compensate for the dramatic retardation with its own means.)

Strauss was indeed concerned to avoid a dramatic retardation. He had always pressed for better climax-building in *Ariadne auf Naxos* and this was obviously a crucial point in the opera from that point of view. But Strauss's setting of the nymphs' passage, whilst fast and lively enough to prevent retardation,

[40] Hugo von Hofmannsthal/Rudolf Borchardt, *Briefwechsel*, p. 69.

is too fast for the words to be audible and so the Circe motif is lost on the audience after all. The impression the audience does receive is of almost irrepressible excitement. This fast pace was not only Strauss's device for avoiding operatic longueurs; it was also requested by Hofmannsthal. In the libretto we read that the nymphs 'treten ... hastig auf' (53). Hofmannsthal's instructions about their delivery are as follows: 'aufgeregt', 'enthusiastisch', 'begeistert' (54). The excitement increases and Dryade 'reißt (Najade das) Wort vom Munde', Najade sings 'eifrigst' and Dryade sings with 'Triumph im Ton' (55). This enthusiasm and excitement from the nymphs is inappropriate for two reasons. It is inappropriate first because it belongs to the structure and ethos of the *Szenarium*, and second because these emotions should not be given to the nymphs at all. These two points need closer comment.

In the *Szenarium* an enthusiastic heralding of Bacchus is called for. The earlier note says 'Chor jubelnd'.[41] In the *Szenarium* the nymphs are full of wonder and praise, and Bacchus is given a hero's welcome even before he has arrived. The nymphs' song fits the structure. In the libretto the archetypal arrival and welcome are retained but the character in question has long since thrown off the unambiguous heroism of an *opera seria* figure. When he arrives on stage having drifted around Naxos for a while, he and the heroine do not fall straight into each other's arms as we expect, but enter on a long and complex misunderstanding. So the underlying structure and related mood of the nymphs' sung narrative arouse certain expectations which are frustrated—a frustration which was not deliberate but came about only because Hofmannsthal did not alter structural foundations when he revised the character Bacchus.

The three nymph figures, who probably also came from Milton's *Comus*,[42] are nature spirits who are supposed to

[41] Appendix A, Note 3.
[42] John Milton, *Comus* (Cambridge, 1927).
    e.g. Sweet Echo, sweetest nymph, that liv'st unseen
            Within thy airy shell ...   l. 230
                I have oft heard
    My mother Circe with the Sirens three,
    Amidst the flowery-kirtled Naiades ...   l. 253
            such court guise   *(continued)*

represent a Heraclitan view of life as flux and change. Accordingly they can accept decay but not death (for this is too absolute) and they can accept infidelity as this is to them part of the rhythm of life (but presumably not fidelity as this is again too absolute). We see this in an early note which elaborates on their reaction to Ariadne's grief, 'Naiade, Echo, Dryade glauben gleichfalls, es gehe ans Sterben. (Ihnen ist Sterben ein Geheimnis, Untreue keines.)[43] In the typed manuscript of *Ariadne auf Naxos* Hofmannsthal wrote the following to Strauss at the end of the first trio for the nymphs. It dwells on the essential impartiality of Nature towards human suffering: 'Die drei letzten Zeilen ad libitum zu wiederholen: durch eine reizende, gaukelnde Stimmführung die lächelnde Gleichgiltigkeit der Natur gegen menschliches Leid ausdrückend. Etwas von Blätterschaukeln, Wellengaukeln schon in der Overtüre.[44] (The three last lines to be repeated *ad libitum*: through a charming, swaying part-writing for voices expressing the smiling indifference of nature to human suffering. Something of the swaying of leaves, the undulation of waves already in the overture.)

Although Strauss did not put the 'Blätterschaukeln' or 'Wellengaukeln' into the overture, he did put them very clearly into this first trio. Strauss manages furthermore to suggest strongly the 'lächelnde Gleichgiltigkeit der Natur gegen menschliches Leid', which is also the nymphs' indifference. If the nymphs are indifferent to suffering then they ought to be indifferent to joy as well. Indifference is not partial and neither should they be, and yet, as we have seen, they are wildly excited at Bacchus' arrival, anticipating his success and Ariadne's joy and happiness. Indeed they almost give the game away.

This contradiction came about once again because Hofmannsthal insisted on retaining his earliest structural organization. The nymphs were made to assume a role which had originally been allotted to a chorus. The result is some odd musical characterization—obviously a small point in itself but

---

As Mercury did first devise
With the mincing Dryades.   l. 262

[43] Appendix A, Note 2.
[44] Appendix A, Note 5.

representative of the faults which found their way into the libretto.

In Ariadne's reaction to Bacchus' voice and to his arrival on stage the *Szenarium* again shows through. In the *Szenarium* Bacchus' voice clearly had a strong, seductive, almost magical power. As he was 'lockend, werbend' so was she 'erschreckt und doch beglückt'. Much use was made of this almost primitive device of the off-stage voice releasing emotional responses in those on stage.[45] In an early note the chorus is entranced by the singing; 'Chor leiser: Oh daß die Stimme weiter tönte.' Another character, most probably Ariadne herself, has the lines 'Töne töne schöne Stimme/schöne Stimme töne wieder'.[46]

In the libretto those on stage still go through precisely the same emotions. Hofmannsthal even uses words from that early note written before 28 May 1911: 'Es greift durch alle Schmerzen. Es ist Auflösung aller Qual.'[47] This becomes 'Es greift durch alle Schmerzen/Auflösend alte Qual' (59). The nymphs are given the song 'Töne, töne, süße Stimme' (53) the verses of which they sing almost as a refrain at intervals during the scene. When Bacchus arrives on stage the shock is too great for Ariadne: 'in jehem Schreck schlägt [*sic*] die Hände vors Gesicht (60). But why, one wonders, should a childish, faintly lisping 'schön halbtraurig Lied' (375), sung in a melancholy voice about some unknown woman, Circe, by an unseen youth, have such an effect on those on stage? Their reactions are appropriate to the earlier Bacchus but improbable where the latter Bacchus is concerned. Ariadne over-reacts. Hofmannsthal has tried to disguise this by a contrived effort at psychodrama in which Ariadne being instantly attracted yet ever faithful gives the man who has attracted her the only name he can have—'Theseus'.[48] But no, she soon realizes her

---

[45] In the 1912 *Ariadne* Bacchus sings his Circe song behind the scenes but for the 1916 version Strauss brought him on stage, although keeping him invisible to Ariadne and the nymphs. This move did not alter the original effect and Hofmannsthal approved it. Bw. 1 May 1916, p. 283 and Bw. 8 May 1916, p. 284.

[46] Appendix A, Note 3.

[47] Appendix A, Note 3.

[48] Daviau and Buelow, however, praise the subtlety of this passage and rightly point out that this is an instance of music being most able to give psychological nuance: the Theseus, Bacchus and Hermes motifs are closely related. Daviau and Buelow, p. 144 and pp. 199–203.

mistake and greets the Messenger of Death with some relief.

Strauss cannot be blamed if he did not straight away appreciate this libretto. It is indeed to his credit that he did not let its winsome aspects blind him to its merits. The following particularly sickly speech by the childish, wistful Bacchus, which is not untypical of the Ariadne–Bacchus exchange, does perhaps explain why the scene did not call forth Strauss's greatest musical inspiration:[49]

> Bacchus
> (ganz jung, zartest im Ton)
> Du schönes Wesen? Bist du die Göttin dieser Insel?
> Ist diese Höhle dein Palast? sind diese deine Dienerinnen?
> Singst du an deinem Webstuhl Zauberlieder?
> Nimmst du den Fremdling da hinein
> Und liegst mit ihm beim Mahl,
> Und tränkest du ihn da mit einem Zaubertrank?
> Und ach, wer dir sich gibt, verwandelst du ihn auch?
> Weh! Bist du auch solch eine Zauberin? (60–1)

> (Bacchus
> (Very young, most tender in tone)
> You beautiful creature? Are you the goddess of this island?
> Is this cave your palace? are these your servant maidens?
> Do you sing magic songs at your loom?
> Do you take the stranger in there
> And lie with him to dine,
> And do you give him a magic potion to drink?
> And ah, he who gives himself to you, do you transform him too?
> Woe! Are you also such an enchantress?)

Not only is the Bacchus in the libretto a confusing double figure but he is further complicated in the final dialogue with Ariadne by being given overtones of the Dionysos in Nietzsche's *Die Geburt der Tragödie*. In particular this is apparent in the pleasure–pain duality, which is not a motif in the *Szenarium* but is worked out in a number of notes after 28 May 1911. According to Nietzsche, in the Dionysian orgiastic state the border line between what is pleasurable and what is painful becomes blurred.[50] One note takes pain as far as

---

[49] See Chapter III, pp. 174–9.

[50] For example, the following passage about 'die wundersame Mischung und Doppelheit in den Affecten der dionysischen Schwärmer . . . jene Erscheinung, daß

Death—and thus makes a link back with Bacchus' supposed identity as Hermes: 'Alles bleibt bei dir. Die Schmerzen unsäglich. Lust erfüllt dich ganz. Du meinst zu vergehen, weil du anfängst zu leben.' (Everything remains with you. The suffering unspeakable. Joy fills you entirely. You think you are passing away because you are beginning to live.) In another note, for reasons which are not quite clear, Ariadne's pain is seen as a secret bond between them: 'Alle die Schmerzen führen dich zu mir. Die Schmerzen sind das große Wunder, mit den Schmerzen warst immer bei mir.'[51] (All the suffering leads you to me. The suffering is the great miracle, with the suffering you were always by me.) These notes are gathered together for the libretto to give such lines as 'Nun steigt deiner Schmerzen innerste Lust / In dein und meinem Herzen auf!' (Now the innermost joy of your suffering fills your and my heart!) and 'die Höhle deiner Schmerzen / Zieh ich zur tiefsten Lust um dich und mich!' (61) (The cave of your suffering is now the cave of our deepest pleasure!) This Nietzschean paraphrase adds nothing either to the *opera seria* figure in the recreated Baroque divertissement or to the dreamy androgynous hero of the 'lyric drama' except perhaps a suggestion of stale eclecticism. The final impression of Bacchus is that of a bundle of very mixed epithets. On top of this there was to be Bacchus' oriental identity. On 15 June 1911 Hofmannsthal wrote to Strauss of 'das Fremdartige, Orientalisch–Märchenhafte, wovon Bacchus umwebt ist' (Bw. 15 June 1911, p. 111). The libretto indicates this only at one point, namely during the 'Zwischenspiel des Orchesters' which was to have followed the Intermezzo and which is marked 'fremdartig, geheimnisvoll' (53). Luckily for the unity of this character the

---

Schmerzen Lust erwecken, der Jubel der Brust qualvolle Töne entreißt. Aus der höchsten Freude tönt der Schrei des Entsetzens oder der sehnende Klagelaut über einen unersetzlichen Verlust'. Friedrich Nietzsche, *Werke in drei Bänden*, Volume I, *Die Geburt der Tragödie aus dem Geiste der Musik,* edited by Karl Schlechta (Stuttgart, 1964), p. 55.

[51] Appendix A, Notes 6 and 7. Of particular interest are the words 'Stampa II' in Note 7. Stiegele has shown that this is a reference to a sonnet by Gaspara Stampa (1523–54) in which a woman laments that her lover has deserted her. Stiegele, pp. 48–9. Here, as with Hofmannsthal's own *Wo ich nahe, wo ich lande* and Milton's *Comus*, poems help the librettist to create atmosphere; an indication of how heavily Hofmannsthal was dependent on literary stimulus.

'Zwischenspiel' was dropped.[52] On the whole, however, Hofmannsthal's badly drawn Bacchus is given back all too faithfully in the music, as shall be seen in Chapter III.

Why was it, though, that the young Bacchus had such personal appeal for Hofmannsthal? Was it not that Hofmannsthal found in him the opportunity of presenting one of his too numerous idealized self-portraits which, as Hermann Broch has suggested, recur in his works in the figure of the 'sehr schöner Knabe'? Broch attributes this over-positive self-image to Hofmannsthal's earlier childhood experience of superiority:

recht bald mußte der Schüler Hofmannsthal herausgefunden haben, wie hoch ihn Begabung und Vorbildung über den Durchschnitt seiner Mitschüler hinaushoben, und das Gefühl der Herausgehobenheit ist mit dem der Überheblichkeit eng verwandt. Er war ja noch ein Kind, und seiner Gaben waren fast allzuviele [sic]. Nicht nur geistig war er weit überlegen, er war auch schöner als die meisten anderen—wie unentwegt ihm diese Kinder–Entdeckung nachhing, bezeugt sich in der Gestalt des 'sehr schönen Knaben', der (mit dieser stereotypen Bezeichnung) sein ganzes Dichterwerk durchwandelt—, und zudem war er mit dem 'Edler von' vor seinem Namen ausgezeichnet, das ihn zu etwas 'Edlerem' stempelte.[53]

(the schoolboy Hofmannsthal must very soon have found out how high talent and early education raised him above the average of his fellows; and the feeling of superiority is closely related to that of arrogance. He was still only a child after all and his gifts were almost too many. Not only intellectually was he vastly superior, he was also more beautiful than most of the others—how unswervingly this childhood discovery followed him can be seen from the figure of the 'very beautiful boy', who (with this stereotyped epithet) is found throughout his literary œuvre—and, what is more, with the aristocratic 'von' in front of his name he was stamped as something more noble.)

Broch's observation is not simply envious or ungenerous. Not only do the large number of beautiful youths such as Octavian or the Composer in the *Vorspiel* back up his observation but the narcissistic isolation of some of Hof-

---

[52] There is no sign of an orchestral interlude in the score. The transition from the Intermezzo to 'Scene III' at No. 188 is abrupt. Thus the musical direction in the libretto (53), not included in the score, is misleading.

[53] Broch, p. 185.

mannsthal's adult life even can best be understood as a consequence of this experience. It could also be pointed out unkindly that Bacchus is 'adelig'; he is the 'Sohn einer Königstochter' (51). Divinity is another feature of the narcissistic self-image. In the *Ariadne Brief* Bacchus is a superior, elect, fated creature with spiritual and ethical capabilities few others possess, and he is divine: 'Bacchus ist Gegenspiel zur gemeinen Lebensmaske Harlekin ... Bacchus ist ein Knabe und schicksalsvoll ... Bacchus ist einziger, ein Gott, auf dem Weg zu seiner Gottwerdung' and he is furthermore 'ein Auserwählter.'[54] All these attributes are measured against the personal qualities of—a Harlekin. The unequal comparison serves only to make Hofmannsthal's claims seem more inflated than they are. In his portrait of the Composer, for example, Hofmannsthal uses affectionate self-persiflage to mitigate the effects of narcissism. Octavian is fleshed out in a number of ways. But Bacchus' narcissism is unrelieved and makes him difficult to take.

It would appear, then, that the shift towards the 'lyric drama' was intimately connected with an increasingly idealized Bacchus whose ethical and spiritual superiority does not augur well for a fair treatment of the original theme of the irony of erotic love and the uncertainty of human fidelity.

As Bacchus grew so Ariadne had to change as well. Originally intended to be a mixture of stylized hauteur and warm psychological realism who rationalizes Theseus' desertion by telling herself he must be dead and whose emotions on Bacchus' arrival are comically ambiguous, she becomes an idealized unrealistic cypher or, as R. Specht calls her, 'eine wandelnde Idee'.[55]

In an earlier note we saw her 'Seelenschwankungen' and found that Ariadne was conscious that she might be falling in love again: 'Wer bin ich wenn ich nochmals liebe? O weh, er kommt hierher! o käm er nie! / O daß er käme!'[56] The note written on 28 May 1911 on the walk with Max Mell presents a very different picture:

---

[54] PIII, pp. 140–1 and p. 142.
[55] Richard Specht, *Richard Strauss und sein Werk*, Volume II, p. 276.
[56] Appendix A, Note 3.

Ariadne
Naiade, Echo, Dryade glauben gleichfalls, es gehe ans sterben
(Ihnen ist Sterben ein Geheimnis, Untreue keines).
Ariadne glaubts bis zuletzt.
Ariadne, Bacchus: Er heißt sie Theseus vergessen. Das scheint
   ihr begreiflich.
Doch will es nicht gelingen: im Gegenteil er entzündet in ihr
   jegliche Erinnerung an Theseus. So fleht sie: mach mich
   geschwind vergessen.
Das Motif des Bacchus.
   Nach dem Duett führt er sie einen kleinen Kreis
   um die Bühne, als ob es schon im Totenreich wäre,
   leise geisterhaft: alles scheint ihr verändert: Meer,
   Bäume, auch Echos Stimme.[57]

(Naiade, Echo, Dryade also believe that it will end in death
(To them death is a mystery but infidelity is not).
Ariadne believes it to the last.
Ariadne, Bacchus: He tells her to forget Theseus. That she can
   comprehend.
But she cannot succeed: on the contrary he awakens in her
   memories of Theseus. So she pleads:
   make me forget quickly.
Bacchus' motif.
   After the duet he leads her in a little circle
   around the stage, as if they were already in the realm of the dead
   quietly ghostlike: everything seems altered to her: sea, trees
   Echo's voice as well.)

Now in order to match Bacchus' spiritual and ethical
superiority, Ariadne must be absolutely faithful. She goes on
thinking of Theseus even though she begs to be made to forget.
If she is to be true to her former lover then she must believe
literally that Bacchus is Hermes and that she is dying, hence
'Ariadne glaubts bis zuletzt'. Since she is able to give herself
entirely to Death the miraculous transformation can take
place. All this is extremely improbable, the more so because
Ariadne herself does not realize what has happened.
   Lyricism intrudes in various guises. Ariadne suffers from
being transposed into 'die vibrierende schattenhafte Totenreich–Atmosphäre, das zarte Lyrisch-Gespenstische'.[58] Just

---

[57] Appendix A, Note 2.
[58] Bw. 15 June 1911, p. 111.

as Bacchus was split so her character is split between realism
and idealism, between allegory and symbolism. The split can
be followed by tracing one particular motif and the way
Hofmannsthal handled it when writing up the *Szenarium*. The
motif is Ariadne's longing for Death. In the *Szenarium* this is
first referred to after the Intermezzo and then only as 'das
ersehnte Todtenreich' (Sz. 290). This is followed by a note
written after 28 May 1911 in which Hofmannsthal establishes
a more specific image of Death. Central to this is the idea of
Death as purification, with fire as the purifying element.
Ariadne is asking herself why Theseus left her: 'Sie fühlt sich
selber nicht mehr rein. Sonst hätte er sie nicht verlassen
können. Ihr Reines ist irgendwo anders. In einer Flamme.'[59]
In the libretto this became the lines:

> Es gibt ein Reich, wo alles rein ist:
> Es hat auch einen Namen: Totenreich.
> Hier ist nichts rein!
> Hier kam alles zu allem! (39)

> (There is a realm where everything is pure:
> And it has a name: realm of the dead.
> Here nothing is pure!
> Here everything became confused!)

In the *Szenarium* the Death motif was insignificant. It had
little in common with the later 'Totenreich'; it was a hook on
which Hofmannsthal could hang a more intricate design. Yet
not only did he make the motif more intricate, he also brought
it well forward in the libretto so that it is introduced in
Ariadne's first recitative and aria *before* the Intermezzo. The
reasons for this are obvious: by sounding it loud and clear,
early in the work, Ariadne's singular fidelity is established and
with it the 'spiritual symmetry' required for the allomatic
transformation.

But unfortunately this motif destroyed the poetic fabric and
made the characterization of Ariadne crumble into a hundred
little parts. Once again the original *Szenarium* character is
overloaded with a new more 'lyrical' yet somehow unsatisfactory nature. The genesis of her double character is reproduced
in miniature in the speeches she has before the Intermezzo

[59] Appendix A, Note 8.

and can again be found using the notes, the *Szenarium* and the libretto. The first speech begins with the lines:

> Ariadne
> (an der Erde)
> Wo war ich? tot? und lebe, lebe wieder
> Und lebe noch?
> Und ist ja doch kein Leben, das ich lebe!
> Zerstückelt Herz, willst ewig weiter schlagen?
>   (Richtet sich halb auf) (36)

> (Ariadne
> (on the ground)
> Where was I? dead? and live, live again
> And live still?
> And it is not even a life that I live!
> Wounded heart, are you going to beat forever?
>   (half raises herself))

From the pathos and resignation in the grand manner and from the merely rhetorical death-wish couched in such stilted language we gather that this must be a realization, and an effective one at that, of the *Szenarium* lines 'Ariadne (richtet sich auf) Große Klage der Verlassenen, pathetisch aber ganz einfach und zum Herzen gehend. Nicht leben—nicht sterben—jammervoll' (Sz. 287). This Ariadne is no more and no less than a mythological person from French Baroque opera.

There is nothing intrinsically wrong either with the continuation of this passage:

> Was hab ich denn geträumt? Weh! schon vergessen!
> Mein Kopf behält nichts mehr;
> Nur Schatten streichen
> Durch einen Schatten hin.
> Und dennoch, etwas zuckt dann auf und tut so weh!
> Ach!

> (What have I dreamt then? Woe! forgotten already!
> My head remembers nothing more;
> Only shadows steal
> Through one great shadow.
> And yet, something flickers up and is so painful!
> Woe!)

Hofmannsthal attempts psychological realism by depicting Ariadne's frail and painfully confused state of mind. A possible flaw in the passage and more especially in the one following it is that it borders on the neurotic. It is especially reminiscent of the neurotic confusion and memory disturbances of the three female leads in *Elektra*. Chrysothemis' lines 'mein Kopf ist immer wüst. Ich kann von heut / auf morgen nichts behalten'[60] (My mind is always confused. I can remember nothing from one day to the next) compare readily with Ariadne's 'Mein Kopf behält nichts mehr; / Nur Schatten streichen / Durch einen Schatten hin.' Both are searching for a self to hold on to. Chrysothemis says 'Ich möchte beten, daß ein Gott ein Licht / mir in der Brust anstecke, daß ich mich / in mir kann wiederfinden.'[61] (I pray that a god would kindle a light in my breast so that I can find myself again.) Ariadne wants back her identity as a young girl before she met Theseus: 'Dies muß ich finden: Das Mädchen, das ich war!' (43). Both desire intensely to forget, as does the thoroughly neurotic and decadent Klytämnestra.[62] Elektra's contrary impulse never to forget is equally neurotic. The motifs of forgetting and remembering and the role of time and memory are central to *Elektra* as indeed they are to *Ariadne auf Naxos*. It is clear from the references to *Elektra* and *Ad me ipsum* and the *Ariadne Brief* and the letter of mid-July 1911 that Hofmannsthal had his earlier work very much in mind when it came to working out the tracery of ideas in *Ariadne*. The neurotic touches given to Ariadne are most noticeable in the choice of such words as 'Schmach', 'zerrüttet', 'verwirrt' (61) and lines such as 'Mein Sinn ist wirr von vielem Liegen ohne Trost!' (61). These seem to have slipped in inadvertently with the more legitimate themes of remembering and forgetting. Nevertheless the speech is still just possible from an *opera seria* figure.[63]

This is not the case with Ariadne's lengthy apostrophe to Death (40). Gone is the pathos of the opening lines, the

[60] DII, p. 20.

[61] DII, p. 20.

[62] Klytämnestra would like to forget the past; it is giving her nightmares: 'Ich habe keine guten Nächte. Weißt du / kein Mittel gegen Träume?'. DII, p. 29.

[63] Del Mar asserts that the similarity of these lines caused Strauss to invent phrases which recall their earlier masterpiece. Del Mar, p. 53. For example, the setting of Ariadne's 'Mein Sinn ist wirr von vielem Liegen ohne Trost!' (No. 285) compares readily with parts of Elektra's great monologue, or with the setting of her lines 'Schleppst du dich hierher, in meinen traurigen Winkel' (No. 128ᵃ).

meaning of which was not only an unequivocal longing to die. Her vision of Death is suddenly so light, lyrical, and airy. This is the vision of the letter of 15 June 1911. Her soul will follow her new lord 'wie ein leichtes Blatt im Winde' (40). Far too many lines are devoted to her vision; gone is the world of heroic mythology, pathetic overstatement, and weary resignation. Instead we have the tripping little voice of an Ariadne just longing to slip away to the Elysian Fields.

From this series of speeches before the Intermezzo we can see how Ariadne started as a realistic allegoric figure but became a brittle symbol instead. Hofmannsthal himself touchingly persisted in the belief that Ariadne was amongst his most human and realistic female portraits. He wrote damningly of the critics' incomprehension: 'Daß die Ariadne, musikalisch wie dichterisch, eine ziemlich komplette Gestalt ist, unendlich gestalteter und kompletter als zehntausend Figuren, die Fräulein Müller oder Frau Meier heißen und deren Adresse und Einkommensziffer wir erfahren, daß sie ebenso "komplett" ist wie Elektra oder Salome, das zu erfassen, sind diese Rüpel . . . unfähig.'[64] (That Ariadne is a decidedly well-rounded figure, in the music and in the poetry, far better fashioned and rounded than many thousand Miss Müllers or Mrs Meiers we get on the stage whose addresses and incomes we are told in detail, no less 'round' than Electra or Salome, this is something which these louts cannot comprehend.)

So Ariadne too was subjected to the lyric treatment but failed to benefit because ultimately the original material was too slight for the subtle finish Hofmannsthal wished to give it. The result, far from being psychological intricacy, is a hollow, second-hand symbolism which is most evident in the third section of the *Oper* after the comedians' Intermezzo. Let us take as an example a short speech of Ariadne's as she is being transformed:

> Gibts kein hinüber?
> Sind wir schon drüben?
> Sind wir schon da?

[64] Bw. 5 Dec. 1912, p. 174. Miss Müller and Mrs Meier were popular sopranos of the day. Elsewhere Hofmannsthal wrote 'Ich glaube, Ihre Musik wird, was die Figur der Ariadne betrifft, es außer allen Zweifel setzen, daß hier nichts Barockes, nichts Verschärftes, sondern Seelenhaft-Wirkliches, Wahres zu geben vermeint war'. Bw. 23 May 1912, p. 159.

Wie konnt es geschehen?
Auch meine Höhle, schön! gewölbt
Über ein seliges Lager,
Einen heiligen Altar!
Wie wunder- wunderbar verwandelst du! (64)

(Is there no going across?
Are we already over there?
Are we already there?
How could it happen?
My cave too, beautiful! arched
Over a blessed bed,
A sacred altar!
How wonder- wonderfully you transform!)

Apart from the conventional use of inarticulateness to convey surprise and wonder which, far from persuading us of the innocent vulnerability of a psyche in a state of upheaval and renewal, alienates us by the weakness of its poetic line and the vacuity and lisping childishness of its sentiment, we are further repelled by the pseudo-religious Wagnerian symbol of the bed as altar which is probably borrowed from the 'Minnegrotte' symbolism in *Tristan und Isolde*. There is also an over-abundance of pseudo-religious vocabulary: the words 'selig', 'heilig', and 'wunderbar' with the root 'Wunder' neatly separated out for us as part of a naïve attempt at intensification all occur within the space of three lines. This is not only a reflection, as Susan Sontag observes, of a modern poverty of religious experience and hence of religious language which in the face of its own pallid identity practises 'a continuing piety toward the grandeur of emotions that went into that vocabulary'.[65] It is also an attitude of spiritual piety on Hofmannsthal's part which results in the over-exquisite spirituality which is the real tenor of the Ariadne–Bacchus transformation. The attitude, the form is there, but emotional substance and content are lacking; the result is sensationalism. The discrepancy between form and content is at the bottom of the inferior, bombastic poetry, which, as G. Marek rightly says, 'is so bad compared with the rest of the opera that it cóuld have been written by a substitute'.[66]

[65] Susan Sontag, *Styles of Radical Will* (London, 1969), p. 69.
[66] Marek, p. 225.

The object of Hofmannsthal's piety emerges in the Ariadne–
Bacchus relationship and its 'negative co-present', the Zerbinetta–Harlekin affair. To discuss this is also in effect to discuss
the genesis of the theme of *Ariadne auf Naxos*.

iii. *Problems of Theme arising in the Shift from the Ironic Allegory*

Love as the ironic emotion *par excellence* was the theme of the
Szenarium. There irony was perfectly sustained at the formal
level; irony being defined in this case as the attitude which
acknowledges the existence of 'the opposite, the complementary impulse'.[67] Hofmannsthal's ironic attitude in the *Szenarium* to the complementary impulses of eroticism and
spirituality serves as a corrective to a single vision of things
and brings about what I. A. Richards calls 'a balanced poise'.[68]
A. Schlegel sees irony in much the same way: '[Die Ironie ist]
ein in die Darstellung selbst hineingelegtes mehr oder weniger
leise angedeutetes Eingeständniß ihrer übertreibenden Einsei-
tigkeit in dem Antheil der Fantasie und Empfindung, wodurch
also das Gleichgewicht wieder hergestellt wird.'[69] (Irony is a
confession, woven into the representation itself and more or
less lightly hinted at, of overcharged one-sidedness in matters
of fantasy and feeling; a confession which thus restores the
balance.) The 'overcharged one-sidedness' of the *opera seria*
and the *opera buffa* is mutually corrected to leave the final
ensemble in a state of happy equipoise—the 'confession' is
implicit in the action.

In the libretto love is regarded not ironically but ethically
and even mystically. The allomatic transformation is symbolic
of higher, purer love, as Hofmannsthal pointed out to Strauss:
'der Schluß [führte] aus dem Spielerischen immer mehr ins
Seelenhafte [hinauf].'[70] Ariadne's and Bacchus' miraculous
love must be freed from the taint of coarse sexuality; eroticism
is permitted so long as it is tinged with the eternal. The
following note which Hofmannsthal did not include, feeling
that the text could be no more than 'Hieroglyphen . . . für ein

---

[67] I. A. Richards, *Principles of Literary Criticism*, 2nd edn. (London, 1926), p. 250.
[68] Richards, p. 250.
[69] August Wilhelm von Schlegel, *Vorlesungen über Dramatische Kunst und Literatur*,
ed. Giovanni Vittorio Amoretti (Bonn, 1923), I, 207–8.
[70] Bw. 5 July 1911, p. 112.

Unaussprechliches'[71] that music alone could decipher, shows the extent to which he protected his serious lovers from charges of ordinary sensuality:

Ariadne–Bacchus (Höhepunkt)
Ariadne: Du hast ein Schiff? Es nimmt mich mit! Das Totenschiff—hinüber
Bacchus: Es gibt kein Hinüber, es ist ein Bleiben, ein Sinken zu tiefster Lust der Ewigkeit—nun ahn ich was Circe mir getan
Ariadne: Alles leer—kein Verbundensein—gelöst und ohne Trauer
Bacchus: Alles in Fülle—verwandelnd verwandelt dunkeläugige Lust.[72]

(Ariadne–Bacchus (climax)
Ariadne: You have a ship? It is taking me with it!
           The ship of death—across
Bacchus: There is no across, there is a remaining, a sinking into deepest pleasure of eternity—now I suspect what Circe did to me
Ariadne: Everything empty—no being bound—released and without grief
Bacchus: Everything in abundance—transforming transformed dark-eyed pleasure.)

Here is a one-sided and overcharged vision of love, which in the libretto does not receive the correction it so sorely needs. Instead the miracle of love becomes the central theme of the 'lyric drama' Ariadne auf Naxos, whereas before it was merely part of a wider theme. Unfortunately it is a theme which, apart from becoming commonplace when dipped in the generalizing current of music, is also one which begs the question. It is begging the question to state that spiritual love is 'higher' than erotic love, and this is what Hofmannsthal is saying at length in the libretto, in the Ariadne Brief with such statements as that Ariadne's love is 'die Wahrheit einer höheren Stufe'[73] and in the mid-July letter where he writes to Strauss 'Was aber ein wirkliches Wunder ist für göttliche Seelen, für die irdische Seele der Zerbinetta ist es das alltägliche' (Bw. mid-July 1911, p. 115). The pretensions of the

[71] PIII, p. 142.
[72] Appendix A, Note 9.
[73] PIII, p. 40.

latter theme spoil the proportions of the original foundations,
as was sensed by the ever perceptive Borchardt:

Ein völliger Ausgleich wollte sich nicht herstellen; was ich als
geniale Skizze, aufs herrlichste angedeutete Ausdeutung eines von
vornherein vieldeutigen 'ewigen Verhältnisses' bewundert hatte,
und was mir als solche vollauf genügt hatte, als Vorgestaltung—wie
den ersten État einer Radierung—einer so weitgefaßten Conception
mir vorzustellen, wie Ihr Schreiben sie entwirft, hat mir nicht
durchweg gelingen wollen.[74]

(I could not quite reconcile the parts; what I admired as an inspired
sketch, a splendidly adumbrated interpretation of an inherently
ambiguous 'eternal relationship' and what as such satisfied me
thoroughly, I could not succeed in imagining as a preliminary plan—
like the first stage of an etching—for such a far-reaching conception
as your letter describes.)

Perhaps a little of the discomfort caused by the 'revised'
theme, if we may call it that, is Hofmannsthal's evident piety
towards the institution of marriage contained in it. The lavish
care which Hofmannsthal took over the staging of this scene
suggests his reverential attitude. First a starry sky and then a
canopy sinks down over the lovers. Other illusionist practices
are enlisted in the service of the mystical:

Hier müssen mir, wenn wir dies je einmal auf die Bühne bringen, der
Maler und der Regisseur alle ihre Kräfte einsetzen, um ein
wahrhaftiges Geheimnis—nicht zu offenbaren, aber zu verherr-
lichen; hier muß die kleine Bühne ins Unbegrenzte wachsen, mit
dem Eintritt des Bacchus müssen die puppenhaften Kulissen
verschwunden sein, die Decke von Jourdains Saal schwebt auf,
Nacht muß um Bacchus und Ariadne sein, in die von oben Sterne
hineinfunkeln, nichts darf vom 'Spiel im Spiel' mehr zu ahnen sein,
Herr Jourdain, seine Gäste, seine Lakaien, sein Haus, alles muß fort
und vergessen sein, und der Zuhörer darf sich dieser Dinge so wenig
mehr erinnern, als wer in einem tiefen Traum liegt, etwas von seinem
Bette weiß.[75]

(If we ever perform this then the scene painter and the director must
really exert themselves in order—not to reveal but—to glorify a
veritable mystery; here the small stage must grow into a limitless
space, at Bacchus' entry the doll-like sets must disappear, the roof of

[74] Hugo von Hofmannsthal/Rudolf Borchardt, *Briefwechsel*, p. 84.
[75] PIII, p. 142.

Jourdain's room rises up, night must enfold Bacchus and Ariadne and stars must shine down from above, no trace may be left of the 'play within a play', M. Jourdain, his guests, his lackeys, his house, everything must be gone and forgotten, and the listener is to remember as little of these things as the person in a deep dream is aware of his bed.)

In Hofmannsthal's high esteem of marriage and his tendency to spiritualize love and sex there is a suggestion of a certain fearful prudishness.[76] Hermann Broch draws attention to the schizoid atmosphere and double morality of Vienna in the 1880s and 1890s, and remarks on the effect this must have had on the young Hofmannsthal: 'Es ist anzunehmen, daß bereits das Kind unter dem Erziehungsbruch—hedonistischer oder zuminderst hedonoider Ästhetizismus bei gleichzeitiger Moralität—gelitten haben mochte und in Verwirrung geraten war.'[77] (It is to be assumed that even as a child he suffered from a double standard in his upbringing—hedonistic or at least hedonoid aestheticism accompanied by morality—and had grown confused.) The tension of a double standard expressed itself in Hofmannsthal in the need to moralize, and to enhance aesthetically what was considered moral. Broch sees in much of Hofmannsthal's writing an attempted 'Sittlichkeits-Ritual'[78] which often takes place in the guise of a dream on a dream-stage. The illusionist dream-stage setting Hofmannsthal envisaged for the Ariadne–Bacchus scene suggests that some kind of 'Sittlichkeits-Ritual' is taking place here. The propinquity of ethics and dreams is in general a mark of Hofmannsthal's most personal style.

The way Hofmannsthal treated the *commedia dell'arte* throws more light on his moral attitudes. In a revealing note in *Ad me ipsum* Hofmannsthal refers to Zerbinetta as 'Tyche', Greek for 'chance': 'Circe, wie Zerbinetta, ist der Weltdämon, Tyche, ein Element gleich dem Efrit.'[79] She is to represent

---

[76] Works with such a treatment of love include *Die Ägyptische Helene, Arabella* and *Der Schwierige. Die Frau ohne Schatten* is more concerned with the moral aspect of human relationships.

[77] Broch, p. 188.

[78] Broch, p. 209.

[79] In order to understand this cryptic note we need to look at an earlier passage from *Ad me ipsum*. Under the heading 'Der Weg zum Leben (und zum Sozialen) durch das Werk und das Kind' there is a group of comments on *Die Frau ohne Schatten* and

(*continued*)

indiscriminate sexuality. Elsewhere the *commedia dell' arte* are referred to as 'gemeine Lebensmasken', 'Zutaten' and 'gemeine Sterblichen'.[80] They are now clearly the morally inferior group and Hofmannsthal keeps his distance from them.

Similarly Hofmannsthal equates 'das Menschliche' with base sexuality. Broch has drawn attention to the difficulty Hofmannsthal had in portraying the human without introducing the debased or immodest: 'wenn das Menschliche . . . zum Vorschein kommt, so deutet es bereits Untermenschliches an, also die teils erschreckenden, teils komischen Eigenschaften der 'untern' Stände, den Mimus, der sich dem Mysterium entgegenstellt, um Scham und Schamlosigkeit—immer noch

---

the idea of fate. Acceptance of fate, of higher necessity, is part of the individual's growth and self-overcoming. Marriage and having children is the ultimate expression of social responsibility:

'Die Frau ohne Schatten': Triumph des Allomatischen.
Allegorie des Sozialen.
    Kreuzung zweier Hauptmotive: Erfassung des
    Schicksalsbegriffes (Schicksal auf sich nehmen
    oder fliehen* und: Sich läutern = sich verwandeln.
        *Sobeïde iterum. 'Tyche'. Das Motif schon
    in 'Tor und Tod'. ('Verworrner Traum entsteigt
    der dunklen Schwelle—und Glück ist alles:
    Stunde Wind und Welle')
        Tyche: die Welt. die das Individuum von sich entfernen
    will, um es zu sich zu bringen. (Auf., p. 218.)

The Dyer's Wife and Sobeide in *Die Hochzeit der Sobeide* try to escape their fates in purely erotic relationships with the Efrit and Ganem respectively. Erotic attachments have a large measure of chance, or 'Tyche' in them. They do not mature the individual in the way a commitment such as marriage does. Claudio in *Der Tor und der Tod* is also unable to commit himself to life (that is, he cannot make the move from 'Präexistenz' to 'Existenz'), and indulges in the aesthete's pursuit of 'Glück' which is necessarily as fleeting as 'Stunde Wind und Welle' (GuLD, p. 275).

Hofmannsthal perhaps had Goethe's poem *Paria* in mind when writing about the Efrit and must have thought of Goethe's *Urworte. Orphisch* when referring to 'Tyche'. However, he modified Goethe's 'Tyche' who is pure chance (or 'Zufälliges', as Goethe wrote in *Über Kunst und Altertum*) and combined her with '*Ananke,* Nötigung' from the fourth stanza of *Urworte. Orphisch*. This new figure, although in the guise of chance, seduces people in order to bring them to their senses and to accept 'Beschränkung', 'Pflicht' or 'Nötigung'. Hence Hofmannsthal writes 'Tyche: die Welt. die das Individuum von sich entfernen will, um es zu sich zu bringen'. 'Tyche-Ananke', unlike Goethe's Tyche, has a place within a benevolent moral scheme.

If we return to the statement about Zerbinetta 'Circe, wie Zerbinetta, ist der Weltdämon, Tyche, ein Element gleich dem Efrit' we see that Circe and Zerbinetta are to join company with the Efrit and Ganem. This makes sense only if we take it to mean Zerbinetta in the 1916 *Ariadne* where we easily imagine that she shall have such a moral effect on the young Composer.

[80] PIII, p. 140. Bw. 28 May 1911, p. 107.

zum Schema der commedia dell'arte gehörig—gegeneinander auszuspielen.'[81] (When the human appears it already means the sub-human, that is, the partly horrifying, partly comical characteristics of the 'lower' orders, of the mimus, who opposes the mystery in order to play off shame and shamelessness against each other—as in the scheme of the commedia dell'arte.) In the libretto to *Ariadne* the division between the two groups, the *opera seria* and the *opera buffa*, is essentially a moral one, then, and at the same time also a moralizing one. If, however, we remember back to the *Szenarium* we find that the division into two groups was essentially a cultural–historical one. In the libretto, out of concern for moral issues, Hofmannsthal does an injustice to the *commedia dell'arte* world by judging it according to a morality which is alien to it. The *commedia*'s sexual ethics, and hence its attitude to 'affairs', partook largely of the Renaissance tolerance and frankness, cult of the body, and ardent sensuality which did not censure ephemeral relationships. The Renaissance was not a prudish age and Hofmannsthal must have been reminded of this in his reading of Monnier. We find the same interpretation of the commedia in Constant Mic's chapter on 'L'élément érotique': 'La saine, fraîche et puissante sensualité de la Renaissance ... ne connaissait pas la pruderie et ne craignait pas la franchise.'[82] Mic goes on to describe its down-to-earth attitude: 'La Comédie italienne est toujours franche, et ceci est, à mon avis, un indice de santé morale et de candeur: elle appelle les choses par leur nom et n'a que rarement recours aux équivoques, aux allusions; de plus, ce ne sont pas tant les paroles, les expressions qui y sont indécentes, mais plutôt les actes et les gestes: la grivoiserie, en somme, est étrangère à l'esprit du Théâtre italien.'[83] (The Italian comedy is always frank and this, in my opinion, is a sign of moral health and candour: the Italians call a spade a spade and only rarely resort to equivocation or allusion; furthermore, it is not so much words or expressions which are indecent but rather actions and gestures: prurience, in short, is unknown to the spirit of the Italian theatre.)

[81] Broch, p. 294.
[82] Constant Mic, *La Commedia dell'arte: ou le théâtre des comédiens italiens des XVIe, XVIIe et XVIIIe siècles*, p. 87.
[83] Mic, p. 88.

Thus it can be said that the author is working out a non-ironic, symbolic complex of themes which can be grouped together under the heading 'transformation' within the formal conventions of an ironic allegory, and that in order to do so he has made several adjustments to the moral world embodied in his piece. Although the audience is led to expect a resolution of the conflict in terms of the *opera seria* and the *commedia dell'arte* Hofmannsthal becomes absorbed in the conflict within Ariadne's soul, frustrating in part the audience's wish for an allegoric resolution. In his critical writings and letters Hofmannsthal was determined to prove that a resolution of Ariadne's problems was inextricably bound up with a resolution of all the tensions in the work. In fact the themes are not so dependent on one another and this is the key to the ending settled on for the 1916 version.

iv. *Alternative Endings to the* Oper

The ending of the *Szenarium* has already been discussed in some detail in Chapter 1. The 1912 *Ariadne* retains the final dance but with the significant difference that the heroic couple have already disappeared from view and do not participate. Nevertheless the *commedia* is there in full force to serve as an ironic corrective to the dream-like, spiritual apotheosis which has just taken place on stage.

In this version, towards the conclusion of their duet Ariadne and Bacchus are carried by the wind into the entrance of Ariadne's grotto. They remain visible for a minute and then they are hidden: 'Weinlaub und Efeu fällt vor, verbirgt sie beide. Ihre Stimmen tönen verflochten' (377). They sing their final lines behind this curtain of vine leaves and ivy. Then all the *commedia* characters and the three nymphs come back on stage. Suddenly Zerbinetta leaps forward 'und wiederholt mit spöttischem Triumph ihr Rondo' (377). There follows a moderately long reprise of her *pièce de résistance*, a coloratura rondo in which she sings of her inability to resist each new lover. The irony of her oblique comment on the recent Ariadne–Bacchus development is heightened by her calling her new lover 'Der neue Gott'. The words of her song can indeed be construed mockingly:

Kommt der neue Gott gegangen,
Hingegeben sind wir stumm!
Und er küßt uns Hand und Wangen
Und wir geben uns gefangen,
Sind verwandelt um und um!
Sind verwandelt um und um! (377–8.)

(When the new god comes along
Captive are we, silent!
He kisses our hand and cheek
And we give ourselves up,
Are transformed over and over!
Are transformed over and over!)

This is a more polished operatic equivalent of her line in the *Szenarium* '(ad spectatores) Wie wir es sagten ist es gekommen' (Sz. 291). Then as in the *Szenarium* they begin their dance and the comedians and the nymphs partner each other. That the Ariadne–Bacchus relationship is ironic and ambiguous is further brought home to the audience by Hofmannsthal's masterly stroke of having Dorantes and Dorimene, who have all along been watching the divertissement, get up during the suspended, magical hush which follows the love duet and walk out on the duped Jourdain. This sudden reminder of the scheming Count Dorantes and his self-interested intriguing for the hand of the widow Dorimene is a powerful ironic corrective after the ecstatic apotheosis of the heroic couple and no doubt also recalls Jourdain's line from the preceding *Bürger als Edelmann*: '[Die Oper] muß ganz und gar auf eine Witwe von vornehmem Stand abgesehen sein, welche zwar darauf beharrt, eine Witwe zu bleiben, welcher es aber doch am Ende schwer gemacht wird, darauf zu beharren' (83). Barbara Könneker draws attention to the nicety of this anti-illusionist device and rightly notes that something is lost by its inevitable omission in the 1916 version.[84] Thus in the 1912 *Ariadne* the form of the allegoric divertissement is preserved and transformation is a sub-theme which is integrated into the theme of the irony of love.

But this integration was precarious. In fact the transformation scene, the climax of the 'lyric drama' and the opera, is too intensely elevated and passionately protracted for any

[84] Könneker, p. 133.

corrective to be possible. Hofmannsthal had over-indulged his lyric vein and Strauss his 'Wagnerian' vein. In the 1912 version this could be contained because the *Bürger als Edelmann* frame imposed discipline on the collaborators. The *Oper* was supposed to be an entertainment given in Jourdain's house and the whole work is concluded by his flat little speech. In the 1916 version, with the Molière frame removed, the authors, particularly Hofmannsthal, with whom the initiative lay, did not feel so much obliged to break the illusion of the transformation scene. The result is that the 1916 *Ariadne* ends with the climactic apotheosis. Bacchus has the last word. This abrupt about-face was caused in part by the authors' quarrelling and confusion as to how to end the new version now that the Molière was gone. In their perplexity they lost sight of the separate problem of the ending for the *Oper*. Much energy was spent deciding if the Major Domo or the Composer should reappear in place of Jourdain and what words he should speak. In the event *no* reference is made at the end to the *Vorspiel*—but neither does the *commedia* make a sufficient reappearance and here the authors threw out the baby with the bath-water. How this came about we shall now examine in detail.

On 6 April 1916 Strauss asked Hofmannsthal to write 'eine kleine hübsche Soloszene (nach "Ariadne"!) . . .: poetisch-melancholisch' with the Composer bursting out in despair 'Was haben Sie aus meinem Werke gemacht' (Bw. 6 Apr. 1916, p. 278). Hofmannsthal reacted with horror to Strauss's 'sehr überraschender Schlußvorschlag' (although he half came round to the idea later). Hofmannsthal felt his Composer had been vulgarly misunderstood by Strauss. So irate was he then that he wrote a letter in which all his true feelings about the ending of the *Oper* emerge:

Dieser Einfall für den Schluß ist geradezu entsetzlich, verzeihen Sie mir, lieber Dr. Strauss—, Sie haben diesen Brief in keinem guten Moment geschrieben. Denken Sie die Höhe der Stimmung, die mühsam erklommen ist, vom Anfang des Vorspiels an, immer höher, in die herrliche Oper hinauf, dann im Kommen des Bacchus, im Duett eine fast mystische Höhe. Und nun, wo die nötige Coda nicht mehr als ein Moment sein darf (so die ganz berühmten Schlußworte des Jourdain), und nun soll solcher Quark wieder sich breitmachen

(auf dem *breit* liegt der Ton): Der Haushofmeister, das Honorar und
der Graf und Tod und Teufel! Und das alles, damit die Rolle ein
Endchen länger wird! Dazu die stilistische Unmöglichkeit, nachdem
das Höchste an Lyrik eben in der Oper selbst gegeben ist, nun in
dem Rahmen wieder 'Lyrisches' zu verlangen. (Bw. 13 Apr. 1916, p.
281.)

(This idea for the end is truly appalling; if you will forgive me, my
dear Dr Strauss, this letter was not written in one of your happiest
moments. Consider the lofty atmosphere which we have been
striving so hard to reach, rising ever higher from the beginning of
the Vorspiel to the glorious opera, then the entrance of Bacchus,
reaching in the duet almost mystical heights. And now, where the
essential coda ought to be over in a thrice (as with Jourdain's famous
last words), now some rubbish of this kind is to spread itself once
more (the emphasis is on *spread*): the major-domo, the fee, the count
and God knows what else! And all this merely to make the part an
inch longer! To say nothing of the stylistic absurdity of this demand
for something 'lyrical' in the framework after the opera has just
reached its greatest lyrical climax.)

Clearly the lyric climax and apotheosis between Ariadne and
Bacchus is of deep importance to Hofmannsthal and even
from this letter it is apparent that Hofmannsthal would have
been happiest to end without any 'coda' at all. The confusion
around the coda arose mainly because the authors still felt
that, as in the 1912 version, the frame ought to encircle the
Oper. At first they did not see that the new *Vorspiel*, being a
totally different form from the adapted *Bourgeois Gentilhomme*,
would allow them to end simply with the opera. It seems to
have been Strauss who first suggested a technical alteration
which opened up the possibility of letting the *Vorspiel* function
entirely as a prologue.

There is unfortunately a gap in the correspondence at this
point. It seems, however, that Ariadne's and Bacchus' presence
on stage at the end of the *Oper* had been seen as a technical
problem which could best be solved by a coda. Strauss must
have suggested surmounting this obstacle by letting these two
exit on board a ship, for on 15 May 1916 Hofmannsthal writes
'Bezüglich Schlusses, wie Ihnen depeschiert, und Ihren
Vorschlägen in der Hauptsache völlig einverstanden; Höhle
verschwindet, beide bleiben sichtbar, hinabschreitend gegen

das Meer und so fort.' (Bw. 15 May 1916, p. 285.) (As I said in
my telegram, I am in complete agreement about the end and
with your suggestions on the main point; the cave disappears,
both remain visible as they step down towards the sea and so
on.) Later this alteration was not incorporated because of the
difficulties of ships on stage.[85] So the plan to have the lovers
depart on Bacchus' ship was replaced in the final version with
the earlier idea of a canopy: 'Ein Baldachin senkt sich von
oben langsam über beide, sie einschließend' (65). Irrespective
of the actual detail of the ending it is clear that their solution
released them from the need to bring back characters from the
Vorspiel. But all this cutting back also made it easier to chop
off more of the *Oper* than ought to have been removed for the
sake of the allegoric and ironic ending. The *Oper* was now
allowed to conclude at its lyric high point with Bacchus having
the final word. The removal of the anti-illusionist return to the
'frame' of the *Vorspiel* had facilitated for its authors a *volte-
face* towards illusion. As Hofmannsthal rightly remarked later
'die heiteren Figuren sind zum Schluß nicht zu ihrem Recht
gekommen'.[86] There is no final joining together of the opposed
forces.

The evidence of the 1916 *Ariadne* suggests that the lyric
aspect was now the dominant one for its authors. Strauss also
seems to have conceived of the work in this way although the
following comment on the 1912 *Ariadne*, written in 1942, may
have been strongly coloured by the 1912 reception and the
1916 experience of the work: 'Die erste Idee war reizend:
anfangend in nüchternster Komödienprosa, durch Ballett und
Commedia dell'Arte in den Höhen reinster, wortloser Musik
geführt, scheiterte sie schließlich an einer gewissen Unkultur
des Publikums.'[87] (The first idea was enchanting: beginning
in soberest comic prose, led through ballet and *commedia
dell'arte* to the heights of purest, wordless music, it came to
grief finally through a certain philistinism of the public.) It
seems that Strauss was never really committed to the original

[85] 'Schiffe auf der Bühne sind recht übel, selbst der furchtlose Reinhardt fürchtet
sie sehr'. Bw. 22 May 1916, p. 288.
[86] 'Die heiteren Figuren sind zum Schluß nicht zu ihrem Recht gekommen, weder
in der Musik noch in der Erscheinung—*sie sind fallen gelassen*—und daraus resultiert
ein Gefühl von Inkomplettheit, leider.' Bw. Oct. 1916, p. 305.
[87] Richard Strauss, *Betrachtungen und Erinnerungen*, p. 195.

plan of the Molière plus a recreated divertissement. But by the same token, Hofmannsthal began very early to reshape and redirect his libretto and, as we have seen, did not leave Strauss much time in which to grow attached to his first ideas.

In fairness it must be added that Hofmannsthal was aware of the original meaning and structure of his little divertissement even in 1916 and that he made some attempt to restore the ironic balance. But from the following letter it emerges that while Hofmannsthal was rationally committed to preserving the balance and the allegorical form he was emotionally committed to the spiritual vision of the 'lyric drama'. In the opening paragraph of this letter we see him forcefully and correctly stating the meaning of the work and acknowledging his duty not to sacrifice Zerbinetta and company for the sake of a 'curtain'. He then states emphatically that Zerbinetta must reappear but makes one concession after the other to his real wish not to have her there at all until he finally declares he would be satisfied if the orchestra drowned her out after the first line and then with her 'symbolisches spöttisches Dastehen und Wiederverschwinden'. One feels that before long he would have considered just her exit quite enough:

Eine völlige Gewissenlosigkeit von mir gegen das Werk und dessen Zukunft wäre es, wollte ich—bequemlichkeitshalber—konzedieren, daß die irdische Gegenstimme (Zerbinetta) gar nicht mehr zu Worte kommt! ... Ich beharre nur darauf, daß die Gegenstimme in der einzigen Figur Zerbinetta am Schluß einen Moment lang zur Geltung kommt. Also etwa so: indessen rückwärts die beiden hinabschreiten, gegen's Meer, und bevor das Orchester zum Nachspiel einsetzt, erscheint rechts vorne, an der Kulisse, aber sichtbar, Zerbinetta, weist spöttisch mit dem Fächer über die Schulter nach rückwärts und fängt an, ihr Couplet zu singen:

'Kommt der neue Gott gegangen, hingegeben sind wir stumm,
Und er küßt uns Stirn und Wangen usw. ... gefangen ...
Hingegeben sind wir stumm!'

Meinetwegen mag sie es nur anfangen, nur die erste Zeile singen—dann mag das Orchester sie zudecken und der Rest mag nur im Textbuch stehen, mir genügt dann ihr symbolisches spöttisches Dastehen und Wiederverschwinden—und mir scheint sogar, daß dieses Würzen des Sentimentalen durch ein widersprechendes Element ganz in Ihrem Geist ist. (Bw. 15 May 1916, pp. 285–6.)

(But—it would be a shameless betrayal of the work and its future for me to concede—out of pusillanimity—that the human counterpart (Zerbinetta) should be deprived of some last word! . . . I will only insist that the counter-voice, represented by the sole figure of Zerbinetta, should be heard at the end for a second. Something like this: while to the rear of the stage the couple step down towards the sea, and before the orchestra opens the epilogue, Zerbinetta appears in front, right, in the wings, but visible, waves her fan mockingly over her shoulder towards the back and proceeds to sing her couplet:

> When the new god comes along, captive are we, silent,
> He kisses our forehead and cheek etc. . . . captive . . .
> Captive are we, silent!

If need be let her only begin to sing, sing the first line—then let the orchestra drown her, so that the rest is to be found only in the libretto; I am satisfied with her symbolic, mocking presence and exit. I am even inclined to believe that such spicing of the sentimental with its opposite is quite in your spirit.)

As shall be seen in the following Chapter Strauss did not in fact spice even this little bit with its opposite and Zerbinetta sings her melody not mockingly but in the same tone of lyric rapture that has pervaded the whole scene. But if Strauss did not write a mocking reprise for Zerbinetta it is because his operatic and dramatic instincts were too sure: there was after all no way to ironize or offset the lyric climax. William Mann recognizes this when he comments on 'how banal and unhelpful any alienation ending would have been'.[88] The authors had gone too far in creating a theatre of illusion. In the 1912 version the original framework ensured at least a semblance of illusion-breaking at the end. In the 1916 version the anti-illusionist device is the merest token gesture. William Mann remarks very aptly 'as we have it *Ariadne II* starts by pricking the balloon and then blows it up to full size.'[89] If the 'lyric drama' offered us true poetic and spiritual insights we might be able to overlook the unresolved allegory but in the absence of these we can only agree with Romain Rolland's trenchant summary of the end to the 1916 version: 'l'impression d'ensemble est une déception . . . Au lieu de terminer, comme il aurait fallu, par un septuor ironique des cinq bouffes et des

[88] Mann, p. 152.
[89] Mann, p. 152.

deux tragiques, les bouffes sont éliminés et l'on nous offre, seule, une tragédie pompeuse et glacée à deux personnages ampoulés.[90] (the impression of an ensemble is deceptive ... Instead of finishing as it should have with an ironic septet of the five buffos and the two tragic characters the buffos are eliminated and we are offered only the pompous, icy tragedy of two bombastic characters.)

The genesis of the 'lyric drama' *Ariadne auf Naxos* using the *Szenarium* and the notes has now been traced in order to show the complications introduced by the authors at the literary level. In matters of theme and characterization there is a shift from the historical and impersonal to the lyric and personal and this shift accounts for some of the faults in the libretto. Before concluding this section by examining the libretto for other lyric features we shall briefly trace the effect of this same shift on Zerbinetta, Harlekin, and the three other male buffos Scaramuccio, Truffaldin, and Brighella. Of these Zerbinetta will be discussed only as a member of the group and not individually; a lengthy analysis of her part follows in Chapter III. It is interesting to observe, however, the absence of any preparatory notes on either Zerbinetta, a main role in the opera, or any of the comedians. This confirms our finding that the real developments and centre of gravity lay with the heroic figures.

v. *The Lyric Treatment of the* Commedia dell'arte

As with Ariadne and Bacchus there is a parallel tendency in Hofmannsthal's development of the *commedia* figures towards lyricism and idealization. Fiedler is the only critic to remark upon this: 'Harlekin und Zerbinetta verschieben sich aber trotzdem zugleich—wenn auch in geringerem Maße als die mythologischen Figuren Ariadne und Bacchus—ins "Seelenhafte" und Symbolische, wie die Figuren der "Frau ohne Schatten", in Hofmannsthals eigenste Sphäre.'[91] (Though to a lesser extent than the mythological figures Ariadne and Bacchus, Harlekin and Zerbinetta also shift into the 'spiritual'

---

[90] Richard Strauss et Romain Rolland, *Correspondance, Fragments de Journal*, pp. 172–3.
[91] Fiedler, p. 65.

and the symbolic, like the figures in the *Frau ohne Schatten*; into Hofmannsthal's most personal sphere.) Fiedler does not elaborate nor does he mention the three other figures.

The *Szenarium* contains a note on the comedians:

> Figuren der commedia
> dell'arte in Callot's
> Manier, bunt, grotesk. (Sz. 286.)

Jacques Callot's *commedia dell'arte* is certainly 'bunt' and 'grotesk'. Further on in the *Szenarium* Hofmannsthal wrote a memo to himself and Strauss, stressing the grotesque element: '(Nicht zu vergessen, daß die 4 *groteske* Gestalten sind: Arlekin ein Gauner, Brighella ein Tölpel, Scaramuccio ein Charlatan und Truffaldin ein grotesker Alter.)' (Sz. 289.) Earlier he writes that the dance that they perform to cheer Ariadne up is 'grotesk-charakteristisch' (Sz. 288). In the libretto these grotesque figures are softened quite considerably as can be seen from the stage direction before the Intermezzo: 'Harlekin, verwegen; Brighella, jung tölpelhaft; Scaramuccio, Gauner, fünfzigjährig; Truffaldin, alberner Alter' (40). They are domesticated versions of their grotesque prototypes and are good-natured, amusing, and lovable. In many ways they resemble Antoine Watteau's drawings of the *commedia dell'arte* rather than Callot's. Their appearance is confirmed by their kind-hearted and sympathetic behaviour towards Ariadne. Harlekin's song is not what might be expected from a sly, rascally lover. Instead he is oddly sensitive to Ariadne's misfortune and his words are suffused with a gentle warmth and philosophical lightness which should not fail to console. It is true that his comment on observing the lack of effect of his song 'Nie hat ein menschliches Wesen mich so gerührt' (39) is quickly undercut by Zerbinetta's quip 'So geht es dir mit jeder Frau' (39); nevertheless there is evidence of a lyricizing of Harlekin's psychological make-up and of the introduction of a new, sentimental streak. Yet even in the libretto Hofmannsthal's Harlekin remains essentially the daring, athletic, amorous type of the Italian comic theatre. Despite lyricism he and the other comedians are very much types belonging to a particular historical context and theatrical convention.[92] It is for this reason that we feel that Hofmannsthal's interpretation of them in the *Ariadne Brief* is as much a begging of the question as was his twisting of the theme of irony. In the following quotation Harlekin is falsely compared with Bacchus: 'Bacchus ist Gegenspiel zur gemeinen Lebensmaske Harlekin, . . . Harlekin ist bloße Natur, ist seelenlos und ohne Schicksal, obschon ein Mann; Bacchus ist ein Knabe und schicksalsvoll, Harlekin ist irgendeiner, Bacchus ist einziger' (140). (Bacchus is the opposite of the common masque Harlekin, . . . Harlekin is mere nature, is soulless and without fate although a man; Bacchus is a boy and full of fate. Harlekin is anyone, Bacchus is unique.) The same false spiritual comparison is implied when Hofmannsthal refers further on to the comedians as 'gemeine Lebensmasken'.

In fact Hofmannsthal gave these figures more personality, stage presence and authenticity than he was perhaps aware of. Above all, in certain passages of the Intermezzo he was able to write perfect, if traditional, comic theatre. Masks, dumbshow, slapstick, and stage acrobatics all contribute to the general gaiety, as do the singing and dancing. Particularly successful is the by-play when Zerbinetta loses a shoe during their dance ensemble: 'Unterm Tanz scheint sie einen Schuh zu verlieren. Scaramuccio, flink, erfaßt den Schuh und küßt ihn. Sie läßt sich ihn von ihm anziehen, wobei sie sich auf Truffaldin stützt, der ihr von der anderen Seite zu Füßen gefallen ist.' (50.). (While dancing she seems to lose a shoe. Scaramuccio nimbly catches the shoe and kisses it. She lets him put it on her, leaning on Truffaldin who has fallen at her feet on the other side.) Their antics continue in this vein. Borchardt was very much impressed by the comic sections of the libretto which he praised in the following terms: 'Keine Ihrer Produktionen ist so ganz und so echt Theatergehorsam, Theaterstil: in der Improvisation, im Waghalsig Hanswurstigen, in der Dreistigkeit der Perfektion, in der Lebensge-

---

[92] It is advisable, however, to be wary of the word 'type' when speaking of the *commedia dell'arte*. As Allardyce Nicoll points out, the commedia figures were not just stock, cardboard characters in the fashion of, say, Victorian melodrama but were aggregate personalities whom the audiences got to know in different plays and different situations, somewhat like modern television serials of domestic life. Nicoll, pp. 20–2. Thus Harlequin, for example, has a distinct personality but he is larger than life and so familiar that it is tempting to call him a type.

wandtheit—allen diesen ganz elementaren und so unentbehr-
lichen Possenreißervoraussetzungen jeder echten komischen
Bühne und jeder echten überhaupt.'[93] (None of your productions is so completely and genuinely suited to the theatre, so
theatrical: in its improvisation, in its clowning, in the
cheekiness of its perfection, in its worldliness—in all these
quite elementary and so indispensable prerequisites of buffoonery, which are essential to any genuine comic stage and to
any genuine stage whatever.)

Yet a feature of the libretto as striking as its theatricality is
its musicality which can be linked with the relative lyricism of
these passages. Two of the three songs which Hofmannsthal
praised to Strauss and to Dora von Bodenhausen as being
incomparable belong to the *commedia*.[94] The one is Zerbinetta's song which we shall discuss later and the other is the
aforementioned 'Harlekins Lied'. Here Hofmannsthal was
deliberately trying his hand at lyric poetry and these poems
are not just isolated moments in the libretto but indicate a
wider preoccupation with lyric forms in both the macrostruc-
ture and the microstructure. The poems are themselves then
woven into the larger poetic tapestry of the Intermezzo.
Borchardt made the following appreciative comment on this
section: 'Ich finde die rhythmischen Partieen der Ariadne
durchaus glücklich und im Sinne der Musicabilität musterhaft,
ein ganz leichtes und lockeres, dabei aber nicht löcheriges
Gewebe in das die Composition nach Bedürfnis füllend
eingreifen kann.'[95] (I find the rhythmic parts of Ariadne
entirely successful and exemplary in their musicality; a light
and loose weave, though without holes, into which the
composition can add its bit where needs be.)

The simple form of Harlekin's three-verse lyric with its
elementary yet pleasing rhythm and metre is perfectly reflected
in the theme which, like the nymphs' philosophy mentioned
earlier, again takes up the Heraclitan view of life as continuity
and renewal. In fact this theme, in itself potentially so lyrical,
had attracted Hofmannsthal as early as 1890 in the ghasel *Den
Pessimisten* which has quite noticeable similarities with

[93] Hugo von Hofmannsthal/Rudolf Borchardt, *Briefwechsel*, p. 68.
[94] See Chapter II, Note 19.
[95] Hugo von Hofmannsthal/Rudolf Borchardt, *Briefwechsel*, p. 70.

Harlekin's song. The texts of the two poems are given here in full:

Harlekin
Lieben, Hassen, Hoffen, Zagen,
Alle Lust und alle Qual,
Alles kann ein Herz ertragen
Einmal um das andre Mal.

Aber weder Lust noch Schmerzen,
Abgestorben auch der Pein,
Das ist tödlich deinem Herzen
Und so darfst du mir nicht sein!

Mußt dich aus dem Dunkel heben,
Wär es auch um neue Qual,
Leben mußt du, liebes Leben,
Leben noch dies eine Mal.

Den Pessimisten

Solang uns Liebe lockt mit Lust und Plagen,
Solang Begeistrung wechselt und Verzagen,
Solange wird auf Erden nicht die Zeit,
Die schreckliche, die dichterlose tagen:
Solang in tausend Formen Schönheit blüht,
Schlägt auch ein Herz, zu singen und zu sagen,
Solang das Lied, das ewge uns umflicht,
Solange werden wirs in Tönen klagen,
Und es erlischt erst dann der letzte Traum,
Wenn er das letzte Herz zu Gott getragen![96]

(Harlekin
Loving, hating, hoping, trembling,
Every joy and every sorrow,
The heart can bear everything
Over and over again.

But neither joy nor pain,
The anguish grown numb,
That is fatal to your heart
And you shouldn't treat me so!

You must pull yourself out of darkness,
Even if to new sorrow,
You must live, dear life,
Live yet once again.

[96] GuLD, p. 145.

To the Pessimists
So long as love entices us with joy and torment,
So long as enthusiasm and despair alternate,
So long will the terrible, unpoetic age
Not dawn on earth:
So long as beauty blooms in a thousand forms
There beats a heart for song and verse,
So long as the eternal song surrounds us,
So long shall we lament it in music,
And the last dream only extinguishes it
When it carries the last heart up to God.)

Harlekin's optimistic philosophy of the emotions is comparable to the optimistic philosophy of the poet who consoles
the 'Kulturpessimisten' with the view that the continuity of
Life guarantees Art. Both share an Orphic view of the
congruity of the world and lyric song; the early poem indirectly
in its praise of 'das Lied, das ewige' and 'Harlekins Lied'
directly by itself being a song. Both furthermore make frequent
use of the long 'a' vowel sound and also of verbal nouns such
as 'Zagen', 'Plagen', and 'Verzagen'. There is also a certain
overlapping of the vocabulary. If Hofmannsthal did not
deliberately incorporate aspects of *Den Pessimisten* into
Harlekin's song he may well have had it at the back of his
mind, and it is significant for our study of the lyric features of
the libretto that there are such evident links between this work
of Hofmannsthal's middle period and one of the early lyric
period.

vi. *Lyric-Dramatic features of the* Oper

Ariadne auf Naxos shares unmistakable structural features
with the lyric dramas. As previously mentioned, Hofmannsthal
himself classified this libretto as a lyric drama.[97] The text
itself is undramatic, anti-naturalistic and symbolic and the
tone is predominantly lyrical and musical. Most important,
however, are the poetic monologues and dialogues which
formed the backbone of such early dramas as *Der Tod des
Tizian, Der Tor und der Tod, Der Kaiser und die Hexe*, to name
but a few. In the stage directions of *Ariadne* alone our attention
is drawn to this feature. Before the heroine's first aria *Ein*

[97] See Chapter II, Note 3.

Schönes war we read the instruction 'vor sich, monologisch' (37). Later the conclusion of her aria from *Es gibt ein Reich* until the Intermezzo is referred to as 'Ariadnes Monolog' (41) and in a letter to Strauss Hofmannsthal refers to Ariadne's final scene as 'dies monologische Abenteuer der einsamen Seele Ariadne' (Bw. mid-July 1911, p. 116). In the first part of the *Oper* she gives voice to her private thoughts, quite ignoring the comedians, and in the third part she sings what amounts to a monologue through her mistake about Bacchus' identity, which makes her comments communications with herself and about herself. In both cases her monologues are examples of the so-called 'lyrischer Monolog' which Gero von Wilpert defines as the 'Selbstoffenbarung der Gefühle eines Helden, auch Ausdruck der persönlichen Auffassung des Dichters'[98] (the self-revelation of a hero's feelings, the expression of the author's personal point of view).

Ariadne is not the only character to hold a monologue. Zerbinetta's previously discussed description of Bacchus' arrival is an example of the 'epischer Monolog' defined as a 'Mittel der Exposition (Plautus, Hans Sachs) Einbeziehung nicht darstellbarer Vorgänge und Vorbereitung neuer Situationen am Aktbeginn oder Zusammenfassung des Bisherigen am Aktschluß'[99] (means of exposition (Plautus, Hans Sachs), a way of including unrepresentable events and a preparation of new situations at the beginning of an act or a summary of what has gone before at the end of an act). Zerbinetta's speech both describes a non-presentable event and prepares for new situations although it is spoken merely at a turn in the action and not at the beginning of an act.

Although Hofmannsthal draws attention to the monologue-like situation of the heroine, the final scene takes the form not of a monologue but of the dialogue poem of which there are a number amongst such early works as *Großmutter und Enkel*.[100]

Using common themes and symbols, the extended lyric dialogue between Ariadne and Bacchus seeks to describe a single complex inner situation and atmosphere and a spiritual event for which there is no real corresponding outer action

[98] Gero von Wilpert, *Sachwörterbuch der Literatur*, p. 494.
[99] Wilpert, p. 494.
[100] GuLD, p. 31.

and thus this dialogue is for two what the lyric monologue was for one. Such dialogues occur most frequently not in individual poems but in the early dramas, such as *Das Bergwerk zu Falun*[101] or *Der Tor und der Tod*.[102]

Apart from these formal features, W. Schuh has made known a source for *Ariadne auf Naxos* which further points to the libretto's affinities with the lyric drama.[103] This is Milton's already mentioned masque *Comus* (1634), itself a verse drama and a historical forerunner of its late nineteenth- and early twentieth-century counterpart.

As W. Schuh's publication makes clear, Hofmannsthal was interested in *Comus* not only because it suggested to him the liaison between Bacchus and Circe, who in Milton's account are the parents of Comus, but also because it suggested the right tone for the Ariadne–Bacchus encounter. Above an excerpt from *Comus*, lines 246 to 252 plus a combination of several other lines,[104] Hofmannsthal noted the words 'Ariadne bez. Bacchus Ton'. The whole of the note is given here:

Notizen I

(Die beiden folgenden Sätze durchgestrichen:)
Ariadne zerstückelten Sinnes verwildert wie ein scheus Thier (*sic*)
Sie liegt starr an der Erde, die drei Nymphen tanzen einen sanften
    traurigen Tanz um sie.

Toll, aber klug!

(Durchgestrichen:)
Als die 5 sich ihr aufdrängen: hält sie beide Hände vor die Augen,
    solche Fratzen ihrer verstörten Phantasie nicht zu sehen.

Die drei Nymphen mit Smeraldina eifrig bemüht, sie zu schmücken
    durch Anhauch wie die homerischen Götter. Man bringt aus der
    Höhle das Goldschimmernde Oberkleid. (orientalisch, blumen-
    bestickt, mit Agraffe. Stirnreif)
Ariadnes schreckhaftes sich entziehen wollen.
Ariadne zu Bacchus
schnell mein Herz bring es hinüber, wo es keiner Anfechtung
mehr ausgesetzt ist.

[101] GuLD, pp. 395–547.
[102] GuLD, pp. 269–92.
[103] Willi Schuh, 'Zu Hofmannsthals "Ariadne"-Szenarium und -Notizen', pp. 88–9.
[104] Milton, *Comus*, lines 246–52, the first half of line 253, line 263, the first half of line 264 and the second half of line 265.

Vorspiel: siehe Mozart. Verkehr mit Sängerinnen

Ceremonie Höflichkeit
Anreden bei Shakespeare
steife Handwerksbräuche
zarteste Convention:
Haltung. Ermöglichung
mit einer Neigung unendlich
viel zu geben. Da
sich das Leben dem
concreten Geben versagt.
Ceremoniel der Tänzerin
Sie gibt was nur sie
geben kann.
Tanzmeister im Vorspiel

Ariadne bez. Bacchus Ton:

Gewiß ein Heilges wohnt in deiner
   Brust
verborgen und bewegt die stille
   Luft
daß sie ihr Zeugnis gebe—
Wie lieblich gleitet dieses auf den
   Flügeln
des Schweigens durch die hochge-
   wölbte Nacht
und streichelt sanft der Finsternis
   ihr Federkleid
bis daß sie lächelt

_____

So süße Bürgschaft wacher
   Seligkeit
vernahm ich nie zuvor. Heil
   fremdes Wunder! (Sz. 291–2.)

(Notizen 1

(The following two sentences crossed out:)
Ariadne, her mind in disarray, wild like a shy animal
She lies rigid on the ground, the three nymphs dance a gentle, sad
   dance around her.

Mad, but clever!

(Crossed out:)
As the five force themselves upon her: she holds both hands in front
   of her eyes so as not to see such grimaces produced by her
   disturbed imagination.

The three nymphs with Smeraldina eagerly busy adorning her by
   breathing on her like the Homeric gods. Out of the cave the
   shimmering gold upper-garment is brought. (oriental, embroidered
   with flowers, with a brooch, tiara)
Ariadne is frightened and wants to escape.
Ariadne to Bacchus
Quickly take my heart across to where it shall no longer
Be exposed to these temptations.

Prologue: see Mozart. Association with singers.

Ceremony politeness
Forms of address as in
  Shakespeare
mechanics' customs
tenderest convention:
bearing. Possibility with an
  inclination of giving
infinitely much. Since life
denies itself actual giving.
Ceremonial of the dancer
She gives what only she can
  give.
Dancing master in the
  prologue

Ariadne and Bacchus tone:
Sure something holy lodges in that
  breast,
And with these raptures moves
  the vocal air
To testify his hidden residence.
How sweetly did they float upon
  the wings
Of silence, through the empty-
  vaulted night,
At every fall smoothing the raven
  down
Of darkness till it smiled!

Such sober certainty of waking
  bliss,
I never heard till now. Hail,
  foreign wonder!)

According to Schuh this note was written before 19 May 1911.
'Das erwähnte Blatt I liegt *vor* der Niederschrift des Szenar-
iums, denn die Gegenfigur zu Ariadne trägt hier noch den
unverbindlichen Namen Smeraldina.'[105] Schuh's deduction is
correct and agrees with our findings about the genesis of the
name 'Zerbinetta'.[106] (The aforementioned sheet dates from
before the time of writing of the *Szenarium*, for Ariadne's
opposite number still bears the non-committal name Smeraldina.) But as there is little or no continuity between the
different parts of the note it can be stated with certainty only
that the part up to the line 'Vorspiel: siehe Mozart: Verkehr
mit Sängerinnen' was written before the *Szenarium*; and, to
judge from motifs such as Ariadne's 'Goldschimmerndes
Oberkleid' which are never again taken up in such detail, this
part may date among the earliest of the notes. Schuh goes on
to make the following comment about the single line which he
claims was added later: 'Zwischen den zur "Ariadne-Oper"
gehörenden Notizen von Blatt I steht unvermittelt der Satz:
'Vorspiel: siehe Mozart. Verkehr mit Sängerinnen.' Er bezieht
sich auf die zwischen "Bürger als Edelmann" und "Ariadne

[105] Willi Schuh, 'Zu Hofmannsthals "Ariadne"-Szenarium und -Notizen', p. 89.
[106] See Chapter I, Note 35.

auf Naxos" vermittelnde Überleitungsszene.'[107] (Between the notes belonging to the Ariadne opera comes unheralded the sentence: 'Prologue: see Mozart. Association with singers.' It refers to the transitional scene between the *Bürger als Edelmann* and *Ariadne auf Naxos*.) It is true that the 'Vorspiel' means the transitional scene written for the 1912 *Ariadne*, and on the basis of the sentence W. Schuh goes on to disprove M. Stern's thesis that the figure of the 'Komponist' was 'eine heimliche Wagner–Karikatur'.[108] However Schuh has failed to notice that the word 'Vorspiel' occurs again in the left-hand column at the end of 'Blatt I'. Furthermore this column, which is in any case obscure, makes no sense at all if it is read as a preparatory note for either *Ariadne* or *Der Bürger als Edelmann*. If, however, it is read in conjunction with the 'Vorspiel'[109] it makes better sense but cannot then have been written before the *Szenarium* as this scene was first mentioned in the correspondence in the following month, June, and cannot have been thought of by Hofmannsthal much before then. The connection between this column of words and the 'Vorspiel' can best be seen from the passage from the letter of 15 June 1911 in which the scene is first planned:

Der Übergang zur eigentlichen Oper vollzieht sich auf offener Szene. Vorher geht eine kleine Überleitung (von mir) in Prosa, eine kleine Szene, worin sich Tanzmeister und Komponist—welche die Arrangeure dieser Opernaufführung in Jourdains Haus sind—über Publikum, Kritik etc. unterhalten. Während dieses Gespräches wird im Saal die Bühne für die Oper aufgestellt, Harlekin und Ariadne schminken sich, andere laufen halb kostümiert hin und wider. Die Lichter werden angezündet, die Musiker stimmen ihre Instrumente, Zerbinetta läßt ein paar Rouladen hören. (Bw. 15 June 1911, pp. 110–11.)

(The transition to the actual opera takes place on the open stage; I shall lead up to it by a short scene in prose in which Dancing Master and Composer—who are responsible for arranging this opera performance at Jourdain's house—talk about the public, critics, etc. During this conversation the stage is being set for the opera in the big hall; Harlekin and Ariadne are making up, others are bustling to

[107] Willi Schuh, 'Zu Hofmannsthals "Ariadne"-Szenarium und -Notizen', p. 89.
[108] Martin Stern, 'Eine heimliche Wagner-Karikatur', p. 3.
[109] The 'Vorspiel' became the transitional prose scene following *Der Bürger als Edelmann* (1911). LIII, p. 146–61.

and fro half dressed for the performance. The lights are being lit, the musicians are tuning their instruments, Zerbinetta tries a few roulades.)

Here we find that Hofmannsthal intended bringing on the Molière character, the 'Tanzmeister'. This explains the phrase 'Tanzmeister im Vorspiel' at the bottom of the column. Other phrases are less easily guessed at but possibly 'steife Handwerksbräuche' refers to the behaviour of the stage-hands whom Hofmannsthal mentions again in a later letter.[110] 'Die Tänzerin' may be a reference to the ballerina who was to dance the part of the 'Küchenjunge'. This role was specially choreographed in 1912 for Hofmannsthal's personal friend, the dancer Grete Wiesenthal, but was planned much earlier. It would fit in with Hofmannsthal's first general conception of the 'Vorspiel' for the 'Tänzerin' to mingle with the backstage crowd and perhaps do a pirouette or two as Zerbinetta practises her roulades.

It seems fairly certain then that this left-hand column was written after the *Szenarium* and after the first part of 'Blatt I'. It could have been written either at the same time as or after the sentence 'Vorspiel: siehe Mozart. Verkehr mit Sängerinnen' which does away with W. Schuh's clumsy and implausible suggestion that this sentence was inserted later. If this is so, however, it means that the right-hand column, the quotation from Milton, must also date from after the *Szenarium* and not before as Schuh claimed. This is significant for our study of the genesis of the libretto because it indicates that Hofmannsthal's search for the right tone in the Ariadne-Bacchus scene dates from around 15 June 1911, namely the time when he was already half-way through realizing the original *Szenarium*.

The tone of this passage from Milton is predominantly lyrical and ethereal, full of breathless wonder. The quasi-religious vocabulary such as occurs in the Ariadne–Bacchus dialogue can be found in this passage, in particular the words 'Heiliges', 'Seligkeit', and 'Wunder'. Bacchus approaches

---

[110] Bw. 23 July 1911, p. 121. Cf. Ernst Stern, *Skizzenbuch von 1912: Notizen für Bühnenbild und Kostüme zu 'Ariadne auf Naxos'*. In his directions for Act 2 of *Der Bürger als Edelmann* Stern notes 'Verwandlung. Zum Theater. Die Bühne wird noch gebaut im rückwärtigen Theil des Saales'. Quoted in Fiedler (147–52), p. 151.

Ariadne in the same attitude of awe and devotion as Comus does his Lady. It seems reasonable therefore to conclude that the tone for which Hofmannsthal was seeking and which he found was the appropriate tone for a high point in a lyric drama. It is thus doubly significant that Hofmannsthal copied out this passage after 15 June 1911 and not before because it confirms our thesis that the lyric aspect was a later development in the genesis of *Ariadne*. Had the passage been copied out at the time W. Schuh suggests, it would have seemed that Hofmannsthal had always had a lyric climax clearly in mind, and this would contradict our earlier findings.

Further evidence of this is the fact that Hofmannsthal did not begin work on the Ariadne-Bacchus scene until the end of June or the beginning of July. On 27 June 1911 he writes that he will turn to the Ariadne–Zerbinetta scene, which immediately precedes the lovers' encounter, on the following day. On 5 July 1911 he informs Strauss that he has just given a last polish to the big scene between Ariadne and Bacchus. It is therefore highly likely that in the middle of June he could have been looking for literary stimulus immediately before writing that passage. It was in this spirit that he turned to Milton's *Comus*, with which he was already familiar.

vii. *Conclusion*

The libretto to *Ariadne auf Naxos* has many literary features in common with the lyric drama and its genesis is a record of a 'Suchen des Geistigen' (Bw. 2 Mar. 1913, p. 187), a search which was in no way tailored to the original measurements of the piece. No one sums it all up better than Strauss's good friend and critic Romain Rolland: 'J'ai le sentiment que Hofmannsthal commence chacun de ses "pastiches" d'un temps passé avec un dessein ironique, mais que son admirable virtuosité les réussit avec tant de succès qu'il finit toujours par les prendre aux sérieux. Et c'est dommage: un sujet-pastiche, comme *Arianna*, n'a toute sa valeur que par l'ironie; et cette ironie doit surtout s'épanouir à la fin.'[111] (I have the feeling that Hofmannsthal begins each one of his 'pastiches' on a past age with an ironic intention but that his admirable virtuosity

---

[111] Richard Strauss et Romain Rolland, *Correspondance, Fragments de Journal*, p. 109.

succeeds so well that he always ends up taking them seriously. And that is a pity: a pastiche subject like *Arianna* only has any value if it is ironic; and this irony must above all open up at the end.)

Nevertheless, despite the fascination of the ahistorical and transcendental, Hofmannsthal continued to endow the little work with historically authentic detail. No doubt the reasons for this can be found once again in the closely defined genesis. There are, for example, the elaborate directions for the stage setting and costumes given by Hofmannsthal and transmitted through the designer Ernst Stern. In the directions for the 1916 *Ariadne*, the so-called 'neue Bearbeitung' which is the more lyrical of the versions, Hofmannsthal gives precise historical information and adds, furthermore, that it is not to be presented as a parody but as a genuine historical recreation:

Die Oper 'Ariadne'

ist, was Dekoration (und Kostüme) betrifft, nicht etwa parodistisch zu halten, sondern ernsthaft im heroischen Opernstil der älteren Zeit (Louis XIV oder Louis XV); ältere vorhandene Dekorationen zu Gluckschen Opern können zur Richtschnur dienen, eventuell wird auch aus solchem Material die Dekoration zusammengestellt werden können. Heroischer Meeresstrand mit einer Höhle; womöglich alte Kulissen (Bäume, Felsen) mit geraden Gassen. Das Ganze dem Poussinschen Stil angenähert. Die Höhle der Ariadne kann entweder plastisch oder flach gemalt sein; in letzterem Fall muß sie aber einen praktikablen Eingang haben. (379–80.)

(The opera 'Ariadne'

is as regards décor (and costumes) not to be treated parodistically but seriously in the heroic opera style of a former age (Louis XIV or Louis XV); any existing décor for Gluck operas can serve as a guideline, possibly the décor can even be made up of such material. Heroic beach with a cave; if possible old scenery (trees, cliffs) at right angles to the stage. The whole approximating to Poussin's style. Ariadne's cave can be either three-dimensional or painted; in the latter case it must have a practical entrance.)

The mention of Louis XIV takes us back to that first note dated 'Paris. Anfang Mai 1911' and the words 'Annäherung an Louis XIV'.[112] We also recall that in the *Szenarium* Poussin was cited as a stylistic model: 'In der Mitte eine künstliche

---

[112] Appendix A, Note 1.

Höhle / Grotte aus Pappendeckel aber architectonisch schön, im Poussin'schen Stil.' (Sz. 286.) And Strauss entered into the spirit when for the 1912 Stuttgart première he insisted that all players use original and very valuable Italian Baroque instruments.[113]

In Stern's own notes for the 1912 *Ariadne*, which were 'nach Besprechung mit Hofmannsthal'[114] and which, to judge from the many abbreviations, were probably taken during conversation, there is painstaking care with historical detail. The following examples are from Stern's costume notes for each of the three groups:

Bei den Schauspielern d.B.G. [des *Bourgeois Gentilhomme*] wären die Trachten v. 1670 etc maßgeblich. Besonders ist Jourdains geschmackloses, knalliges Kleid zu berücksichtigen ... Die Sänger d. Oper sind im Geschmack d. Opern + Balletaufführungen am Hofe z. Versailles gekleidet und zwar Echo, Dryade, Nayade Reifröcke. Ariadne u. Bacchus möglichst nackt und mit Schleiern. Die Comödianten d. Comödia del Arte tragen die entsprechenden Costüme ihrer Rolle in absolut anderem Material als die Sänger, die sehr reich gekleidet erscheinen.[115]

(For the actors in the *Bourgeois Gentilhomme* costumes of 1670 etc. should serve as models. Special attention must be paid to Jourdain's tasteless, gaudy coat ... the opera singers are dressed in the fashion of opera and ballet productions at the Court of Versailles, that is, Echo, Dryade, Naiade in crinolines. Ariadne and Bacchus as naked as possible and with veils. The comedians of the commedia dell'arte wear costumes appropriate to their roles in absolutely different material from the singers, who appear very richly dressed.)

Stiegele rightly points out that Stern was intent upon accuracy down to the smallest detail of the costumes.[116] Even the briefest glance at the *Skizzenbuch* reveals this, as do the following instructions about the buttons on the ladies' costumes: 'Knöpfe bei feinen Westen gelb, aurora, weisse Seide, die Besatzknöpfe aus Holz mit Seidenstoff oder mit Silberdraht.'[117]

[113] Richard Strauss, *Betrachtungen und Erinnerungen*, p. 84. See also Chapter IV, Note 33.
[114] Fiedler, p. 151.
[115] Fiedler, p. 148.
[116] Stiegele, p. 62.
[117] Fiedler, p. 149.

In his autobiography Stern gives as the sources for his drawings first a reprint of a lavish book, *La mode au XVII Siècle*, based on contemporary engravings from the collection of Monsieur Liez, and, second, illustrated works on architecture and theatre from Hofmannsthal's own library.[118] Stern's sketches for *Ariadne* have all been preserved in a portfolio which was requested from him by Strauss's publisher, Adolf Fürstner, and which became part of the copyright of the 1912 version. Stern comments: 'Alle Theater, die in Zukunft die Oper "Ariadne" aufführen wollten, mußten sie zusammen mit dem "Bürger als Edelmann" spielen, hatten also die Mappe zusammen mit Aufführungsrecht zu erwerben.—Die einzigartige Stellung, die Strauss in Deutschland einnahm, ermöglichte ihm solche diktatorischen Bestimmungen.'[119] (All theatres that in future wished to perform the opera 'Ariadne' had to do it together with the 'Bürger als Edelmann', so they had to apply for the portfolio with the performing rights.—The unique position which Strauss held in Germany permitted him such dictatorial stipulations.)

In this portfolio there was also found a reproduction of one of the Félibien etchings for *George Dandin* by Molière from the official description of the *Grande Fête de Versailles*. As Fiedler observes, it is fascinating to see how a minute detail such as the suspended chandeliers in the etching found its way into Stern's notes. In Stern's 'Allgemeine Bemerkungen' we find 'Beleuchtung: Kronen mit Kerzen', and later in the transitional scene 'Diener entzünden die Kronleuchter'.[120]

A final example of historical accuracy is the description of the male *commedia* costumes from the instructions to *Ariadne* itself: Harlekin is wearing a patchwork costume, a variant of the more traditional loose-fitting, lozenge costume, and has on a little cape.[121] The countrified Brighella has on a straw hat:

[118] See Chapter 1, Note 41.
[119] Ernst Stern, *Bühnenbildner bei Max Reinhardt*, p. 97.
[120] Fiedler, p. 147 and p. 151.
[121] The costumes were historically authentic, as Nicoll's description of Harlequin's costume shows: 'By the second half of the seventeenth century the patches had developed into regular triangles or lozenges, arranged with precision all over his dress and often set off with strips of ribbon; and by that period his mask was innocent of any hirsute appendages. Throughout the century following, this was Harlequin's familiar uniform.' Nicoll, pp. 69–70.

'Harlekin im bunten Lappenkostüm, Pritsche, Larve, Män-
telchen. Brighella, jung, tölpelhaft, bäuerlich. Narcissimo
Kostüm Strohhut. Scaramuccio. schwarz gekleidet, Degen,
Larve. Truffaldino. Entweder Harlekin Abart oder Polichinelli. Larve.'[122] (Harlekin in a colourful patchwork costume,
whip, mask, little cloak. Brighella, young, foolish, countrified.
Narcissus costume with straw hat. Scaramuccio. dressed in
black, dagger, mask. Truffaldino. Either a variant of Harlekin
or Polichinelli. Mask.) Stern was clearly a conscientious
researcher with a genuine feeling for period work. That he
could combine these qualities with a capable artistic imagination and a sense of humour assured him of his permanent
position as Reinhardt's stage and costume designer. This
combination of qualities, not least among them his historical
accuracy, also recommended Stern to Hofmannsthal, and
Hofmannsthal was prepared to defend his choice in the face
of some attacks from Strauss.[123]

One surprising remark which Hofmannsthal does make
about Stern in the correspondence was that his décor was to be
'half-historical, half-anachronistic': [Stern] hat auf geistreiche
und halb historische, halb anachronistische Weise verschie-
dene geistige Welten gegeneinanderzuhalten, zeichnerisch
und durch die Farbe.' (Bw. 21 Apr. 1912, p. 151.) (Stern's
designs and colours must, in a spirited, half-historical, half-
anachronistic manner, balance against each other two different
conceptions of the world.) This is the first mention that has
been made of anachronism and in the face of all the evidence
which weighs so heavily on the side of historicism we cannot
but be suspicious of its sudden appearance. The word is not
mentioned again in connection with Stern's design. Certainly
Stern does not use it in his own notes to himself. In a later
letter to Strauss, Hofmannsthal uses the word a second time
when complaining about the 'scharfer Anachronismus' of
having the King, alias Louis XIV, remark in *Der Bürger als*

122 Fiedler, p. 152.
123 Strauss preferred the designer Roller. He regarded Stern's work as 'genialer
Kitsch' and said that it looked as if it had been dashed off quickly for cheapness. Bw.
19 Apr. 1912, p. 149. It is true that Stern's sketches have a certain freedom, even
looseness of form, but it was most probably Reinhardt's last-minute rushes which
were responsible for poorer work from Stern. For Hofmannsthal's point of view see
Bw. 21 Apr. 1912, p. 151.

Edelmann that all modern opera lacks melody when it is commonly known that Louis XIV patronized *only* what was modern. All other anachronisms in the 1912 *Ariadne*, according to Hofmannsthal, are mild in comparison with this one, and he insists that it be removed (Bw. 14 June 1912, p. 157).

If Hofmannsthal is as shy of anachronisms in general as he is of this one it is hard to believe he would have tolerated as much as half of the décor being anachronistic. Hofmannsthal's relationship to anachronism is a difficult one. We need only note that the Stern comment is an instance of Hofmannsthal's theorizing complicating the issue. As far as the *appearance* of *Ariadne auf Naxos* was concerned he was still intent on recreating a Baroque divertissement. This is in itself an illustration of Hofmannsthal's double and parallel intentions in the libretto. A lengthy theoretical discussion of anachronism such as Gräwe gives in his Introduction cannot be anything but a critical red herring or failure to understand this work's genesis.

So far the libretto of *Ariadne auf Naxos* has been dealt with on its own, an arbitrary procedure since Hofmannsthal was not writing in isolation from Strauss, but justified because ultimately much of the artistic initiative lay with the librettist. In the following Chapter we turn to a complete genesis of the opera and hence of the libretto in its proper capacity as one part of a full music drama. This will also be an account of those complications brought about by the unique circumstances of the close and sometimes over-defined genesis which were so influential in shaping this work.

Chapter III

The Genesis of the Opera

During the crucial first months of work on *Ariadne*, in which the *Oper* assumed almost its final form, Hofmannsthal was under pressure from Strauss to produce the libretto quickly. It was Strauss's custom to devote the summer months to composing and the remaining months of the year to conducting and related duties. As the summer of 1911 approached and Strauss was about to withdraw to his house in Garmisch-Partenkirchen he found that he had no fresh material to compose and that writing symphonies no longer appealed to him. On 17 March 1911 he wrote inquiring after the Molière scheme: 'Ich bin sehr gespannt, was Sie mir vom "Steinernen Herzen" und der kleinen Molièresache zu erzählen haben. Vergessen Sie nicht, ich habe für den Sommer noch nichts zu arbeiten. Symphonien schreiben freut mich gar nicht mehr.' (Bw. 17 Mar. 1911, p. 95.) (I am most anxious to hear what you have to tell me about *Steinernes Herz* and the little Molière piece. Don't forget: I still have no work for the summer. Writing symphonies doesn't amuse me at all any longer.)

Das steinerne Herz was the early name for *Die Frau ohne Schatten*. From the correspondence of this month we may conclude that Hofmannsthal had two irons in the fire: the Molière piece and *Das steinerne Herz*. Neither was at a more advanced stage than the other but Hofmannsthal regarded *Das steinerne Herz* as potentially the greater and more serious work. For this reason he would not be hurried on it: 'An einem schönen Stoff, wie die "Frau ohne Schatten" es ist, das reiche Geschenk einer glücklichen Stunde, an einem solchen Stoff, so fähig, Träger schöner Poesie und schöner Musik zu werden, an einem solchen Stoff wäre es ein Frevel, wollte man hasten, wollte man sich forcieren.' (Bw. 15 May 1911, p. 98.) (The fact is that with so fine a subject as *Die Frau ohne Schatten*, the rich gift of a happy hour, with a subject so fit to become the vehicle of beautiful poetry and beautiful music, with a subject such as this all haste and hurry and forcing oneself would be a crime.) Therefore when in May Strauss applied real pressure, mentioning that he had been in touch with d'Annunzio and a playwright by the name of Levetzow in the hope of finding new libretti and repeating that he was very anxious to hear something from Hofmannsthal, the latter decided that rather than endanger *Die Frau ohne Schatten* in any way it was time to down tools and concentrate entirely on the 'Zwischenarbeit'.

Strauss was not deceiving Hofmannsthal with his approaches to d'Annunzio and Levetzow.[1] He was well within his rights in seeking new libretti wherever he could find them and he was open with Hofmannsthal about it. Moreover Hofmannsthal was under an obligation if the partnership was really to become a long-term one to make sure that Strauss had a new libretto at the time he was free to compose. Hofmannsthal was aware of this obligation and took no umbrage at Strauss's pressure or at the mention of the other two authors. In any case it was d'Annunzio who approached Strauss first and not vice versa.[2]

Hofmannsthal decided, then, that he would set to work on *Ariadne* but even once this choice was made Strauss had to wait for each new instalment of the text and there are numerous points in the correspondence where Strauss's impatience is only thinly disguised.[3] During the first months, May, June, and July Hofmannsthal was being almost continuously prodded. In early July this came to a head and there was a minor eruption as Strauss waited for the conclusion of the libretto:

Lieber Dichter! Sie sind komisch. Sie wollen von mir was hören! Aber ich will von Ihnen was lesen, dann erst können Sie von mir was "hören"! Also dichten Sir und warten Sie! Jedenfalls schicken Sie baldigst alles Gedichtete! Ich bin bis 8. August hier in Garmisch,

---

[1] The nature of the subject matter Strauss requested from d'Annunzio—'einen ganz modernen Stoff, sehr intim und von nervösester Psychologie'—suggests that without Hofmannsthal Strauss would have continued to devlop in the direction of *Salome* and *Elektra*. Bw. 15 May 1911, p. 97.

[2] Cf. Del Mar: 'Strauss only used d'Annunzio's offer as a lever to extract material from Hofmannsthal, never as a serious proposal.' Del Mar, p. 3.

[3] For example, Bw. 22 May 1911, p. 102; Bw. 27 May 1911, p. 106 or Bw. 1 June 1911, p. 108.

dann teils in München, um zu dirigieren! Jetzt will ich fest arbeiten!
Also schicken Sie, dann hören Sie! (Bw. early July 1911, p. 112.)

(Dear Poet. You are funny. You want to hear something from me!
But I want to read something from you, and only then will you be
able to 'hear' something from me. Go write your poetry, please, and
wait! In any case send me all the poetry you've written without
delay! I'm here in Garmisch till 8th August, then part of the time in
Munich conducting! Now I want to work hard! So please deliver:
then you'll hear!)

   Part of the agitation and rush seems to have arisen out of a
failure to agree upon deadlines. In a letter in May Hofmannsthal promised Strauss the full libretto 'für Anfang Juli
... vielleicht auch für Ende Juni'. This, he added, would give
Strauss work for July and August. In all fairness it must be
noted that Hofmannsthal delivered the final manuscript of the
full libretto to Strauss on 12 July, thus only a little later than
his own estimate. But Strauss it seems was working to a much
tighter schedule (possibly because August was to be interrupted
by the Munich engagement). On 27 May 1911 he wrote to
Hofmannsthal that he hoped to have *Ariadne* all ready by July
1 and that the overture and first dances and quite a bit besides
were already sketched out. As Strauss did not finish the
unscored version until October 1911 it seems that he had
miscalculated the time he would need even if Hofmannsthal
had delivered the libretto more rapidly.[4]

   Hofmannsthal was then writing the libretto to *Ariadne auf
Naxos* under pressure of time. During the period of actual
work on the *Oper* from the day the *Szenarium* was posted off
on 19 May 1911 to the day Strauss was sent the final part of the
libretto on 12 July 1911 Hofmannsthal did not have much
time to plan or reassess his work. The implications of this do
not need to be further spelt out; but this accounts largely for
Hofmannsthal's relying so heavily on the *Szenarium* and the
Notizen for the libretto.

   Of more significance here is the fact that Strauss was
composing the first parts of the libretto without having seen

---

[4] After the heated letters of July there is a break in the correspondence until
October when Hofmannsthal, on holiday in Neubeuern, learnt from the *Münchner
Neueste Nachrichten* that Strauss had finished. Hofmannsthal could begin immediately
on the transition scene. Bw. 22 Oct. 1911, p. 125.

the last. By his own admission he did not even understand the last scene when it arrived.[5] Clearly this piecemeal method of working was a risky one and lack of direction resulted in some curious faults. Later Hofmannsthal criticized this method of working in *Der Rosenkavalier* and refused to let Strauss have the first act of *Die Frau ohne Schatten*, that work which was so dear to him, before the other acts were completed (Bw. 12 June 1913, p. 200). Perhaps he had learnt too from the *Ariadne* experience. It seems fairly certain, whatever the case, that this was a method of working that Hofmannsthal would not have permitted in 1911 had not all parties concerned thought that this was to be a thirty-minute chamber opera. The early contract thus allowed a method of working which would not normally have pleased this fastidious librettist.

What is curious, however, is that it was Hofmannsthal himself who failed to notice that because he and Strauss were working too closely together the opera acquired two female leads, Ariadne and Zerbinetta, and so two centres of gravity—one of the opera's least satisfactory features. Furthermore the one female lead, Zerbinetta, is a part fraught with contradictions. There are of course no purely operatic rules determining the number of female leads in one opera but it is rare to find two main parts as stylistically and dramatically independent and yet as equally weighted as these two. One of the few critics to remark on this at all is Michael Kennedy who does not however inquire into the causes. Nor does he quite put his finger on the problem but senses 'the dichotomy of Hofmannsthal's concern for the deep seriousness of his treatment of the Ariadne legend, with its basic theme of fidelity, and Strauss's delight in the *commedia dell'arte* characters, particularly Zerbinetta'.[6]

i. *The Genesis of Zerbinetta's Part*

The star role for Zerbinetta originated in the following way. In the letter of 19 May 1911 accompanying the *Szenarium* Hofmannsthal requested Strauss to indicate where he meant

[5] For example, Bw. 19 July 1911, p. 117. Here Strauss speaks with veiled irony of his own incomprehension: 'ganz überzeugte mich aber das Werk erst nach dem Lesen Ihres Briefes, der so schön ist und den Sinn der Handlung so wundervoll erklärt, wie er mir oberflächlichem Musikanten allerdings nicht aufgegangen war.'

[6] Michael Kennedy, *Richard Strauss*, p. 157.

to have set numbers: 'Zu Nummern, Duetten, Terzetten, Quintetten, Sextetten ist reichlich Gelegenheit.—Sie werden gut tun, mir anzudeuten, an welchen Stellen Sie präzise Nummern legen wollen, an welchen Sie diese Form nur effleurieren wollen, so wie dies im "Rosenkavalier" mehrmals geschehen ist.' (Bw. 19 May 1911, p. 100.) (There is ample opportunity here for set numbers: duets, trios, quintets, sextets. It would be good if you were to indicate to me where you mean to place definite *numbers,* and where you intend merely to suggest them as you did repeatedly in *Rosenkavalier.*)

Hofmannsthal's wish to have the set numbers marked in was part of his original desire in writing *Ariadne auf Naxos* to experiment with the libretto as a genre. The interest in set numbers *per se* was furthermore a reflection of that simplicity, here at the technical level, which was the defining characteristic of the original plan. This is confirmed in the letter in which Hofmannsthal calls the *Szenarium* 'diese kleine Unterlage für Ihre Musik' (Bw. 19 May 1911, p. 100).

Strauss entered the set numbers into the margin of the *Szenarium* itself and these can be seen in Appendix B. The *Szenarium* was not, however, returned to Hofmannsthal immediately[7] and meanwhile Strauss sent off a letter with a plan of the set numbers in a more detailed form than that of the marginalia. In this same letter of 22 May 1911 Strauss also indicated the voice ranges for each part. These are much the same as those in the final score except that Ariadne was later given to a soprano and not a contralto. Zerbinetta remained a coloratura soprano. In the letter Strauss indicates 'Zerbinetta (Paraderolle) . . . hohe Koloratursängerin'. The ever-practical Strauss then suggests Kurz, Hempel, and Tetrazzini as three possibilities for the part. Thus even at this early stage it is clear that Strauss was concerned to differentiate between the two female voices. What also emerges is that Strauss thought of Zerbinetta as the main part and 'Paraderolle' in the *Oper*. This becomes even clearer if we compare Strauss's descriptions of the set numbers:

a) Rezitativ und Arie der Ariadne

---

[7] Bw. 25 May 1911, p. 104. Hofmannsthal requested that his original draft be returned.

b) Lied des Harlekin
c) große Koloraturarie und Andante
und dann Rondeau, Thema mit Variationen und allen Koloratur-
späßen (womöglich mit obligater Flöte) der Zerbinetta, wo sie von
ihrem Ungetreuen spricht (Andante) und dann Ariadne zu trösten
sucht: Rondeau mit Variationen (zwei bis drei).
Paradenummer.
d) Männerquartett (Harlekin): "komm mit mir", geht in Quintett
mit Zerbinetta über.
e) Männerterzett (buffo), wenn Harlekin und Zerbinetta verschwunden sind.
f) Das Finale (geschlossen und fortlaufend) beginnt mit der
Meldung der Najade. (Ein hymnenartiges Marschthema, dazu
Duett: Ariadne, Zerbinetta, steigert sich und schließt mit dem
Eintritt des Bacchus ab.)
Liebesduett.
Schlußensemble. (Bw. 22 May 1911, p. 102.)

(a) Recitative and aria of Ariadne,
 b) Harlekin's song
 c) Great coloratura aria and *andante,*
then rondo, theme with variations and all coloratura tricks (if
possible with flute *obbligato*) for Zerbinetta, when she speaks of her
unfaithful lover (*andante*) and then tries to console Ariadne: rondo
with variations (two or three).
A *pièce de résistance.*
 d) Male quartet (Harlekin): 'Komm mit mir' going over into
quintet with Zerbinetta.
 e) Male trio (buffo), after Harlekin and Zerbinetta have
disappeared.
 f) Finale (unbroken and continuous), beginning with the Naiad's
warning. (A hymn-like march theme, add the duet of Ariadne
and Zerbinetta, rising towards a climax and concluding with
Bacchus' entry.)
Love duet.
Final ensemble.)

The composer in Strauss had clearly been most attracted by
the role of Zerbinetta and her number is described in by far
the most musical detail. It is the only one for which an actual
instrument, the flute, is mentioned. Indeed many of these first
ideas, including the flute *obbligato*, were carried almost intact
into the final score. In comparison with the bare and matter-
of-fact 'recitative and aria for Ariadne' Zerbinetta's number

is teeming with ideas. Being composed of a long aria, an *andante*, and then a rondo with variations broken by another rondo, it is also longer than Ariadne's main solo section and a veritable *pièce de résistance*.

At this stage there is no reason why Strauss should not have given Zerbinetta the star part. In terms of the 'lyric drama' which the libretto then became his decision is less understandable. But his plan of the set numbers was drawn up on the basis of the *Szenarium* only and before 28 May 1911, the date on which Hofmannsthal had so many new, more personal thoughts about *Ariadne auf Naxos*.

Thus Hofmannsthal's acceptance of Strauss's plan for the part of Zerbinetta must be taken at face value. Hofmannsthal himself did not yet have any ideas about the spiritual or symbolic antithesis of the two female leads and so would not have had any objections beyond the surprise he indicates: 'Daß Sie Zerbinetta so ganz ins stärkste musikalische Licht stellen wollen, war mir zuerst überraschend, dann sehr einleuchtend' (Bw. 25 May 1911, p. 103). There is no reason to doubt Hofmannsthal's conviction as Stiegele does when she attributes his acceptance to his obligingness: 'Seine bewußte Gutwilligkeit ließ Hofmannsthal auch die von Strauss beabsichtigte Verlagerung des musikalischen Schwergewichts von Ariadne auf Zerbinetta nach kurzem Zögern akzeptieren.'[8] (Hofmannsthal's conscious desire to oblige led him after a brief hesitation to accept Strauss's intended displacement of the musical centre of gravity from Ariadne to Zerbinetta.) It is furthermore quite incorrect that Ariadne had been agreed on as the musical centre of gravity for *no* such decisions had been made about the little divertissement.

Daviau and Buelow, who are often too keen to play up disagreements in the collaboration, entirely distort this issue: 'Hofmannsthal, however, was shocked to learn of the composer's immediate decision to emphasize Zerbinetta in a way fully beyond the poet's intentions: "That you intend to place Zerbinetta so distinctively in the musical limelight surprised me at first . . ."'[9] The relevant sentence is not quoted

---

[8] Stiegele, p. 52.
[9] Daviau and Buelow, p. 185.

in full, and in any case when Hofmannsthal was 'shocked' he did not put it so mildly.

In most ways Strauss's decision did in fact fit in with Hofmannsthal's conception of *Ariadne* thus far. This slight and simple divertissement was intended partly as an opportunity for Strauss to write some attractive music on a reduced scale. In the same letter of 25 May 1911 in which Hofmannsthal approves Strauss's plans for Zerbinetta he writes 'hier soll alles nur wie ein Drahtgestell sein, um Musik gut und hübsch daran aufzuhängen'. Strauss's description of Zerbinetta's solo certainly sounded light-hearted and appealing.

More specifically it was always Hofmannsthal's intention to learn more about a set number technique through *Ariadne auf Naxos*, and this learning process focused itself on Zerbinetta's part. The opening paragraph of the letter of 25 May 1911 warmly welcomes Strauss's plan of set numbers: 'Der Überblick über die geschlossenen Nummern, die Sie wünschen, ist mir fördend und *suggestiv*, desgleichen alles, was Sie mir noch an speziell musikalischen Wünschen und Absichten mitteilen werden. Nur so ist Zusammenarbeiten möglich.' (Bw. 25 May 1911, p. 103.) (Your list of the set numbers you would like is helpful and stimulating, and the same will certainly be true of all other specific musical wishes and intentions you may communicate to me. This is the only way to collaborate.) After agreeing to Zerbinetta's part Hofmannsthal then goes on in this letter to say he will make himself thoroughly acquainted with the formal requirements of coloratura. Strauss had referred him to a number of well-known coloratura arias including the aria from Hérold's *Zweikampf*, Gilda's aria from *Rigoletto*, or some Mozart rondos. Hofmannsthal was very conscientious about studying these texts and possibly also the music. There is no record of what he obtained, but from the letter of 28 May 1911 it is clear he tried to find some of the arias listed by Strauss; he asks for the appropriate aria text from the *Zweikampf*. Enclosed in the same letter was a libretto, the title of which we do not know, which Hofmannsthal was sending Strauss so that he could mark in the aria and rondo. He was persistent in his desire to learn.

But Strauss felt that such earnest study would not be truly

helpful. He wrote back 'Ich habe eine Dummheit gemacht, als ich Sie auf die blöden Koloraturarien verwies, aus deren Texten Sie nichts entnehmen können. Ich wollte Sie nur auf das musikalische Schema verweisen, wie es sich etwa in der Briefarie der Donna Anna, in der Arie der Gilda ("Rigoletto") darstellt.' (Bw. 1 June 1911, p. 108.) (It was foolish of me to refer you to those idiotic coloratura arias from whose texts you can't learn a thing. I merely wanted to refer you to the musical scheme as it emerges, for instance, from Donna Anna's letter aria, or in Gilda's aria (*Rigoletto*).)

If Hofmannsthal took this advice and was not directly influenced by any particular texts it does appear that he was influenced by the ethos of the eighteenth-century Italian opera when writing the words for Zerbinetta's aria: her enumeration of her former lovers—'So war es mit Pagliazzo / Und mit Mezzetin!' (44)—bears a strong resemblance to Leporello's catalogue aria Number 4 *Madamina* from *Don Giovanni*[10] which was one of the operas Strauss suggested. Yet this aria could just as well be modelled on Ochs's aria in their own *Der Rosenkavalier* in which Ochs lists all his wenches. Strauss suggested this aria as a stylistic model in his letter of 1 June 1911. But it could be argued that both Ochs's and Zerbinetta's arias are indebted to Leporello. The Mozartian influence in both these operas was strong. In any case G. Polower's suggestion that Zerbinetta's was modelled on Gilda's *Caro nome che il mio cor?* from *Rigoletto* is quite incorrect and presumably based on a superficial reading of the correspondence.[11]

Thus far there had been no problems surrounding Zerbinetta's role. On 28 May 1911 Hofmannsthal began devising those 'seelische Motive der Sache' which were to transform the *Szenarium* and which were discussed in so much detail in Chapter II. The paragraph following the one outlining the primary relationship of Bacchus and Ariadne was not quoted earlier and reads as follows:

So sehe ich die Arbeit "Ariadne"—über deren Zutaten, Zerbinetta,

---

[10] The first lines of Leporello's aria from Act 1, Scene 2 are 'Madamina, il catalogo è questo / Delle belle, che amò il padron mio.' *Don Giovanni*, Opera in two Acts by W. A. Mozart, Vocal Score by Ernest Roth, London, 1953, p. 49.

[11] Genie Edith Polower, 'Hofmannsthal as Librettist', p. 76.

etc., wir ja ganz d'accord sind. Bietet Ihnen mein Text, wenn er vor Ihnen liegt, [keine Anziehung,] so lassen Sie ihn in Frieden und Freundschaft unkomponiert, denn auf das Zentrale bei einer Sache kommt es an, und die Schnörkel dürfen von zwei Leuten, die etwas können, zwar nicht geringgeschätzt werden, können aber die Hauptsache nicht ersetzen. (Bw. 28 May 1911, p. 107.)

(That is how I feel about *Ariadne*—and about the trimmings, Zerbinetta, and so forth, we are in any case already entirely *d'accord*. But if my libretto, when you have it, does not attract you in this way, then by all means leave it alone; there will be no hard feelings. What matters is the central idea of the piece and though two men like us who know their job should not despise the flourishes, they can never be a substitute for the real thing.)

Here is an example of the complicated genesis leaving its mark on the work. Hofmannsthal's fundamentally conflicting intentions about Zerbinetta make her at one moment the legitimate moral antithesis of the heroic ideal, and at the next one of the dispensable 'Zutaten'. The one Zerbinetta belongs to that stratum laid down by the *Szenarium* and on it, with the librettist's agreement, Strauss based his musical numbers. The other is the figure from the 'lyric drama' who in the 1916 *Oper* in particular is forgotten in the final scene and then given a token reappearance. In the final version, especially, the audience may be puzzled as to why this character should have such a large and magnificent solo in the middle of the work; Zerbinetta does in some way bear witness to Hofmannsthal's relative lack of experience as a librettist.

    Strauss's decision to favour Zerbinetta was quite legitimate from a reading of the *Szenarium*. Influenced in part by his dislike of the early sketch, Strauss, the experienced man of the theatre, felt that without glittering 'Paraderollen' *Ariadne* might be a flop: '[Es] müssen ein paar Paradegesangsrollen drin sein, denn die Handlung an sich interessiert nicht, ebensowenig wie interessante Kostüme den Ausschlag geben. Mich persönlich interessiert die Sache auch nicht gerade übermäßig, darum bat ich Sie, Ihren Pegasus etwas zu stimulieren.' (Bw. 27 May 1911, p. 106.) (There must be some star singing parts in it, for the plot as such holds no interest and interesting costumes won't turn the scale either. Personally, I am not particularly interested by the whole thing myself:

that was why I asked you to spur your Pegasus a bit.) Stiegele, for one, feels that Strauss was being justifiably practical here.[12]

On quite another level than these 'practical' considerations Strauss's choice of bel canto for Zerbinetta was a masterly and intuitive piece of musical characterization and counts amongst his best inspirations. From the *Szenarium* alone Strauss must have constructed in his imagination a figure full of flirtatious verve, self-irony, and humour, who could best be captured in the brilliant roulades, tricks, and musical self-mockery of a sophisticated pastiche of eighteenth-century coloratura. Strauss wrote to Hofmannsthal that this had sprung to his mind 'unwillkürlich' and this unwittingness was surely the sign of an unconscious creative process within him. In the same letter despite his obvious enthusiasm for Zerbinetta he endearingly reassures Hofmannsthal that of course Ariadne and Bacchus are the 'Hauptsache'. His reassurance is endearing because after all at this stage there was still no libretto and all Strauss had to work on were Hofmannsthal's sometimes obscure and sometimes overwrought letters which he received with almost unfailing patience. His acquiescence in the importance of Ariadne and Bacchus did, however, compound the problem of the two female leads. Strauss's letter begins by reopening the discussion of coloratura aria texts:

Mir fiel die Form von Koloraturvariationen unwillkürlich ein, als ich Ihren Entwurf der ersten Zerbinetta-Arie las. Lassen Sie sich also nicht weiter irritieren. Ich dachte mir die erste Rede der Zerbinetta, wo sie sich bei Ariadne einzuschmeicheln sucht, als Rezitativ mit langsamer Begleitung, dazu dann die Rede der vier Männer, am Schluß dann Allegro mit Variationen, wo sie an jedem der vier etwas unwiderstehlich findet. Es genügt aber für Sie vollkommen, wenn Sie alles dies mit ein paar wohlklingenden Versen (à la Mägdeerzählung des Ochs) charakterisieren. Das andere ist dann meine Sache. Die Hauptsache ist natürlich dann Ariadne und Bacchus. (Bw. 1 June 1911, p. 108.)

(The form of coloratura variations sprang to my mind unwittingly as I read your draft of Zerbinetta's first aria. So please, don't let them confuse you any further. I pictured Zerbinetta's first speech—when she tries to ingratiate herself with Ariadne—as recitative with slow

[12] Stiegele, p. 52.

accompaniment, added to it then the speech of the four men, and
finally an allegro with variations as she finds something irresistible
in each of the four. But as far as you are concerned, it's quite enough
if you characterize all this with a few melodious verses (in the
manner of Ochs's account of his wenches). The rest will be up to me.
The main thing, of course, is Ariadne and Bacchus.)

The correspondence and the *Szenarium* do not suggest that
there might be a jewel hidden in this part. Yet it *is* reckoned
amongst critics as being a jewel and certainly ranks as one of
Strauss's most delightful and witty roles.[13] How is it that this
is a part otherwise so easily passed over?

The explanation lies in the extreme symmetry of the
Szenarium, discussed previously in connection with the ironic
allegory. The interpretation of the *Szenarium* presented in
Chapter II, being mainly concerned with the allegory, gave as
neutral and unbiased a picture of the two sides as possible.
There was no doubt that Hofmannsthal definitely intended a
neutral symmetry for his little divertissement. However, even
the brief *Szenarium* is open to two different readings. Just as
with the *Vexierbild* or those optically illusory drawings of
puzzle boxes which seem now to come forward and now to go
back, so the perfect regularity and symmetry of the *Szenarium*
allows it to be read now one way and now another. This
ambiguity hinges on the interpretation of Zerbinetta's character, particularly of the single line '(ad spectatores) Wie wir
es sagten ist es gekommen [*sic*]' (Sz. 291). Is this line spoken in
full awareness of the irony of Ariadne's falling in love with
Bacchus? There is nothing in the *Szenarium* to suggest that
Zerbinetta is not aware of the irony of erotic love although she
is at the same time subject to it. She may well be a knowing
participant and thus be in a detached position enabling her to
offer a final summing up of the divertissement for the audience,
although within the allegory she is merely the representative
of infidelity. The same line may however be read as a piece of
banal non-comprehension on Zerbinetta's part. She may have
no perception of the irony of the situation and her comment is

[13] Cf. Daviau and Buelow, p. 184. 'The great scene for Zerbinetta, one of the most
challenging vocal parts ever created for coloratura soprano, demonstrates Strauss's
virtuoso style at its most extraordinary. In her music Zerbinetta projects a personality
that is flashily brilliant, witty, yet surprisingly compassionate.'

then spoken without a knowing undertone. Irony is not absent but turns against her because she, the common soubrette, can see only the sexual and not the spiritual aspect of love.

The two readings depend then on whether Zerbinetta is taken to be an intelligent, knowing character capable of ironic insights and hence also of self-irony since her insights do not free her from the paradoxes of human emotions, or whether she is taken to be a very shallow, superficial character with a frivolous view of the world.

In a letter of 13 April 1916 Hofmannsthal indicated that there had been some profound disagreement in the conception of this character (Bw. 13 Apr. 1916, p. 281). Strauss replied 'Über die Zerbinettafigur kann man schließlich zweierlei Meinung sein' (Bw. 16 Apr. 1916, p. 282). Although there is no proof of it Strauss may well have been referring to the ironic and non-ironic interpretations.

Strauss was temperamentally disposed to make the first reading. His fascination with the feminine psyche so evident in the figures of Salome, Elektra, and the Marschallin was ready to find stimulus in erotic complexity, even if this complexity were open and cheerful rather than decadent.[14] An ironic Zerbinetta promised him these things not because there was anything *risqué* about a coquette—the 'servetta' of the *commedia dell'arte* is too down-to-earth a role for that—but because she is intelligent and witty, unlike Ariadne.

Daviau and Buelow note that 'this character aroused Strauss to an intensity and spontaneity of musical ideas that he found nowhere else in the libretto'.[15] Ideas for Zerbinetta's recitative and aria in Strauss's first plan of numbers were abundant. Beyond his sympathy for the character Strauss was drawn musically to an ironic interpretation because it would allow him to use those devices in music such as stylistic imitation, burlesque send-up, musical quotation, humour, and musical parody which were amongst his most individual gifts as a

[14] See Patrick J. Smith, *The Tenth Muse*, pp. 361–83, for an excellent chapter on Hofmannsthal in which the six libretti are treated as an *œuvre* unified by the theme of love. Smith traces the development and efflorescence of this theme. It is interesting to note that all six Strauss-Hofmannsthal operas have women in the main roles and that in five of the six the woman is referred to in the title.

[15] Daviau and Buelow, p. 184.

composer.[16] By these means can irony and wit, usually restricted to conceptual or representational arts, be conveyed in music. Hans Mayer writes of Zerbinetta's aria: 'Bewußt schuf [Strauss] diesmal Kunst einer Spätzeit mit Imitationen, Parodien, musikalischen Zitaten.'[17] (This time Strauss deliberately created art of the end of an age, with imitations, parodies, musical quotations.) The word 'Spätzeit' suggests however a self-consciousness and mistrust of simple feeling which are for the most part belied by the zest and freshness of the Zerbinetta passages.

Not only was Strauss temperamentally inclined to see an ironic Zerbinetta; he also had cultural tradition on his side. His view of the *commedia dell'arte* character is closer than the other to the original type. Actually Zerbinetta was not a well known 'servetta' in the *commedia*. But according to Allardyce Nicoll she was a variant of the much better known Colombina who is Pulcinella's sweetheart.[18] Colombina herself emerged in the seventeenth century from the older Franceschina, and from the following description a picture of Zerbinetta can be built up as well:

At this age she [Colombina] reveals herself as sprightlier and perter, a girlish character whose merry wit easily defeats the efforts of older lovers . . . This young servetta dresses more daintily than the older Franceschina, and the daintiness becomes more pronounced after Caterina Biancolelli, at an early age, appeared at the Théâtre Italien as Colombina. Vivacious and buoyant, an incorrigible flirt, lively and animated, this Colombina is Watteau's heroine, and not only chance leads her to vary her name by appearing on occasions as Arlecchina.[19]

In this it is difficult to see an unintelligent, superficial character, particularly if we keep in mind the sophistication of the *commedia* personalities, who, far from being mere buffoons or stock types engaged in purely farcial improvised plots, were well-thought-out, psychologically persuasive personalities,

---

[16] Bw. 5 June 1916, p. 290. 'Ich bin doch schließlich jetzt der einzige Komponist, der wirklich Humor und Witz und ein ausgesprochen parodistisches Talent hat . . . Ja, ich fühle mich geradezu berufen zum Offenbach des 20. Jahrhunderts.'

[17] Mayer, p. 22.

[18] Nicoll, p. 96.

[19] Nicoll, p. 96.

usually well-read, generally intelligent, and taking part in a highly skilled comedy. This in itself is perhaps no guarantee of Zerbinetta's ironic insights, but it should be remembered that the Renaissance to a greater degree than any other age had a sharp nose for human weaknesses and a gleeful self-irony. When presented with the relatively bare *Szenarium* Strauss was then fully entitled to make the interpretation he did.

If Strauss had strong feelings about Zerbinetta we know that after 28 May 1911 Hofmannsthal did not. Up until that date he regarded *Ariadne auf Naxos* as such a secondary venture that he had no strong feelings about *any* of the characters. But later, although he was intensely involved with other characters, writing analyses of them in letters and *Notizen*, there were no notes on Zerbinetta at all and few mentions in the correspondence.

Yet as a result of the contract and the method of working he found himself in the false position of having to write a large part which would furthermore lend itself to the strict requirements of the coloratura aria for a character who did not greatly interest him—beyond her symbolic value as the antithesis of Ariadne, the real heroine of the 'lyric drama'.

Without being aware of the shape his libretto was taking and at the same time without caring enough to develop the character of Zerbinetta, Hofmannsthal attempted to get out of this awkward position by simply writing Zerbinetta's part from the *Szenarium* and the *Notizen* in front of him. And in so doing, fortunately for Strauss and posterity, he transferred the original ambiguity almost intact. Zerbinetta in the libretto can be read as a merely human, trivial and very common person, which was Hofmannsthal's theoretical interpretation of her, or indeed as those things mentioned above, which is perhaps the less contrived reading. Here are the opening lines of her recitative:

Zerbinetta

(beginnt mit einer tiefen Verneigung vor Ariadne)
Großmächtige Prinzessin, wer verstünde nicht,
Daß so erlauchter und erhabener Personen Traurigkeit
Mit einem anderen Maß gemessen werden muß
Als der gemeinen Sterblichen.—Jedoch

(Einen Schritt näher tretend, doch Ariadne achtet in keiner Weise
    auf sie)
Sind wir nicht Frauen unter uns, und schlägt denn nicht
In jeder Brust ein unbegreiflich, unbegreiflich Herz? (43.)

                    (Zerbinetta
(begins with a deep bow before Ariadne)
Great Princess, who could fail to see
That such a noble and illustrious person's sorrow
Has to be measured by another standard
Than that used for normal mortals.—Yet
(Coming a step closer, but Ariadne does not take the slightest notice
    of her)
Are we not women together, and does there not beat
In every breast an incomprehensible, incomprehensible heart?)

This is a free realization of the *Szenarium* lines 'Zerbinetta
nähert sich Ariadne, sucht sich einzuschmeicheln. Sie verstünde zu trösten' (Sz. 288). The very formal address may, as
indicated, have been a realization of the line 'Anreden bei
Shakespeare' (Sz. 292).

Are Zerbinetta's lines to be interpreted as a vulgar attempt
to ingratiate herself with her superior by flattering titles, self-
abnegation, and false familiarity? Is the plea of 'ein unbegreiflich Herz' merely an absence of dignity and moral integrity?
Or is Zerbinetta's address humorously mock heroic with a
mock pathetic reference to herself as a 'mere mortal'? And
does she have any real knowledge about 'the mysteries of the
heart'? Our interpretation depends almost entirely on whether
we are sympathetically disposed towards this character or not.

The following section of the recitative cleverly imitates the
historical sources of the original divertissement:

            Sie wollen mich nicht hören—
            Schön und stolz und regungslos,
            Als wären Sie die Statue auf Ihrer eigenen Gruft—
            Sie wollen keine andere Vertraute
            Als diesen Fels und diese Wellen haben? (43.)

            (You do not wish to hear me—
            Beautiful and proud and motionless,
            As if you were the statue on your own tomb—
            You do not want any other confidante
            Than this cliff and these waves?)

Here the stylized Antiquity of French Baroque is suddenly stressed and must surely accord with the actual décor of the opera although it is a visual world one tends to forget in the excesses of the transformation scene.

The entire text of Zerbinetta's recitative and aria proves itself amenable to the two interpretations and need not be presented in detail. The recitative continues in a tone that may be interpreted as playful rhetoric or bad taste. But the final stanza before the first Arietta *Noch glaub ich dem einen* begins to present such a differentiated sensibility that it seems wrong-headed to persist in seeing a spiritually inferior, vulgar, unimaginative Zerbinetta. She describes how easily the heart is swayed:

> Eine kurze Nacht
> Ein hastiger Tag
> Ein Wehen der Luft
> Ein fließender Blick
> Verwandelt ihr Herz!
> Aber sind denn wir gefeit
> Gegen die grausamen-entzückenden,
> Die unbegreiflichen Verwandlungen? (44.)

> (A short night
> A hurried day
> A wafting air
> A fleeting glance
> Transforms her heart!
> But are we invulnerable
> To the terrible—enchanting,
> To the incomprehensible transformations?)

There is something of the atmosphere of Schnitzler's *Anatol* here. Zerbinetta reveals not only an erotic suggestibility but also an erotic sensibility which leads her to complex emotional paradoxes:

> Ja, halb mich wissend und halb in Taumel
> Betrüge ich endlich und liebe noch recht! (44.)

She is in this a more complicated and more interesting character than Ariadne. There follows a list of her former lovers: Pagliazzo, Mezzetin, Cavicchio and others. But

although one could see in this nothing but coarse sexuality
there is an accompanying emotional urgency:

> Immer ein Müssen!
> Immer ein neues
> Beklommenes Staunen
> Daß ein Herz so gar sich selber,
> Gar sich selber nicht versteht! (45)

> (Always a compulsion!
> Always a new
> Uneasy amazement
> That a heart so utterly,
> So utterly does not understand itself!)

This may be an expansion of the line in the *Szenarium:* 'Sie
wundert sich über ihr eigenes Herz, das immer Vorsätze der
Treue, der Enthaltsamkeit macht und sie so wenig zu halten
weiß' (Sz. 289).

In the expansion from the *Szenarium* to the libretto which
Hofmannsthal had to undertake because of the agreement
about set numbers it seems that he created a character who
was very open to the *Szenarium* interpretation. The witty
exchanges with Harlekin elsewhere confirm this. Hofmannsthal too appears to have been in sympathy whilst
writing the part if only because in the course of writing such
a long number he had put something of himself into it. We
know that he had taken particular care over the verses because
in a later letter he told Strauss that Zerbinetta's song would
one day be amongst his most famous (Bw. 23 July 1911, p.
119). In the letter to Dora von Bodenhausen Hofmannsthal
included it as one of the three 'kleine Gedichte'.[20] It would
seem that in these two instances he temporarily lost sight of
the proportions of the coloratura aria he had willingly written
and was mainly thinking of the text's indisputable poetic
merit. However to champion Zerbinetta's aria only as a lyric
poem as Gräwe does is unfair: 'Das ausladende Rondo mit
Koloraturvariationen wird dem "französischen Rondeau"
Hofmannsthals nur eine oberflächliche formale Entsprechung,
ein überdimensionales, die Proportionen entstellendes Kostüm. Der Rhythmus der zyklischen, variierenden Wieder-

[20] See Chapter II, Note 19.

kehr, bei Hofmannsthal leise und bezwingend wirksam, wird bei Strauss unter dem wuchernden musikalischen Überbau erstickt.[21] (The lengthy rondo with coloratura variations bears only a superficial, formal resemblance to Hofmannsthal's 'French Rondeau'; it is a costume cut too large that distorts the proportions. The rhythm of the cyclic, varied recurrence, in Hofmannsthal's hands quietly and forcefully effective, is suffocated in Strauss's under the rampant musical superstructure.) Gräwe has forgotten or is unaware of the fact that Hofmannsthal himself had undertaken to write a text for coloratura rondo with variations. Strauss's music is not in fact a stifling superstructure: it is quite a feat of *legerdemain* and furthermore Hofmannsthal was trying to respond formally to Strauss's demands by providing a lot of repeatable lines. Finally the passage which Gräwe refers to as a French Rondeau, presumably the last thirteen lines of *Als ein Gott kam jeder gegangen* down to 'Hingegeben war ich stumm!', is so only in a very loose sense.[22] Gräwe is then interpreting the aria too much in the light of Hofmannsthal's comment about poems in *Ariadne auf Naxos*.

But if Hofmannsthal was in sympathy with Zerbinetta whilst writing her part he was definitely out of sympathy when he came to give his theoretical interpretation.[23] This rightly belongs amongst the third set of complicating factors, to be discussed in Chapter IV; but it has been the basis of critical accounts of Zerbinetta in both text and music, and as her

[21] Gräwe, p. 246.

[22] Gero von Wilpert gives the following definition of the French Rondeau: 'franz, Gedichtform aus mindestens 8, meist 13 Zeilen zu 8–10 Silben mit nur zwei Reimen in Gruppen zu 5,3 und 5 Zeilen. Die Anfangsworte der 1. Zeile kehren in der Mitte der 8. und am Schluß in der 13. Zeile als ungereimter Refrain wieder und gliedern das einstrophige Gedicht in zwei oder drei Teile (Couplets).' Hofmannsthal's thirteen-lined strophe has only two rhymes but the division is into 5, 4 and 6 lines of repetition and the opening words do not reappear as unrhymed refrain in lines 8 and 13. Gero von Wilpert, *Sachwörterbuch der Literatur*, p. 663.

[23] Hofmannsthal's theoretical interpretation of Zerbinetta and her relationship to Ariadne was shaped in part by his concurrent work on his novel *Andreas* (1912). Largely influenced by Morton Prince's *Dissociation of a Personality* (1906) which he was reading at the time, he evolved a theory of antithetical yet paradoxically, even mystically, related personalities. Maria and Marquita in *Andreas* are such a secretly identified pair and their psychology is drawn in some detail. In theory Hofmannsthal believed in what Könneker calls 'die gleichzeitige Identität und Nichtidentität von Ariadne und Zerbinetta', but this theory was not fully realized in the opera and is but one more confusing stratum. Könneker, p. 129.

music is shortly to be examined in detail it would be clearer to
state the 'official' interpretation here so that it can be measured
against the alternatives.

The letter of 28 May 1911 referring to Zerbinetta as
'Zutaten' has already been discussed. In the letter of mid-July
1911 Zerbinetta is not much more than a witless prostitute:
'Es steht hier die Gruppe der Heroen ... gegen die
menschliche, nichts als menschliche Gruppe der leichtfertigen
Zerbinetta und ihrer Begleiter, dieser gemeinen Lebensmasken. Zerbinetta ist in ihrem Element, wenn sie von einem zum
andern taumelt.' (In the present case we have the group of
heroes ... facing the human, the merely human group
consisting of the frivolous Zerbinetta and her companions, all
of them base figures in life's masquerade. Zerbinetta is in her
element drifting out of the arms of one man into the arms of
another.) Further down in the same letter Hofmannsthal
continues with that begging of the question which has
previously been criticized. Divine love, we are told, is more
divine than earthly love. The two groups, instead of being
plausible human representatives of two sides of an emotion,
have become extreme representatives of what scarcely seems
the same emotion: 'Was aber ein wirkliches Wunder ist für
göttliche Seelen, für die irdische Seele der Zerbinetta ist es das
alltägliche. Sie sieht in dem Erlebnis der Ariadne das, was sie
eben darin zu sehen vermag: den Tausch eines neuen
Liebhabers für einen alten.' (Bw. mid-July 1911, p. 115.) (But
what to divine souls is a real miracle, is to the earth-bound
nature of Zerbinetta just an everyday love-affair. She sees in
Ariadne's experience the only thing she *can* see: the exchange
of an old lover for a new one.) From the preceding discussion
we know that this both oversimplifies and belittles Zerbinetta
as she appears in the text. And yet it has become the standard
view of her character. This may have come about from the
frequent malpractice of quoting Hofmannsthal's letters indiscriminately in programme notes[24] and critical literature. Even

---

[24] For example, see the programme of the Royal Opera House 1976/7 production
of *Ariadne auf Naxos* conducted by Edo de Waart, programme notes compiled by
Noël Goodwin: the letter of mid-July 1911 is quoted at length. Similarly the
programme of the 1975 production by the Australian Opera at the Sydney Opera
House conducted by Edward Downes, programme notes by Wenzel de Neergaard,
quotes this letter and no other.

such an otherwise reliable critic as Norman Del Mar quotes only the letter of mid-July including those lines given above as his sole illustration of 'the crucial opposition in outlook between Ariadne and Zerbinetta'.[25] Daviau and Buelow in the only single full-scale study of *Ariadne* likewise begin their chapter on the 'Interpretation of the Opera' by quoting this letter.[26] After getting caught up in a long-winded discussion of the symbolic meaning of the opera they conclude: 'while Zerbinetta's simplified analysis of Ariadne's problem and its solution—surrender to another man—proves eventually to be correct, there is a qualitative difference in the occurrence far beyond her comprehension.'[27] In other words they too are suggesting a non-ironic Zerbinetta.

ii. *Strauss's Musical Interpretation of Zerbinetta*

Does Strauss's music suggest that she is lacking in comprehension? The structure of Zerbinetta's number has been variously presented. Daviau and Buelow give it as recitative, first secco and then accompagnato (F major), two part aria (D flat major, D major), and rondo with variations (D major).[28] Del Mar retains this plan but rightly prefers to see the second section as two ariettas rather than as a two-part aria.[29] These two short ariettas *Noch glaub' ich* (No. 109 – 9 bars) and *So war es mit Pagliazzo* (No. 117 – 6 bars) do not have the elaborate musical structure of the aria and there is also the modulation from D flat major to D major and the change from 3/4 to 6/8 time which does not suggest that they are parts of one aria. Gräwe agrees with Del Mar but gives a more detailed and accurate account of the recitative which is indeed a splendid show-piece in itself. He divides it into recitative secco with piano accompaniment (No. 99 – 9 bars to No. 101), recitativo accompagnato with a quaver motif and arioso-like qualities (No. 101 to No. 105), recitativo accompagnato proper (No. 105 to No. 107) with another more melodic arioso concluding section (No. 107 to No. 109).[30] Full-scale descriptions of all of

[25] Del Mar, p. 25.
[26] Daviau and Buelow, p. 125.
[27] Daviau and Buelow, p. 125.
[28] Daviau and Buelow, p. 182.
[29] Del Mar, p. 36.
[30] Gräwe, p. 242.

Zerbinetta's pieces can be found in the above critics as well as in W. Mann[31] and will not be given here. Only those points necessary for a general understanding leading into an interpretation of the musical characterization will be raised.

Of special interest is the use of the piano as the accompanying instrument for the *commedia dell'arte* throughout. It is jaunty and refreshing after the harmonium and viola of the *opera seria* accompaniment and more readily associated with comic theatre than most other instruments. The other interesting feature is Strauss's generous use of recitativo accompagnato. This type of recitative is dramatic rather than declamatory and is more strictly measured than parlando. (The throbbing quaver motif has this effect.) Not only is Strauss's setting of Zerbinetta's recitative very dramatic and in itself strong evidence of the dramatic flair which Hofmannsthal especially praised in him[32] but it is also a deliberate imitation of an earlier style. The Harvard Dictionary entry for recitativo accompagnato reads: 'It assumed considerable importance in eighteenth-century opera, where it was usually reserved for the climactic scenes of the drama and served to introduce the most brilliant arias of the work.'[33] Strauss is using it here with precisely that function and the whole of Zerbinetta's number is based on the eighteenth-century bel canto recitative and aria practice. Thus Strauss employs historical imitation in his characterizations.

The recitative opens with a rhetorical flourish. The voice falls an octave and a third over an arpeggio-like figure which is intended perhaps to illustrate Zerbinetta's 'tiefe Verneigung vor Ariadne' (Ex. 1). The sense of space created by the sparse chordal accompaniment on the piano and the wide-ranging, rapid vocal line suggest that this opening section, which is a setting of the elaborate formal address (43), is intended to be humorously grandiose rather than vulgar and ingratiating. This is confirmed by the setting of the words 'gemeinen Sterblichen'. The short melisma on 'gemeinen' extending

[31] Daviau and Buelow, pp. 181–94. Del Mar, pp. 35–40. Gräwe, pp. 230–3, 242–50. Mann, pp. 161–2.

[32] Hofmannsthal wrote 'von uns beiden haben Sie, ganz abgesehen vom Maß der Begabung, den stärkeren dramatischen Instinkt, ohne jeden Zweifel.' Bw. 22 Dec. 1912, p. 179.

[33] Willi Apel, *Harvard Dictionary of Music*, p. 718.

Ex. 1

down into the low reaches of the soprano's register to show quite how 'base' they are and the tripping rhythm ♪· ♪♪ which has the effect of a cheeky smile suggest that Zerbinetta is acting and is being deliberately mock-pathetic rather than self-abnegating. The following phrase 'Jedoch, sind wir nicht Frauen unter uns?' could be interpreted as either false familiarity or an indication of shared experience. Strauss sets this line with great simplicity and delicacy. Over a dominant seventh chord marked *piano* which seems the more intimate for coming after the playful, robust setting of 'gemeinen Sterblichen' Zerbinetta climbs the scale interrogatively (Ex. 2). This line also indicates her tentative step forward ('einen Schritt näher tretend') and the run is continued by the piano with four delicate staccato notes in such a charming fashion that the over-all impression is of a delicate, never false, but slightly pert character.

Ex. 2

The setting of the following lines 'und schlägt denn nicht / In jeder Brust ein unbegreiflich, unbegreiflich Herz?' reveals a sudden flash of feeling in Zerbinetta which leads us to believe that she *is* initiated into the mysteries of erotic love and is not just a common coquette (Ex. 3). Not only is the sudden modulation from F major to E major on 'unbegreiflich' a

Ex. 3

musical pun, depending on the ambiguity of the chord on C,[34] but it is also a shift into one of the more lush and sensuous of the Straussian keys.[35] Furthermore there are the marking 'espressivo' in the accompaniment, the intensified string texture, the increase in dynamics from 'mf' to 'f' and the high top G sharp held against the inverted dominant seventh resolved on 'Herz' which all suggest that Zerbinetta is capable of moments of genuine feeling.

The texture lightens and the flute, chosen by Strauss in imitation of eighteenth-century practice as the *obbligato* instrument,[36] is introduced at this early stage with a very fast motif consisting of a rising fourth and a falling octave (Ex. 4).

Ex. 4

Daviau and Buelow claim that this motif represents Zerbi-netta's 'Knix'.[37] Whilst this is certainly true at first, the motif is used so extensively throughout this second section of the

[34] Daviau and Buelow mistakenly claim that the modulation itself is incomprehensible; in fact, it is quite conventional, p. 187.

[35] There is no doubt that Strauss associated some keys and groups of keys with certain moods and psychological states. Edmund Wachten has made a fascinating 'psychographic' study of Strauss's use of tonality, rhythm, harmony, and melody but wisely does not attempt to find a system of deliberate correlation between tonality and mood. Nevertheless E major seems often to be used by Strauss for optimistic sensuality, cheerfulness, or courage, and is associated in *Ariadne* with the *commedia dell'arte*. The key of D flat major, for Strauss a more sombre, intense, erotic tonality, is reserved for the *opera seria*. Edmund Wachten, *Der einheitliche Grundzug der Strauss'schen Formgestaltung*, p. 257 ff.

[36] See Bw. 22 May 1911, p. 102.

[37] Daviau and Buelow, p. 186.

recitative that it takes on other meanings. In its leaping, volatile character it could equally well be an illustration of the words 'Und zuckt uns nicht der Sinn danach?' The total effect of this motif is of an intense white flame leaping through the score.

Hofmannsthal's sudden return in the text to an historically authentic description of the *opera seria* stage[38] now provides Strauss with an opportunity for marvellously witty characterization. Zerbinetta in a good imitation of the heroic style sends up her rival group (Ex. 5).

Ex. 5

There are heavy chords in the bass on the strings under a triadic melody. Melodic movement around the triad is usually associated in Strauss with moments of high or serious feeling and is used extensively for example in Ariadne's aria *Du wirst mich befreien*. The tempo is ponderous and we are in the 'heroic' tonality of E flat major, the key of Ariadne's recitative and aria. The word 'regungslos' is taken advantage of for a stylized piece of word-painting: the accompaniment does not move at all in this bar. Zerbinetta is obviously clever and witty to be able to produce such a good imitation for these lines. The music continues over the motif used for Ariadne's vision of death[39] and concludes with another piece of word-painting on the word 'Wellen' which enhances the archaic, historicizing atmosphere of this passage (Ex. 6).

Ex. 6

[38] See Chapter III, pp. 142–3.
[39] Del Mar, Ex. 22, p. 33, No. 62.

The third section of the recitative (No. 105 to No. 107), which Gräwe calls the recitativo accompagnato proper, can only be construed as playful rhetoric and deliberately exaggerated gesture. The voice rises and falls rapidly through its range coming to a climax on the high A flat of 'unzählige' and 'mehrere'. The opening three words 'Verlassen! in Verzweiflung! ausgesetzt!' are each time set in mock pathetic overstatement which is successfully undercut by the humorous staccato runs on the piano played during the rests in the vocal line. By the end of this section the aloof Ariadne has completely disappeared into her cave. Alone Zerbinetta enters upon the final section, the words of which from 'Eine kurze Nacht' to

Ex. 7

'Die unbegreiflichen Verwandlungen' have already been discussed.[40] These words, more reflective and private than the rest, express something of the atmosphere of Zerbinetta's erotic life and of its emotional urgency. The chromatically shifting arpeggios in the piano accompaniment convey the breathless haste and urgency of 'Eine kurze Nacht, ein hastiger Tag'. Transience and impressionistic elusiveness of experience are both suggested by this technique (Ex. 7). There is nothing frivolous or flirtatious about this passage. Nevertheless with one of the quick changes of mood that mark this recitative it culminates in a sudden piece of self-irony: the motif used for 'unsere Schwachheit' (No. 102 to No. 104) is incorporated into

[40] See Chapter III, pp. 143–4.

Ex. 8

the long melisma on 'Verwandlungen' (Ex. 8). On the one
hand the melisma is ridiculously long and winding. Zerbinetta
is obviously enjoying every 'transformation' as it comes her
way. On the other hand the musical reference to 'the weakness
of the female sex' implies that she 'just can't help it'.
Zerbinetta's irony consists here of saying one thing but
meaning another. She has acute self-awareness as well as a
sense of fun—but it is doubtful whether Strauss's complex
piece of characterization could be appreciated by the unaided
listener.

The music now modulates into the key of D flat major for
the first arietta. This lyric number, which is in ternary form
and preserves the reduced texture of the chamber orchestra, is
pretty but not particularly memorable. Although there are
melismas on words such as 'gelogen' and 'schlecht' it does not
have the pyrotechnic bravura of the following arietta or the
rondo but neither does it have the melodic distinctiveness of
Ariadne's arias nor are there enough chromatic harmonies to
convey the shifting, elusive, disturbingly paradoxical lines:

> Ja, halb mich wissend und halb im Taumel
> Betrüge ich endlich und liebe noch recht! (44.)

> (Yes, half aware of my motives and half in a whirl
> I deceive him finally and still love him well!)

In fact the second line is sung to an inappropriately heroic and
diatonic melody (No. 114−2 bars to No. 115). In short this
arietta is a transitional number which does not succeed in
being anything in itself.

The second arietta in D major is by contrast a sheerly
extrovert extravaganza full of breathtakingly virtuoso roulades
and leaps, chromatic runs and trills. It is concluded by an
exceedingly demanding unaccompanied cadenza leading into
the rondo. The impression of the whole when performed by a
singer with a technique equal to the task is of a *joie de vivre*,
even a reckless exuberance, only just held in check by the
pronounced rhythm of the opening bars. The piece is marked

Ex. 9

'allegro scherzando' and is in a lilting 6/8 time (Ex. 9). This type of light-hearted virtuoso display is appropriate for the words which recount Zerbinetta's virtuoso love life although the setting of the lines 'Doch niemals Launen / Immer ein Müssen',[41] in which the roulades become more and more taxing might perhaps have been done more sensitively.

Particularly in the second half of this arietta as well as in parts of the rondo the voice is treated in an instrumental fashion. This can be seen in the five bars preceding the cadenza (Ex. 10). Gräwe claims in respect to this passage: 'Die völlige Instrumentalisierung entfernt deren Trägerin vom individuell Menschlichen.'[42] He compares Zerbinetta's part with Papageno's in *Die Zauberflöte*, quoting at length from Kierkegaard's 'Die Stadien des Unmittelbar-Erotischen' with a view to showing that just as Papageno's ceaseless, cheerful twittering is an adequate expression of his essential being so

Ex. 10

[41] See Chapter III, p. 144.
[42] Gräwe, p. 248.

are Zerbinetta's instrumental passages an adequate expression of her poorly developed individuality.[43]

That this approach is not satisfactory as an over-all interpretation becomes clear from the clearly differentiated sections of her rondo. Although it is true that there is something of the mechanical songbird about Zerbinetta a more apt comparison might be with the automaton in Offenbach's *The Tales of Hoffman* than with Papageno; and we remember that Brighella calls her 'die hübsche Puppe' (50). But it should also be kept in mind that Strauss was here deliberately imitating and also parodying coloratura style with its florid ornamentations.

Ex. 11

The rondo with variations which forms the final part of this number was, like the first arietta, cut quite considerably in the revision for the 1916 *Ariadne*. The form of the rondo in the 1912 version was ABA (variation 1) CA (variation 2) coda, and in the 1916 version ABA (variation 1) coda, which is really only modified ternary form. The 1916 coda is half the length of the original coda.

The principal subject of the rondo is introduced straight away. It is a catchy melody enhanced by a lively figure (a) on the violins (Ex. 11). The rondo material is light-hearted and outgoing, and is an example of the freshness and zest which is a corrective to the more self-conscious musical pastiche. The first episode (B) is strongly contrasted to it. Marked 'tranquillo' (No. 123 to No. 126), it is the lyrical answer to A and provides a tender, meditative interlude in this difficult number as well as shading Zerbinetta's personality and contrasting with the

[43] Sören Kierkegaard, 'Die Stadien des Unmittelbar-Erotischen oder Das Musikalisch-Erotische', in *Entweder-Oder* p. 78. Quoted in Gräwe, p. 248.

Ex. 12

passage of instrumental vocalization (Ex. 12). Figure (x) is a
spun out version of the figure in the second arietta *So war es
mit Pagliazzo*. The strings provide a soft, sustained chordal
background whilst the solo 'cello accompanies Zerbinetta's
new thematic material on the words 'Jeder wandelt mich um'
(between Nos. 123 and 124). The latter part of this episode is
distinguished by a beautifully mellifluous imitation of the
vocal line on solo woodwinds, particularly the flute (No. 125).
The voice winds in a leisurely fashion through embellishments
on 'gefangen' and 'gegeben' and after a short accelerando
moves into the first variation.

At this point Strauss began cutting the 1912 version. This
was done partly in order to make the area less taxing and for
this reason the second arietta and the rondo were dropped a
tone from E major to D major thus avoiding a high F sharp
which is not within the range of most sopranos.[44] The cuts
were made more particularly because Strauss had been carried
away with rather too self-conscious parodies of the admittedly

[44] Hans Mayer suggests, incorrectly, that Strauss would not drop this aria down a
tone and that the top note was always a high E: [Hofmannsthal] versuchte . . .—
selbstverständlich ohne Erfolg—von Strauss eine Erleichterung der Zerbinetta-Aria
zu erreichen, damit nicht bloß höchst virtuose, aber einigermaßen überreife
Koloratursoprane (er dachte an Margarethe Siems und Selma Kurz), sondern wirklich
anmutige junge Sängerinnen die Rolle singen und spielen könnten. Strauss gab nicht
nach und tat recht daran, denn als der Brief geschrieben wurde, gab es bereits das
Wunder Maria Ivogün: Anmut, Leichtigkeit und Unfehlbarkeit der Koloratur, die
jedoch überall, bis hinauf zum hohen E, so wie Strauss es gewollt hatte, dem
musikalischen Ausdruck diente.' Mayer, p. 22.

farcical excesses of eighteenth-century operatic practice. As well as being 'discursive and almost formless',[45] as Del Mar says, the rondo had become a laboured operatic in-joke and this did little for the musical characterization of Zerbinetta.

Accordingly Strauss made a 39 bar cut in variation 1 at No. 126 after the formal return of the main subject. This cut included a parody of a classical practice which Del Mar describes in the following terms:

Star singers of the seventeenth and eighteenth centuries were wont to omit part of their vocal line in order to return with greater effect at the cadenza. Strauss satirizes this tradition with delightful wit: Zerbinetta misses an entry and, then observing that the clarinet is prompting her, maliciously leaves the part entirely to him with a great show of good humour, merely joining in for the last half-dozen notes of the final cadence.[46]

The rest of the cut was of an elaborate middle section. The remaining portion of variation 1 comprises only 6 bars from No. 126 to No. 127 and is a parody of the more naïve classical melodies and harmonies of a Bellini or a Donizetti. The groups of three accents are a clever touch (Ex. 13). These accents indicate that the phrase is to be sung in an exaggerated manner to bring out the banality of the musical invention. We can enjoy the joke with Zerbinetta without it becoming tedious.

Ex. 13

Strauss now made a second cut of approximately 40 bars which did away with the second episode C, variation 2, and the coda (which was however replaced). Del Mar notes that the second episode did not contain much new material but

[45] Del Mar, p. 73.
[46] Del Mar, p. 38.

that there were numerous clever imitations of Zerbinetta's *fioriture* on the flute also in the manner of Bellini or Donizetti.[47] After the final return to the rondo theme Strauss launches into the coda, which contains another self-conscious joke: there is a farcical *contretemps* between Zerbinetta and the orchestra as both parties compete in reaching a climax. Del Mar writes: 'For a short time Zerbinetta battles bravely but finally gives up in despair. The orchestra, observing her dismay, hurries on to a conventional 6/4 chord and pauses expectantly. At this Zerbinetta makes an extravagant 'thank you' gesture to the conductor and embarks on her great cadenza.'[48]

The new coda extends from No. 127 to No. 130 and is followed by a brief reprise of the rondo theme. The coda is better shaped than the earlier one and includes a Donizetti-like duet for flute and voice in the style of the passage cut in the second episode (Ex. 14).

Ex. 14

The entire number is concluded by an amusing setting of the last line 'Hingegeben war ich stumm, stumm . . .' with Zerbinetta literally 'stumm' on the final cadence of the number on the first beat of No. 144. To a snap chord on the second beat Harlekin springs out of the wings and begins their recitative.

[47] Del Mar, p. 39.
[48] Del Mar, p. 39.

In this brilliant mixture of parody, sophisticated pastiche, and original invention, pruned in the 1916 version of its excesses, Strauss gives a musical portrayal of a witty, vivacious character capable of satire and self-mockery, occasionally inclined to show off, occasionally giving way to moments of deeper feeling but always able to enjoy herself and her skill. Zerbinetta is theatrical but she is warm and compassionate. She is ironic and clever but she is also sincere. In short Strauss created a character of considerable complexity and interest and a musical centre of gravity in the opera.

Hofmannsthal was unable either to see or to appreciate Strauss's musical creation. W. Mann is probably right to conclude that Hofmannsthal regarded the part as 'vulgarly exhibitionistic',[49] although he never said so in so many words. Egon Wellesz reports that in a conversation in 1918 Hofmannsthal said that Zerbinetta was too 'marionettenhaft'.[50] And in a letter to Strauss in 1918 Hofmannsthal suggested that Strauss write the part anew in the melodious style of the Incidental Music to *Der Bürger als Edelmann*: 'wenn die im Text so vielfach rhythmisch streng auseinandergehaltenen Teile dieser Arie ... von Ihnen mit der melodiösen Biegsamkeit, welche die bezaubernde 'Bourgeois'-Musik aufweist, neu komponiert würden, [würde] das Ganze sich mit einem Ruck tiefer ins Verstehen der Menschen und in ihr lustvolles Verstehen einschmeicheln' (Bw. 8 July 1918, p. 350). (If ... you were to write new music of the smooth melodiousness of *Le Bourgeois* for its various phases with their distinct variation in rhythm, the whole aria would, I imagine, all at once gain a firmer hold on people's understanding and make this understanding a delight.) Hofmannsthal's own understanding at this point was perhaps hampered by his lack of musical training, which he openly acknowledged, and by his conservative tastes. In a letter written shortly before his death he confessed to Carl

---

[49] Mann, p. 184.

[50] Wellesz asked Hofmannsthal 'was ihn dazu bewogen habe, der Oper "Ariadne" das Vorspiel vorangehen zu lassen. Er sagte, die Figur der Zerbinetta mit ihrer großen Koloraturarie sei ihm marionettenhaft erschienen, es fehlte ihr die menschliche Wärme, die eine Figur wie die Philine in Goethes "Wilhelm Meister" so bezaubernd mache; deshalb habe er den Gedanken gefaßt, der Oper eine Szene vorangehen zu lassen.' Egon Wellesz, 'Hofmannsthal und die Musik', p. 237.

Burckhardt[51] that he had never really cared much for Strauss's music although he professed the opposite to Strauss and at that time he listened repeatedly and with great pleasure to Verdi.[52] However the depression and despair of the final years may have brought out a nostalgia that remained latent in better times.

iii. *Zerbinetta's Place within the* Oper

But no matter how much Zerbinetta may be vindicated as a character in her own right the fact remains that within the framework of the 'lyric drama', which was the form towards which Hofmannsthal's libretto seemed ultimately to aspire, she is a superfluous figure. The 'lyric drama', with its themes of love and mutual transformation, memory and individuality, is focused upon Ariadne and Bacchus. The presence of the *commedia* group can be justified as the symbolic antithesis to the heroic group and this argument in various guises is one of the main ones in Hofmannsthal's own theoretical interpretations of *Ariadne*. But the fact remains, despite all arguments, that the *commedia* is not *necessary* to the 'lyric drama'. Hofmannsthal half sensed this when he wrote on one occasion that the coloratura did not form 'eine wesentliche Stärke des Ganzen' (Bw. 8 July 1918, p. 350). This part which is almost as long as Ariadne's recitative and aria, and is the longest uninterrupted solo in the opera is then dramatically superfluous, it adds no movement to an already static action and entitles R. Specht to his opinion that *Ariadne auf Naxos* is a 'Vokalkonzert im Kostüm'.[53]

[51] Hugo von Hofmannsthal / Carl J. Burckhardt, *Briefwechsel*, p. 103. See also Egon Wellesz, 'Hofmannsthal und die Musik', p. 236.

[52] Burckhardt tells the following story about Hofmannsthal: 'Hofmannsthal verbrachte drei Monate des kalten Winters 1929, vom Januar an, bei mir auf dem Schönenberg, in einem für den Sommer gebauten Landhause. Wir waren tief eingeschneit und saßen den ganzen Tag am Ofen. Damals schrieb er die Oper "Arabella" zu Ende. Allabendlich las er ein kurzes Stück daraus vor. Er sprach viel über die Oper als Kunstform, Verdi beschäftigte ihn in jenen Monaten sehr. Er hatte eine Anzahl von Platten aus den Opern des großen Italieners gekauft; als er die Arie "Credo in un dio crudel" anhörte, fiel dieses merkwürdig Steinerne, Maskenhafte auf sein Gesicht; er ließ die Platte nochmals laufen, lauschte mit gespanntester Aufmerksamkeit und sprach lange nicht. Er zog sich in sein Zimmer zurück und wollte dann keine Musik mehr hören.' Carl J. Burckhardt, 'Erinnerung an Hofmannsthal', p. 144.

[53] Richard Specht is critical of Hofmannsthal's libretto, or 'Dichtung': 'Ihre Wirkung, die fleckenloseste, die er geübt hat, ist vollkommen die der reinen Musik.

Nevertheless one of Hofmannsthal's first intentions with *Ariadne* was to provide Strauss with a 'Drahtgestell' on which to hang the music well and prettily. This was an open invitation to a 'Vokalkonzert im Kostüm'. And a star part for Zerbinetta was part of the original spirit of the thing. So if discussions of this opera seem to go round in circles this should be taken as proof in itself of its twisted and complicated genesis from fundamentally simple beginnings.

Since the *commedia dell'arte* and Zerbinetta *are* present in this libretto it is best to treat them in accordance with the argument that justifies their presence, namely to treat them as an antithetical group which is in effect an extension of the idea of opposed forces in the allegory. Zerbinetta, it is true, is too individualized to be an allegorical figure, but this can be passed off if the allegorical structure, especially the united happy end, is retained. Then the theme of erotic love is sustained at the formal level as well and the whole piece succeeds in achieving some balance and artistic unity.

An attempt was made at preserving the allegorical structure in the 1912 *Ariadne*. The libretto allowed for this; but the lyric climax of the opera, the transformation scene occurring just before the end, was too overpowering and in the 1916 version the allegory was sacrificed to the 'lyric drama' although Hofmannsthal tried to conceal this fact.

The original text made provision for an adequate reappearance of the *opera buffa* troupe. This was concluded by a symbolic dance in which all characters were involved:

Zerbinetta
(vor und wiederholt mit spöttischem Triumph ihr Rondo)
Kommt der neue Gott gegangen,
Hingegeben sind wir stumm!
Und er küßt uns Hand und Wangen,
Und wir geben uns gefangen,
Sind verwandelt um und um!
Sind verwandelt um und um!

Die dramatische schweigt. Ich habe die Empfindung: ein Vokalkonzert im Kostüm. Ich bedarf der Szene nicht, ja sie stört mich eher in ihren Barock-Velleitäten—ich schließe die Augen und öffne die Seele so weit ich kann, um die edlen Worte und die erlauchte Musik über sie hin—und tief in sie hineinfluten zu lassen.' Richard Specht, *Richard Strauss und sein Werk*, Volume II, p. 286.

(Sie reicht die Hand dem Harlekin, desgleichen die übrigen
paarweise. Zerbinetta singt und tanzt mit ihrem Partner.)
So war es mit Pagliazzo!
   (Ein Knicks)
Und mit Mezzetin!
   (Ein Knicks)
Dann mit Cavicchio,
Dann Burattin!
   (Ein Knicks)
Doch niemals Launen,
Immer ein Müssen,
Immer ein neues
Beklommenes Staunen:
Daß ein Herz so gar sich selber
Gar sich selber nicht versteht. (378.)

                    (Zerbinetta
(comes forward and repeats her rondo in mocking triumph)
When the new god comes along
Captive are we, silent!
He kisses our hand and cheek
And we give ourselves up,
Are transformed over and over!
Are transformed over and over!
(She gives Harlekin her hand, the others do the same in pairs.
Zerbinetta sings and dances with her partner.)
So it was with Pagliazzo!
   (A curtsy)
And with Mezzetin!
   (A curtsy)
Then with Cavicchio,
Then Burattin!
   (A curtsy)
But never a whim,
Always a compulsion,
Always a new
Uneasy amazement
That a heart so utterly,
So utterly does not understand itself!)

Many of the *commedia* motifs creep back in, and there are
a number of references to the themes of the rondo as well as to
the *buffa* ensembles.[54] The stage grows lighter and the climax

[54] For a good summary, see Del Mar, p. 55.

Ex. 15

is reached with the repetition of the waltz theme used in the
buffa quintet *Hübsch gepredigt aber tauben Ohren* (Ex. 15).

This is in the same family as the Breakfast Waltz from *Der
Rosenkavalier*, and many of Strauss's Viennese waltzes which
were still to follow. It is not hard to hear in it the jubilant
harmonious mood of a happy finale as well as simple dance
music. As a conclusion the final group ensemble of the 1912
version captured some of the ambience of the original thirty
minute divertissement and helped restore the balance after
the lyric apotheosis.

In Chapter II it was suggested that when the Molière frame
was removed the authors felt less obliged to break the illusion
of the transformation scene and that the removal of the anti-
illusionist frame was indeed taken advantage of as a way of
letting the 'single vision' stand uncorrected. Hofmannsthal's
letter of 15 May 1916 was quoted, in which he declared himself
satisfied with Zerbinetta's 'symbolisches spöttisches Dastehen
und Wiederverschwinden'. At the same time the allegorical
substructure demanded more than just a symbolic gesture and
of this Hofmannsthal was also aware. In reply to Hofmannsthal's proposal Strauss wrote: 'Ihr Wunsch ist mir
Befehl: Zerbinetta tritt Ziffer 326 leise aus der Kulisse und
singt spöttisch: "Kommt der neue Gott gegangen, hingegeben
sind wir stumm—stumm—", das Fagott deutet dazu das
Rondothema der Arie an, sie verschwindet Ziffer 327.' (Bw.
18 May 1916, p. 287.) (Your wish is my command: at Number
326 Zerbinetta shall softly step from the wings and sing
mockingly: 'When the new god comes along, captive are we,
silent—silent—'; the bassoon hints at the rondo theme from
her aria, and at Number 327 she vanishes.) But although
Strauss did carry out the command to the letter he was not true
to the spirit of it. Zerbinetta's line from her aria which was
intended to be mocking and the opposite of sentimental is
augmented and modified into eight bars of sheer lyricism and
overlaid on a magical, tender orchestral interlude in the

Ariadne–Bacchus duet. Ariadne has just finished singing the lines 'Was hängt von mir' down to 'Laß meine Schmerzen nicht verloren sein!' (65). This is accompanied throughout by the nymphs singing off-stage the third and final repetition of their *Töne töne süße Stimme*.[55] Still in the rich warm key of D flat major the interlude begins with a motif of bell-like fourths (x) on celeste, harps, and piano. The delicate orchestration is reminiscent of the tinkling music of the Rose Presentation in *Der Rosenkavalier*. The gentle staccato rhythm ♪♪♪ in the passage No. 326 to No. 327 is part of the original motif (x) and adds to its fragile charm.

Ex. 16

The second half of this orchestral interlude from No. 327 to No. 328, marked 'poco meno lento', continues in the same tranquil mood, solo cello and viola alternating with an augmented version of the motif which Del Mar calls Bacchus' love melody.[56] The first half of this gently rising theme is given (Ex. 16) in the form it appears in during the interlude. At No. 328 Ariadne and Bacchus sing the final part of their duet *Laß meine Schmerzen*.[57]

Over the first part of this interlude Strauss has Zerbinetta sing her mocking reprise of her rondo. It is cleverly done but, as we shall see, not in the spirit of the solution. The whole passage from No. 326 + 1 bar to No. 327 is quoted (Ex. 17).

[55] This verse has not been printed in *Lustspiele* III. Although it was a textual addition made by Strauss, it must have been approved by Hofmannsthal and ought to have been included there. LIII, p. 65.

[56] Del Mar, Ex. 48, p. 51.

[57] Again, the version of the libretto in *Lustspiele* III does not agree with the score: at No. 328 Bacchus' two lines, 'Deiner habe ich um alles bedurft! / Nun bin ich ein anderer, als ich war', are sung against the two lines of Ariadne's speech preceding Zerbinetta's re-entry. Zerbinetta's and Ariadne's lines should be transposed and some indication of a duet should be given. LIII, p. 65.

Ex. 17

We note that in the score the directions are 'Zerbinetta (leise und diskret)', whereas in the libretto they read: 'Zerbinetta ... wiederholt mit spöttischem Triumph ihr Rondo' (65). The first is certainly the more accurate description. Hofmannsthal's request for a mocking, unsentimental presence has been ignored. From the quotation (Ex. 18) of the actual rondo theme in D major it can be seen that Strauss transformed it into a lyrical form at No. 326 through augmentation of the opening phrase:

Ex. 18

The second part of the phrase at No. 326 is a very free modification of the closing bars of the rondo. Even the bassoon, an instrument used in this opera in its traditional role of comedian of the orchestra,[58] is handled in a lyric way. Its hints at Zerbinetta's aria which we might expect to be ebullient or comical are in fact 'zart hervortretend'. They are the most discreet hints imaginable. During this entire passage the bell-like fourths sound quite clearly.

Daviau and Buelow are the only critics to realize that Zerbinetta's final entry is not mocking and that it is not an

[58] For example, the bassoon features in the principal theme of the Intermezzo, which first appears at No. 79.

ironic corrective. They do not see that the passage's lyricism is a result of Strauss's opportunistic handling of an orchestral passage and thus draw false conclusions about the 'meaning' of this entry and exit: 'Zerbinetta leaves the stage musically at least a wiser woman.'[59] The truth of the matter is that Strauss was fundamentally disinclined to break operatic illusion and musical characterization *is* sacrificed for a curtain.

iv. *'Scene III' and the Transformation*

It was alleged in Chapter I that Strauss was at his most Wagnerian in the lyric climax of the *Oper*. The transformation itself cannot be examined separately from the whole of the third scene which begins after the Intermezzo as this scene firstly is 'durchkomponiert' and secondly has a complex interlocking structure. This structure is tripartite and thus reflects the tripartite form of the *Oper*. Norman Del Mar suggests that the music for the third scene was sketched out before Strauss had actually composed up to it. He points out that it is entitled 'III Scene' whereas there are no other such demarcations, and also includes as evidence the abrupt transition from D major in the previous section to a fanfare opening in C sharp major. He rightly states that here virtue is being made of complete contrast regardless of what might have been composed for the gap.[60] The structure and key schemes of the scenes are best given in Daviau and Buelow who divide this scene into the section before Bacchus' voice is heard which is the nymphs' expository trio, the section from Bacchus' off-stage song *Circe, Circe* until his arrival on stage and the final section from Ariadne's *Ich grüße dich* down to and including the orchestral coda.[61] This division seems

---

[59] Daviau and Buelow, p. 217.

[60] Del Mar, p. 43.

[61] Daviau and Buelow, p. 201. Part of their chart is given here:

Section III:

1a. Ariadne (Ich grüße dich)		B flat
1b. Bacchus (Du schönes Wesen)		B flat
1c. Ariadne (Ich weiß nicht, was du redest)		g
1d. Bacchus (Wie kennst du mich denn?)		g–b
2. *The Transformation*		
Ariadne (Nein, nein)		g
Bacchus (Wer bin ich denn?)		b
Ariadne (Du bist der Herr)		b
Bacchus (Ich bin der Herr)		g

unexceptionable as do their indications of primary tonalities. Once again musical detail which is readily available elsewhere will not be dwelt on here. Instead, an interpretation will be made in the light of our previous concerns.

The nymphs' opening trio *Ein schönes Wunder* was discussed in Chapter II as being an account of Bacchus' individual history, necessary for the sake of the psychological symmetry of the plot.[62] The criticism, best expressed by R. Borchardt, that this narrative exposition is both clumsy and retarding so late in the piece, was something of which Strauss was already aware for his setting of the text is extremely rapid and dramatic. The tempo marking is 'Sehr schnell M♩=138'. Further to avoid dramatic longueurs Strauss let Najade, Dryade and Echo sing in a tone of almost irrepressible excitement and in this instance he was faithfully obeying Hofmannsthal's directions. The mood of excitement is created by the fanfare-like motif (x) on the trumpet, quivering tremolos on the violins (y), and a vocal line reflecting the fanfare. The opening of the trio is given in Ex. 19. The theme sounding in the bass here is meant to suggest Bacchus' attractive personality and culminates in another fanfare-like flourish (Ex. 20). The fanfare is generally associated with Bacchus. The sense of scurry and buoyancy of this section is later highlighted by the surging harp arpeggios beginning at No. 189.

	Ariadne (Nimm mich hinüber)	?
	Bacchus (So willst du mit mir gehen auf mein Schiff?)	?
	Ariadne (Ich bin bereit)	D flat–f
	Bacchus (Sprach ich von einem Trank?)	?
	Ariadne (Ich weiß, so ist es dort)	A flat–D flat
	Bacchus (Bin ich ein Gott)	A–D flat
	Ariadne (Das waren Zauberworte)	c sharp–E
	Bacchus (Ich sage dir)	b
	Ariadne (Lag nicht die Welt auf meiner Brust?)	E flat–F
	Ariadne (Gibt es kein Hinüber)	C–?
	Bacchus (Du, alles du)	A
3a.	Bacchus (Höhle deiner Schmerzen)	D flat
3b.	Ariadne + Trio (Töne, töne)	D flat
3c.	Zerbinetta (Kommt der neue Gott gegangen)	D flat
3d.	Ariadne, Bacchus Duet	D flat
3e.	Bacchus (Durch deiner Schmerzen bin ich reich)	D flat
3f.	Orchestral coda	D flat

[62] See Chapter II, pp. 81–2.

Ex. 19

But amidst all this excitement the words, and with them the precious symmetry needed for an allomatic transformation, are almost lost. Perhaps for this reason the trio strikes the listener as a sudden, sensational outburst. But the momentum of the scene is not held up.

Ex. 20

In Chapter I it was noted that such emotional display as is evident in this trio is alien to the nymphs' natures. They are supposed to represent 'die lächelnde Gleichgiltigkeit der Natur gegen menschliches Leid'.[63] In their first trio, *Wie der Blätter leichtes Schaukeln*, they do represent this. But not only is the second trio out of character: it also contributes to the confusion surrounding Bacchus. This trio is, in effect, a triumphant heralding of the conqueror. Bacchus' success in love is anticipated in a transparent way and an image of him is instantly built up. This image corresponds to the first of the two Bacchus figures discussed in Chapter II, that is, to the strong romantic hero of the *Szenarium* and not the later dreamy adolescent.

[63] Appendix A, Note 5.

Bacchus, when his voice is first heard, conforms to the image the nymphs have created. He takes up the fanfare motif with a vengeance. His melody is built almost entirely around the fifth and its inversion, the fourth, which is the most basic interval of the fanfare or heraldic call. The rhythm ♩♩ | ♩· is the same as in the preceding trio. The orchestration, with its emphasis on the brass, but still with harps and violin tremolos, continues to convey exalted excitement and triumph. The opening of Bacchus' song is given here and the square brackets indicate phrases built around the fourth or fifth (Ex. 21).

Ex. 21

Strauss's Bacchus is strongly reminiscent of the Wagnerian 'Heldentenor', a type he professed not to like.[64] The other Wagnerian touch is the deliberate quotation of the 'Zaubertrank' leitmotif from *Tristan und Isolde* to illustrate Circe's magic potion.[65]

It requires a great leap of the aural imagination to understand how Strauss could ever have prefaced the first strophe of this heroic song with the words 'jung, zauberhaft, träumerisch' (at No. 215). The second strophe which continues

[64] George Marek is most critical of Bacchus: 'Unfortunately the opera begins to go to pieces with the arrival of Bacchus. From here to the end we are in German Olympus, and a noisy one too. Strauss turns Wagnerian, and that fatal *Tristan* chord makes its appearance. The young god turns out to be a *Heldentenor*. The upwelling at the end, Ariadne's and Bacchus's apotheosis, is meant to be mystically soaring, but lands flat footed in bombast.' Marek, p. 225.

[65] See Daviau and Buelow, p. 204.

at No. 224 in the same tempo, key and mood, except that the tenor, now approaching the top of his tessitura with a high 'a', is sounding even more ecstatic, has an equally inappropriate marking; 'schwermütig, lieblich'. The third strophe, which is 'schneller als die erste Strophe' and continues in the same vein, is marked 'fröhlicher mit etwas graziösem Spott'. These markings were of course Hofmannsthal's own. It is obvious that Strauss took the atmosphere from the *Szenarium* from which he had drawn up the plan of set numbers rather than from the libretto. In the *Szenarium* the scene is conceived of as a continuous ('fortlaufend') movement which builds up to a climax at the end. Strauss outlined this simple structural dynamic in his letter of 22 May 1911:

f) Das Finale (geschlossen und fortlaufend) beginnt mit der Meldung der Najade. (Ein hymnenartiges Marschthema, dazu Duett: Ariadne, Zerbinetta, steigert sich und schließt mit dem Eintritt des Bacchus ab.)
Liebesduett.
Schlußensemble. (Bw. 22 May 1911, p. 102.)

(f) Finale (unbroken and continuous), beginning with the Naiad's warning. (A hymn-like march theme, add the duet of Ariadne and Zerbinetta, rising towards a climax and concluding with Bacchus' entry.)
Love duet.
Final ensemble.)

The hymn-like march theme was replaced by the fanfare theme and the duet between Ariadne and Zerbinetta was cut from the 1912 *Ariadne*.[66] Otherwise Strauss retains the principles of continuity and crescendo and subordinates the parts to these principles.

The nymphs' two strophe song *Töne töne süße Stimme* is used by Strauss both to punctuate the verses of Bacchus' Circe song and also to provide contrast within this continuous fabric. The song is sung partly in unison and partly in close and simple harmony and is first heard at No. 221. Del Mar writes: 'Strauss was perfectly well aware that this charming little melody comes straight from Schubert (from the *Wiegenlied* 'Schlafe, schlafe'), much as the little duet for Sophie and

---

[66] See Del Mar, pp. 48–50, for a full musical description of the dressing scene.

Octavian at the end of *Der Rosenkavalier* which it recalls.'[67] In fact the reference was probably unconscious; Strauss refers only to the first five notes of the Schubert melody so that the trio cannot be regarded as a full quotation. It is rather a generalized stylistic imitation, made probably because for Strauss nature, and creatures of nature such as the nymphs, were associated with the music of Schubert.[68] Others have approved of the trio on the grounds that it provides a tranquil interlude as well as binding the scenes together.[69] However, these refrains can also seem like layers of over-sweet, artificial cream in an already rich cake. There is furthermore a mildly ridiculous discrepancy between their description of Bacchus' song and the reality. The words of the almost identical strophes are as follows:

Najade, Dryade, Echo
(leise, zaghaft)
Töne, töne, süße Stimme,
Fremder Vogel, singe wieder,
Deine Klagen, sie beleben,
Uns entzücken solche Lieder! (59)

Najade, Dryade, Echo
(nachdem die Stimme zu verstummen scheint, leise)
Töne, töne, süße Stimme,
Süße Stimme töne wieder!
Deine Klagen, sie beleben!
Uns entzücken deine Lieder! (59)

(Najade, Dryade, Echo
(softly, timidly)
Sing, sing, sweet voice,
Strange bird, sing again,
Your laments, they enliven,
Such songs delight us!

Najade, Dryade, Echo
(after the voice seems to fade, softly)
Sing, sing, sweet voice,

[67] Del Mar, note 29, p. 48.

[68] I am indebted to Derrick Puffett for drawing my attention to these points about the Schubert song.

[69] For example, 'The nymphs' chorus is both an aural oasis and a musical *point d'appui* in this through-composed finale.' Patrick J. Smith, *The Tenth Muse*, p. 241.

Sweet voice sing again!
Your laments, they enliven!
Such songs delight us!)

Chapter II showed how Hofmannsthal made use of the
primitive device of the off-stage voice releasing emotions in
those on stage. That device was seen as an instance of the
relatively elementary structure and characterization of the
original sketch. Just as it was appropriate for the chorus to be
'jubelnd' when Bacchus' arrival was announced so was it
appropriate that his seductive voice should provoke all those
enraptured, enthusiastic responses. But Bacchus' voice in the
Circe song is neither seductive nor sweet and it seems far-
fetched to react to him as to some exotic song bird. The
nymphs' response is inappropriate. Furthermore the trio
might be objected to on the grounds that the contrast it
provides is too strong, thus exposing Bacchus' forced exaltation
particularly at the second change-over at No. 224 where there
is a sudden, ugly transition from D flat major to A major.
Bacchus becomes a ridiculous, wooden figure.

Ex. 22

After the nymphs' second strophe there follows Ariadne's *Belade nicht zu üppig* (A major and b minor). At No. 274 the dressing scene between Ariadne and Zerbinetta was cut and instead the music moves straight into Bacchus' arrival (Ex. 22). This passage is heavily orchestrated to convey a sense of shattering chaos. Percussion instruments are used for the first time. Timpani, tambourine, snare drum, and glockenspiel add exotic colour and bring out the syncopated rhythms of the first part of Bacchus' theme which is booming all through this passage. Against Bacchus' theme parallel fourths in shifting, mysterious tonalities portray Bacchus' incessant footsteps.

This passage, with its syncopations, percussion, and tonal chaos, bears a very close resemblance to Klytämnestra's entrance in *Elektra*. One can almost hear Klytämnestra's whips being cracked and see her decadent retinue staggering after her. It also resembles the Recognition Scene in *Elektra*, particularly when the music subsides after Ariadne's cry, 'Theseus', into a lyrical passage of peaceful beauty at No. 278. Del Mar calls it a 'Little Recognition Scene' and rightly mentions the paradox of Ariadne's disconcerting *lack* of recognition.[70]

Taken as a whole, the passage may strike the listener as slightly sensational. Bacchus' arrival cannot equal Orestes' return home in dramatic intensity and impact. Possibly Strauss was calling on stock-in-trade for the setting of a part of the libretto which did not directly inspire him.

However, it may well have been that Strauss's interpretation of Bacchus' arrival as a primitive Dionysian irruption onto the stage was encouraged in part by the *Szenarium* and the first of the Bacchus images. Particularly the line 'Triumphierendes Heranschreiten (nun in der Musik)' (Sz. 291) must have determined Strauss's first musings. But the phrase 'Triumphierendes Heranschreiten' can only be associated with the first Bacchus, and it is disconcerting to find after this primitive irruption Bacchus 'zartest im Ton' naïvely enquiring if Ariadne is 'die Göttin dieser Insel'. Bacchus continues 'schüchtern, im Tiefsten verwirrt durch das Abenteuer mit Circe, das erste in seinem Leben'[71] but Strauss's attempts at

---

[70] Del Mar, p. 50.
[71] These words appear in the score at No. 282, but not in LIII.

portraying the shy, inexperienced youth seem altogether lame in the section from No. 282 to No. 284.

The actual transformation begins at No. 289 with Ariadne's *Nein, nein* and extends to No. 320 with Bacchus' *Du alles du.* This section makes extensive use of opposing key centres for Ariadne and Bacchus as a means of portraying their lack of understanding of each other.[72] (We recall that Ariadne persists in her belief that Bacchus is Hermes until the end.) Strauss is wise enough to let the music settle into one key for the finale (D flat major again), thus securing Ariadne's happiness in the music at least.

W. Mann, whilst acknowledging the effectiveness of the device, feels that the music is uninspired: 'The final duet of Bacchus and Ariadne is a lengthy failure; their mutual misunderstanding is effectively conveyed by bitonality (D flat and A major, for the most part, but more generally the contrast of a flat and a sharp key) ... but there are signs that Strauss was not working at full inspirational stretch here.'[73] This duet (by this W. Mann means the transformation scene) is certainly lengthy, taking up approximately twenty minutes of an opera that is not quite one and a half hours long. The 'misunderstanding', lasting for ten of those twenty minutes, is tediously protracted.

If the music is uninspired this may well have been because Hofmannsthal's libretto did not set Strauss's imagination on fire. The relatively poor quality of the poetry has already been mentioned.[74] There is also a lack of lively dramatic climax such as Strauss understood it, and it must be remembered that Strauss had fairly traditional views of what comprised an operatic climax. On 14 July 1911 Strauss wrote: 'Nur die Aussprache zwischen Ariadne und Bacchus hätte ich mir noch bedeutender gewünscht, mit lebhafterer innerer Steigerung. Das muß noch mehr in die Höhe gehen, wie der Schluß der *Elektra*, sonniger, dionysischer.' (Bw. 14 July 1911, p. 113.) (Only I should have preferred the dialogue between Ariadne and Bacchus to be rather more significant, with livelier

---

[72] Daviau and Buelow, p. 212. See also Chapter III, Note 89.

[73] Mann, p. 116. Strictly speaking, the term 'bitonality' should not be used as it means the *simultaneous* sounding of different keys. Ariadne and Bacchus sing consecutively in different keys.

[74] See Chapter II, pp. 94–5.

emotional *crescendo*. This bit must soar higher, like the end of *Elektra*, sunnier, more Dionysian.) In his letter of mid-July 1911 Hofmannsthal agreed in principle to climax-building although he stated that the manner and degree of it should still be settled.[75] After the explanations of the mid-July letter and after another look at the now typed manuscript, Strauss wrote that he had got a much better impression of the whole but added that he still needed a bigger *crescendo* for the conclusion (Bw. 19 July 1911, p. 116). As Hofmannsthal did not rewrite the conclusion Strauss could arrive at his *crescendo* only by musical means. But without real dramatic substance as a base it inevitably became what M. Kennedy describes as a 'conventionally rhetorical ending'.[76] P. Heyworth calls it an 'inflated and rhetorical finale'.[77]

An example of this empty rhetoric is Bacchus' *Du alles du* (No. 318 − 4 bars to No. 322). Before discussing this passage in more detail we should mention that the word 'Wagnerizing' used by both A. Einstein[78] and G. Marek[79] in conjunction with this passage is not meant to imply direct imitation of Wagner's style, for as W. Schuh points out Strauss does not transform the leitmotif as Wagner does and Strauss by the time he wrote *Der Rosenkavalier* had individualized the orchestral voices to a far greater degree than Wagner ever did; it implies that Strauss was indulging in those abuses, usually to do with size in all respects, which Wagner is commonly held to have initiated.[80] For that reason 'pseudo-Wagnerian' was preferred as a term here.

[75] Hofmannsthal replied: 'Eine Steigerung des Schlusses in der von Ihnen angedeuteten Weise wird sich gewiß finden lassen.' Later, he added, they could settle 'das Wieviel und Wie einer solchen Steigerung'. Bw. mid-July 1911, p. 115.

[76] Michael Kennedy, *Richard Strauss*, p. 159.

[77] Peter Heyworth, *Observer*, 20 Dec. 1976, p. 22.

[78] Einstein asks 'Ist man sich darüber im klaren, daß Strauss die tiefe Lehre dieser 'singenden Blume' (wie Hofmannsthal sie auffaßte) mißverstand, daß er sie ihres wahren Inhalts beraubte, sie wagnerisierte und mit Ornamenten überdeckte?' Albert Einstein, 'Strauss und Hofmannsthal', p. 133.

[79] Marek, p. 225.

[80] Willi Schuh, replying to Mayer's accusation that Strauss uses a 'Wagnerorchester' in *Der Rosenkavalier*, says: 'Zwischen dem Wagnerorchester und dem "Rosenkavalier"-Orchester liegt das "Salome"-Orchester, in welchem die Individualisierung der Orchesterstimmen, die schon in der "Feuersnot" zu beobachten ist, voll ausgebildet wurde.' He goes on to explain that Strauss, unlike Wagner, does not transform his motifs. Willi Schuh, *Hugo von Hofmannsthal und Richard Strauss: Legende und Wirklichkeit*, p. 12.

The opening bars up to No. 320 are sung over Ariadne's
theme which Del Mar says expresses her relief at having shed
her sufferings and which is closely related to Elektra's great
lyric theme.[81] Bacchus' vocal line is vulgarly heroic and
vaunting. His self-realization after being transformed by
Ariadne's love amounts to the unsubtle triumph of a young
Siegfried (Ex. 23). The passage continues in this manner until

Ex. 23

a canopy sinks over his head. Another similar passage runs
from No. 299 to No. 305 with Bacchus' *Bin ich ein Gott* and is
marked 'etwas feierlich gemessen'. Bacchus is 'tief erregt,
unbewußt feierlich'. The main problem with the passage is
that it attempts to be solemn and measured and deteriorates
into the static. The accompanying figure of a triplet followed
by a dotted minim ♪♪♪ ♩. is a variant of the nymphs' trio
theme and refers to Bacchus' upbringing and his divinity.[82] It
is used throughout the section yet in itself the material is too

[81] Del Mar, p. 53.
[82] Del Mar, p. 45.

slight to be so extended. The tinkling orchestration, celeste, harps, and violin tremolo do not help to sustain the bass. The sequential use of a fragment of the motif indicating Bacchus' immunity to Circe's charms at No. 301 likewise sounds thin and repetitive. Against this static, thin, and tinsel background Bacchus is straining in his upper register to sound dignified and deeply serious. The discrepancy between the sustained and forced elation of the upper line and the insubstantial bass reaches a peak in the final eight bars (Ex. 24).

Ex. 24

The musical climax of the whole third scene is the final brief duet in D flat major (No. 328 to No. 330) and Bacchus' solo *Durch deine Schmerzen bin ich reich*. Although the duet is too lushly orchestrated it is redeemed by Ariadne's melody, originally in E major, which expresses her relief at seeing the end of her sufferings.[83] This broad, sweeping, almost instrumental melody has marked similarities with Elektra's great reconciliatory theme.[84] Del Mar notes that in the 1912 version this section 'resolves on to a mighty orchestral tutti in which no less than three of Bacchus' themes ... are played simultaneously and also combine with the stately Hermes theme.'[85] The 1916 version was provided at this point with an

[83] Ariadne's theme is in E major and is based on a triplet rhythm in both voice and orchestra. The clearest statement of the theme is from No. 306 to No. 307.
[84] Elektra's theme is first heard at Bar 221 and is likewise based on a triplet rhythm.
[85] Del Mar, p. 45.

equally heavily orchestrated coda. Here Strauss is using his chamber orchestra of thirty-six players at full stretch. Tremoli, massive block chords, and heavy reliance on the keyboard instruments including the piano which had previously been restricted to the *opera buffa* sections assure Strauss of a volume and texture equal to that of the full symphony orchestra. Gräwe aptly comments: 'Längst wurde das Kammerorchester nicht mehr als solches behandelt, längst mußten die akkord-mächtigen Tasteninstrumente ergänzen, was dem Ariad-neorchester zum Zarathustraorchester fehlte. Die Begleitung zu Bacchus' Abgesang aber demonstriert nichts anderes, als daß die Hypertrophie der Sinfonischen Dichtungen mit den reduzierten Mitteln des Ariadneorchesters ebensogut zu bewerkstelligen ist.'[86] (The chamber orchestra has long since ceased to be treated as such, long since have the keyboard instruments, with their full chords, had to supply what the Ariadne orchestra lacked to make it a Zarathustra orchestra. The accompaniment to Bacchus' final solo demonstrates merely that the hypertrophy of the symphonic poems can be accomplished just as well with the reduced means of the Ariadne orchestra.)

Strauss achieved the Wagnerian operatic climax that he desired for this work from the outset. In the following excerpt from his *Betrachtungen und Erinnerungen* Strauss admits this desire and adds that he was not unduly restricted by his chamber orchestra:

Auch das Operchen ging flott von statten, bis zum Auftritt des Bacchus, wo ich fürchtete, daß für meine dionysischen Gelüste das kleine Kammerorchester nicht ausreichen würde. Ich teilte Hof-mannsthal meine Besorgnisse mit und frug ihn, ob ich von da ab nicht zum 'großen Orchester', allenfalls hinter der Bühne, übergehen könne. Allerdings ein recht blöder Gedanke! Hofmannsthal be-schwor mich, davon abzusehen, unter dem wohltätigen Zwang ist trotzdem die zweite Hälfte charakteristisch genug ausgefallen.[87]

(The little opera also went without a hitch until Bacchus' entry, where I feared that the little chamber orchestra would not satisfy my dionysian appetites. I told Hofmannsthal of my concern and asked him if I couldn't go over to the 'full orchestra', at all events backstage.

[86] Gräwe, p. 279.
[87] Richard Strauss, *Betrachtungen und Erinnerungen*, p. 195.

Granted it was a very stupid idea! Hofmannsthal begged me to give it up and under this salutary restraint the second half turned out characteristically enough in any case.)

But it is not enough to push all the blame for the ending of *Ariadne* on to Strauss as Gräwe does by calling it 'dieser massive Nachhall spätromantischer Götteropern'[88] (this massive echo of a late Romantic opera about the gods). First we must remember that Strauss was very much in the orbit of the nineteenth century and that his interpretation of a Bacchus was likely to be as 'dionysian' as Wagner's, Nietzsche's, or later Thomas Mann's. Strauss had one foot firmly in this tradition. To persuade him to give a different musical interpretation of Bacchus Hofmannsthal needed to present him with a much more unified and persuasive alternative than the eclectic double Bacchus who appears in this opera.

Second, and more fundamentally, this ending, heavily Romantic, too richly orchestrated, and protracted beyond the limits of its originality, is but a reflection in Strauss's own terms of a pattern already present in Hofmannsthal. Just as Hofmannsthal had to move from the historicizing and impersonal *Szenarium* to the personal statements of the 'lyric drama', so Strauss moved from a deliberately archaic musical style to full-blown Wagnerizing. Strauss later viewed this, as we have seen, as an image of progress, progress from prose to the heights of pure music,[89] and reveals again his traditionalism in this aesthetic equivalent of the nineteenth-century Ideal of Progress. In this he was reflecting or rather interpreting *one*, but only one, of Hofmannsthal's own explanations of *Ariadne*, which he presented as a progression from the prosaic and incidentally amusing to the spiritual.[90] Rudolf Borchardt who during this period had a remarkable intuitive sympathy with all Hofmannsthal wrote and who can be regarded often as an extension of Hofmannsthal's own voice also saw *Ariadne* in terms of progress: 'Ich habe das geistreiche Werk, das in so unvergleichlicher Weise vor den Augen des Zuschauers,

[88] Gräwe, p. 297.
[89] See Chapter II, p. 106.
[90] For example, Hofmannsthal wrote 'der Schluß [führt] aus dem Spielerischen immer mehr ins Seelenhafte [hinauf].' Bw. 5 July 1911, p. 112. See also Bw. 18 Dec. 1911, p. 129.

durch die Aktion seiner Handelnden, das zarteste und schönste
Seelengebild aus einer Absurdität herausholt, das mit dem
ganzen Zauber der übermutigen Skizze vom Abgeschmackten
ins Mysterium fortwandelt, mit dem größten Glücke genos-
sen.'[91] (I enjoyed with extreme pleasure your inventive work,
which through the action of the characters turns an absurdity
into the most delicate and beautiful spiritual thing in such an
incomparable way in front of the spectator's eyes; your work,
which with all the magic of your audacious sketch progresses
from the vulgar to the miraculous.)

Certainly the pressure of time and the instalment method of
working combined to make it appear as if *Ariadne* was a
deliberate paradigm of progress and it is more than understandable that Strauss should have brought his own nineteenth-
century aesthetic notions to bear on it.[92] Nevertheless it must
be said against Strauss that if he had had a clearer and more
tenacious grasp of the original idea he might have dissuaded
Hofmannsthal from straying so widely from it or, better still,
have insisted on major revision to accommodate Hofmannsthal's new leanings in the work. As it is, there is in
Ariadne a distinct pattern of smaller, older forms giving way
to larger ones. These more archaic forms are restricted to the
incidental music for *Der Bürger als Edelmann* and the overture
to the *Oper*. The overture is quite remote in style from the
finale. Oddly, this 'stylistic progression' from archaizing
miniatures through pastiche to a Romanticism which doesn't
quite succeed in parodying itself has not been remarked upon
in previous critical studies.

v. *The Incidental Music to 'Der Bürger als Edelmann' and the
Overture*

The nature of the original *Ariadne* scheme was such that
Strauss could begin sketching the incidental music almost as
soon as Hofmannsthal had settled on the Molière play. On 15
May 1911 Hofmannsthal wrote recommending the Bierling
translation and told Strauss he would find it in Cotta's
Bibliothek der Weltliteratur, Molière, Volume 3, *Der adelige
Bürger*. In the same letter he briefly outlined how he proposed

---

[91] Hugo von Hofmannsthal / Rudolf Borchardt, *Briefwechsel*, p. 68.
[92] See Richard Strauss, *Betrachtungen und Erinnerungen*, p. 197.

to concentrate the five acts into two, omitting, of course, the Turkish Ceremony (Bw. 15 May 1911, p. 99).

Strauss offered one or two suggestions in his reply and agreed for the most part with the plans. Shortly after 20 May 1911 he received a rough sketch of the two-act adaptation. The correspondence during the next week was taken up entirely with discussions of the *Szenarium* which Hofmannsthal had posted off on 19 May 1911; but a postscript to Strauss's letter of 27 May 1911 contains the information: 'Ich hoffe, "Ariadne" fix und fertig bis 1. Juli zu haben. Ouvertüre und erste Tänze und manches andere ist schon skizziert.' (Bw. 27 May 1911, p. 106.) (I hope to have *Ariadne* all ready by 1st July. Overture and first dances and quite a bit besides already sketched out.) It is important to note that this music was sketched out whilst Strauss must surely have had in mind the small-scale historicizing ambience of the *Szenarium*. Indeed the music itself is proof of this. We do not know which dances Strauss sketched first although on 1 June 1911 Strauss wrote that he had done 'die Tänze der Schneider etc.' As all this music is homogeneous in style, this is, however, of little importance; it bears the stamp of the *Szenarium*.

The form in which this incidental music is most often heard is the orchestral suite, *Der Bürger als Edelmann* (op. 60), first presented by Strauss in Salzburg on 31 January 1920. The suite, which is an expanded version of the original music, was written to save the latter from extinction after the Molière play had been severed from the *Oper* in 1916. Although it is more developed and sophisticated it remains a good example of Strauss's best quality pastiche and of his spiced neo-classicism. A most adequate discussion of the suite is given in an article by Alfred Rosenzweig entitled 'Les adaptions de Lulli et de Couperin par Richard Strauss'.

Del Mar gives a full account of the version of the incidental music we are concerned with.[93] Although this first version, unlike the suite, did not use Lully's incidental music which had been performed at the original production of *Le Bourgeois Gentilhomme* at Chambord on 14 October 1670 and then in the following month in Paris,[94] it is nevertheless in the classical

[93] Del Mar, pp. 11–24.
[94] Alfred Rosenzweig, 'Les adaptations de Lulli et de Couperin par Richard Strauss', p. 34.

manner. The use of small string ensemble and continuo as well as numerous compositional devices such as imitation and *solfeggi,* four- and eight-bar phrases, simple melodies and harmonies occasionally embellished with unusual harmonic twists, all give a distinctive archaic flavour to this music which is yet also sincere and delightful. It is an example of what Borchardt aptly terms 'genuines Archaisieren'[95] and corresponds entirely to the original plan of the imaginative recreation of a divertissement. Here the first bars of the overture are given. Del Mar rightly draws attention to the falling flattened seventh (x) as an example of an unexpected melodic twist (Ex. 25). Each of the incidental numbers is short

Ex. 25

and witty. Strauss used older forms such as the minuet, the gavotte, and the polonaise, and treated them as miniatures, for amongst other things he did not want to retard the action of a Molière play he already felt to be undramatic.[96] H. Mayer comments correctly that Strauss wrote music 'die—durchaus im Sinne der Tradition—das Zeremoniell erhöhte, ohne das eigentliche Schauspiel nennenswert zu stören'[97] (which—in a thoroughly traditional manner—heightened the ceremonial without disrupting the actual play to any extent worth mentioning). Strauss evidently found composing it a diverting task, for he wrote in his memoirs 'die Komposition der Schauspielmusik machte mir viel Spaß und wurde wie fast alles, was ich so unbesorgt mit der 'linken Hand' hinschrieb, so gut, daß sie später als kleine Orchestersuite ein recht erfolgreiches Weiterleben führte'.[98] (Composing the music for

---

[95] Hugo von Hofmannsthal, / Rudolf Borchardt, *Briefwechsel*, p. 56.

[96] For example, Bw. 20 May 1911, p. 101: '"Gentilhomme" gelesen . . . die zweite Hälfte ist mager, und meine ich, [*sic*] Sie müßten da noch manches hinzudichten, was die Handlung besser abrundet und zuspitzt.'

[97] Mayer, p. 21.

[98] Richard Strauss, *Betrachtungen und Erinnerungen*, p. 195.

the play was great fun and like almost everything that I dashed off it was so good that it later led a most successful independent existence as an orchestral suite.)

The style of the incidental music was carried over into the overture to the *Oper* which Strauss had sketched as early as 1 June 1911. This was before Hofmannsthal had even sent off the first instalment of the libretto and obviously before Strauss could begin to understand the theme of transformation and the other subtleties of the text. In a letter of 10 June 1911 Strauss again mentions the overture and asks whether Hofmannsthal agrees to having one. Hofmannsthal replied on 15 June 1911 that he did agree but sensibly suggested that Strauss might leave the writing of this until the very end; Hofmannsthal seems, however, to have forgotten that Strauss had already sketched it and he did not pursue the matter as he ought to have.

Strauss's earliest ideas for the overture[99] have been preserved in the hand-written marginal note on the *Szenarium*. But this note was not passed on to Hofmannsthal in the letter of 22 May 1911 containing the list of set numbers. It reads as follows:

> a = c
> Einleitung melancholisch G moll, dann
> b leidenschaftlich / Tränen pizzicati /
> Bratsche Meereswogen. (Sz. 287.)

> (a = c
> Introduction melancholy G minor, then
> b passionately / pizzicati tears /
> viola waves.)

Strauss kept quite closely to the note. The overture is in G minor. The opening bars portray the desolate, melancholy mood of the abandoned Ariadne sitting alone on Naxos (Ex. 26). The dotted rhythm suggests Ariadne's sobbing and perhaps was substituted for the pizzicati tears. The melancholy is further conveyed by the extremely sparse orchestration. The entire overture is treated with great restraint in this respect as

---

[99] Del Mar prefers to call it a 'Prelude' but there is no reason for not using Strauss's own 'overture'—in any case a more Baroque term. Del Mar, p. 28.

Ex. 26

is fitting for a chamber orchestra. In the first seventeen bars Strauss seems to underline the idiom he has chosen by using only a string sextet and three other instruments (bassoon, clarinet, and flute) in moderation. The closely controlled chordal texture, full of harmonic and melodic dissonances such as seconds and sevenths, the absence of bass support (the cello plays in its upper range and the double bass has only one note) all suggest plaintive emotions. At the same time this rather stylized portrayal of grief could have been directly inspired by the Baroque doctrine of the affections and Strauss is thus historicizing here as Hofmannsthal was in the *Szenarium*. This first section in G minor moves into a contrasting middle section in E flat major based on material that is later used in Ariadne's aria *Ein schönes war*.[100] This middle section suggests the warmer, happier days of Ariadne's and Theseus' love and the orchestral colours become more glowing. French horn and solo cello, harmonium and woodwind, all contribute to this.

At No. 6 Strauss takes up material which had appeared as an answer to the opening eight-bar subject. In its minor form the dotted rhythm was thrown into relief particularly by the falling parallel fourths (No. 1). In the major version octaves are used in preference to the fourths, lending the melody a more joyful turn, but the fourths reappear as the music modulates back to G minor in preparation for the final section (Ex. 27). The final section, which is in the home key and thus secures for the overture a traditional tripartite form, is a direct realization of the words 'Bratsche Meereswogen'. Here is a miniature piece of marvellous tone painting such as the Baroque period adored. In the manner of that age in which

---

[100] Daviau and Buelow have mistaken the order of composition of the overture and the aria: 'Strauss lifted this entire middle section almost note for note from that portion of Ariadne's first aria beginning *Ein Schönes war*.' In fact it was the other way round. *Ein Schönes war*, composed later, was taken from the overture. Daviau and Buelow, p. 168.

Ex. 27

natural events correspond with an *Affekt*, the violence of the
waves is also a sudden violent manifestation of Ariadne's
grief. This section is characterized by an upsurging wave-like
motif on the cellos and the bassoons which gives way to a
pounding, driving rhythmic development of the same motif.
The wave motif Daviau and Buelow maintain comes from
Ariadne's aria *Ich will vergessen*[101] but as it is unmistakably
'Meereswogen' the aria material must surely have been taken
from the overture and not vice versa. This would confirm the
suspicion that Strauss composed the overture in an unorthodox
and reverse order. No music critics have commented at all on
the significance of Strauss's little note. The wave motif is
given in Ex. 28.

Ex. 28

The climax of this passage is reached at No. 10 as G minor
reappears after the music has gone through a number of
chromatic progressions which possibly evolved out of the
chromaticism of the wave motif itself. Parallel fourths are
again used as the music subsides from No. 10 onwards. Here
the section No. 9 to No. 10 is given in Ex. 29. Octaves are used
to give a broader, more emphatic sound. The curtain rises as

[101] Daviau and Buelow, p. 169.

Ex. 29

a flowing, undulating clarinet passage plays around the G minor chord. The nymphs recapitulate the opening theme of the overture and the arpeggio-like runs continue in the bass. The mood is again the restrained, sorrowful pathos of the opening with the chamber idiom strictly upheld.

With this overture Strauss has written a period piece. It is pastiche in the same vein as the incidental music to *Der Bürger als Edelmann* and is also an aural extension of it. In its economy of form and expression it leads the listener to expect a chamber opera at most and at least a musical divertissement. It is a work of delightful and ingenious historicizing but its aesthetic and intellectual horizons are not wide and certainly the listener is not told that he is being presented with more than an amusing (if 'serious') trifle.

vi. *The Nymphs' Dialogue and Trio*

The same musical idiom is sustained in the opening number of the *Oper* which is made up of the nymphs' dialogue and then their trio *Ach wir sind es eingewöhnet. Wie der Wellen sanftes Gaukeln*. On the typescript of the libretto Hofmannsthal had written the following note: 'Die letzten drei Zeilen ad libitum zu wiederholen: durch eine reizende, gaukelnde Stimmführung die lächelnde Gleichgiltigkeit der Natur gegen menschliches Leid ausdrückend. Etwas von Blätterschaukeln, Wellengaukeln schon in der Overtüre.'[102] (The three last lines to be repeated ad libitum: through a charming, swaying part-writing for voices expressing the smiling indifference of nature

---

[102] Appendix A, Note 5.

to human suffering. Something of the swaying of leaves, the undulation of waves already in the overture.)

There was no suggestion of the rustling of leaves or the rippling of waves in the overture but very probably this inspired the accompaniment to the nymphs' recitative which serves as a transitional passage between the overture and the first operatic number, their trio (Ex. 30). There is a much more

Ex. 30

obvious depiction of 'Blätterschaukeln' and 'Wellengaukeln' in the weaving vocal lines of the trio. The long melismas, the uninterrupted babbling of the music turning into pure vocalization from No. 21 to No. 23 and the warm key of G major combine to give an impression of 'lächelnde Gleichgil-tigkeit' so unlike the enthusiasm of *Ein schönes Wunder*. The trio is lightly scored for woodwind and strings. In Ex. 31 a part of their free vocalization is given:

Ex. 31

The trio concludes with a restatement of the opening motif of the overture at No. 24 in the original key of G minor. A sparse chordal accompaniment on viola and harmonium leads into Ariadne's recitative *Ach wo war ich*.

The chamber idiom and the idea of set numbers are retained more or less throughout this large section although this is more evident at the beginning than the end. The Baroque atmosphere is however soon lost and it is fair to say that historical authenticity is not preserved by Strauss beyond the nymphs' trio.

vii. *The Lack of Sustained Idiom in the 'Oper'*

The section of Ariadne's aria *Ein schönes war* is derived from overture material as mentioned above and not surprisingly the opening idiom is best sustained in it. At No. 33 there is a passage for string sextet alone and throughout the aria the accompaniment repeats the opening material with little variation. A good example is the use of dotted rhythm at No. 36. The 'Meereswogen' motif and the pounding rhythm are also used to good effect from No. 40 to No. 46 to express Ariadne's sudden agitation as she tries to find another identity for herself now Theseus is gone. It could also be suggested that the ostinato bass at No. 50−4 bars and at No. 53 is an imitation of a Baroque device.

Otherwise Ariadne's aria becomes more lush and more elaborate as the various sections follow one another with Harlekin's song sandwiched in between, leading to the melodic highlight of the whole number *Du wirst mich befreien* at No. 70 (Ex. 32). This is a beautiful, soaring melody but it must be noticed that it is pure Strauss and could be taken from the music of any of his noble and passionate heroines.

Ex. 32

Strauss's departure from ironic pastiche was prompted in part by instructions received from Hofmannsthal. The first problem was that this *opera seria* character was to be 'ganz *wirklich*, so wirklich wie die Feldmarschallin' (Bw. 19 May 1911, p. 100), and it was difficult for Strauss to try and fit emotional realism into a historicizing divertissement. He could perhaps have done it by giving another imaginative account of a Baroque *Affekt*, but the libretto itself was a problem, being first too long and second full of psychological nuance such as her obscure 'Nicht noch einmal', which required elucidation from Hofmannsthal (Bw. 15 June 1911, p. 111), and heavy symbolism such as occurs in the section *Es gibt ein Reich*. The profound significance of the psychological nuances and the meaning of the Ariadne–Bacchus relationship had been hammered home to Strauss in the letter of 28 May 1911 dispatched in advance of the libretto (sent off in early June); other such didactic letters must have been arriving as Strauss composed Ariadne's number. Indeed there was little left for Strauss to do in the face of these conflicting instructions except to decide to be himself, within limits, and to aim for a general heroic mood. This is in fact what he did.

Zerbinetta's coloratura aria, for all its brilliance both as pastiche and characterization, must also be judged historically inauthentic as indeed must the *Oper* from the nymphs' trio onwards. Bel canto belongs after all to the eighteenth century and it is anachronistic to connect it with Molière. As we have mentioned, there is a self-conscious element to Zerbinetta's aria which suggests that Strauss was moved in part by a desire for formal play with art for its own sake. Nor should we overlook the parodist in Strauss which was always a very strong element in him from the early symphonic poems through to *Capriccio*. It seems, then, that although Strauss could see the need for historicizing pastiche at first, he lost sight of it when Hofmannsthal did. That Strauss had given up the 'alte historisch gewordene Formen' and thus upset the proportions of *Ariadne* was the gist of one of Hofmannsthal's most perceptive criticisms of the opera made in 1920:

Ich habe die Ariadne sehr lieb, es ist doch ein Wesen besonderer Art. Sie hätte leicht viel schöner werden können, wenn ich mehr Verständnis für die besonderen Bedingungen der Modernen Musik— meine Fantasie verweilt immer bei den alten, historisch gewordenen Formen—oder wenn Strauss mehr Voraussicht und Einsicht in das Ganze eines Kunstwerkes besäße. Manches war berechnet, spiel-uhrhaft vorbeizuklingen, und nun da es große, wenn auch nicht laute Musikstücke geworden sind, hat der Text nicht den Gehalt und die Tragkraft, es ist wie wenn man ein Vogelhaus mit seinen dünnen Stäbchen und Drahtzierarten zu den Dimensionen eines von Menschen bewohnten Lusthauses vergrößerte, das ist nicht schön. Es hätte der Musiker voraussehen müssen, daß er ein großes Menschenlusthaus daraus zu machen nicht umhin können würde— dann hätte man das Project, den Bauplan ändern müssen, und alles wäre schöner geworden. Immerhin ist es ja so, daß man es wohl liebgewinnen kann.[103]

(I am very fond of Ariadne; it is an entity of a special sort. It could have become much more beautiful if I had better understood the special requirements of modern music—my imagination always remains with the old, historical forms—or if Strauss had had more foresight and insight into the totality of a work of art. Much was calculated to sound like a musical clock and now that the pieces have become large, if not loud, the text does not have the content or the strength to support a load; it is as if one enlarged a birdcage with its thin bars and wire ornaments to the dimensions of a pleasure house inhabited by human beings: that is not beautiful. The musician should have foreseen that he could not make a human pleasure house just like that—then one would have had to alter the project, the plan of construction, and everything would have grown more beautiful. Nevertheless, it is still something that one can become fond of.)

Of course Hofmannsthal sees it from his own point of view and lays far too much of the blame at Strauss's door. But the basic analysis is right and *both* parties were guilty of the same mistakes.

In this section it has emerged that the opera *Ariadne auf Naxos* was complicated during its genesis by bad collaboration on both sides. Because of the lack of an initial over-all plan two centres of gravity, one represented by Zerbinetta and one by Ariadne, make the work more static than it might otherwise have been. The character of Bacchus also exhibits signs of some curious mutations. The ending of the *Oper* both in its 1912 and 1916 versions was found to be less than satisfactory, with the reprise of Zerbinetta's rondo adding to, rather than subtracting from, the Romantic vision of the lovers' closing scene. Finally, structural and other remnants of the original allegory were found to show through in the later version of the drama without being properly incorporated. In short *Ariadne*

---

[103] Quoted in Rudolf Hirsch, 'Auf dem Weg zu "Ariadne": Aus neugefundenen Briefen mitgeteilt', *Neue Zürcher Zeitung*, 15 Nov. 1970, p. 49.

auf Naxos lacks artistic unity. It is difficult to synthesize critically, and its much-praised ambiguity[104] is often only a result of the accretions of meaning and intention that went into its genesis. Had various outward circumstances of the collaboration not been present such as the 'contract' and an exacting third partner the authors might have got down to a grass-roots assessment of the work at some time during the genesis. This, and this alone, could have corrected the work's basic weaknesses.

[104] One of the earliest critics to praise the irony was Bernhard Diebold, 'Die ironische "Ariadne" und der "Bürger als Edelmann"'. See also Könneker, p. 126, p. 128 and p. 131, and Fiedler, p. 136. A full discussion of irony follows in Chapter IV.

Chapter IV

Critical Interpretations and the Decision
to Revise

i. *Interpretation*

The genesis of *Ariadne,* which we have analysed in all its
complexity, is reflected in the interpretative difficulties
associated with this work. The most serious of these difficulties
spring from a tendency to speak about the 1912 and 1916
versions as if they were one opera. These difficulties have been
aggravated by the number of Hofmannsthal's own interpretative comments in the correspondence with Strauss.

The crucial question in any interpretation of *Ariadne* and
the one which often proves the stumbling-block in critical
argument is why is there this mixture of *opera seria* and *opera
buffa,* of seemingly unrelated *tragédie lyrique* and *commedia
dell'arte,* in the *Oper?*

In Chapter I historical authenticity was given as the most
likely explanation. It was proposed that the 1912 combination
of play plus opera was originally constructed as a Molière
adaptation, with the appended *Zwischenspiel* and especially
the *Oper* as historical recreations of a Molièresque prologue
and divertissement respectively, in which continuity of style,
idiom, and ambiance were paramount. The proximity of *opera
buffa* and *opera seria* thus receives historical legitimation. It is
a light-hearted cultural joke.[1] The wider, symbolic significance
which was overlaid on this scheme when Hofmannsthal
wished to diverge into a 'lyric drama' was not thematically
incompatible with the original ironic allegory, but, as was
seen, entailed a sacrifice of formal unity.

The historical, divertissement origins of the *Oper* have not
always been recognized.[2] Hans Mayer is one of the few to do

---

[1] See Bw. 26 Dec. 1911, p. 135.
[2] Fiedler gives the best account of the divertissement origins of *Ariadne,* however,
as we have already remarked, he is mainly concerned with historical documentation

so: 'Die Oper war dann eigentlich bloß als Finale und Divertissement gedacht.[3] (The opera was intended in fact merely as a finale and divertissement.) This does not prevent Mayer, however, from being side-tracked into the issue of the simultaneous versus the successive appearance of the *opera seria* and *opera buffa*. He begins, rightly, by seeing *Ariadne* as a new stage in the Strauss–Hofmannsthal collaboration but makes some odd deductions about the genesis of the text:

Die neue Etappe heißt *Ariadne auf Naxos*. Scheinbar abermals eine Griechenoper von Richard Strauss, dennoch vergleichslos gegenüber allem, was Strauss vorher geschaffen hatte. Hofmannsthal übernahm die Führung. Er wollte erreichen, daß nun nicht mehr, wie beim *Rosenkavalier,* die scharf vom Librettisten umrissenen Eigentümlichkeiten der geistigen und sprachlichen Bereiche durch lyrische Symphonik fortgewaschen wurde. Bei der Wiener Komödie war der Dichter daran gescheitert, daß die ständisch und sprachlich voneinander gesonderten Figuren gleichzeitig *miteinander* auf der Szene agieren mußten, wobei es dem Komponisten weder gelang noch wichtig schien, abgesehen von leitmotivischen Themen, dieses Gegeneinander in der Gleichzeitigkeit musikalisch auszudrücken. In der Ariadne-Oper stellte daher Hofmannsthal die Welten der Heroine und der Zerbinetta auf das Prinzip des Nebeneinander und Nacheinander. Es durfte niemals zu einem wirklichen Gespräch zwischen Ariadne und Zerbinetta kommen. Die Führerin des Buffo-Quintetts durfte zwar die Tragödiengestalt anreden, bekam aber keine Antwort. So konnte auch im musikalischen Ausdruck die scharfe Eigenart der Sphären gewahrt bleiben.[4]

(The new stage is called *Ariadne auf Naxos*. To all appearances another opera based on Greek mythology by Richard Strauss, yet beyond comparison with everything that Strauss had previously done. Hofmannsthal took the lead. He wanted to make sure that this time the characteristic ideas and language so sharply outlined by the librettist would not be washed away by lyrical symphonic writing. In the Viennese comedy the poet came to grief because the characters, separated from each other by class and language, had to act on stage *together*. The composer neither managed nor did it seem important to him to express in music this opposition within simultaneity, except by leitmotivic themes. In the Ariadne opera Hofmannsthal

and with Hofmannsthal's relation to Molière and so does not follow through his findings into the region of literary criticism.

[3] Mayer, p. 21.
[4] Mayer, p. 20.

therefore based the worlds of the heroine and Zerbinetta on the principle of proximity and succession. Never should it come to a real conversation between Ariadne and Zerbinetta. The leader of the buffo quintet might address the tragic figure, it is true, but she received no reply. So in the music as well the distinct nature of the spheres could be preserved.)

This is an original account, but Mayer's evaluation of musical differentiation in *Der Rosenkavalier* is in itself dubious,[5] and the claim concerning the separation of the two spheres is incorrect: in the scene between Ariadne and Zerbinetta in the 1912 version there is quite a lengthy exchange, just as the two groups intermingle in the 1912 dance finale. Mayer's underlying observation, that the two spheres in *Ariadne* are musically distinct, is however quite valid.

W. Mann suspects historical precedent in the choice of *opera buffa* and *opera seria* and makes an educated, but incorrect, guess:

I would not be surprised if *Ariadne* was inspired by Hofmannsthal's ponderings on the balance of serious and comic, formal and uninhibited elements in *Don Giovanni* and perhaps *Figaro,* then on the two art forms, *opera seria* and *opera buffa,* that are married in heaven by these great works, and thence as a bland confrontation of both elements as a technical experiment.[6]

Gräwe, in an otherwise excellent study, entirely misses the point of historical authenticity: 'Hofmannsthal bringt ungeachtet ihrer stilistischen und geschichtlichen Zugehörigkeit Molière, Commedia dell'arte, barocke Affektenoper und sich selbst auf die Bühne.'[7] (Hofmannsthal brings onto the stage, regardless of whether they belong together stylistically and historically, Molière, commedia dell'arte, baroque opera and himself.) Further on Gräwe elaborates:

Im Jahre 1912 endlich standen Ariadne und die wüste Insel im Zentrum der Dichtung und der Bühne. Die Anwesenheit der drei Naturwesen Najade, Dryade, Echo und die Ankunft des Gottes Bacchus waren mythologisch legitimiert; die Interventionen der

barocken Commedia-Figuren dagegen erschienen als vernunftwid-
rige, anachronistische Mutwilligkeiten, die störten. Vollends die
Einbettung der Oper in eine Molière-Komödie war ein kompliziertes,
scheinbar hergeholtes, unsinniges und willkürliches Verfahren.[8]

(In 1912 at last Ariadne and the desert island were in the centre of
the libretto and the stage. The presence of the three nymphs Najade,
Dryade and Echo and the arrival of the god Bacchus was
mythologically legitimate; the intervention of the baroque commedia
figures, on the other hand, seemed to be an unreasonable,
anachronistic mischievousness that distracted the audience. To have
embedded the opera in a Molière comedy was altogether a
complicated, apparently far-fetched, unreasonable and arbitrary
procedure.)

This contradicts the findings presented in Chapter I.

The same misapprehension leads both Gräwe and Stiegele
into giving interesting but superfluous accounts of the
commedia dell'arte revival which took place in the early
twentieth century, beginning in Russia but spreading throughout Europe.[9] This renaissance of interest in the *commedia* can
be seen as part of a larger anti-naturalist, anti-symbolist
theatrical movement, initiated by such famous figures as
Stanislavski, Meyerhold,[10] and Tairov[11] who in 1913 founded
a Moscow studio for teaching *commedia dell'arte* techniques,
and influencing such various works as Stravinsky's *Petrushka*
(1911), Vollmöller's translation of Gozzi's *Turandot* produced
by Max Reinhardt in 1911 (which Hofmannsthal knew),
Schönberg's *Pierrot Lunaire* (1912), Arthur Schnitzler's pan-
tomime *Der Schleier der Pierrette,* which Meyerhold staged in
Petersburg in the winter of 1910/11, Busoni's operas *Arlecchino*
and *Turandot,* both written in 1917, and of course Puccini's
Turandot, based on Gozzi which was premièred in 1926.

This renaissance, although doubtless part of Hofmannsthal's

[8] Gräwe, p. 35.
[9] Gräwe, pp. 39–42; Stiegele, pp. 5–7.
[10] Meyerhold the producer, like Brecht after him, would not permit his audience to
sink back into theatrical illusion. That theatre is only theatre, that theatre is
entertainment, not real life, was his credo. Vsevold Meyerhold, *Le théâtre théatral*
(Paris, 1963).
[11] See Alexander Tairov, *Das entfesselte Theater,* Collection Theater (Cologne,
1964).

general cultural milieu, has little bearing on the inclusion of the *commedia dell'arte* in *Ariadne*.[12]

Leaving aside historical legitimation or, rather, going beyond it, we may formulate several symbolic interpretations of the mixture of *opera seria* and *buffa,* not least convincing of which is that favoured by R. Specht: 'man könnte die beiden ineinander geschobenen Spiele ebenso gut als das Symbol unsrer eigenen hohen und skurrilen Stunden auffassen, die einander ablösen und durchdringen.'[13] (One could just as well take the two interlocking actions as the symbol of our own elevated and ribald hours, which follow and permeate one another.) Daviau and Buelow give a metaphysical slant to what we have so far viewed only in terms of ironic equipoise:

The diverse styles—the lofty emotions of the *opera seria* and the grotesque buffoonery of the *commedia dell'arte*—oppose and at the same time supplement each other in a logical and consistent manner. As a result the opera embodies in its very structure the union of opposites, the *coincidentia oppositorum,* which in Hofmannsthal's opinion constituted the fundamental unity of the world.[14]

K. J. Krüger[15] likewise bases his interpretation on the *coincidentia oppositorum,* which is certainly one of the mystic concepts running through Hofmannsthal's work.[16]

The critical interpretations so far have not been extraordinary or untenable, but we now come to deal with a group of related interpretations which may at first seem extraordinary in the light of what has been established in the genetic analysis. This new interpretation suggests that in *Ariadne,*

[12] For Max Reinhardt's relationship to the *commedia dell'arte* revival, which, ironically, he came to through, 'Ariadne auf Naxos', see *Max Reinhardt und die Welt der Commedia dell'arte: Text- und Bilddokumentation,* edited by Edda Leisler and Gisela Prossnitz.

[13] Richard Specht, *Richard Strauss und sein Werk,* Volume II, p. 276.

[14] Daviau and Buelow, p. 130.

[15] 'Daß die unsinnige Laune eines Idioten das gleichzeitige Abspielen der seria und buffa veranlaßt, bringt gerade erst Sinn in das Ganze! Denn dadurch erst wird die kosmische Einheit all dessen, was Leben heißt, nicht als Konstruktion eines Literatengehirns, sondern als Erfüllung des über dem Leben thronenden Gesetzes erwiesen! "Das alles ist geheim, so viel geheim," Es ist gewissermaßen eine *coincidentia oppositorum!*', Krüger, p. 137.

[16] For example, 'Die einzige Gleichheit, die vor dem tiefer eindringenden Blick besteht, ist die Gleichheit des Gegensätzlichen', *Buch der Freunde,* Auf., p. 36. Also, from the poem 'Ein Traum von großer Magie' the line 'Ihm war nichts nah und fern, nichts klein und groß', GuLD, p. 22.

particularly in the *Oper* with its mixture of *opera buffa* and *seria*, there is evidence of a kind of novel montage technique, a compositional technique in which various contrasting styles, genres, or worlds are arbitrarily juxtaposed in order that the author, by a passive synthesis of these heterogeneous elements, may arrive at a fresher, more arresting insight or artistic statement than is possible with traditional homogeneous stylistic methods.

The synthesis occurs without the author's active intervention in the irony of these juxtapositions, and hence it seems fair to term the whole technique 'formal irony'. It is suggested amongst other things, then, that those two groups, the *opera seria* and *buffa*, whose co-existence we were so much concerned to ground historically, are being deliberately contrasted as part of a formal technique—a step beyond seeing them symbolically in a union of opposites.

Formal irony, which excuses the author from direct personal statement, is a technique corresponding closely to a procedure best formulated by the New Critics. The following is a definition of irony as they understood it. In it 'styles' can be read as 'points of view':

In the first half of the twentieth century the word 'irony' was again used (after Schlegel) of literature which, for various reasons, juxtaposes without comment opposite or merely different points of view. The object of this ironic procedure might be to achieve a balanced all-round view, to express one's awareness of the complexity of life or the relativity of values, to express a larger and richer meaning than would be possible with direct statement, to avoid being over-simple or over-dogmatic.[17]

So far we have suggested irony only at the thematic level in *Ariadne*, which this new view does not dispute. In the above quotation irony is being put forward at an all-pervasive formal level and becomes a compositional principle. The first person to interpret *Ariadne* in this way was Hofmannsthal himself in a letter to Strauss dated 18.XII.(1911):

Es ist diese 'Oper' mit ihrer raffinierten Stilmischung, ihrem unterm Spiel versteckten tiefen Sinn, ihrer Einrahmung in den Molière,

---

[17] D. C. Muecke, *Irony*, The Critical Idiom, 13, edited by John D. Jump (London, 1970), p. 24.

welche wieder als symbolisch gedacht ist (Jourdain—das Publikum),
eines der allerheikelsten Gebilde, der allerinkommensurabelsten. Es
ist eine meiner persönlichsten und mir wertesten Arbeiten; als ein
aus Teilen komponiertes Ganzes gedacht, kann sie nur dort
existieren, nur dort zur Entstehung kommen, wo ein höheres
theatralisches Genie Teile zum Ganzen zu formen imstande ist.
(Bw. 18 Dec. 1911, p. 129.)[18]

(This 'opera', with its subtle stylistic make-up, with its profound
meaning hidden beneath the playful action, framed as it is by the
Molière piece, a fact itself symbolic in intention (for Jourdain stands
for the public), is a conception of the most fragile, the most
uncommensurable kind. It is one of my most personal works and one
I cherish most highly. It is conceived as a whole composed of several
parts, and can only exist, or come into being, where a theatrical
genius of a superior order knows how to weld the parts together.)

Gräwe likewise detects signs of formal irony: 'In "Ariadne"
... wird die Willkür, die "Unmöglichkeit" der Konfrontation
zweier a priori disparater Welten geradezu Stilprinzip.'[19] (In
'Ariadne' ... arbitrariness, the 'impossibility' of the confrontation of two a priori disparate worlds almost becomes a
stylistic principle.) And the most illustrious of all critics to
write on this opera, A. Einstein, is of the same opinion;
Strauss, he is arguing, failed to understand the deeper meaning
of transformation:

Der Grund lag darin, daß der Dichter, der sich langsam und schwer
beladen rückwärts wandte, alles in einem Spiegel darstellte, in einem
barock umrahmten Spiegel, in einem fast unvorstellbaren Stilge-
misch, das es möglich machte, auch das Ernsteste, Tiefste und
Erlesenste offen zu sagen, und daß das Stück in dem Komponisten
die besten Kräfte ausrief ... Ist man sich darüber im klaren, daß er
die tiefe Lehre dieser 'singenden Blume' (wie Hofmannsthal sie
auffaßte) mißverstand, daß er sie ihres wahren Inhalts beraubte, sie
wagnerisierte und mit Ornamenten überdeckte?[20]

(The reason was that the poet, who, slowly and heavily laden, turned

---

[18] This ties in well with one of Hofmannsthal's most famous statements about
himself as a librettist: 'Meine Qualität als Librettist [ist] vielleicht nicht schwer zu
definieren ... -, daß ich es auf Kontraste, und über den Kontrasten auf Harmonie das
Ganze anzulegen weiß'. Qualities of a general artistic order, as Hofmannsthal
acknowledges. Bw. 15 June 1911, p. 111.

[19] Gräwe, p. 102.

[20] Albert Einstein, 'Strauss und Hofmannsthal', p. 133.

to look behind him, presented everything in a mirror, in a baroque-framed mirror, in an almost inconceivable mixture of styles, which made it possible to say even the most serious, profound, and elevated things openly; it was also that the piece called forth the composer's best abilities ... Are we fully aware that he misunderstood the profound message of that 'singing flower' (as Hofmannsthal conceived it), that he robbed it of its true content, Wagnerized it, and covered it over with ornaments?)

Einstein takes the *Ariadne* message very seriously and is correct in saying that it has been 'Wagnerized', but the gist of his analysis, which concerns us here, is that this message is given obliquely through the medium of an elaborate montage.

B. Könneker is the critic who gives the most extended interpretation of *Ariadne* in the light of formal irony. Her argument is that the essential quality of the libretto is not its 'meaning', which can be reduced to the theme of transformation, but its subtle mixture of styles which makes our traditional values relative while creating a new balance in a mutual reflection and interpenetration of opposites:

Dieses Eigentliche und Wichtige aber ist zweifellos die durch die Verknüpfung von entgegengesetzten Form- und Stilelementen bewirkte Vertauschbarkeit der Sphären und Ebenen, die Verflüchtigung der Wertgrenzen und die Aufhebung eindeutig festlegbarer Sinnbezüge, ist das gegenseitige Sichspiegeln von Scherz und Ernst, Tiefsinn und Frivolität im Zusammen- und Widerspiel der Figuren.[21]

(This essential and important quality is, however, doubtless the exchangeability of the spheres and levels effected by the connection of opposed formal and stylistic elements, the vanishing of absolute values and the removal of unequivocally fixed referential frames; it is the mutual reflection of jest and seriousness, profundity and frivolity in the interplay and counterplay of the figures.)

In line with the New Critics, Könneker sees irony and the ironic procedure as equal to the task of expressing the complex truths of our age.[22] Symbol and symbolic meaning are replaced

[21] Könneker, p. 129.
[22] 'Wahrheit aber ... ist in heutiger Zeit etwas so Komplexes geworden, daß sie sich in der Kunst nicht mehr in direktem Zugriff, mittels des unterscheidenden und wertenden Begriffs oder des sinnträchtigen Symbols erfassen läßt.' Könneker, p. 138.

by an evocative theatrical montage of language, gesture, figures and styles:

Als Dichtung aber will die *Ariadne* im Grunde nicht mehr befragt werden auf ihren konkret formulierbaren und begrifflich zu fixierenden 'Sinn', der sich ummünzen ließe in Lebenshilfe oder Lebensrezept, sondern ist umgekehrt ein—sich spielerisch gebender—Versuch, die Kompliziertheit der modernen Welt, die sich solcherart Sinnfragen gerade entzieht, einzufangen und in Sprache, Gestik und Konstellation der Figuren widerzuspiegeln. Dabei wird diese Kompliziertheit weder direkt formuliert noch programmatisch verkündet, sondern ist, hinter mythischem Tiefsinn und frivolem Getändel verborgen, identisch mit dem Konstruktionsprinzip der Handlung selbst, wird sichtbar allein in jener raffinierten, weil scheinbar absichtslosen Verknüpfung heterogener Elemente, Stile und Ebenen, die die Unmöglichkeit, ja Hinfälligkeit eindeutiger Aussagen ebenso leichthin wie eindringlich dokumentiert.[23]

(As poetry *Ariadne* fundamentally refuses to be questioned about its concretely formulatable and conceptually fixable 'meaning', meaning which can be recoined as tips or formulae for better living. It is on the contrary an—apparently playful—attempt to reflect in language, gesture and the constellation of the figures the complexity of the modern world, which evades precisely these questions. Nevertheless, this complexity is neither formulated directly nor proclaimed programmatically; hidden behind mythical profundity and frivolous trifling, it is identical with the principle of construction of the action itself. It becomes visible only in that sophisticated—because apparently unintentional—connection of heterogeneous elements, styles and levels which reveals casually and yet forcibly how impossible, indeed how futile, it is to make unequivocal statements.)

Two reservations may be expressed about Könneker's interpretation without damning the idea of montage technique. First, despite all juxtaposing and contrasting, the emotional apotheosis at the end of the *Oper,* particularly in the 1916 version, tends to cancel the effects of those elements, either formal or thematic, which would otherwise show up as relative the noble principle or its utterance, and to endorse various absolute values ('Wertgrenzen') and referential frames ('Sinnbezüge'), which together may be summarized as romantic idealism. This is the fundamental weakness of *Ariadne* upon

23 Könneker, pp. 140–1.

which most criticism lights, although phrasing its insights quite differently. It is not true, then, that we should not enquire into the 'meaning' of *Ariadne;* thus the state of ironic suspension and balance which is the goal of this montage can be only imperfectly realized. Second, it is not true that Hofmannsthal abstains from using traditional symbols or evaluative concepts to arrive at his meaning, as Könneker suggests elsewhere.[24] *Ariadne* is full of symbols, from the 'wüste Insel', which is Ariadne's loneliness, to the action itself, which may be symbolically understood. Hermann Broch rightly speaks of the 'Charakter- und Handlungssymbol' in *Ariadne* and of the 'dichtes Allegoriengewebe, dem es obliegt, die Handlung zu tragen, um eben hierdurch von ihr erklärt zu werden',[25] (close allegorical texture, which must bear the action in order to be explained by that action).

Yet there is much to recommend Könneker's view. If there are reservations, it may well be because this is an instance of the interpretation reflecting the genesis. Here the symbolic 'lyric drama', a problematic stratum in *Ariadne,* is clearly intruding. But how are we to reconcile formal irony in general with the genetic interpretation of *Ariadne,* which establishes it as a stylistically homogeneous, historical rather than artificial or eclectic, formally traditional recreation, with secondary lyric attributes?

The answer emerges, I suggest, if we distinguish clearly between the 1912 and 1916 *Ariadnes* and hence between the two different frames, or, better, contexts, for the *Oper,* that section of the work round which all interpretation revolves. The answer, in brief, is that the 1912 *Ariadne* is primarily a straight literary adaptation of a Molière *comédie-ballet* with an original transitional scene and divertissement. The play, taking up three-fifths of the evening, is therefore the major enterprise, and must determine the audience's impression of the remaining evening's entertainment. The *Zwischenspiel* is in every way contrived to preserve stylistic continuity, and we

[24] Könneker states sweepingly that since the *Chandos Brief* Hofmannsthal no longer believed in the power of the symbol. Whilst the *Ariadne* libretto is clearly more symbolic in some parts than in others Könneker is treading on unsafe ground when she claims 'Nichts hatte [Hofmannsthal] hier tatsächlich ferner gelegen, als ein symbolträchtiges Kunstwerk zu schaffen'. Könneker, p. 129.

[25] Broch, p. 233.

arrive at the *Oper* thoroughly transported into the world of Louis XIV and French Baroque, and this world will not be shattered by anachronism. We cannot therefore view the *Oper, Ariadne auf Naxos,* as other than an attempted historical recreation, albeit one treating a timeless theme which attracted the librettist personally. To claim a novel montage technique for the 1912 version is to claim, then, that the whole of the two act *Bürger als Edelmann* is just one of many heterogeneous stylistic elements, and this seems far-fetched; the play, both by its duration and by its methods, establishes itself as an unquestioned dramatic reality and not as an ironically selected world with which the audience should not fully identify itself. Through the authenticity of the Molière adaptation we see the *Oper* in historical, not eclectic, terms. The way the *Oper* is seen is therefore determined by its, in this case, historical context. But in the 1916 version the *Vorspiel* does not force the audience to see the *Oper* in a primarily historical light. This is because, although authentic in much of the detail one might expect to find in a backstage scene in Maria Theresian Vienna, it is a sometimes piquantly anachronistic dish. Furthermore its loose structure as a prologue merely leading up to the *Oper,* although preparing for the latter and reflecting it in a hundred clever ways, including the brief affair between the Composer and Zerbinetta, does not imply the following work as an historical form in the way that the *comédie-ballet* implies the divertissement. The *Vorspiel* is a less specifically historical and less 'individual' work (indeed, apart from the *commedia,* the characters do not have names). The *Oper* in the 1916 version, although not freestanding, can be more easily separated in the imagination from its context, and hence becomes amenable to interpretations in terms of montage or formal irony. *Opera seria* and *opera buffa* are then dead styles, used artificially and eclectically in deliberate formal play. Furthermore the very obvious, sometimes even stereotyped, realism of the *Vorspiel,* which expands into the warm emotional realism of the Composer-Zerbinetta passage, throws the *Oper* into relief as art and artifice and suggests that here formal irony is being used to illustrate a theme already prefigured on a realistic level. The *Vorspiel* is thus itself in a contrastive style and contributes to the whole montage. This the contiguous *Bürger als Edelmann* clearly could not do.

Hofmannsthal's interpretation of *Ariadne* in terms of montage or 'raffinierte Stilmischung' was made on 11 December 1911, six months after he had completed the first libretto, at a time when he was having doubts about the experimental combination of play and opera, and was looking at the *Oper* as a separate entity to see how he could save it. His interpretation was made *ex post facto* about a work he was already revising in his head. It is certainly wrong to present formal irony either as an intention or as an interpretation of the 1912 *Ariadne,* as Hofmannsthal does in this *post hoc* analysis, but it is an indication of something there *in potentia* and which Hofmannsthal was probably developing in his creative unconscious. Thus, when *Ariadne* received its disappointing première at the *Königliches Hoftheater, Kleines Haus,* in Stuttgart on 25 October 1912, Hofmannsthal was not caught entirely unprepared and in the short space of two months had advanced a plan for revision, which, predictably, entailed severing the *Oper* from the 'Bourgeois' and which placed it in a context that used its potential as montage. Hofmannsthal should receive all praise for recognizing and developing the possibilities of his material; experimenting and continuous reshaping are the hallmarks of creativity and we are the richer for it by having two works in place of one.

However, others approaching this work from outside, and with more critical detachment than Hofmannsthal, should keep the two versions distinctly apart in their minds and not use the montage interpretation indiscriminately in blanket references to both. Here we see how an interpretative difficulty reflects the genesis, for the genesis was not the logical fruition of a single idea but a story of continual shifts and realignments, which results in *Ariadne* interpretations being also ultimately historical.

ii. *Revision*

There is no doubt that Hofmannsthal was most influenced in his decision to revise by the hostile reception given to *Ariadne.* Whether he was right in reacting to circumstances and

criticism as violently as he did we shall shortly consider.[26]
Whatever the case, any secret doubts he may have had before
1912 became corrosive after that date, and the next four years
find him struggling to carry his point. Strauss, ironically now
quite converted to the work, did not want to make changes.

Once again external factors had a hand in the genesis.
Problems began in Stuttgart, which was not a good place to
have chosen for the première. A prevailing provincialism
caused resentment at the *Kleines Haus* against the famous
outsiders, Reinhardt and his ensemble, who put local talent in
the shade. In his autobiography Ernst Stern tells of the lengths
to which the Stuttgart company went in their efforts to hinder
the production.[27] Not least humorous amongst them is the
anecdote about the Director of the Hoftheater, who objected
to Stern's palm trees for the island of Naxos because they were
painted pink. Had it not occurred to Stern that they might
want to use the palm trees in other plays? (The truth was that
the Director had had his eyes on them for a forthcoming
production of *A Midsummer Night's Dream*.) Furthermore on
the night of the première Lortzing's *Undine* was being
performed in the *Großes Haus* in Stuttgart, and the regular
back-stage crew of the *Kleines Haus* was suddenly required to
go there and help out. As a result the performance was
technically less professional than usual. We are told that the
première was in any case badly rehearsed.[28] That last-minute
rush, the one aspect of Reinhardt's methods Strauss detested,
was not avoided after all.[29] On this occasion Reinhardt was
not successful in timing the different parts to coalesce at the
eleventh hour: his own ensemble was well prepared for the
Molière and was led by an impressive line-up of stars including
Victor Arnold and Rosa Bertens as M. and Mme Jourdain[30]
but the *Oper* was less thoroughly rehearsed, although the cast

---

[26] Daviau and Buelow in their Chapter "'A Curse on all Revision'", pp. 70–86,
present as usual a great number of facts and quotations but once again their lack of
a thesis prevents them from properly assessing their material. It is not clear, for
example, whether they consider revision necessary or in what critical regard they hold
the 1912 version.

[27] Ernst Stern, *Bühnenbildner bei Max Reinhardt*, pp. 99–101.

[28] Gräwe, p. 53.

[29] See Bw. 19 Apr. 1912, p. 149.

[30] See Appendix C.

included such famous singers as Maria Jeritza as Ariadne and Margarete Siems as Zerbinetta. There was thus a noticeable difference in the quality of the two parts of the evening's entertainment.

Although *Ariadne* had received a lot of publicity in the press[31] and although the pre-publication of the libretto in the *Neue Freie Presse* in May 1912 as well as the publication of the essay 'Ce que nous avons voulu en écrivant "Ariane à Naxos"'[32] and the *Ariadne Brief* had secured the libretto a measure of understanding, the evening, in spite of enormous expense and lavishness,[33] was a failure. Strauss gives two reasons for this: first that the audience was impatient to hear the new Strauss–Hofmannsthal opera and so found the Molière boring, and second that they were made even more impatient by the protracted *cercle* held by the King of Württemberg. Strauss was less disturbed than Hofmannsthal by the initial critical reception and considered that, apart from these two points, the evening went smoothly:

Der Abend selbst verlief normal! Aber zwei Dinge waren nicht bedacht worden. 1. daß das Publikum auf die 'Straussoper' so gespannt war, daß es dem prächtigen (von Reinhardts Schauspielern, besonders dem genialen Arnold, herrlich gespielten) Molière nicht das nötige Interesse entgegenbrachte, 2. daß der liebenswürdige König Karl von Württemberg nach Molière in bester Absicht einen $\frac{3}{4}$ stündigen Cercle abhielt, der die $1\frac{1}{2}$ stündige 'Ariadne' etwa $2\frac{1}{2}$

---

[31] See Gräwe, pp. 56–61 and Daviau and Buelow, pp. 60–5.

[32] See Chapter I, Note 20.

[33] The Berlin newspaper *Welt am Montag* savagely attacked the forthcoming *Ariadne* for its extravagance and exclusiveness, and for the high price of the tickets: 'Hier Ariadne auf Naxos, Neuestes vom Neuesten, noch nie dagewesen, alles echt, Musik, Libretto und Billettpapier, und der Platz kostet nur 50 Mk. Eine Bagatelle für das, was geboten wird. Da können sich Metropoltheater und Komödienhaus verstecken. Also immer ran, meine Herrschaften . . . Und was wird geboten? 0—man strahlt vor Stolz: viel Geld, viel Geld! Hier, sehen Sie mal: das ist der Stoff zum Mantel der Primadonna, nach alten Mustern eigens für dies Stück in schwerem Damast gewebt. Die Kostüme der Diener in Weiß und Erdbeer sind beinahe so schön wie die der Kellner aus dem grillroom "Rosenkavalier" (nächstneueste création in Berlin-Schöneberg), und Monsieur Jourdains Schlafrock ist dem des großen Louis XV. stilgerecht nachgebildet! Aber das ist alles noch nichts. In den drei Festvorstellungen werden vom Orchester alte italienische Streichinstrumente gespielt, deren Gesamtwert 300 000 Mark beträgt . . . Na, was sagen Sie nun? Darunter eine Stradivari für 40 000, eine Guarneri für 30 000 und eine Amati für 25 000 Mark. Und der ganze übrige Zimt macht trotz der hohen Eintrittspreise auch noch ein paar Hunderttausend Mark Unkosten' *Welt am Montag*, 29 Sept. 1912, p. 7.

Stunden nach Theateranfang beginnen ließ, vor einem bereits etwas
verstimmten und ermüdeten Publikum. Der Erfolg war trotzdem
gut, obschon es sich herausstellte, daß der Abend im ganzen zu lang
war.[34]

(The evening itself went according to plan! But two things had not
been taken into consideration. 1. that the public would be so eager
for the 'Strauss opera' that it would not be sufficiently interested in
the splendid Molière (wonderfully acted by Reinhardt's actors,
especially the brilliant Arnold) and 2. that dear King Karl of
Württemberg with the best of intentions held a $\frac{3}{4}$ hour long reception
after the Molière, which meant that the $1\frac{1}{2}$ hour long 'Ariadne'
began about $2\frac{1}{2}$ hours after the curtain first went up before an already
somewhat peevish and weary public. It was a good success all the
same, even though it turned out that the evening as a whole was too
long.)

A final factor which Strauss considered had prejudiced
Ariadne's chances was the inexplicable last-minute cut made
in the *Zwischenspiel*—the spoken scene which 'explained' the
Oper. It is not certain who was responsible for this cut, but it
was probably Reinhardt. How Hofmannsthal could have
agreed to this tampering with his work is incomprehensible.

Those reviewing the opera generally praised Strauss's music
as being his best and most original to date, a judgement some
still make today.[35] But the mixture of *opera seria* and *opera
buffa* estranged many critics, and Sonne, of the *Leipziger
Illustrierte Zeitung,* is representative of them: 'Die enge
Verschmelzung einer seriösen Handlung . . . mit dem boshaf-
ten Spiel einer derbwitzigen Gauklerbande wirkt in der
unzureichend motivierten Sprunghaftigkeit ermüdend. Hier

---

[34] Richard Strauss, *Betrachtungen und Erinnerungen,* pp. 196–7. Walter Panofsky
also mentions the King of Württemberg's unfortunate reception: 'Zu allem Malheur
fiel as dem König von Württemberg, Wilhelm II., ein, in der Pause vor *Ariadne*
ausgedehnt Cercle zu halten. Ermüdet, als hätte es den ersten Akt der Götterdäm-
merung zweimal hintereinander erlebt, ließ das Publikum nach dem *Bürger als
Edelmann* nun auch noch die Oper *Ariadne* über sich ergehen. Da halfen alle
Regiekünste Reinhardts nichts, da konnte der dirigierende Komponist alle Schön-
heiten seiner Musik enthüllen: am Premierabend schon ist klar, daß die Schlacht
verloren wurde.' Walter Panofsky, *Richard Strauss: Partitur eines Lebens* p. 183.

[35] Strauss himself was enamoured of his *Ariadne* music: 'Die gestrigen ersten
Orchesterproben von *Ariadne* abends von 7–9 Uhr waren mir die große Genugtuung,
Es klingt prachtvoll, schöner als alles, was ich bisher gemacht habe. Ein ganz neuer
Stil und neue Klangwolken.' Richard Strauss, *Eine Welt in Briefen,* p. 199.

nun tritt Richard Strauss als Sieger und Retter auf den Plan.[36] (The close fusion of a serious action ... with the mischievous play of a group of coarse buffoons is tiring because of its insufficiently motivated jerkiness. Richard Strauss now steps up as victor and rescuer.) The connection between the Molière and the *Oper* was generally considered to be slight and at best the work was accepted as a 'Kulturkuriosum'.[37]

Hofmannsthal felt badly misunderstood and continued to defend *Ariadne,* but in a letter of 9 December 1912 he refers favourably to a suggestion of Strauss's made in conversation concerning the casting of the *Zwischenspiel:* 'Bin recht froh über unser Gespräch neulich, Ihren glücklichen Einfall mit den Secco-Rezitativen (werde zu diesem Zweck die kleine Szene umarbeiten, alle Anspielungen, die auf den Molière zurückdeuten, ausmerzen).' (Bw. 9 Dec. 1912, p. 175.) (I was very glad of our talk the other day, and about your happy idea concerning the *secco* recitatives (in view of this I shall recast that brief scene and cut out all allusions which refer back to the Molière).) On 9 January 1913 Hofmannsthal outlined the action of the *Vorspiel* for Strauss. It was to take place behind the *Ariadne* stage in a hall of a nameless Maecenas' house in which dressing-rooms have been improvised. The Maecenas does not appear but has a servant transmit his bizarre commands. The focal point is to be the young Composer 'als Verliebter, Genarrter, als Gast, Kind, Sieger und Besiegter in der irdischen Welt' (Bw. 9 Jan. 1913, p 180). The whole *Vorspiel* will run for about thirty minutes.[38] Strauss expressed no interest whatever in the scheme; he did not so much as mention it until six months later. On 3 June 1913 Hofmannsthal, still fulminating about ignorant newspaper critics and upset by bad performances in a number of German cities including Munich, informed Strauss that the only solution to the *Ariadne* problem, namely the *Vorspiel,* was sitting on his desk and that he was just typing it up. He added 'Mir wälzen Sie einen Stein vom Herzen, und glauben Sie mir, sich auch, wenn erst die widernatürliche Verkuppelung des Toten mit dem Lebendigen gelöst ist (ich glaubte das Tote durch die

[36] O. Sonne, *Leipziger Illustrierte Zeitung,* 31 Oct. 1912, p. 804.
[37] Wilhelm Mauke, *Münchener Zeitung,* 26 Oct. 1912, p. 213.
[38] The performance time of the completed *Vorspiel* is approximately one hour.

Bühne zu galvanisieren, aber das Instrument versagte!)' (Bw. 3 June 1913, p. 199.) (It will take a real load off my mind, and, believe me, off yours too, once that unnatural connection between the dead and the living has been severed (I thought the stage would enable me to galvanize the defunct, but the instrument failed me!)) Only in this new form could he regard *Ariadne* as complete, Hofmannsthal concluded. Strauss did not take to the *Vorspiel* at all; he said quite frankly that he could only regard it as a dreary and uninteresting task. He found the prospect of setting the Composer downright distasteful and refused to consider the revision as a possible definitive version:

[Ich habe mich] in unsere erste Arbeit derart hineinverbissen, und halte sie im Aufbau und in der Idee für so glücklich, daß mir die neue Fassung immer wie ein Torso vorkommen wird, zu dessen Herstellung mich kein inneres Bedürfnis, sondern nur eine äußere Notwendigkeit bringen wird, die auch vorläufig nicht vorliegt. (Bw. 15 June 1913, p. 201.)

(I now cling so obstinately to our original work, and still regard it as so successful in structure and conception, that this new version will always look to me like a torso. And to produce such a thing, for which I have no inner urge, I would have to be driven by pressure of circumstances—which, at the moment, is not the case.)

On 15 December 1913 Strauss made another impassioned and, for him, lengthy plea for the first version. He was stung into this outburst by the brilliant success of Wolf-Ferrari's new opera *L'Amore Medico* based on Molière's *Le médecin malgré lui,* which was not only hailed as the long-awaited musical comedy of the day (this barely two years after the first performance of *Der Rosenkavalier*) but was performed at Dresden in the costumes of *Ariadne!*

As Del Mar has pointed out, Strauss agreed to compose the *Vorspiel* in 1916 only because of the war.[39] Here was Strauss's 'äußere Notwendigkeit'. Although a final draft of *Die Frau ohne Schatten* was ready by 1915, there was no hope of getting it, or any other major opera, staged. So, faced again with the prospect of the summer months without work, Strauss took up the prologue, knowing that in a revised and less hybrid form he could easily secure further performances of *Ariadne.*

[39] Del Mar, p. 60.

Whilst the 1916 *Ariadne auf Naxos* cannot then be regarded as the definitive version, it is the one which has been preferred by opera companies and by opera-going publics over the last sixty years. No doubt there are practical reasons for this: a first-rate double cast is no longer needed and the staging is less complicated and costly. But, as we shall see in the next Chapter, the *Vorspiel,* particularly the wonderfully deft parlando setting, is in a class of its own and must surely have survived on its merits. Nevertheless the 1912 *Ariadne* is not without its supporters. The earlier version is an original experiment and has the merit of being firmly grounded in an historical tradition on the one hand and a comedy of character on the other. Amongst its supporters was Sir Thomas Beecham who conducted it in the spring of 1913. In his autobiography *A Mingled Chime,* published in 1944, he wrote:

During the late spring, by way of an interlude, I gave the *Ariadne auf Naxos* of Strauss at His Majesty's Theatre in conjunction with Sir Herbert Tree, who himself played the part of Monsieur Jourdain in the comedy. The work was given in English, translated from the German through the French by Somerset Maugham, whose equanimity was on more than one occasion disturbed by the actor-manager's propensity to forget his lines and substitute an improvised patter for the polished verse of that distinguished master of the vernacular. Otherwise Tree, who in this line of broad and fantastic comedy had hardly a rival, was capital, and the whole production was adjudged superior to the original given at Stuttgart in the previous year. In this, the earlier version of *Ariadne,* I have always considered that the musical accomplishment of Strauss attained its highest reach, yielding a greater spontaneity and variety of invention, together with a subtler and riper style, than anything that his pen had yet given to the stage . . . It has to be admitted that it is neither an easy nor practicable sort of piece to give in an ordinary opera house, as it postulates the employment of a first-rate group of actors as well as singers; and for this reason, no doubt, the authors re-wrote it at a later period, making a full-flown opera of the old medley and thinking probably that they were making a very good job of it. The result has been doubly unfortunate, for the later version has not only failed to hold the stage, but has dimmed the public recollection of the superior and more attractive original.[40]

---

[40] Thomas Beecham, *A Mingled Chime,* p. 117. Beecham was not to know that after 1945 the revised *Ariadne* would become increasingly popular.

At a special performance in 1947 Beecham gave excerpts from *Ariadne I* and in 1950 there was a full production at the Edinburgh Festival, at which Miles Malleson assisted Beecham. Yet despite the points Beecham is able to raise in its favour an attempt in Stuttgart in October 1962, fifty years after the première, to re-introduce the public to the original was a failure. The occasion was the opening of the rebuilt *Kleines Haus* and a top cast was assembled under the direction of Günther Rennert. It was hoped furthermore that widespread prosperity in Germany would make audiences better disposed towards this 'aristocratic'[41] aesthetic experiment. But Stuttgart was once again impatient with the Molière and delighted with the Strauss–Hofmannsthal contribution. History repeated itself—but at least it *could* do so. Both versions have strengths and weaknesses; but both versions are available to us and we are enriched by the choice.

[41] See Bw. 4 Mar. 1913, p. 187.

Chapter V

The *Vorspiel*

i. The Text

(1) *Changes from* Zwischenspiel to Vorspiel

Hofmannsthal first thought of writing the *Zwischenspiel* on 23 July 1911 after the libretto of the *Oper* had been so coolly received by Strauss and after the letter of mid-July 1911, that forerunner of the *Ariadne Brief*. The scene would explain the meaning of the *Oper* and Hofmannsthal wrote to Strauss 'Auch habe ich noch ein Vehikel, um [den] Hauptpunkt den Leuten näherzubringen: nämlich die der Oper vorhergehende Prosaszene.' (Bw. 23 July 1911, p. 121.) (I have, furthermore, another vehicle to bring home to people this central idea; I mean the big prose scene which is to precede the opera.) Strauss was enthusiastic and wrote back with suggestions. But Hofmannsthal delayed actually writing the scene until March/April 1912,[1] to Strauss's slight annoyance, even though there was nothing in it for music. The text was sent off on 24 April 1912 and was well received by Strauss.

Most of the earlier *Zwischenspiel* was incorporated verbatim into the *Vorspiel*. The largest alterations are to the part of the First Lackey, who conveys his master's bizarre command about the order of the entertainments. This part is expanded into that of the pompous, condescending Major Domo who uses Latin phrases ('summo et unico loco' (11)) and calls works of art 'Kunstfertigkeiten' (10). He conveys the same message as the lackey. One or two of the other longer speeches in the *Zwischenspiel* are cut to make it suitable to be set to music. Hofmannsthal thought it wise to sacrifice the following speech by the Dancing Master which is actually a sardonic comment on operatic malpractices in the seventeenth century. It is a speech that would have been worthy of Molière. The Dancing

---

[1] See Bw. 7 Nov. 1912, p. 144.

Master is persuading the Composer to make some cuts in
Ariadne:

Tanzmeister
Fragen Sie ihn, ob er seine Oper lieber heute ein wenig verstümmelt
hören will, oder ob er sie niemals hören will.
(Zum Komponisten)
Es sind gerade die Striche, durch welche eine Oper sich empfiehlt,
und die vorzüglichsten Theater rechnen es sich zum Verdienst an,
durch ihre Striche mindestens ebensoviel zum bleibenden Erfolg
eines musikalischen Werkes beigetragen zu haben, als der Komponist durch das, was er an Arbeit hineingetan hat. Das erste, wonach
der Herr Generalintendant der Königlichen Vergnügungen zu
fragen pflegt, ist, ob eine Oper auch recht gute Striche enthält, und
es wäre an der Zeit, daß ein geschickter Musikus die Bequemlichkeit
annähme und komponierte ein gut Teil ordentlicher Striche von
Anfang an in die Partitur hinein. (153–4.)

(Dancing Master
Ask him if he wants to hear his opera today in a slightly mutilated
form or if he never wants to hear it.
(to the Composer)
It is precisely the cuts which recommend an opera and the best
theatres pride themselves on having contributed just as much to the
enduring success of a musical work by their cuts as the composer by
his labour. The first thing that the Director of Royal Entertainment
asks about is whether an opera contains some good cuts, and it is
about time that a clever musician availed himself of this convenience
and composed a good portion of cuts into the score from the outset.)

The new part of the *Vorspiel* is the greatly expanded 'Blick
hinter die Kulissen' (9–19) which is placed before the
transposed *Zwischenspiel*. In the *Zwischenspiel* there is also a
glimpse of the jealousies, foibles and preoccupations of
backstage life; for example, in the quarrel between the
Primadonna and Zerbinetta about the respective merits of
their own pieces (147) or in the episode where the Composer
is made to cut his opera with both parties competing to have
the other's parts reduced (153–5). In the *Vorspiel* Hofmannsthal
adds colour and detail and introduces two more characters,
the Officer and the Wigmaker. The *Vorspiel* achieves a briskly
paced, kaleidoscopic effect through these sketch-like additions; it receives a certain allure from the knowledge that here
we are seeing people without their masks on, and a certain

depth from the gap we suspect lies between the unmasked person and the dramatic *persona*.[2] Hofmannsthal has preferred to operate with stock types and situations, realizing how it would overload an already complicated programme to introduce psychological intricacy. The apparent clichés he is using are handled with skill, and the original idea of including some humorous 'Selbstpersiflage', whilst not achieved in quite the specific way Strauss would have liked,[3] comes off well as a gentle satire on the vanities and excesses of theatrical life.

This additional section also gives Hofmannsthal room to paint a fuller portrait of the Composer, which was one of the main objectives of the revision. On 3 June 1913 Hofmannsthal could write '[Ich habe] die Garderobeszene mit großer Frische und Laune umgeschrieben: der Komponist steht jetzt ganz in der Mitte.' (Bw. 3 June 1913, p. 198.). (I have rewritten the Vorspiel, the dressing-room scene, with great zest and vigour; the Composer now occupies the very centre of the scene.) At one point the Composer tries to call the violinists together for a last-minute rehearsal only to be told roughly by a lackey that they are playing table-music for the assembled company. Here the youthful Composer emerges in all his naïve credulity, innocent of the vulgarity of the common herd:

Komponist
(kommt eilig von rückwärts)
Lieber Freund! Verschaffen Sie mir die Geigen. Richten Sie ihnen

[2] No doubt the motif of the person and the *persona* of the actor was one which fascinated Molière and led him to write the *Impromptu de Versailles*, a work which may well have influenced the *Vorspiel*. In fact this motif is part of the larger theme of masks and reality. In *Men and Masks: A Study of Molière* Lionel Gossman sees this as the most fundamental theme in Molière's work and *Le Bourgeois Gentilhomme* is itself about exposing the deluded Jourdain. In his first adaptation Hofmannsthal includes all the scenes in which Jourdain is duped but excludes all the schemes to unmask Jourdain and hence also the Turkish Ceremony. This unwise omission deprives the comedy of its moral climax and hence of a happy dénouement. Hofmannsthal must have felt the imbalance of folly and wisdom in his earlier version for the Turkish Ceremony is reinstated in the 1918 *Bürger als Edelmann*.

[3] Cf. Bw. 24 July 1911, p. 122. 'Lassen Sie da Ihren ganzen Witz schießen, lassen Sie auch einige Bosheiten über den "Komponisten" einfließen, das amüsiert das Publikum am meisten, und jede Selbstpersiflage nimmt der Kritik die stärksten Waffen aus der Hand. Das Molièresche Stück ist etwas dumm: es kann ein Schlager werden, wenn Sie die beiden Rollen des Komponisten und Tanzmeisters so ausbauen, daß alles darin gesagt ist, was heute über das Verhältnis von Publikum, Kritik und Künstler zu sagen ist. Es kann das Gegenstück zu den "Meistersingern" werden; 50 Jahre später.

aus, daß sie sich hier versammeln sollen zu einer letzten kurzen Verständigungsprobe.

Der Lakai

Die Geigen werden schwerlich kommen, erstens weils keine Füß nicht haben, und zweitens, weils in der Hand sind!

Komponist

(naiv, belehrend, ohne sich verspottet zu glauben)

Wenn ich sage: die Geigen, so meine ich die Spieler.

Der Lakai

(gemein, von oben herab)

Ach so! Die sind aber jetzt dort, wo ich auch hin sollt! und wo ich gleich sein werd—anstatt mich da mit Ihnen aufzuhalten.

Komponist

(ganz naiv, zart)

Wo ist das?

Der Lakai

(gemein, plump)

Bei der Tafel!

Komponist

(aufgeregt)

Jetzt? Eine Viertelstunde vor Anfang meiner Oper beim Essen?

Der Lakai

Wenn ich sag: bei der Tafel, so mein ich natürlich bei der herrschaftlichen Tafel, nicht beim Musikantentisch. (12–13)

(Composer

(comes quickly from behind)

Dear friend! Get me the violins. Tell them that they are to assemble here for a last short rehearsal.

The Lackey

The violins can hardly come, firstly, because they have no feet, and secondly, because they are in the hand!

Composer

(naïve, instructive, not thinking that he is mocked)

When I say 'the violins' then I mean the players.

The Lackey

(coarsely, condescendingly)

Oh indeed! But they are now where I should also be! and where I soon shall be—instead of wasting time with you.

Composer

(quite naïve, tender)

Where is that?

The Lackey

(coarse, tactless)

At table!
    Composer
    (excited)
Now? At a meal a quarter of an hour before the beginning of my opera?
    The Lackey
When I say 'at table' then of course I mean at the master's table not at the musician's table.)

The volatile Composer is also seen in the throes of creation; one moment he is fuming at an impertinent lackey and the next a lovely melody occurs to him. A little later he sings this to an improvised text 'Du, Venus' Sohn' (18).

In this first section Hofmannsthal takes the opportunity to prepare the ground for the fleeting encounter between Zerbinetta and the Composer. Zerbinetta catches the young man's notice and he asks his Music Teacher 'Wer ist dieses entzückende Mädchen' (16). The question adds shades of situational irony for this is just the moment the Music Master is about to break the news that *Ariadne* will be followed by a comic intermezzo.

Finally the additions to the *Vorspiel* allow for a more thorough exposition of the actual mechanics of the plot. The Maecenas' commands are clearly heard. The story of *Ariadne* has to be told to the *commedia dell'arte* and we learn what their plan of action is. This is a valuable though superficial aid to understanding the *Oper,* and obviously something which can rightly be expected of a prologue.

The additions to the end of the *Vorspiel* comprise the encounter already mentioned (30–1), which it should be noted is prefigured, be it ever so briefly, in the *Zwischenspiel,* and the text to the Composer's 'Ode to Music' *Musik ist heilige Kunst* (33). The Zerbinetta-Composer affair was first suggested, partly in jest, in a letter by Strauss.[4] Hofmannsthal certainly did not take up this suggestion in earnest until 1913 but in 1912 he created between them a moment of transient attraction in which there is a strong erotic element. The Composer is

---

[4] 'Diese Szene vor der Oper muß das eigentliche Stück werden. Zerbinetta kann ein Verhältnis mit dem Komponisten haben, wenn derselbe nicht zu porträtähnlich mit mir wird.' (Bw. 24 July 1911, p. 123.)

defending his work against what he sees as Zerbinetta's trivializing version of it:

> Komponist
> (Springt auf)
> Sie machen mir eine wahnwitzige Posse aus dem einzigen Traum meiner Seele. Schütten den Kehrricht der Straße in ein himmlisches Gemach. Ich muß mich zur Wehr setzen.
> (Zerbinetta tritt zu ihm, sieht ihm in die Augen)
> Komponist
> Ein Lebendiges ist es, ein Atmendes, fließend geschmiedet Glied an Glied—wie das da—
> (Er ergreift ihre Hand, fährt sanft den Arm aufwärts)
> —und Ihr wollts auseinanderreißen. Eure infamen Affenstreiche dazwischen treiben. Mörder seid ihr alle miteinander. (158.)

> (Composer
> (Jumps up)
> You are making a mad farce out of the only dream of my soul. You are emptying the rubbish from the street into a heavenly dwelling. I must be on my guard.
> (Zerbinetta steps up to him, looks him in the eye)
> Composer
> Its a creature that lives and breathes, smoothly joined limb to limb— like that there—
> (He grasps her hand, feels softly up her arm)
> —and you want to tear it apart. To bring in your apish pranks. You're murderers, the lot of you.)

There is obvious ironic ambiguity in the Composer's saying he must offer resistance—is it to Zerbinetta's triviality or to her sexual charms? Then his violent words and gentle gestures undercut each other. The emotional extremes of ardent youth are presented in a single concentrated episode.

Cut from the *Vorspiel* is the final dialogue between Dorantes and Dorimene who plan to steal away at the end of the coming performance. Dorimene who is not aware that Jourdain and not Dorantes is footing the bill asks innocently 'Auf diese Weise könnten wir uns den langweiligen Komplimenten Ihres Strohmannes entziehen?' (161). Dorantes has other reasons for wanting to avoid Jourdain. Their disappearance at the end of the *Oper* creates a dramatically effective pause and eases the transition back into the Molière frame, and the sacrifice of this scene was one of the losses already mentioned in conjunction with the revision of the 1912 version.[5]

The Vorspiel ends as the comedians rush on stage not yet quite dressed. The Composer utters a cry of despair at the cruel, philistine world. He vents his rage on his long-suffering Music Teacher:

> Komponist
> (rasend)
> Ich durfte es nicht erlauben! Du durftest mir nicht erlauben, es zu erlauben! Wer hieß dich mich zerren, mich! in diese Welt hinein? Laß mich erfrieren, verhungern, versteinern in der meinigen!
> (Läuft vorne ab, verzweifelt.
> Musiklehrer sieht ihm nach, schüttelt den Kopf.
> Vorhang (fällt schnell.) (34.)

> (Composer
> (frantic)
> I shouldn't have allowed it! You shouldn't have allowed me to allow it! Who told you to drag me, me! into this world? Let me freeze, starve, turn to stone in my own world!
> (Runs off frontstage, in despair.
> Music Teacher glances after him, shakes his head.)
> Curtain (falls quickly.))

This provides the *Vorspiel* with an effective curtain.

The other major alteration Hofmannsthal made was to bring the whole scene about seventy-five years forward. The *Vorspiel* takes place in Vienna as there was no real reason for keeping a French location. But in order to find a comparable social situation in which private houses might offer such lavish entertainments it was necessary to move to the Vienna of Maria Theresia.[6] Thus we find in the 'Angaben für die Gestaltung des Dekorativen in Ariadne (neue Bearbeitung)' that the *Vorspiel* may also take place in a room in the Rococo style: 'Ein großer Saal im Barock oder Rokokostil' (379). Rococo is not considered to have begun until 1715 although it started in 1700 in France.[7]

---

[5] See Chapter II, p. 103.

[6] This was for Hofmannsthal one of the great periods in Austrian history. See his sensitive, devoted appreciation of this matriarchal figure, *Maria Theresia* (1917), PIII, pp. 387–400.

[7] *The Oxford Companion to Art*, ed. Harold Osborne, (Oxford, 1970), pp. 985–8.

Distinctively Viennese touches occur mainly in the servant types. Stiegele rightly points out that the typical Viennese humour of these figures places them in the company of Nestroy's comic characters.[8] One example, the lackey's exchange with the Composer, has already been quoted.[9] Another is his clever word-play when the Officer gives him an unjust shove on his way to an assignation with Zerbinetta: 'Das its die Sprache der Leidenschaft, verbunden mit einem unrichtigen Objekt' (12). The Major Domo's stiff arrogance draws laughs against, not with, him. But in him too there is something typically Viennese; the ridiculous manner of the self-important subaltern.[10]

One or two other small touches add to the Austrian flavour. There are, for example, certain details of the Zerbinetta-Officer affair which could not come from Versailles, such as his kissing her hand and her being 'noch sehr im Negligé' (15). Then there is the language of the Wigmaker with more overtones of Viennese officialese, for example, 'Dero miß-helliges Betragen kann ich belächelnd nur einer angenommen-en Gemütsaufwallung zurechnen!' (15). Gustav Görlich was the first to point out that these words were actually written in a letter by one of Beethoven's copyists who had just been hauled over the coals: 'Was ferneres das sonstige mißhellige Betragen gegen mich betrifft, so kann ich belächelnd selbes nur als eine angenommene Gemütsaufwallung ansehen ... übrigens nehmen Sie die Versicherung, daß, auch nur um eines Körnleins wert, ich nie Ursache habe, meines Betragens willen vor Ihnen erröten zu müssen.'[11] (As for the rest of the unpleasant behaviour to me, I can only regard it indulgently as a fit of temper ... Furthermore, you may rest assured that I have never had the slightest cause to blush in front of you for my behaviour.) Stiegele draws attention to this copyist's Viennese turn of phrase.[12] An example of Austrian dialect is

[8] Stiegele, pp. 77–8.

[9] See Chapter V, pp. 213–5.

[10] Gräwe suggests that the Major Domo is the mouthpiece of an arbitrary, absurd authority *in absentia* and that the *Vorspiel* is therefore an allegory of an absurd and cruelly misruled world. Gräwe, p. 299. Although the Maecenas uses his power capriciously are we not meant to laugh at his pretentions rather than shudder as if he were, for example, Camus' Caligula in a moment of didactic teasing?

[11] Gustav Görlich, 'Aus der Werkstatt des Librettisten', p. 33.

[12] Stiegele, p. 78.

the Music Teacher's sentence 'Mein Freund, ich bin halt dreißig Jahrln älter als wie du (19). The diminutive, 'Jahrln', and the comparative, 'als wie', are unmistakable South German traits.

The genesis of the *Vorspiel* from the *Zwischenspiel* thus involved firstly expansion and secondly a change of time and place. Some aspects of characterization have been mentioned in passing and these are now attended to in more detail.

(2) *Characters in the* Vorspiel
The Music Teacher and the Dancing Master are, as previously noted, two characters taken from Molière's *Le Bourgeois Gentilhomme*. Hofmannsthal rounds them out and makes them distinguishable from one another. In *Der Bürger als Edelmann* (1912) they are jealous rivals, not individuals but representatives of their art; their defence of their respective arts bears witness to Molière's mastery of elegant wit and the formal cut and thrust of clever dispute:

Musiklehrer
Ohne die Musik kann ein Staat unmöglich bestehen.
Tanzmeister
Ohne das Tanzen kann ein Mensch nichts Rechtes ausrichten.
Musiklehrer
Alle Unordnungen, alle Kriege in der Welt rühren von nichts anderm her, als daß die Leute nicht Musik lernen.
Tanzmeister
Alles Leid der Menschen, alle Unglücksfälle, mit denen die Historie angefüllt ist, alle Fehler der Staatsmänner, alle Vergehungen der größten Helden kommen bloß daher, weil sie nicht tanzen konnten.
Jourdain
Wie denn so?
Musiklehrer
Rührt der Krieg nicht daher, weil die Menschen nicht miteinander harmonieren?
Jourdain
Das ist wahr!
Musiklehrer
Wenn nun alle Leute die Musik lerneten, wäre das nicht das beste Mittel, miteinander zu harmonieren und einen allgemeinen Frieden in der Welt zu stiften?
Jourdain
Sie haben Recht.

Tanzmeister

Wenn jemand einen Fehler in seiner Aufführung begangen hat, entweder in seiner Familie, oder in Staatssachen, oder auch im Felde, sagt man nicht allemal: Der oder der hat bei dieser oder jener Gelegenheit einen Fehltritt getan?

Jourdain

Ja, so sagt man.

Tanzmeister

Kann aber denn ein Fehltritt anderswoher rühren, als weil man nicht tanzen kann?

Jourdain

Das ist wahr. Sie haben alle beide recht. (78)

(Music Teacher

Without music it is impossible for a state to exist.

Dancing Master

Without dancing a person can do nothing right.

Music Teacher

All disorders, all wars in the world stem from the fact that people do not learn music.

Dancing Master

All human suffering, all the misadventures with which history is full, all statesmen's mistakes, all the great heroes' violations arise merely because they cannot dance.

Jourdain

How is that?

Music Teacher

Doesn't war stem from people not being able to harmonize with each other?

Jourdain

That is true!

Music Teacher

If all people learnt music wouldn't that be the best means of promoting harmony and the general peace of the world?

Jourdain

You are right.

Dancing Master

If someone has made a mistake in his conduct either in his family or in affairs of state or even on the field doesn't one always say this or that man has on this or that occasion made a false step?

Jourdain

Yes, that is what one says.

Dancing Master.

But can there be any other reason for a false step than that one

doesn't known how to dance?
    Jourdain
That is true. You are both right.)

This rivalry continues in the *Vorspiel* between the two theatrical groups headed by the Music Teacher and the Dancing Master. There is no single direct confrontation between them as in the above quotation but there are numerous barbed attacks such as the Dancing Master's 'was die Einfälle anlangt, so steckt in meinem linken Schuhabsatz mehr Melodie als in dieser ganzen "Ariadne auf Naxos"' (16).

When Hofmannsthal decided to place the Composer at the centre of the *Vorspiel* it was an obvious step to bring out the relationship between the Composer and the Music Teacher, who is the person closest to him, and thus to emphasize the proud, protective feelings of the teacher towards his gifted protégé. Hofmannsthal's Music Teacher seems older than Molière's rather stuffy 'Maître de Musique' and often behaves like an affectionate grandfather. He is pragmatic enough to remind the Composer of the fifty ducats he stands to lose if he will not compromise his work, but is sufficiently sensitive to want to spare the Composer the Dancing Master's criticisms about longueurs in *Ariadne* (25). He takes a tolerant, if mildly ironic, view of the Composer's temperamental genius and comes across as a kind-hearted mentor.

The Dancing Master is quite another kettle of fish. Just as the Music Teacher's nature aligns him with the noble world of *tragédie lyrique* so the Dancing Master's makes it right that he should be associated with the *commedia dell'arte*. He is a showy, breezy, sometimes brittle character, inclined to punctuate his blunt assertions with a pirouette (24). Not unlikable, he has, however, no time for profundities and like Zerbinetta has some of the brilliance and extroversion of a virtuoso temperament. It is a most rewarding part to play in the theatre, especially if the actor uses ballet movements to show up the Dancing Master's physical vanity.

The disdainful Primadonna is Hofmannsthal's own creation. The Primadonna's operatic partner, the Tenor (who later sings Bacchus), is equally superior and conceited, as the incident with the Wigmaker shows (14). These two characters who make only the briefest of appearances cannot be developed within that space into anything more than two easily recognizable types.

The remaining figures are the *commedia dell'arte* who, in accordance with Italian tradition, play themselves whether on stage or off.[13] They contribute to the theatrical effectiveness of the *Vorspiel* in a number of mimic and pantomimic gestures. Their first entrance is comic enough: 'Harlekin, Scaramuccio, Brighella, Truffaldin sind im Gänsemarsch aus Zerbinettas Zimmer gekommen' (18). When Zerbinetta puts on her make-up all four buffos find it necessary to help her: 'Zerbinetta hat auf dem Strohstühlchen rechts im Vordegrund Platz genommen, schminkt sich zu Ende, von ihren Partnern bedient; Harlekin hält das Licht, Brighella den Spiegel' (19). Their final entrance is pure slapstick: Zerbinetta comes on stage backwards, Harlequin runs on doing up his belt and the other three come on still getting dressed (33).

These then are the supporting characters and types who are glimpsed behind the scenes. Their clear contours and their uninhibited zest secure a dynamic realism for the *Vorspiel*.

The main characters are the Composer and Zerbinetta. The source for the Composer was Molière's 'Élève du Maître de Musique' in *Le Bourgeois Gentilhomme*. But this pupil appears so briefly that Hofmannsthal was able to create him afresh. Hofmannsthal may also have been prompted in his decision to have a Composer by an inaccurate translation by Bierling of 'Maître de Musique' and 'Élève du Maître de Musique' as 'Ein Komponist' and 'Ein Schüler des Komponisten'.[14] This piece of information about the Bierling translation helps incidentally to follow Hofmannsthal's otherwise incomprehensible letter of 22 October 1911 in which he mentions a 'Composer's pupil':

Welches Stück lassen Sie denn in der Anfangsszene des 'Bourgeois Gentilhomme' dem Jourdain vom Komponisten vorführen?? (An Stelle jenes musikalischen Gesprächs?) Das muß ich wissen, daran muß ich anknüpfen. Ich lasse in dieser Szene den Schüler des Komponisten als überflüssig fort, vielleicht verwende ich ihn auch

---

[13] Hence the Dancing Master's remark about Zerbinetta: 'Sie ist eine Meisterin im Improvisieren; da sie immer nur sich selber spielt, findet sie sich in jeder Situation zurecht' (26).

[14] Bierling, p. 59.

gerade als junges musikalisches Genie und lasse ihn den Autor der
'Ariadne' sein, denn mit der Figur des Komponisten selbst, behäbig
und bürgerlich, wie Molière ihn hingestellt hat, da ist wenig
anzufangen, die Figur ist gar nicht biegsam. (Bw. 22 Oct. 1911, pp.
125–6.)

(What is it that the Composer plays for Jourdain in the opening
scene of *Le Bourgeois Gentilhomme* (instead of that conversation
about music)? I must know this in order to refer to it. In this scene
I am leaving out the Composer's pupil, who is not wanted; or
perhaps I shall use him as a young musical genius and make him the
author of *Ariadne,* because the figure of the Composer himself, smug
and bourgeois as Molière has made him, is of little use—the character
is so inflexible.)

Hofmannsthal is of course referring to the 'Maître de Musique'
and his pupil. His own warm, humane Music Teacher must
have evolved as a reaction to Molière's unsympathetic
prototype. The piece about which he is asking Strauss is the
air for a serenade which Molière's 'élève' has been set to
compose while the assembled company waits for Jourdain to
get up one morning. In *Der Bürger als Edelmann* (1912) the
Composer has just composed an ariette. Hofmannsthal
decided to write new words and produced some suitably
mannered verses to Cupid:

> Du, Venus' Sohn, gibst süßen Lohn
> Für unser Sehnen und Schmachten.
> Dir sei geweiht mein junges Herz,
> Und all mein Sinnen und Trachten.
> O du Knabe! du Kind! du mächtiger Gott! (75)

> (Venus' son, you give sweet reward
> For our longing and languishing.
> My young heart is dedicated to you
> And my every thought and wish.
> Oh you lad! you child! you mighty god!)

This is sung by a 'Sängerin' with the Composer accompanying
on the piano. In the *Vorspiel* the Composer is actually in the
process of composing this song and its genesis runs through
this section from the overture onwards. True to his intentions
Hofmannsthal also made the Composer the author of *Ariadne*.
   The outlines for the Composer Hofmannsthal borrowed

from Molière. The personality of the naïve, spontaneous, idealistic youth Hofmannsthal added himself. It was partly a self-portrait of the young 'Loris' but more specifically a portrait of Mozart, as W. Schuh proves conclusively using the *Notizen von Blatt 1* which we have already discussed. W. Schuh rightly rejects M. Stern's suggestion, endorsed by H. Mayer, that the Composer is a secret caricature of Wagner:[15]

Zwischen den zur 'Ariadne-Oper' gehörenden Notizen von Blatt 1 steht unvermittelt der Satz: 'Vorspiel: siehe Mozart, Verkehr mit Sängerinnen.' Er bezieht sich auf die zwischen 'Bürger als Edelmann' und 'Ariadne auf Naxos' vermittelnde Überleitungsszene. Durch diesen Satz dürfte Martin Sterns Vermutung, Hofmannsthal habe beim 'Komponisten' zeitweilig eine Wagner-Karikatur im Sinne gehabt, in Frage gestellt sein. Der Hinweis auf Mozart erfährt übrigens durch einen handschriftlichen Zusatz in dem für den Komponisten bestimmten Maschinenexemplar des 'Vorspiels' der 'Neuen Bearbeitung' eine Bestätigung. Zu den ersten, an den Lakaien gerichteten Sätzen des Komponisten, der 'eilig von rückwärts auftritt', fügt Hofmannsthal dort die Bemerkung: 'umflossen mit Grazie, trotz der scheinbaren Trockenheit'. Das deutet gewiß nicht auf Wagner, sondern auf eine dem jungen Mozart angenäherte Figur.[16]

(Between the notes belonging to the 'Ariadne opera' on page 1 suddenly there is the sentence: 'Prologue: see Mozart, converse with singers.' It refers to the transitional scene linking the 'Bürger als Edelmann' and 'Ariadne auf Naxos'. This sentence puts in question Martin Stern's conjecture that Hofmannsthal had a Wagner caricature somewhere in mind when writing the part of the 'Composer'. The reference to Mozart is confirmed, furthermore, by a handwritten comment in the typed copy of the Prologue of the new version meant for the composer. To the first of the Composer's lines, addressed to the lackeys as he 'rushes on from the back of the stage', Hofmannsthal adds the comment: 'graceful in spite of the apparent dryness'. That suggests surely not Wagner but a figure based on the young Mozart.)

W. Schuh puts his finger on it: Hofmannsthal's Composer has

---

[15] See Chapter II, p. 119.

[16] Willi Schuh, 'Zu Hofmannsthals "Ariadne"-Szenarium und -Notizen', p. 89. Strauss took the point and later described the Composer as a young 'Mozart, etwa am Hofe von Versailles oder bei den Banausen des Münchner Hofes, für den [er] als 16 jähriger "Idomeneo" komponiert hat'. (Bw. 16 Apr. 1916, p. 282.) (Strauss made a slight error: Mozart was twenty-four, not sixteen, when he composed *Idomeneo*.)

too much genuine charm to be a caricature. The Composer is like a young animal taking his first steps—one may laugh at him but he is not a proper subject for ridicule.

The Composer is young enough to be sexually ambiguous. Strauss's suggestion made on 6 April 1916 that the part be given to a soprano (he had the accomplished Mlle Artôt in mind) does not therefore seem in bad taste. Strauss's choice of the *Hosenrolle,* actually first suggested by the conductor, Leo Blech,[17] was furthermore the result of very real casting difficulties; neither a first-rate tenor nor a baritone would be interested in such a short part. Even if Strauss could have secured a good tenor or baritone the deeper voice range would have made the Composer seem too old; and there was always that other risk with Strauss's tenors, a register he did not care for, that they would turn into the *Heldentenor,* just as Bacchus had almost done. Strauss arrived at his choice by a process of elimination and rightly asked Hofmannsthal 'Was bleibt übrig, als das einzige Sängergenre, das in "Ariadne" nicht vertreten ist, mein Rofrano, der überall in einer intelligenten Sängerin vorhanden [*sic*].' (Bw. 16 Apr. 1916 p. 282.) (What is left to me except the only genre of singer not yet represented in *Ariadne,* my Rofrano, for whom an intelligent female singer is available anywhere.) Hofmannsthal was dismayed. This would reduce the part, he feared, to a *travesti* role, reminiscent of operetta.[18] But Strauss insisted and on the whole it turned out very well, as Hofmannsthal must have felt.

Max Reinhardt also had a large part in shaping this figure.[19] In fact Reinhardt's contributions to the Composer in the *Zwischenspiel* and the 1912 version gave Hofmannsthal many ideas for the *Vorspiel.* As W. Stiegele points out in her useful discussion of this matter, Hofmannsthal was not very interested in the Composer in the 1912 *Bürger als Edelmann:*

[17] Ernst Krause, *Richard Strauss: Gestalt und Werk,* p. 374.

[18] Bw. 13 Apr. 1916, p. 280–1. 'Ich fürchte, hier hat Sie der Theateropportunismus total auf den Holzweg gebracht. Zunächst ist mir die Besetzung des jungen Komponisten mit einer Dame völlig gegen den Strich. Dieses Verniedlichen gerade dieser Figur, um die der "Geist" und die "Größe" wittern sollen, in eine immer leise operettenhafte Travestie, das ist mir, verzeihen Sie meine Offenheit, greulich. Ich kann mir leider nur denken, daß unsere Auffassung dieser Figur hier sehr weit auseinandergeht, leider Gottes, wieder einmal, wie bei Zerbinetta! O Gott, wäre es mir gegeben, Ihnen das Eigentliche, Geistige der Figuren ganz deutlich zu machen.'

[19] See Chapter I, pp. 20–1.

he does not even indicate when the Composer should leave the stage during Act 1.[20] Reinhardt worked backwards from the *Zwischenspiel* and filled in this non-speaking role with music and gesture. For example, in Act 1, when Jourdain's four teachers, the Music Teacher, the Dancing Master, the Fencing Master, and the Philosophy Teacher begin to brawl after each arguing that his branch of learning is the highest, Reinhardt has the Composer, oblivious of the tumult, put the final touches to a composition: 'Er hat auf einen Notenblatt indessen etwas beendet, pfeift es leise vor sich hin, scheint nicht unbefriedigt, sieht sich um, geht ab, da er die anderen nicht mehr sieht.'[21] (Meanwhile he has finished something on a sheet of manuscript, whistles it softly to himself, seems not dissatisfied, looks around, goes off because he no longer sees the others.) Reinhardt establishes the artist's detachment from the world, a detachment which by its comic juxtaposition with a brawl brings out the Composer's innocence, gives Hofmannsthal the idea of having the genesis of 'Du, Venus' Sohn' spread over the *Vorspiel,* and also solves very nicely the problem of the Composer's exit. Reinhardt adds some other ingenious touches. When Jourdain appears in his splendid new coat the Composer does not notice him: 'Er schlägt leise einige Tasten an, (und erst als der Musiklehrer ihm die Hand auf die Schulter legt), fährt er auf, blickt verwirrt um sich und verneigt sich linkisch.'[22] (He plays a few notes (and only when the music teacher puts his hand on his shoulder) he starts up, looks dazedly about and bows awkwardly.) When Jourdain is bored by his ariette and yawns openly, the Composer cannot believe people are so insensitive: 'Er sieht den Tanzmeister an, er setzt sich hoffnungslos resigniert, er rauft sich die Haare, er gibt Zeichen von Aufregung, stöhnt, glotzt Jourdain an.'[23] (He looks at the Dancing Master, he sits down hopelessly resigned, he tears his hair, he shows signs of agitation, groans, stares at Jourdain.) Here is the figure of both the *Zwischenspiel* and the *Vorspiel.*

Zerbinetta is the only character who is developed in both

---

[20] Stiegele, p. 25.
[21] Max Reinhardt, *Regiebuch zu Ariadne auf Naxos,* p. 23.
[22] Reinhardt, p. 19.
[23] Reinhardt, p. 20.

the *Vorspiel* and the *Oper*. It has been claimed that one of the reasons Hofmannsthal wrote the scenic prologue was to give Zerbinetta a second chance, so to speak. Egon Wellesz reports that in conversation Hofmannsthal once said that Zerbinetta was too like a marionette and that he had written the *Vorspiel* in order to make a warmer, more human figure of her. Wellesz records:

Ich fragte ihn [Hofmannsthal] einmal, was ihn dazu bewogen habe, der Oper 'Ariadne' das Vorspiel vorangehen zu lassen. Er sagte, die Figur der Zerbinetta mit ihrer großen Koloraturarie sei ihm marionettenhaft erschienen, es fehlte ihr die menschliche Wärme, die eine Figur wie die Philine in Goethes 'Wilhelm Meister' so bezaubernd mache; deshalb habe er den Gedanken gefaßt, der Oper eine Szene vorangehen zu lassen, in der Zerbinetta für einen Augenblick ein zartes Gefühl für den jungen Komponisten zeigt; dieser Moment genüge, um die Figur der Zerbinetta lebendig zu machen.[24]

(I asked him [Hofmannsthal] once what had moved him to allow the *Vorspiel* to precede the opera 'Ariadne'. He said that the figure of Zerbinetta with her great coloratura aria had seemed marionette-like to him, she lacked the human warmth which made a figure like Philine in Goethe's 'Wilhelm Meister' so enchanting; so he had had the idea of letting the opera be preceded by a scene in which Zerbinetta shows for one moment a tender inclination for the young Composer; this moment would suffice to make the figure of Zerbinetta come alive.)

But this is a one-sided, retrospective account of the genesis of the *Vorspiel*. There were other much more important reasons for writing it. Moreover, as indicated in Chapter III, Zerbinetta is a much more successful, rounded figure in the *Oper* than Hofmannsthal thought. She is ironic and complex but she is also alive and capable of warm feelings. Nevertheless the above quotation does indicate the direction which Zerbinetta's character took in the *Vorspiel* and this will be discussed in the following section.

Firstly, a possible source of the *Vorspiel* not mentioned earlier: the *Vorspiel auf dem Theater* from Goethe's *Faust*. If

[24] Egon Wellesz, 'Hofmannsthal und die Musik', p. 237.

not a direct source, and there is no real evidence that it is,[25] it nevertheless has so many parallels with Hofmannsthal's *Vorspiel* that it can serve only as an excellent illumination of the latter.

In Goethe's *Vorspiel auf dem Theater* a Theatrical Manager, a Poet and a Comedian (in German a 'Lustige Person' who is a Hanswurst or Pickelhering figure) are arguing about the play to follow. The Poet, a figure reminiscent of Hofmannsthal's Composer, wishes to uphold the higher principles of Art. He worships the Muses and despises the common run of men:

> O sprich mir nicht von jener bunten Menge,
> Bei deren Anblick uns der Geist entflieht.[26] (ll.59–60.)

> (O speak not of the crowd, the motley-hued,
> The sight whereof drives reason from my side!)

The Poet is treated ironically by Goethe and does not come off well in the dispute in which the Theatrical Manager has the last word. This Manager is as apparently cynical about artistic standards as ever the Dancing Master, the Major Domo, or the Maecenas were. He advocates stuffing the audience with a variety of scenes:

> Wird vieles vor den Augen abgesponnen,
> So daß die Menge staunend gaffen kann,
> Da habt Ihr in der breite gleich gewonnen,
> Ihr seid ein vielgeliebter Mann. (ll. 91–4)

> (and if with incident you cram the stage,
> And hold entranced the staring populace,
> You're certain then to score a huge success,
> And be acclaimed the wonder of the age.)

The Comedian is a less cynical, more happy-go-lucky person who suggests that what the audience wants is a slice of life:

> In bunten Bildern wenig Klarheit

[25] Hofmannsthal would have known the *Vorspiel auf dem Theater* as part of *Faust* but it is unlikely that he knew of the suggestion that Goethe had originally written the *Vorspiel* as a prologue to his libretto *Die Zauberflöte*. Nevertheless Hofmannsthal had a most profound admiration for Goethe's 'Singspiele' and clearly sought to emulate Goethe the librettist. See Hofmannsthal's *Einleitung zu einem Band von Goethes Werken, enthaltend die Opern und Singspiele*, PIV, pp. 174–81.

[26] *Goethes Werke*, ed. Erich Trunz, 14 vols (Hamburg, 1960), III, 10–15. *Goethe's 'Faust'*, translated by John Shawcross (London, 1959).

Viel Irrtum und ein Fünkchen Wahrheit
So wird der beste Trank gebraut,
Der alle Welt erquickt und auferbaut. (ll. 170–4)

(Gay gaudy pictures, but bewildering too:
Much that is false, a little that is true.
Of such ingredients must the drink be brewed,
That edifies and cheers the multitude.)

Here, as in the *Vorspiel* to *Ariadne,* the purist argument vies
with the argument favouring multiplicity and variety. Zerbinetta's line 'Und wenn ich hineinkomme, wirds schlechter?'
(30) comes to mind. And *Faust* like *Ariadne* is made up of
heterogeneous scenes, styles, and moods. But here the
similarity ends, for Goethe's prologue is actually an *apologia*
added by the Classical Goethe for the open Shakespearean
form of *Faust*,[27] whereas the *Vorspiel* turns on the issue of the
mixture of high tragedy and low comedy which is only part of
Goethe's wider concern.

(3) *An Interpretation of the Text*
One of the functions the *Vorspiel* has in common with the
Zwischenspiel is to explain the meaning of *Ariadne.* The
following dialogue which perfectly captures the ironic theme
was transposed *in toto* from the *Zwischenspiel.* The Major
Domo has made his announcement and now the story must be
explained to Zerbinetta:

    Tanzmeister
  (zu Zerbinetta, lustig geistreich)
Diese Ariadne ist eine Königstochter. Sie ist mit einem gewissen
Theseus entflohen, dem sie vorher das Leben gerettet hat.
    Zerbinetta
  (zwischen Tür und Angel)
So etwas geht selten gut aus.
    Tanzmeister
Theseus wird ihrer überdrüssig und läßt sie bei Nacht auf einer
wüsten Insel zurück!
    Musiklehrer
  (links leise gleichzeitig zum Komponisten)
Noch das, es muß sein!

---

[27] For a useful analysis of form in *Faust* see Eudo C. Mason, *Goethe's Faust: Its
Genesis and Purport* (Berkeley, 1967).

Zerbinetta
(verständnisvoll)
Kleiner Schuft! (27.)

(Dancing Master
(to Zerbinetta, amusingly witty)
This Ariadne is the daughter of a king. She has fled with a certain
Theseus, whose life she saved earlier.
    Zerbinetta
    (from the door)
That sort of thing never ends well.
    Dancing Master
Theseus gets tired of her and leaves her one night on a desert island.
    Music Teacher
    (standing to the left, aside to the Composer)
That too, it has to be!
    Zerbinetta
    (knowingly)
Little rascal!)

Zerbinetta and the Dancing Master treat it as an everyday
affair. Theseus' and Ariadne's behaviour is reduced to its most
banal as Zerbinetta determinedly shows how 'transparent' it
all is. The conversation continues and the Composer and the
Music Teacher spring to Ariadne's defence. They are as
solemn and elevated as the first pair are trivial:

    Tanzmeister
Sie verzehrt sich in Sehnsucht und wünscht den Tod herbei.
    Zerbinetta
Den Tod! Das sagt man so. Natürlich meint sie einen anderen
Verehrer.
    Tanzmeister
Natürlich, so kommts ja auch!
    Komponist
    (hat aufgehorcht, kommt näher)
Nein, Herr, so kommt es nicht! Denn, Herr! sie ist eine von den
Frauen, die nur einem im Leben gehören und danach keinem mehr.
    Zerbinetta
Ha!
    Komponist
    (verwirrt, starrt sie an)
—keinem mehr als dem Tod.

Zerbinetta
(tritt heraus)
Der Tod kommt aber nicht. Wetten wir. Sondern ganz das Gegenteil.
Vielleicht auch ein blasser, dunkeläugiger Bursche, wie du einer
bist.
Musiklehrer
Sie vermuten ganz recht. Es ist der jugendliche Gott
Bacchus, der zu ihr kommt! (28.)

(Dancing Master
She is consumed with longing and wishes for Death.
Zerbinetta
Death! That is what people say. Of course she means another
admirer.
Dancing Master
Of course, that is how it turns out too!
Composer
(has pricked up his ears, comes nearer)
No Sir, that is not how it turns out! Because, Sir! she is one of those
women who only belong to one man in their lives and after that to no
other—
Zerbinetta
Ha!
Composer
(confused, stares at her)
—no other than Death.
Zerbinetta
(steps out)
But Death doesn't come. Let's bet on it. On the contrary quite the
opposite. Perhaps even a pale, dark-eyed lad like you.
Music Teacher
You guess quite correctly. It is the youthful God Bacchus, who
comes to her!)

The Music Teacher inadvertently betrays the Composer here
and shows that even he cannot grasp the finer points of
transformation. Zerbinetta's comment also rightly identifies
Bacchus as the Composer's self-projection, a point which
Strauss underlines in his score.[28] The Composer tries to
explain that Ariadne thought Bacchus was Death and that this
makes a world of difference:

[28] A 6/8 version of Bacchus' triplet motif, first appearing at No. 189+4 bars,
accompanies the Music Teacher's lines from No. 78.

Zerbinetta
(fröhlich, spöttisch)
Als ob man das nicht wüßte! Nun hat sie ja fürs nächste, was sie braucht.
Komponist
(sehr feierlich)
Sie hält ihn für den Todesgott. In ihren Augen, in ihrer Seele ist er es, und darum, einzig nur darum—
Zerbinetta
(aus der Tür)
Das will sie dir weismachen.
Komponist
Einzig nur darum geht sie mit ihm—auf sein Schiff! Sie meint zu sterben! Nein, sie stirbt wirklich.
Zerbinetta
(indem sie was überwirft)
Tata. Du wirst mich meinesgleichen kennen lehren!
Komponist
Sie ist nicht Ihresgleichen!
(Schreiend)
Ich weiß es, daß sie stirbt.
(Leise)
Ariadne ist eine unter Millionen, sie ist die Frau, die nicht vergißt.
Zerbinetta
(tritt heraus)
Kindskopf. (28–9.)

(Zerbinetta
(merrily, mockingly)
As if one didn't know that! Now she's got what she needs.
Composer
(very solemnly)
She takes him for the God of Death. In her eyes, in her soul he is that, and for that reason, only for that reason—
Zerbinetta
(from the door)
She wants you to believe that.
Composer
Only for that reason does she go with him—on his ship! She believes she is going to die. No, she really does die.
Zerbinetta
(slipping something on)
Come, come. You're trying to teach me to know my own kind!

                    Composer
She is not your kind!
    (shouting)
I know that she dies.
    (softly)
Ariadne is one in a million, she is a woman who doesn't forget.
        Zerbinetta
        (steps out)
Silly fool.)

In the above dialogue the ironic mutual non-comprehension of
the two groups is elegantly and skilfully presented. This same
ironic non-comprehension is present in the ironic allegory in
the *Szenarium*. Both groups have taken up extreme positions
about an issue whose inherent irony they unwittingly embody.
Both groups need each other as correctives whether or not
they can accept each other as such. Clearly the irony in this
dialogue, unlike the formal irony discussed in Chapter IV, is
purely thematic. Here the *Vorspiel* is not explaining by analysis
but is explaining by example; the non-comprehension in the
Oper will be a repetition of the above scene and will
presumably help towards a better understanding of the theme.
    The other significant scene in the *Vorspiel* is the encounter
between Zerbinetta and the Composer, first suggested by
Strauss, and already discussed in its *Zwischenspiel* form (158–
59).[29] These lines were expanded and altered from Zerbinetta's
question about the improvisations she will be making in
Ariadne:

        Zerbinetta
Und wenn ich hineinkomme, wirds schlechter?
        Komponist
        (vor sich)
Ich überlebe diese Stunde nicht!
        Zerbinetta
Du wirst noch ganz andere überleben.
        Komponist
        (verloren)
Was wollen Sie damit—in diesem Augenblick—sagen?
        Zerbinetta
        (mit äußerster Koketterie, scheinbar ganz schlicht)

[29] See Chapter V, pp. 215–6.

Ein Augenblick ist wenig—ein Blick ist viel. Viele meinen, daß sie mich kennen, aber ihr Auge ist stumpf. Auf dem Theater spiele ich die Kokette, wer sagt, daß mein Herz dabei im Spiel ist? Ich scheine munter und bin doch traurig, gelte für gesellig und bin doch so einsam.

Komponist
(naiv entzückt)
Süßes, unbegreifliches Mädchen!

Zerbinetta
Törichtes Mädchen, mußt du sagen, das sich manchmal zu sehnen verstünde nach dem einen, dem sie treu sein könnte, treu bis ans Ende.—

Komponist
Wer es sein dürfte, den du ersehnest! Du bist wie ich—das Irdische unvorhanden deiner Seele.

Zerbinetta
(schnell, zart)
Du sprichst, was ich fühle.—Ich muß fort. Vergißt du gleich wieder diesen einen Augenblick?

Komponist
Vergißt sich in Äonen ein einziger Augenblick?
(Zerbinetta macht sich los, läuft schnell in ihr Zimmer nach rechts.) (30–1.)

(Zerbinetta
And if I come in does it get any worse?

Composer
(to himself)
I won't survive this hour!

Zerbinetta
You will survive hours quite different from this.

Composer
What do you mean—at this moment—by that?

Zerbinetta
(extremely coquettish, apparently quite straightforward)
A moment is little—a glance is much. Many think that they know me but their eyes are blind. In the theatre I play the coquette; who says that my heart is in it? I seem merry and yet I am sad, pass as sociable and yet I am so lonely.

Composer
(naïvely enchanted)
Sweet, incomprehensible girl!

Zerbinetta
Silly girl, you should say, who sometimes longs for the man to whom

she could be true, true to the end.—
    Composer
What a privilege to be that man! You are like me—earthly things
have no power over your soul.
    Zerbinetta
    (quickly, tenderly)
You say what I feel.—I must go. Shall you forget this moment
straight away?
    Composer
Is a single moment forgotten in aeons of time?
    (Zerbinetta breaks loose, runs quickly into her room on the right.))

It is necessary to quote at such length here because the passage
is in itself an 'infinite moment', a moment of perfect emotional
and spiritual intimacy the congruence of which cannot be
appreciated unless these two beings are seen first moving
towards and afterwards away from one another. The movement is greater on Zerbinetta's side. Indeed she covers too
much spiritual ground and so can only retreat. At first during
this conversation she retains her identity as a flirtatious
coquette. She is clever enough to sense which line to take with
each new person, and with the Composer chooses a version of
the 'unhappy clown'; she plays the would-be faithful coquette.
The stage direction 'mit äußerster Koketterie, scheinbar ganz
schlicht' (30) is a clear instruction from the author to the
actress that she is to dissimulate. The Composer is taken in, as
we gather from the stage direction 'naiv entzückt'. Zerbinetta
then touches the heart of the matter: if only she could find
someone to be faithful to forever. The Composer continues to
take her seriously and perhaps this is the act of faith needed to
liberate a hitherto dormant spirituality. She cannot put it into
words herself; the Composer expresses it for her: 'Du bist wie
ich—das Irdische unvorhanden deiner Seele' (31). Stage
directions once again indicate beyond doubt the actress's
psychological state. Her next speech is 'schnell, zart'. There is
no need to suspect Zerbinetta of dissimulation here. She has
been genuinely and deeply touched.[30] The Composer has
articulated something vaguely felt: 'Du sprichst, was ich

[30] Several critics claim that in this duet Zerbinetta is at no time sincere. Könneker
regards it ultimately as a 'Mißverständnis' on the Composer's part. Könneker, p. 138.
Del Mar likewise condemns Zerbinetta for her insincerity. See Chapter V, pp. 256–7.

fühle.' But it would not be wrong to say either that this feeling has been repressed, for whatever reason, and that it therefore now threatens her personality or that it is a new feeling, equally subversive, which she would prefer to ignore. Whatever the case, her response is equally appropriate—and predictable: 'Ich muß fort.' She must escape to save Zerbinetta the frivolous flirt. But she cannot suppress a parting question to this past-master of fidelity and therefore of remembering: 'Vergißt du gleich wieder diesen einen Augenblick?' The Composer answers with an emphatic, ecstatic negative: not only will he not forget but he presents her with a whole new world-order in which forgetting does not exist. He presents her with a world of eternal remembrance, a self-remembering world which is necessarily also a faithful world. No wonder then that Zerbinetta must flee back into her own territory: 'Zerbinetta macht sich los, läuft schnell in ihr Zimmer nach rechts' (31). She moves away from the Composer but there is no doubt that they have shared a moment of spiritual closeness.

As indicated, Zerbinetta is the only figure from the *Oper* to be developed in the *Vorspiel*. Does she stay in character in this new addition to the libretto? The lines 'Ich scheine munter und bin doch traurig, gelte für gesellig und bin doch so einsam' (31) are worth considering. Even if spoken 'mit äußerster Koketterie' her next lines show that what she said had an element of truth in it. Zerbinetta the coquette is playing a role. Her real self longs for a different life. Hofmannsthal is adding a sentimental dimension akin to the pathos of the 'sad clown' figure. Zerbinetta in the *Vorspiel* is a coquette by circumstance and not by conviction. But in the *Oper* she is a coquette by conviction and not circumstance. Her ironic self-knowledge and her willing, healthy enjoyment of her way of life, even if shaded by a complex erotic sensibility and an awareness of paradox, make her one with her role and exclude her from the sentimental dilemma of the *Vorspiel* Zerbinetta who would be good if she could. The *Vorspiel* Zerbinetta is a pathological coquette and must have a bad conscience about it into the bargain. The *Oper* Zerbinetta is not pathological because her irony and insight have detached her from what could be a compulsion and have made her into the conscious artist of herself. This finds symbolic expression in her virtuoso song.

The *Vorspiel* Zerbinetta is then reduced in stature and potential although she is the cause of the musically delightful scene with the Composer and a means of characterizing him further. The genesis of Zerbinetta in the *Oper* was, as we have seen, full of unintentional felicities which allowed the authors' genius to come to the fore sometimes in spite of themselves, but in the *Vorspiel* the authors missed the opportunity of capitalizing on these felicities and instead stepped down to the sentimentally 'human'.

So far this encounter has been looked at only from Zerbinetta's side. From the Composer's side it is rich in irony. Not two seconds before falling in love with Zerbinetta the Composer was outraged and exasperated by the prospect of her and her low partners being mixed up in his *Ariadne*. She was to him nothing but an uncomprehending comedienne, and then suddenly he finds her irresistibly attractive. Here the theme of the irony of love which is behind the whole work is presented in terms of realistic rather than stylized characters. But the irony is identical with that of Ariadne falling in love again.

There is also gentle irony in the observation of the emotional sequence following the Composer's love scene with Zerbinetta. During a little interlude the cast assembles itself on stage and Zerbinetta reappears having recovered herself enough to blow the Composer a saucy kiss. The Composer, in a touching state of elation and joy after his recent experience, 'umarmt den Musikmeister stürmisch' (32). He is inspired with confidence in his art and sings:

(Mit fast trunkener Feierlichkeit)
Musik ist heilige Kunst, zu versammeln alle Arten von Mut wie Cherubim um einen strahlenden Thron! Das ist Musik, und darum ist sie die heilige unter den Künsten! (33.)

((With almost intoxicated solemnity)
Music is a holy art that gathers all kinds of courage like cherubim around a radiant throne! That is music and that is why music is holy amongst the arts!)

The Composer is in what William James, one of Hofmannsthal's most revered authors, would refer to as a 'faith state'. This state 'may be a mere vague enthusiasm, half spiritual, half vital, a courage and a feeling that great and wondrous things are in the air'.[31] It is a state well known to lovers, here gently satirized by Hofmannsthal and neatly undercut by the rude entrance of the comedians (33). His enthusiasm turns just as quickly to despair. Who are these creatures, he cries. The *Vorspiel* ends with the Composer's pathetic overstatement:

Ich durfte es nicht erlauben! Du durftest mir nicht erlauben, es zu erlauben! Wer hieß dich mich zerren, mich! in diese Welt hinein? Laß mich erfrieren, verhungern, versteinern in der meinigen!
    (Läuft vorne ab, verzweifelt.) (34.)

W. Mann is of the opinion that the *Vorspiel* ought to end with the Composer's paean to music and omit the return to a vulgar reality.[32] If, however, the full sequence of the Composer's emotions and moods were curtailed, his changeability would not be fully portrayed in all its endearing and humorous aspects.

Before discussing the full significance of the Zerbinetta–Composer episode we might turn our attention to other possible interpretations of the Composer whose part has now been presented in its entirety. E. Krause postulates direct social and political relevance: 'Er [der Komponist] ist der Exponent des sich aus feudalistischen Fesseln befreienden Künstlertums, der seine Werke nach eigener Überzeugung schaffen will.'[33] (He [the Composer] is the exponent of an artistic world freeing itself from feudal bonds and he wishes to create his work according to his own convictions.) The problems of patronage in the *Vorspiel* are not feudal in the strict sense for the 'richest man in Vienna' could also be a 'bourgeois gentilhomme'. Nevertheless the question of artistic freedom in a quasi-feudal environment is central to the Composer's situation.

The implications of this character for Hofmannsthal's total *œuvre* are to be found in a critical insight offered by H. Broch. In order to overcome the decadent aestheticism prevalent in the Austria of his youth, Hofmannsthal, Broch suggests, made

---

[31] William James, *Varieties of Religious Experience* (London, 1910). p. 210.
[32] Mann, p. 158.
[33] Ernst Krause, *Richard Strauss: Gestalt und Werk*, p. 374.

the stage into an ethical forum in which occurs a 'Ritual der Sittlichkeit'.[34] But he could never quite renounce the cult of beauty which was also part of his heritage. As Broch comments, 'Das Wörtchen "schön" blieb eines der häufigsten seines Vokabulars'.[35] The theatre then becomes the place where Hofmannsthal can reach a compromise between ethics and beauty. This compromise is effected by the author, who becomes a figure on the stage and thus is a personified mediator between the beauty of the theatrical dream and illusion and the moral demands which he has accepted as part of his social definition of theatre:

Die Welt—'Wie schön ist diese Schlacht'—wird zum schönen Theater, das der Künstler eben dieser selben Welt vorzuführen hat, er, ihr idealer Zuschauer und infolgedessen zugleich auch ihr idealer Darsteller, so daß er auf seinem Parkettplatz innerhalb der Menge sitzend . . . sich zugleich auch in der Abgesondertheit und Einsamkeit der Bühne befindet. Die Doppelstellung des Innen und Außen zugleich, die der Dichter im 'szenischen Gedicht' imaginär ausfüllt, wird auf die Bühnenrealität übertragen und muß hier—wie alles auf der Bühne—handfeste Gestalt annehmen: das ist der Grund, um dessentwillen der 'Prologus' und 'der Dichter' schier unentbehrliche Figuren der Hofmannsthalschen Personenverzeichnisse sind, der eine als Vor-Kommentator für das Dichtergeschäft, der andere beauftragt . . . das Kompromiß zwischen Schönheit und Sittlichkeit als szenisches Ritual vor den Augen des Zuschauers zu vollziehen.[36]

(The world—'How beautiful is this battle'—becomes beautiful theatre, which the artist has to present in turn to this same world; he, the ideal spectator and therefore also the ideal performer: and so when he sits amongst the crowd in the stalls . . . he also feels the remoteness and loneliness of being on stage. The double position of inside and outside, which the poet occupies in his imagination in the 'scenic poem', is transferred to the stage reality and here it must— like everything on the stage—assume tangible shape; that is the reason why the 'prologus' and 'the poet' are quite indispensable figures in the Hofmannsthalian list of dramatis personae: the one as an 'advance commentator' on the business of writing poetry, the other charged with . . . effecting the compromise between beauty and morality as a scenic ritual before the spectator's eyes.)

[34] Broch, p. 199.
[35] Broch, p. 199.
[36] Broch, pp. 199–200. (The line 'Wie schön ist diese Schlacht' is from *Das kleine Welttheater*, GuLD, p. 375.)

The Composer, although an ironic portrait, is like the 'Dichter' and the 'Prologus' in being an embodiment on stage of the artist and so making palpable this compromise between 'inner' dream and 'outer' morality. But he is more than just a token figure symbolizing a struggle: his own work, *Ariadne auf Naxos,* epitomizes the compromise, for in it he tries to conjure up a moral apotheosis. Its final wonderful, magical dream-sequence, which comes to a climax in a moment of beautiful illusion as the lovers embrace against a starry sky, has supposedly been made legitimate by being closely but not always comfortably bound in with moral issues. The Composer's romantic apotheosis makes an uneasy settlement with his moral idealism.

The final significance of the Zerbinetta–Composer scene lies, however, in the Composer as a symbol of the antitheses in the *Oper*. As Hofmannsthal wrote to Strauss, 'Der Komponist ... ist rein symbolisch halb tragische, halb komische Figur, die Antithese des ganzen Spiels (Ariadne, Zerbinetta, Harlekins Welt) ist jetzt in ihm verankert.' (Bw. 3 June 1913, p. 198.) (The Composer ... is, symbolically, a figure half tragic, half comic; the whole antithesis of the action (Ariadne, Zerbinetta, Harlekin's world) is now firmly focused on him.) The affair with Zerbinetta helps the Composer towards this tragi-comic identity because in it he, the romantic idealist, embraces his opposite, the light-hearted realist. The mixture of tragic *opera seria* and comic *opera buffa* in the *Oper,* and all mixed forms of art thus find, momentarily at least, the right to exist in this embrace. As Könneker says, the question of the mixed art form or 'Gesamtkunstwerk' becomes thematic in the *Vorspiel*. She adds:

Diese Synthese zwischen Seelendrama und Posse, Tiefsinn und Frivolität, Illusion und Skepsis, banaler äußerer Wirklichkeit und höherer Wirklichkeit in der Kunst, wie sie sich in der endgültigen Fassung des Vorspiels vollzieht—sie wird geleistet von dem jungen Komponisten, dem Schöpfer der tragisch heroischen Oper, bewirkt und gestiftet aber wird sie von keinem anderen als der 'gemeinen Lebensmaske' Zerbinetta.[37]

(This synthesis between spiritual drama and buffoonery, profundity

[37] Könneker, p. 136.

and frivolity, illusion and scepticism, banal external reality and higher reality in art, this synthesis as it is realized in the final version of the prologue—is achieved by the young Composer, the creator of the tragic heroic opera, but it is caused and produced by none other than the 'common masque' Zerbinetta.)

ii. *The Music*

The *Zwischenspiel* was not set to music, neither was any incidental music to be played during it. The idea of expanding this scene and composing music for it came with the decision to revise. In a conversation (of which there is no record) Strauss suggested using secco recitatives for the new *Vorspiel*. On 9 December 1912 Hofmannsthal wrote 'Bin recht froh über unser Gespräch neulich, Ihren glücklichen Einfall mit den Secco-Rezitativen' (Bw. 9 Dec. 1912, p. 175). On 22 December 1912 he wrote '[ich will] auch das Vorspiel zur 'Ariadne' vornehmen und ein bißchen durchgehen, ... so daß das Ganze für eine Behandlung mit Secco-Rezitativen als bleibendes Piedestal 'Ariadne' möglichst gut wird' (Bw. 22 Dec. 1912, pp. 179–80).

In fact the *Vorspiel* is not written in secco recitative style proper.[38] This kind of operatic recitative was developed in the eighteenth century and was used in *opera seria* and the operas of Mozart and Rossini. In contrast to the aria it is a fast and unmelodious parlando clearly intended as a vehicle for the narrative sections of the libretto. The Harvard Dictionary of Music notes under the term recitativo secco 'It. secco, dry— with reference to its lack of expressiveness'. Most importantly the recitativo secco was sung to a thorough-bass accompaniment only.

An example of this type of recitative can be found in the *Oper* and has already been discussed. This is the opening bars to Zerbinetta's great solo scene beginning *Großmächtige Prinzessin* (No. 101–9 bars).[39] The accompaniment (on the piano) is sparse and chordal and the repeated notes in the vocal line give it its characteristic 'patter'. Daviau and Buelow rightly suggest that this recitative was the source of inspiration

---

[38] A point not brought out by Daviau and Buelow, pp. 223–4.

[39] See Chapter III, pp. 148–9. Good examples of secco recitatives in the *Vorspiel* are to be found in Zerbinetta's part from No. 83 to No. 84 and from No. 26 + 1 bar to No. 27.

for the *Vorspiel*.[40] But Strauss also provided the scene with recitativo accompagnato (a more strictly measured recitative, dramatic rather than declamatory, having an instrumental accompaniment), lyric arioso episodes, songs, a love duet and spoken dialogue in the first section, and an ariette. There are numerous examples of secco recitative, such as part of the Composer's conversation with the lackey about the violins starting from 'Wenn ich sage: die Geigen, so meine ich die Spieler' (No. 15 to No. 17). A further example is the setting of the Wigmaker's line 'Dero mißhelliges Betragen kann ich belächelnd nur einer angeborenen Gemütsaufwallung zurechnen' (No. 24+4 bars), in which the accompaniment, although on the strings, is so thin as not to count for more than a continuo Ex. 33.

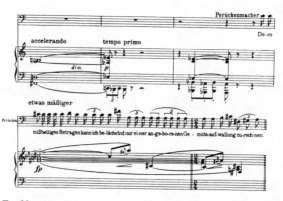

Ex. 33

When Strauss uses recitativo accompagnato—the most frequent style in the *Vorspiel*—then he almost invariably employs a motif technique in which motifs from the overture to the *Vorspiel* and more importantly from the *Oper* are used either as directly referential quotation or as wittily ironic commentary. This brings us to an unusual feature of the *Vorspiel,* namely that as a result of the opera's complicated genesis it was composed last not first. The full ingenuity of the motif treatment in the *Vorspiel* cannot be appreciated by anyone who does not know the *Oper* very well indeed.

[40] Daviau and Buelow, p. 224.

Nevertheless Strauss's *Vorspiel* although composed in this esoteric way is immediately enjoyable in its own right and has the merit of being a seminal preparation for the *Oper:* the melodic fragments are given in the first half and in the second half the listener has the pleasure of being reminded of them and of hearing them in their new yet proper context. This motivic preparation is essentially the same as that employed in many operatic overtures (for example the overture to *Der Freischütz* (1821)). Daviau and Buelow make the additional point that this use of motivic material in the *Vorspiel* musically integrates the two parts of the work.[41]

There are examples of the purely referential quotation of *Oper* motifs on nearly every page of the score. Needless to say, there is hardly a mention of 'Ariadne' or the comic 'Nachspiel' which does not prompt an appropriate motif from the orchestra. For instance there is the Music Master's introduction of Zerbinetta to the Composer:

Musiklehrer
Es ist die Zerbinetta. Sie singt und tanzt mit vier Partnern das lustige Nachspiel, das man nach deiner Oper gibt.
Komponist
(zurückprallend)
Nach meiner Oper? Ein lustiges Nachspiel? Tänze und Triller, freche Gebärden und zweideutige Worte nach 'Ariadne'! Sag mirs!
Musiklehrer
(zaghaft)
Ich bitte dich um alles.—
Komponist
(tritt von ihm weg; edel)
Das Geheimnis des Lebens tritt an sie heran. (17.)

(Music Teacher
That's Zerbinetta. With four partners she sings and dances the comic after-piece, which is to follow your opera.
Composer
(recoiling)
After my opera? A comic after-piece? Dances and trills, saucy gestures and suggestive words after 'Ariadne'! Is that what you mean?

[41] Daviau and Buelow, p. 220. See Del Mar for an analysis of the musical motifs in the *Vorspiel*.

Music Teacher
(cautiously)
I beseech you.—
    Composer
   (steps away from him; nobly)
The secret of life touches her.)

The first line with its reference to the 'Nachspiel' is set against the principal theme of the Intermezzo which first appears at No. 79 in the *Oper* on the piano and pizzicato strings (Ex. 34).

Ex. 34

Here the theme is allowed to climb the E major scale with a dramatic twist on B sharp which gives an impression of the mounting tension inside the Composer as he hears this news. At No. 30 he burst out 'zurückprallend' and 'heftig bewegt' with an unaccompanied 'Nach meiner Oper' (Ex. 35). Then the words 'Tänze und Triller, freche Gebärden' are set to the

Ex. 35

dance theme of the Intermezzo finale. At the mention of 'Ariadne' her theme from the *Oper* overture is quoted. At No. 31 in response to the words 'Das Geheimnis des Lebens', meaning transformation, one of Bacchus' motifs sounds forth in the bass.

At No. 33 + 4 bars at the words 'Ein heiteres Nachspiel! Ein Übergang zu ihrer Gemeinheit!' the dance theme quoted above reappears. The mention of Bacchus at No. 22 brings forth his little triplet motif. And at No. 52 the line 'Ariadne ist das Losungswort' is set to her 'Befreiungsmotif'[42] which the Music Teacher sings in a consciously grand manner.

Humorously or ironically used motifs occur less often but once recognized they add a little more spice to the already exotic *Vorspiel*. At No. 65 the Dancing Master, persuading the others to make a few judicious cuts in the *Oper,* sings 'Die Oper enthält Längen—gefährliche Längen'.[43] This too is set to the 'Befreiungsmotif', one of the most serious and sublime moments in Ariadne's tragic monologue. The implication is of course that she is not grand but simply boring. And Strauss may even be making fun of his own heroic melodies here. At No. 50 the Dancing Master humorously sings Zerbinetta's name to an imitation of one of her roulades and at No. 43 + 5 bars the Primadonna answers her own question 'Weiß man hier nicht, wer ich bin?' in spite of herself—Strauss has her sing it to a main motif from Ariadne's aria. At No. 67 this same Ariadne motif turns into the comedians' dance motif (Ex. 36). The full speech of the Dancing Master runs 'Fragen Sie ihn, ob er seine Oper lieber heute ein wenig verstümmelt hören will, oder ob er sie niemals hören will. Schaffen Sie ihm Tinte, Feder, einen Rotschift, was immer! (Zum Komponisten) Es handelt sich darum, Ihr Werk zu retten' (25). Here the Dancing Master is clearly saying that the *commedia dell'arte* with its fund of practical common sense will help rescue 'Ariadne'. Therefore the Ariadne motif can be taken over or 'rescued' by the *buffa* motif. But at the same time, ironically, the heroic dimension is thus made harmless and trivial. Here

---

[42] See Chapter III, p. 188.
[43] This is another instance of a minor change by Strauss not being recorded in LIII; Strauss reduced the longer line 'Es sind Längen in der Oper—gefährliche Längen' (25).

Ex. 36

is a musical reinforcement of that ironic non-comprehension already discussed in connection with the *Vorspiel*.[44]

At No. 69 there is an ironic 'in-joke' about the sacrifice of the 1912 *Bürger als Edelmann*—which an audience could surely not appreciate without studying the score of both versions. The Dancing Master is singing the words 'Hundert große Meister, die wir auf dem Knien bewundern, haben sich ihre erste Aufführung mit noch ganz anderen Opfern erkauft' (26). At the word 'Opfer' there is a quotation of the Dinner Music which was one of the incidental pieces for *Der Bürger als Edelmann* all of which were sacrificed in favour of the *Vorspiel*.

Occasionally Strauss uses motifs non-ironically to give a deeper psychological meaning to the text being sung. This is the case at No. 79 when the Composer's line 'Sie hält ihn für den Todesgott' (28) is set over the Bacchus motif which features so prominently in the 'Verwandlung' in Scene III of the *Oper*. The mysterious identity of Death and transformation are thus proclaimed even in the *Vorspiel*.

Much of the new material for the *Vorspiel* draws on the two key motifs of the Composer (Ex. 37). These are used in

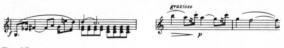

Ex. 37

[44] See Chapter V, pp. 229–33.

accordance with the Romantic psychological tradition. The
first motif is built on an initial leap of a major seventh with the
minor sixth E flat acting as a grace note followed by a leap of
a minor seventh (F sharp to E natural with A and G as passing
notes). It is clearly vital, thrusting and spontaneous in
character. The second is a feminine counterpart with the
falling seconds conveying sorrow, a sob in the throat or
sighing. Strauss uses both these motifs, but especially the first,
at all those points in the libretto which seem psychologically
typical of the young Composer, where he is acting or reacting
in a way that is unique to himself and in which his character
seems to be particularly concentrated. Thus Strauss underlines
these separate instances and gathers them into a composite
characterization by means of these motifs. One example is the
Composer's refusal to compromise 'Ariadne' after the Major
Domo's second announcement. All his resistance and impet-
uous idealism culminate in the word 'Fort!' which is also a cry
to action. Under the vocal line is a clear statement of the
Composer's first motif (Ex. 38). At No. 64 the Composer's

Ex. 38

outrage at the common, vulgar world explodes with the
rhetorical 'Wozu leben in ihr' (25). This is set over the first
motif. At No. 69 the same motif appears softly in a minor key
illustrating the Composer's helpless queries about whether he
ought to change his work. At No. 85 — 5 bars the second motif
accompanies the words 'Sie gibt sich dem Tod hin—ist nicht
mehr da—weggewischt' (30). The expressive, sad quality of
this motif is here exploited to the full. The second motif is used
at No. 88 to convey quite a different feeling: outrage at the
buffoons. At No. 108 following the Composer's 'conversion'
through his affair with Zerbinetta both motifs are used to

express the passionate enthusiasm of the Composer's new faith in life.

By appearing at different psychological moments these motifs acquire multiple shades of meaning and conversely each repetition of the motif must adumbrate the other moments. Del Mar's epigrammatic summary of the motifs, the first delineating 'the impetuosity of the boy himself' and the second 'representing his instinctive protest against the buffo characters'[45] is too narrow and, a more serious criticism, implies a technical procedure which was not Strauss's: Del Mar implies that the Composer's motifs are fixed in meaning from the outset and that they are merely cited where possible whereas Strauss's motifs are fluid, acquire meaning gradually from their contexts and come to stand for the Composer's many-faceted character.

Near the opening of the *Vorspiel* there is a section of alternating spoken and sung parts. The *Vorspiel* turns temporarily into a kind of Singspiel.[46] The device of spoken dialogue is dramatically effective in the *Vorspiel* for it underlines the character of the 'prosaic' Major Domo, that 'Prosamensch' who represents an unpoetic world. His presence is a reminder of this world outside, which even in the 1916 version is there as an imaginary frame. The contrast between the clearly enunciated, pompously delivered words and the flexible, light secco recitative only serves to reinforce the gap between the worlds and to make the bizarre command more credible. It has been objected that the Major Domo's part is a 'Stilbruch'[47] but the *Vorspiel* is essentially such a mixture of styles that this objection does not carry much weight. Furthermore the prose passages have the advantage that the information given by the Major Domo, so vital to the plot, can be perfectly understood by the audience.

[45] Del Mar, pp. 62–3.

[46] Del Mar refers to the opening as 'a form of fragmentary melodrama' and adds that Strauss had had some practice with this form years earlier in *Enoch Arden* (1898). Del Mar, p. 64. But, strictly speaking, melodrama is a stage representation intermediate between play and opera, and consists of a spoken text and background music. Singspiel on the other hand consists of alternating spoken and sung passages as in Mozart's *Die Entführung aus dem Serail* (1782) and therefore I have preferred it as a term.

[47] Eugen Schmitz, 'Die Neubearbeitung der *Ariadne auf Naxos*', p. 718.

But Hofmannsthal did not want the *Vorspiel* to consist entirely of recitatives and spoken dialogue. On 3 June 1913 he wrote to Strauss 'damit es nicht ganz secco [*sic*], sind kleine witzige Anlässe zur Arie geschaffen' (Bw. 3 June 1913, p. 198). And on 12 June 1913 when sending off the corrected copy of the *Vorspiel* Hofmannsthal expanded on this point:

Das Ganze ist für Seccorezitativ gedacht, nur um die Figur des Komponisten witternd ein Höheres: Musik. Hierzu meinerseits folgende Anhaltspunkte: Zuerst die Findung der Melodie ('O, Du Venussohn') aus dem 'Bourgeois', diese Findung zweimal: ferner am Schluß das Zwiegespräch mit Zerbinetta, der Aufschwung zu etwas Höherem als bloßes Parlando: Vielleicht mündet das Ganze in ein winziges Duett, nicht eigentlich eine *Nummer,* oder ähnlich, auf die letzten Sätze des Textes, die lyrisch gehalten sind. Endlich drittens der lyrische Höhepunkt (zu welchem die obige Melodie als zu zart und zahm erschien)—der Ausbruch des Komponisten: 'Musik'! (Bw. 12 June 1913, p. 199.)

(Everything is intended for *secco* recitative, only round the figure of the Composer a glimmer of something more: music. For this I have provided the following *points d'appui:* first the genesis of the tune ('O, Du Venussohn') from the *Bourgeois*—this twice; then at the end the conversation with Zerbinetta, rising emotionally to something more than mere *parlando;* perhaps the thing might lead up to a tiny duet or something of the kind, but not a proper *number,* on the last few sentences of the text, which are lyrical in tone. Thirdly and finally: the lyrical climax (for which the above melody is probably too tender and tame); I mean the Composer's outburst: 'Music!')

The song *Du Venussohn* is based on a lovely lilting sicilienne (Ex. 39). This melody is first heard on the oboe at No. 20 after

Ex. 39

the Composer's contretemps with the lackey. His expression changes from one of anger to reflection and his next line 'O ich möcht vieles ändern noch in zwölfter Stund' (14) suggests that he would like to incorporate the melody into his opera. He suddenly remembers what is going to be done to his work that very evening and forg ats his melody. Then at No. 21 Strauss adds a direction not given in the libretto: 'er nimmt die Melodie, die ihm eingefallen war, wieder auf.' Interrupting the melody to make its genesis seem even more immediate was thus Strauss's own original contribution. Strauss introduces another nice touch at No. 25 + 2 bars: The Composer asks the Wigmaker for 'ein Stückerl Schreibpapier' (15) and a new part of the sicilienne is suggested both in the vocal line and in the accompaniment (Ex. 40). At No. 37, our appetites whetted, we are allowed to hear the song in full. It comes as a welcome relief to the ear after the rapid flow of recitatives.

Ex. 40

The next 'oases' were added by Strauss entirely on his own initiative. The first is a miniature piano sonata at No. 44 accompanying Zerbinetta's complaints about how difficult it will be to amuse the audience after 'Ariadne'. The vocal line is in itself not very melodic and the musical relief is provided by the piano. This instrument features largely in the second 'oasis' which is the Dancing Master's ariette. This is based on material from the incidental music to *Der Bürger als Edelmann* and its fresh appealing chamber idiom will be recognized as the major influence on the *commedia dell'arte* music in the *Oper*. Del Mar points out a detail which well illustrates this point: the comedians' dance motif[48] is actually an inversion of a motif heard at bar 60 of the orchestral introduction to the second act of *Der Bürger als Edelmann*.

Hofmannsthal gave quite detailed instructions about the

---

[48] Quoted in Chapter V, p. 244.

'Ode to Music' and continued in the letter of 12 June 1913:

Hier müßte der Text zur Findung einer neuen schönen Melodie
anregen, feierlich schwungvoll, hoffentlich tut er seine Schuldigkeit:
(Richtig in Zeilen gesetzt)

> 'Musik ist eine heilige Kunst
> zu versammeln alle Arten von Mut
> um einen strahlenden Thron!
> Das ist Musik!
> Und darum ist sie die Heilige unter den Künsten!'

(Ich empfand den Text als etwas der Art, wie Beethoven nicht
ungern zu Grunde legte.) (Bw. 12 June 1913, pp. 199–200.)

(Here the words ought to inspire you to find a new, beautiful melody,
solemn and ebullient; let's hope they accomplish their object:

> (Properly organized in lines)
> Music is a holy art
> that gathers all kinds of courage
> around a radiant throne!
> That is music!
> And that is why music is holy amongst the arts!

(This struck me as the kind of text Beethoven might have liked to
use.))

Hofmannsthal was no doubt thinking of Schiller's 'Freude,
schöner Götterfunken' and the aria begins with a Beethovenian
enough opening in A flat major following the introductory
'Mut ist in mir' No. 112 which ends on a chord of E flat used
as the dominant of A flat. But from there on Strauss gives free
rein to his own personal style. The melody begins peacefully
yet ebulliently. Fittingly, the Composer's motifs can be heard
in the orchestra. However the artificiality of this euphuistic
text to someone like Strauss who was first and foremost a
music dramatist and in any case not an idealist soon begins to
take its toll and the music deteriorates into bombast after No.
115. The hackneyed climax of the aria is typical of Strauss at
his worst and all the danger signs such as octaves, over-
orchestration, fingered tremoli, lack of rhythmic variety and
banal diatonicism are there.

A section of the *Vorspiel* music vital to the interpretation of
the whole work is the setting of the Zerbinetta–Composer
encounter. Hofmannsthal had definite ideas about this scene

as he made clear in the already quoted letter of 12 June 1913:
'Ferner am Schluß das Zwiegespräch mit Zerbinetta, der
Aufschwung zu etwas Höherem als bloßes Parlando: Vielleicht
mündet das Ganze in ein winziges Duett, nicht eigentlich eine
Nummer, oder ähnlich, auf die letzten Sätze des Textes, die
lyrisch gehalten sind' (Bw. 12 June 1913, p. 199). He did not
regard this scene as the lyric climax of the *Vorspiel.* The 'Ode
to Music' seemed more important to him. But Strauss's
instincts as an operatic composer told him that musically,
psychologically, and emotionally this encounter was crucial
and bound to be more effective on stage than a solo aria.
Strauss found an opportunity here for a lyrical, sentimental
interlude. Hofmannsthal himself made a sentimental interpretation possible but in the letter of 12 June 1913 he stresses
that it must be kept within bounds and refers only to the last
few sentences of the text as being lyrical in tone. In the libretto
Zerbinetta and the Composer do share a moment of spiritual
intimacy but at the beginning of their conversation Zerbinetta
preserves her identity as a coquette. She is full of dissimulation
until the sudden reversal of the last few lines, which she speaks
sincerely, thereby losing the self-irony of the Zerbinetta in the
Oper. Strauss however allowed no room for psychological
development and Zerbinetta in the music is sincere from the
outset.

In order to establish this point her aria *Ein Augenblick ist
wenig* is quoted from at length (Ex. 41). Everything about the

Ex. 41

music contradicts the direction 'scheinbar ganz schlicht, mit
äußerster Coquetterie'. As Daviau and Buelow write, 'the
music is incandescently sensuous, and the aria is the most
passionate and compelling of its type in either act.'[49] At No.
91 there is a perfect cadence from the dominant B major into
the rich warm key of E major. Zerbinetta's long, winding
melody plays around the tonic triad and then grows more
complicated as the aria passes through various modulations
returning to E major at the Composer's next entry. The
dynamic markings are pianissimo, espressivo, and molto
espressivo. The tempo marking is 'ruhig bewegt' with the
instruction that rubato should be freely used. The orchestration
is vibrant and full, with an exquisite solo violin part making
frequent use of poignant unresolved appoggiaturas (x) rising
an octave. A tiny motif from Zerbinetta's coloratura aria *So
war es mit Pagliazzo*,[50] one of her most devilishly flirtatious
and difficult passages, is here transformed beyond recognition
into a wistful melodic turn (y). Further on in this aria the
Composer's two motifs are augmented and take on such a
quiet, lyrical hue that they are no longer recognizable either.

Strauss is transforming motifs belonging to both Zerbinetta
and the Composer which were originally dynamic and
extravert into their lyrical, introspective antitheses; he is
clearly suggesting an equivalent spiritual transformation. Thus
Strauss lets Zerbinetta 'drop the mask' much sooner than
Hofmannsthal and the music continues as a full-blown love
duet.

The Composer's reply to Zerbinetta 'Süßes, unbegreifliches
Mädchen!' (31) is melodiously triadic and remains in E major.
His theme played on the strings begins a chromatic descent to
the key of D flat major and at No. 95 there is a sudden
melancholy shift to a dominant seventh chord on E flat which
draws the listener up short for Zerbinetta's next sentence:
'Törichtes Mädchen, mußt du sagen, das sich manchmal zu
sehnen verstünde nach dem einen, dem sie treu sein könnte,
treu bis ans Ende.—' (31). Here Strauss has added the explicit
and revealing direction 'einfach und ruhig'. When Zerbinetta
comes to the word 'sehnen' the key of D flat (as Daviau and

[49] Daviau and Buelow, p. 237.
[50] See motif x in the musical example quoted in Chapter III, p. 154.

Buelow point out, significantly the key of Ariadne's transformation[51]) is finally established and she is instructed to be 'sehr innig'. Her aria becomes more and more sincere and moving and reaches a climax on the word 'treu' sung first on a high G flat and then a high B flat (No. 97).

The Composer is understandably carried away and tells her they are kindred spirits as indeed Strauss's music has made them. Now come those last few lines, which Hofmannsthal considered lyrical enough for something more than mere parlando but not for a proper number. Zerbinetta sings 'schnell, zart'. The Composer has moved her deeply but she must escape this emotion. Obviously Strauss is now building up to the climax of this episode and is not going to sacrifice

Ex. 42

any possible effect. Lyrical expansion is the order of the day and a moment which ought to be fleeting and shy is drawn out into a heartfelt declaration (Ex. 42). Many features in this passage account for its emotional richness. The effective, poignant appoggiaturas are now in the voice part as well as in

[51] Daviau and Buelow, p. 238.

the orchestra. The markings are pianissimo subito, espressivo and larghetto ('etwas breit'). The bass is made up of long sustained chords. There is an exceptionally beautiful melisma precisely on the word 'fühlen'. At (x) the violins come in with an ornamented version of the Composer's second motif. But although they are marked 'ziemlich lebhaft' and although they should be fast and lively, expressing Zerbinetta's desire to escape, these violins play slowly in comparison with what has passed before in the *Vorspiel* and convey no urgency. In the next bar the music and the words are distinctly at odds. The three words 'ich muß fort' although marked 'schnell' are sung to notes with long values. The dotted minim on 'fort' is particularly weak, regardless of how much rubato is used. After an orchestral bar marked espressivo the music moves to Zerbinetta's parting question 'Vergißt du gleich wieder diesen einen Augenblick?' (31). The climax of the entire duet is reached at No. 102 when the Composer, 'hingerissen, schwärmend', sings his answer. This was one of the passages that Hofmannsthal in response to a request from Strauss designated as suitable for lyrical expansion:

Folgende zwei Stellen sind zu einer lyrischen, d.h. musikalischen Verbreiterung geeignet:

1. Die Stelle: 'Vergißt sich in Äonen ein einziger Augenblick!' Duett über diese Zeile, als Text, die unzähliger Wiederholung mit verschiedenstem Ausdruck fähig ist.
2. 'Laß mich verhungern, versteinern, erfrieren in der meinigen!' als rührende, klagende kleine Arie auszudehnen. (Bw. 8 May 1916, p. 285.)

(The following two passages are suitable for lyrical, i.e. musical expansion:
1. The passage: 'Is a single moment forgotten in aeons of time!' Duet on this line, capable of endless repetition in various moods.
2. 'Let me starve, turn to stone, freeze in my own world!' could be expanded into a touching, plaintive little aria.)

But Strauss did not need such elaborate expansion now and merely drew out the line into an eleven-bar melody made up of a seven-bar and then a four-bar phrase. This number ends quietly on an E major chord with the violins holding a top B and the mood is rudely interrupted by the comedians bursting onto the stage for the final scene (No. 104−1 bar).

Most critics have recognized that Zerbinetta steps out of character in this scene. W. Mann refers to their duet as being 'in melody and harmony and orchestral texture of intoxicating voluptuousness so that we like the Composer are enchanted by the magic spell of Zerbinetta's sexuality'.[52] Daviau and Buelow present a similar argument: 'We are carried away with Zerbinetta's charms for she has become what she was not meant to be: a genuinely tender, misunderstood woman whose magnetic personality is more than anyone could resist. Because of the music, the audience cannot make the necessary distinction between what she appears to be and what Hofmannsthal intended her to be.[53] Ernst Krause is of the same opinion although he qualifies it by suggesting that Zerbinetta is deceiving herself—which does not fit in with the musical analysis given above: 'In diesem Duett findet Strauss für sie Töne eines bezaubernd reinen Gefühls. Sie ist gar nicht die treulos Schwankende der Hauptoper. Sie ist, wenn auch vielleicht nur in einem Augenblick der Selbsttäuschung, sehr wohl einer wahren Liebe wert.'[54] (In this duet Strauss finds for her notes of enchantingly pure feeling. She is not at all the faithless, fickle woman of the main opera. Even if only for a moment of self-deception, she is very worthy of true love.)

But Del Mar, in spite of his insights into the discrepancies between the libretto to the *Vorspiel,* the character built up in the *Oper* and the music to this scene, misinterprets it by claiming that at *no* time is Zerbinetta genuine. It is as if Del Mar is trying to compensate for, and correct, Strauss's lyrical excesses by injecting a dose of pragmatism into his analysis. He writes: 'It is difficult to realize that she and the Composer are not singing a love duet. On the contrary Zerbinetta's remarks are extremely cynical and provocative.'[55] We have seen that they *are* singing a love duet and that only some of Zerbinetta's remarks in Hofmannsthal's text may be described as cynical or provocative. Further on Del Mar adds: '(Perhaps

[52] Mann, p. 158.
[53] Daviau and Buelow, p. 239.
[54] Ernst Krause, *Richard Strauss: Gestalt und Werk,* p. 375.
[55] Del Mar, p. 69.

Circe's seduction of Bacchus was hardly fundamentally different from Zerbinetta's of the Composer in the present scene, and was certainly no more sincere.) The entranced Composer sees in Zerbinetta a kindred spirit; she shrewdly plays on his loyalty, extracts his enduring faithfulness and makes her escape.'[56] We have seen that Zerbinetta was not behaving in such a calculated way at all. Simply to dismiss Zerbinetta's behaviour as 'duplicity' as Del Mar does is to miss the essence of this scene.[57]

But few if any critics have examined the implications of these discrepancies in terms of the meaning of the *Vorspiel*. In the libretto the Zerbinetta–Composer encounter prefigured the irony of Ariadne's falling in love again and the Composer symbolized the antitheses of the *Oper*. He is a tragi-comic figure and his affair with Zerbinetta is a symbolic union of opposites which in a sense justifies the strange mixture of *opera seria* and *opera buffa* in the following work.

In the music, however, Zerbinetta responds to the Composer in like coin. She is no longer the comic coquette but reveals her idealistic, true self. The antitheses are then cancelled out and there is nothing ironic in the Composer's loving her; she is not his opposite. Once again in the Strauss–Hofmannsthal collaboration romantic idealism has asserted itself a little too forcefully. And it is at this point that the deficiency of an analysis of the libretto alone, such as Könneker gives, becomes apparent: a final interpretation of the *Vorspiel* must take the music into account.

iii. *Concluding Remarks on the* Vorspiel

The revised version of *Ariadne auf Naxos: Oper in einem Aufzuge nebst einem Vorspiel* had its première on 4 October 1916 at the K.K. Hof-Operntheater in Vienna under Franz Schalk.[58] It was not an immediate success but has grown steadily more popular. The *Vorspiel* itself, however, has always been appreciated in its own right. Whilst it is not independent enough to be performed without the *Oper* it is so distinctive

---

[56] Del Mar, p. 71.
[57] Del Mar, p. 72.
[58] See Appendix C.

and self-contained that it can earn praise regardless of whether or not the *Oper* finds favour.

Part of this distinctiveness lies with Strauss's neo-classical treatment of the chamber orchestra and his innovative use of recitatives. Recitative, being furthermore less formed or formal than aria, is a fitting musical mode for the backstage milieu of the *Vorspiel*. By seeming natural itself it suggests a certain realism which is in sharp contrast to the obvious art of the *Oper*. The lyrical episodes in the *Vorspiel* provide variety and give it a heterogeneous format which fits the variety of character and incident occurring in it.

The chamber orchestra is handled with great brilliance and imagination and the texture is always clear and sparkling. The pace is extremely rapid; episodes follow one another in dazzling succession, yet characterization is not sacrificed to technique. Gräwe aptly describes the *Vorspiel* as 'ein bizarres Impromptu, das Kulinarismus mit Ironie, schönen Schein mit jäher Ernüchterung, emphatischen Schwung mit Trockenheit verbindet'[59] (a bizarre impromptu that combines a culinary art with irony, beautiful appearance with sudden disenchantment, forceful verve with dryness). All in all, the *Vorspiel* is one of Strauss's and Hofmannsthal's most deft and most 'modern' creations. Drawing on the incidental music to *Der Bürger als Edelmann* which in its imitation of Lully and Couperin, its use of the early suite form, its reduction of orchestral resources and colours is pronouncedly neo-classical, Strauss went on to compose a neo-classical piece free from the unrestrained emotionalism of late Romanticism yet able to accommodate some passages of typically Straussian warmth and sentiment. The *Vorspiel* is the more remarkable in that it was completed two years before Prokofiev's Classical Symphony (1918) and four years before Stravinsky's ballet *Pulcinella* (1920), these works being commonly cited amongst the earliest examples of neo-classicism. Hofmannsthal's libretto with its reliance on variety of incident and type, its for him unusually loose and straightforward form, its lack of pretension and its value as theatre of entertainment rather than theatre of illusion made possible Strauss's new style.

[59] Gräwe, p. 319.

Ironically, plot and characters of a restricted, even stereotyped, nature make, as is so often the case, very good opera.

Strauss, who at first had not been enthusiastic about writing a prologue, was delighted with the results and came to set great store by them. He saw this new style as a way to develop beyond his previous 'Wagnerian' phase and wrote to Hofmannsthal early in September 1916 in connection with *Die Frau ohne Schatten:* 'Ihr Notschrei gegen das Wagnersche 'Musizieren' ist mir tief zu Herzen gegangen und hat die Tür zu einer ganz neuen Landschaft aufgestoßen, in der ich, von 'Ariadne' und besonders dem neuen Vorspiel geleitet, mich ganz ins Gebiet der unwagnerschen Spiel-, Gemüts- und Menschenoper zu begeben hoffe.' (Bw. early Sept. 1916 pp. 303–4.) (Your *cri-de-coeur* against Wagnerian 'note-spinning' has deeply touched my heart and has thrust open a door to an entirely new landscape where, guided by *Ariadne* and in particular the new Vorspiel, I hope to move forward wholly into the realm of un-Wagnerian emotional and human comic opera.) Hofmannsthal's experiment with set numbers and historical recreation had paid off this far; Hofmannsthal had in some ways anticipated the neo-classical libretto and had helped Strauss to break new ground, so leading him away from the 'Wagnerschen Musizierpanzer'. But the *Vorspiel* proved after all not to mark a radical change in Strauss's style. Instead, as Fähnrich has outlined, Strauss synthesized his neo-classical or 'Mozartian' style with his Romantic heritage.[60] Nevertheless the *Vorspiel* enabled Strauss to extend his language as a composer and Hofmannsthal might feel with some justification that he had guided his partner in matters of style and taste. Only with his last opera *Capriccio* (1942), written with Clemens Krauss, did Strauss return to a modified form of the *Vorspiel;* but the emphasis here is on 'modified' and one of the greatest similarities between the two works is that their plots are about artists and art.

Essentially then the merits of the *Vorspiel* are the results of the authors' economy: Strauss is sparing with his orchestration and Hofmannsthal does not saddle his characters with obscure psychological or metaphysical symbolism. But neo-classicism

[60] See Introduction, pp. 9–10.

could not be a lasting direction for Strauss and Hofmannsthal: sparseness and economy of that sort are modern virtues and this collaboration had its roots in the rich and generous soil of the nineteenth century. Furthermore many of the Vorspiel's virtues come from its being just that; a prologue, a lightweight, economical introduction. It was an interesting byway in the collaboration; it contains much that is beautiful; but it skirts the contentious artistic issues whereas the *Oper Ariadne auf Naxos* confronts them and discloses incidentally a great deal about the collaboration.

The *Vorspiel* is made relatively self-contained by the unifying presence of the young Composer who stands in the centre of the action and the symbolism. He is a delightful and gently satirical portrait of young genius and Strauss's interpretation of this character in the music is masterly. The Composer's fleeting affair with Zerbinetta is needed in the *Vorspiel* for a variety of reasons, not least as a way of fleshing out this youthful character. A single objection to this episode is that it introduces a note of sentimental pathos into Zerbinetta's otherwise ironically self-conscious character but this is perhaps a small loss compared with the musical and structural gains.

Within the 1916 version the Composer has the added function of acting as an ironic disclaimer for the admitted 'Länge' of his opera; these longueurs arise not only from static Baroque conventions but also from the theme of transformation. By making 'Verwandlung' the Composer's own pet theme Hofmannsthal can detach himself from it. Possibly an audience seeing *Ariadne* for the first time might among all the distractions forget that the *opera seria* has been written by the Composer. Nevertheless this ironic disclaimer adds to the many levels of irony in the 1916 version. The *Vorspiel* is itself a kaleidoscopic mixture of moods and incidents. Together the *Vorspiel* and the *Oper* present many shades of thematic, formal, and situational irony. Moreover the *Vorspiel,* as we saw in Chapter IV, allows us to view the *Oper,* with its juxtaposed styles and worlds, as a comment on the rich and complex unity of life. It seems fair to say that the 1916 *Ariadne auf Naxos* through its *Vorspiel* and the young Composer may appear to an audience familiar with this difficult work to possess a joyful, ironic unity, making its many internal problems and contradictions less significant. This may be seen as an advantage which the 1916 version has over the earlier *Ariadne,* in which there is a perturbing lack of artistic unity.

Conclusion

In conversation with Luden, Goethe is reported to have said: 'In der Poesie gibt es keine Widersprüche. Diese sind nur in der wirklichen Welt, nicht in der Welt der Poesie. Was der Dichter schafft, das muß genommen werden, wie er es geschaffen hat. So wie er seine Welt gemacht hat, so ist sie. Was der poetische Geist erzeugt, muß von einem poetischen Gemüt empfangen werden.'[1] (In poetry there are no contradictions. These exist only in the real world, not in the world of poetry. What the poet creates must be taken as he has created it. His world is as he has made it. What the poetic mind conceives must be received by a poetic soul.) Goethe is requiring of his reader or audience more than just a passive suspension of disbelief; the reader must bring his own poetic imagination to the task of appreciation. If in such a mood of creative receptivity we were to see either of the *Ariadne* versions for the first time, what might our impression be? No doubt both versions would delight our senses with their colourful variety, with the pellucid charm of the *commedia dell'arte* music and Zerbinetta's vocal display, with their contrasting moods and characters, and they might touch the heart in the love scenes between the Composer and Zerbinetta or Ariadne and Bacchus. The over-all impression would be of a light-hearted, superficial entertainment with a certain fragile, ironic beauty—a stage-world of fleeting impact. Certainly *Ariadne* would not seem to be a work fraught with contradictions; contradictions can exist only within a whole and to find any sort of unity in *Ariadne* is a task well beyond the poetic sensibility. The authors have not created 'eine Welt', certainly not one in the Goethean sense. In Romain Rolland's words, 'l'impression d'ensemble est une déception

[1] Heinrich Luden, *Rückblicke in mein Leben: Das Faustgespräch* (Berlin, 1916), p. 52.

. . . Point de parti décidé dans l'idée générale, le drame, le style musical'.[2] (The impression of an ensemble is deceptive . . . There is no definite direction in the over-all idea, the drama, the musical style.)

But since the aesthetic function in man strives for unity the audience suspects that the authors, or more specifically the librettist whose initial task it was, had 'eine Welt' in mind. If imagination fails, it is then up to the critical, analytic mind to establish what this world was. A genetic criticism makes it possible to see what historical, ironic, dramatic, and musical unities were envisaged for *Ariadne auf Naxos* and where and why the finished work fell short of its ideal form.

Yet although *Ariadne* lacks unity and is far surpassed in this respect by both *Elektra* and *Der Rosenkavalier*, compared with *Die Frau ohne Schatten* or *Die Ägyptische Helena* it is a more popular and in many ways a superior work. *Arabella*, which Hofmannsthal did not live to see completed, redeems the collaboration but has, as Del Mar says, suffered the stigma of being thought an inferior sequel to *Der Rosenkavalier*.[3] There is no doubt, however, that *Arabella* is the most unabashedly nostalgic and backward-looking of the entire six. *Ariadne* on the other hand is forward-looking in its neo-classical aspects although it was not the Mozartian number opera that Hofmannsthal had hoped for. Indeed some of its artistic weaknesses are those common to many neo-classical works; they arise from the attempt to put new wine into old bottles, and Strauss and Hofmannsthal clearly put too much new wine into *Ariadne*. Furthermore, the 1916 version, interpreted in the light of formal irony, has much in common with early twentieth-century avant-garde montage techniques employed by such authors as Eliot and Joyce and more recently perhaps by the composer Peter Maxwell Davies.[4] In short *Ariadne* has a number of positive aspects and these, as we have seen in

[2] Richard Strauss et Romain Rolland, *Correspondance, Fragments de Journal*, p. 172.

[3] Del Mar, p. 436.

[4] For example, in his *St. Thomas Wake: Foxtrot for Orchestra on a Pavan by John Bull* (1969) Peter Maxwell Davies plays with different styles and materials without parodying them. John Bull's pavan is juxtaposed and mixed with five foxtrots played by a small band in the orchestra. Peter Maxwell Davies's aesthetic play, his music through music, can be regarded as a late and abstract extension of formal irony.

examining the genesis, it owes to its interim, experimental nature.

On the negative side *Ariadne auf Naxos* is symptomatic of the weaknesses which beset the next two operas: parts of it are over-literary, artificially symbolic, undramatic, inflated, and self-consciously profound. These are the limitations of the moralizing phantasmagoria, *Die Frau ohne Schatten*, an opera overburdened with symbolic meaning, whose genesis imitates *Ariadne*'s to a disturbing degree. Once again it was to be an opera about allomatic transformation, this time in eleven scenes with a double transformation worked out between the two couples coming from an upper, spiritual, and a lower, earthly, sphere: 'Es sind elf bedeutende, fast pantomimisch prägnante Situationen—durch ihre Verbindung aber—indem in ihnen zwei Welten, zwei Menschenpaare, zwei Konflikte ineinander wechselweise sich ablösen, einander spiegeln, einander steigern und schließlich einander aufheben—, ist ein Ganzes hergestellt.' (Bw. 20 Jan. 1913, p. 182.) (There are eleven significant, almost pantomimically incisive situations, but it is their combination—in which two worlds, two pairs of beings, two interwoven conflicts take their turn, reflect each other, enhance each other and eventually find their equilibrium—which gives unity to the whole work.) But although *Die Frau ohne Schatten* began as a fairytale it became a rationally and eclectically constructed myth. Again the trouble started when Hofmannsthal wrote the libretto from the scenario. Too many ideas occurred to him and this time even Hofmannsthal had to recognize that they were not suitable for the stage. Instead he put the new material into an 'Erzählung' bearing the same title as the opera.[5] But this did not prevent the third act from becoming ever more psychologically abstruse and contrived. The effect of the libretto on Strauss was not inspirational:

The fact has to be faced that as in all Strauss's most pretentious and high-minded works, the often fine music contains much that is striking and memorable, something even that is touching, but also a considerable amount that is merely bombastic and, especially in the all-important moments of Transfiguration, distressingly banal. How else could it be when he became bogged down by the spurious

[5] Ez., pp. 254–375.

symbolism and endless insoluble intricacies of the extraordinary text? Not since *Zarathustra* had Strauss encountered a subject the philosophies of which he understood less, and *Zarathustra* had at least been his own choice for music treatment. It is ironic that Hofmannsthal should have planned such a work just when he had mapped out for Strauss a future modelled on Mozart and Offenbach.

The effect, so far from inspiring him to lighten his style, was on the contrary to pitchfork him into the creation of a music drama more heavily overladen with Wagnerian motifs and psychological cross-references than ever before.[6]

As in *Ariadne* it seems that Strauss Wagnerized where he found the libretto obscure or lifeless. Unfortunately, however, the initial plan to use a chamber orchestra for the ethereal world and a full orchestra for the human world came to nothing and *Die Frau ohne Schatten* lacks that contrasting lightness of touch which characterizes the comic sections of *Ariadne*. First performed in 1919, *Die Frau ohne Schatten* has met only limited success.

Shaken perhaps by the difficulties and disappointments of their third and fourth offspring Strauss and Hofmannsthal now let their operatic collaboration slide into an eight-year abeyance. After this time the subject which attracted them was the myth of Helen of Troy and her reconciliation with her husband Menelaus after the fall of Troy. Once again the opera began life as a light-hearted work—Hofmannsthal referred to it as an 'operetta'—and Strauss must have thought at once of Offenbach's *La Belle Hélène*. But Hofmannsthal grew serious and ambitious about his libretto and it turned into a complex dialectical piece for which he made researches into Bachofen's studies on myth and Strindberg's marital dramas. Particularly the second act of *Die Ägyptische Helena* suffers from Hofmannsthal's need to raise the level to something more rarefied and lyrical. Willi Schuh remarks on this, although with no critical intent, in his comment on the *Ariadne Szenarium*;

[Das Szenarium] läßt, obwohl einige wichtige Momente und Bezüge noch kaum angedeutet sind, und der spielerisch-leichte Ton eines Impromptus durchaus vorherrscht, doch bereits ahnen, daß die Dichtung sich schließlich—wie später die zuerst auch als 'Farce'

---

[6] Del Mar, p. 215.

angelegte 'Ägyptische Helena'—ins 'höhere Lyrische' werde erheben müssen.[7]

(Although several important moments and connections are as yet scarcely hinted at and the playfully light tone of an impromptu still predominates, it is foreshadowed in the Szenarium that the libretto will eventually climb to 'higher lyricism'—as did later the 'Ägyptische Helena', another libretto conceived as a 'farce'.)

Again the obscure passages in the text call forth Strauss's Wagnerian *durchkomponiert* style.[8] And the shift in emphasis in the opera from the comic to the high-minded again leaves some odd relics washed up on its shore: in this case a giant, all-knowing conch out of which a voice speaks distortedly as if through a telephone—an embarrassing object on stage in any but the most determined of operettas. *Die Ägyptische Helena*, first performed in 1928, has met with least success of all the Strauss–Hofmannsthal operas.

In three operas, then, the genesis followed a distinct pattern: Hofmannsthal took something originally light-hearted or ironical too seriously, jeopardized the form of the work and left his composer floundering and dissatisfied. Romain Rolland, ever perceptive and helpful, suggests that Strauss was incapable of sharing Hofmannsthal's kind of seriousness. The following quotation from a work written in 1924 refers to the two *Ariadnes* and *Die Frau ohne Schatten* but is equally applicable to *Die Ägyptische Helena*: 'Tous les pastiches: ce ne serait rien encore; mais Hofmannsthal, esclave de sa virtuosité, finit par les prendre au sérieux. Et Strauss ne le peut pas.'[9] (All the pastiches: they are of no account; but Hofmannsthal, slave to his virtuosity, ends up taking them seriously. And Strauss is not able to do that.)

The problem of *Ariadne*, *Die Frau ohne Schatten*, and *Die Ägyptische Helena* can be stated plainly: by 1911 Hofmannsthal

---

[7] Willi Schuh, 'Zu Hofmannsthals "Ariadne"-Szenarium und -Notizen', p. 85.

[8] See Del Mar, p. 317. Willy Haas, who is more sympathetic towards Hofmannsthal than Strauss and fails to see the limitations of this libretto as a comedy, gives a different account: '*Die Ägyptische Helena*, eines seiner besten Libretti, war als Komödie und Zauberspiel gedacht—Richard Strauss hat es durch seine pompöse wagnerianische Musik geschmacklos auf den Kopf gestellt, und Hofmannsthal, müde geworden und hilflos, protestierte nicht mehr.' Willy Haas, *Hugo von Hofmannsthal*, p. 29.

[9] Richard Strauss et Romain Rolland, *Correspondance, Fragments de Journal*, p. 173.

felt secure enough as a librettist to allow his poetic gifts greater freedom. In 1912 he even referred to the *Ariadne* libretto as his 'Gedicht'. But, as we have seen, Hofmannsthal's verse dramas are essentially undramatic. There is no doubt that Hofmannsthal experienced immense difficulty with dramatic forms; the endless revisions, for example of *Der Turm*, the fragments and even the Molière adaptations attest this.[10] Yet for Strauss an opera was a music drama: he might agree about 'prima la musica e dopo le parole' but he would never agree that the *drama* should stand in second place.[11] How Strauss must have welcomed Stefan Zweig's view of a good libretto: 'Ich halte eigentlich ... nur jenen Operntext [für gut], den man auch ohne Textbuch versteht—jeder andere, den man vorauslesen oder während der Musik mitlesen muß, will mir Belastung des Werkes, Zerspaltung der Aufmerksamkeit zu bedingen scheinen.'[12] (I consider ... only those libretti good, which one understands without a copy in one's hand—those, which one has to read beforehand or during the music, seem to me to encumber the work and to divide one's attention.)

Although Hofmannsthal was not a born dramatist—he once wrote to Strauss 'von uns beiden haben Sie, ganz abgesehen vom Maß der Begabung, den stärkeren dramatischen Instinkt' (Bw. 22 Dec. 1912, p. 178)—he was very much a man of the theatre with a finely developed instinct for what could be done on stage. Much of his work for the stage, including that which went into the *Salzburger Festspiele*, was shaped by the Austro–Bavarian Baroque ideal of 'Festlichkeit'. *Ariadne* profited from Hofmannsthal's love of theatre and of theatrical display. It is not surprising, then, to find Hofmannsthal writing to Borchardt of opera not as drama plus music but as 'Theater plus Musik'; should he not use this combination and 'hiebei sein Gedicht, versteht man nur, um was der Handel geht, vor

---

[10] For a sharp comment on Hofmannsthal's introspective bent, see H. F. Garten, *Modern German Drama* (London, 1959), pp. 75–6.
[11] For this reason suggestions that Strauss or Hofmannsthal fundamentally doubted or questioned the genre opera should be treated with extreme caution. Peter Conrad, for example, asserts that *Ariadne* is a 'disquisition on the operatic idea'. Peter Conrad, *Romantic Opera and Literary Form*, p. 6. Egon Vietta likewise falls for the idea of aesthetic self-reflection in *Ariadne* and speaks of 'die Zerstörung des Opernlibrettos durch die Reflexion'. Egon Vietta, 'Die Entstehung der "Ariadne"', p. 10.
[12] Richard Strauss / Stefan Zweig, *Briefwechsel*, p. 10.

wesentlichen Verzerrungen und Verschüttungen doch retten und ihm zugleich einen langen Bestand und wahrhafte Popularität sichern'?[13] (so long as the nature of the bargain was understood, to rescue his poem from distortions and from being buried alive and at the same time to assure it of a long life and true popularity). But success did not rush to greet the three libretti in which Hofmannsthal had not paid scrupulous attention to dramatic qualities. What Romain Rolland said of *Die Frau ohne Schatten* could equally have been said of the other two: 'le poème de Hoffmansthal [*sic*] affirme l'incapacité scénique de l'écrivain. Son obscure pensée traîne une ombre glacée. Elle pèse sur la passion.'[14] (Hofmannsthal's poem proves the writer's scenic inability. His obscure turn of mind casts an icy shadow and stifles passion.) By *Arabella* Hofmannsthal had learnt the lesson that a libretto is not a lyric drama and from his early story *Lucidor* built up a romantic drawing-room comedy with a number of lifelike characters. As Del Mar says, for the first time in seventeen years Strauss felt he understood exactly what the libretto was about and that he could contribute on an equal footing to a true joint effort.[15]

But clearly Hofmannsthal was not the only one to blame for the weaknesses of their collaboration: had Strauss stood his ground over the question of the too abstruse and undramatic texts, instead of setting them in a half-hearted manner, he might have helped his librettist to still greater things than their first two operas. But by not consistently demanding the highest, by giving Hofmannsthal the lead in matters of taste and fancy, Strauss also betrayed the collaboration. Strauss was a composer standing at the end of a tradition: his weakness was a tendency to write kitsch. How much greater a danger of this he ran by composing in a genre about which he himself could ask 'wo hört der Kitsch auf und wo beginnt die Oper?'[16]

Ariadne auf Naxos is important within the collaboration, then, because during its uniquely long and well-documented genesis these problems emerge for the first time. A critical account of the work's composition shows how the issues of the

[13] Hugo von Hofmannsthal / Rudolf Borchardt, *Briefwechsel*, p. 87.
[14] Richard Strauss et Romain Rolland, *Correspondance, Fragments de Journal*, p. 175.
[15] Del Mar, p. 389.
[16] Richard Strauss / Stefan Zweig, *Briefwechsel*, p. 87.

literary librettist and the too complaisant composer affected the final work. It appears that the geneses of *Die Frau ohne Schatten* and *Die Ägyptische Helena* followed the same course for the same reasons of dramatic insufficiency, but that is a suggestion which has yet to be worked out in detail. What is certain is that genetic criticism, although unlikely to be of use to collaborators on past or future 'Ariadnes', does give a better understanding both of what this particular opera claims to be and what has been claimed for it.

Appendix A

Hofmannsthal's Unpublished Notes

Note 1   Arbeit: alles künstlich, abgewonnen, gezüchtet.
Racine spielen, die Annäherung an Louis XIV.
Pyrrhus ein Prinz von Geblüt, Orest ein Herzog—
Das Gesicht des Schauspielers, nichts ist da,
alles strebt irgendwohin,
das Unpräcise das Beste an dieser Maske.

Decoration kleine Felsen wie Modelle für Nymphenburger
Porzellan, verbunden durch Guirlanden und dazwischen
Candelaber.

Note 2   *Ariadne*
Naiade, Echo, Dryade glauben gleichfalls, es gehe
ans Sterben.
(Ihnen ist Sterben ein Geheimnis, Untreue keines)
Ariadne glaubts bis zuletzt.
Ariadne, Bacchus: Er heißt sie Theseus vergessen.
Das scheint ihr begreiflich.
Doch will es nicht gelingen: im Gegenteil er
entzündet in ihr jegliche Erinnerung an Theseus.
So fleht sie: mach mich geschwind vergessen.
Das Motiv des Bacchus.
Nach dem Duett führt er sie einen kleinen Kreis um
die Bühne, als ob es schon im Totenreich wäre,
leise, geisterhaft: alles scheint ihr verändert:
Meer, Bäume, auch Echos Stimme.

Note 3   Nymphe: meldet von Bacchos. Chor jubelnd.
Ariadne: ablehnend.
Ein Schiff liegt in der Bucht, ein Einzelner
ist gelandet.
Er ist herrlich, ist unwiderstehlich.
Ariadne: in dumpfem Hinbrüten.
Bacchos Stimme: Wo ich nahe, wo ich lande—
Mannes Stimme, Raubtierstimme.

Ariadne: Es ist in mir. Es greift durch alle
Schmerzen. Es ist Auflösung aller Qual.
Es ist der Götterbote, der mich zu den Schatten holt.
Die Stimme weiter. Ariadne gelöst. Zu den Nymphen.
Chor leisest: Oh daß die Stimme weiter tönte.
Stimme schweigt, Ariadne erstarrt. Chor betrübt.
Stimme ertönt wieder. Ariadne gelöst, zu den Nymphen.
Töne töne schöne Stimme,
schöne Stimme töne wieder! Bacchos:
Deine Klagen sie beleben,
uns entzücken solche Lieder!
darauf entsetzt: Wer bin ich, wenn ich nochmals liebe?
O weh, er kommt hierher! o käm er nie!
O daß er käme!
Zerbinetta schmückt sie. Ariadnes Erwägungen für uns
gegen Schmuck. Bacchos *heftig* zieht die sich wehrende
mit sich: um Deiner Schmerzen willen.

Note 4   Hineinwühlen in den Schmerz. Fingiertes Gespräch
mit dem Abwesenden. Sag doch, du hast mich verachtet.
Sind Männer so anders als Frauen—nein, du bist tot!
gewiß!

Note 5   Die letzten drei Zeilen ad libitum zu wiederholen:
durch eine reizende, gaukelnde Stimmführung die
lächelnde Gleichgiltigkeit der Natur gegen menschliches
Leid ausdrückend. Etwas von Blätterschaukeln,
Wellengaukeln schon in der Overtüre.

Note 6   Alles bleibt bei dir. Die Schmerzen sind unsäglich.
Lust erfüllt dich ganz. Du meinst zu vergehen,
weil du anfängst zu leben.

Note 7   Alle die Schmerzen führen dich zu mir. (Baruzi II)
Die Schmerzen sind das große Wunder, mit den
Schmerzen warst immer bei mir.

Note 8   Sir fühlt sich selber nicht mehr rein. Sonst hätte
er sie nicht verlassen können. Ihr Reines ist
irgendwo anders. In einer Flamme.

Note 9   Ariadne Bacchus (Höhepunkt)
Ariadne: Du hast ein Schiff? Es nimmt mich mit!
Das Totenschiff—hinüber

Bacchus: Es gibt kein hinüber, es ist ein Bleiben,
ein Sinken zu tiefster Lust der Ewigkeit
—nun ahn ich was Circe mir getan

Ariadne: Alles leer—kein Verbundensein—gelöst
und ohne Trauer

Bacchus: Alles in Fülle—verwandelnd verwandelt
dunkeläugige Lust.

Appendix B

The *Szenarium* and Two Notes to *Ariadne auf Naxos*

[SZENARIUM] (1911)

[Durchgestrichen:] (Die Musiker möchte Reinhardt
gern auf der Bühne haben, – womöglich – mit dem
Capellmeister am Spinett)

Die Bühne aufgestellt in Jourdains großem Saal. Anstatt der
Coulissen abwechselnd Orangenbäumchen in Kübeln und Cande-
laber mit brennenden Kerzen. In der Mitte eine künstliche
Höhle/Grotte aus Pappendeckel aber architectonisch schön, im
Poussin'schen Stil.

Die heroischen Figuren		Die Figuren des Intermezzo	
Ariadne	*Alt**	Zerbinetta	*Coloratur*
der Fremdling (Bacchos)		Arlekin	*Bariton*
	lyrischer Tenor	Scaramuccio	*Tenor*
Naiade	*Sopran*		4 Männer
Dryade	*Sopran*	Brighella	*Baß*
Echo		Truffaldin	*Baß*

durchaus edel, im Stil
der Louis XIV-Antike

Figuren der commedia
dell'arte in Callot's
Manier, bunt, grotesk.

Bacchos   lyrischer Tenor (Spieltenor) [*Durchgestrichen:*]
oder Alt??

*[Die Besetzungsangaben sind von Strauss' Hand.]

Scenarium für Ariadne auf Naxos

[von Strauss' Hand.]
a = c
Einleitung melancholisch Gmoll, dann
b leidenschaftlich/Tränen pizzicati/
Bratsche Meereswogen

Ariadne vor ihrer Höhle.
Naiade links vorne an den Stufen des Podiums gelagert.
(Dort eine Andeutung der Meereswellen aus bläulichem Silberstoff.)
Dryade rechts vorne an eines der Orangenbäumchen gelehnt.
Echo rückwärts halbverborgen an die Höhle geschmiegt.
Zerbinetta, Arlekin, Brighella, Truffaldin, Scaramuccio außerhalb
der Bühne postiert, hinter den Bäumchen, gucken gleichsam
zwischen den Coulissen hervor.
Introduction.   Dann: Naiade, Dryade, Echo.
    Naiade: Sie schläft!
    Dryade: Sie weint!
    Zu dreien: Ariadne!

(eine kurze Scene)

Ariadne (richtet sich auf) Große Klage der Verlas-   *Recitativ u.*
senen, pathetisch aber ganz einfach und zum Herzen   *Arie**
gehend. Nicht leben – nicht sterben – jammervoll.
Naiade – Dryade – Echo: leise, discret mischen sich
ein, nehmen manches auf. Sie wissen daß sie hier zu
trösten unvermögend sind.

Die italienischen Figuren, zwischen den Coulissen
hervor, sprechen ihr Bedauern über den Gemütszu-
stand der Dame aus.
Arlekin versucht es mit einem Liedchen.   *Lied*

Ariadne scheint seiner gar nicht zu achten.
Echo wiederholt leise den Refrain seines leichtfertig
tröstlichen Liedchens.

Ariadne achtet es nicht, starrt vor sich hin. Stille
(absolute Stille: ein paar Zwischenbemerkungen der
Zuschauer: Hoffnung, daß diese Verlaßne doch
irgendwie werde Trost annehmen) *Intermezzo*: Zer-

---

*[Die kursiv gesetzten Marginalien, die sich auf die musikalische Formgestaltung
beziehen, sind von Strauss' Hand.]

binetta und ihre 4 Begleiter besteigen von vorne die Bühne und präsentieren sich Ariadne. Sie aufzuheitern, unternehmen sie einen Tanz. (Furlana) grotesk-charakteristisch.

Ariadne achtet es nicht, sieht über sie hinweg wie über leere Luft.

Die 4 Männer treten bei Seite.

Zerbinetta nähert sich Ariadne, sucht sich einzuschmeicheln. Sir verstünde zu trösten. Auch ihrem Herzen sei Kummer des Verlassenwerdens nicht fremd. Den Brief eines nie vergessenen Ungetreuen (ihres *ersten* Liebhabers) trage sie immer am Herzen. Zieht ihn hervor, schickt sich an, ihn vorzulesen. Ariadne, belästigt, erhebt sich lautlos, (dies in Bewegungsteile zerlegen) geht in die Grotte. Zerbinetta wagt es nicht ihr nachzugehen, bleibt am Eingang der Grotte stehen und liest (= singt) den Brief des Ungetreuen. Sie ist zu Ende. Ariadne gibt keinen Laut, kein Zeichen. *Arie. Variationen mit Coloraturen*

Zerbinetta: solche Untreue hat mein Herz erlitten. Bin ich nicht wert, Ihre Freundin zu werden? Die 4 Männer geben Zeichen der Ungeduld. Sie wollen Zerbinetta von der Grotte weghaben. »Laß das undankbare Geschäft, eine Verzweifelte zu trösten. Komm mit mir. *Männerquartett*

(Jeder: mit mir – mit mir – mit mir.)

Arlekin: sieh die Insel! sieh die Früchte

Scaramuccio: sieh die Blumen! die Rasenplätze

Arlekin: Genieße sie mit mir!

jeder: mit mir!

Zerbinetta findet an jedem der 4 etwas unwiderstehliches. Einen sanft, einen wild, einen hoheitsvoll, einen feurig. Keinem kann sich ihr Herz ganz entziehen. Sie wundert sich über ihr eigenes Herz, das immer Vorsätze der Treue, der Enthaltsamkeit macht und sie so wenig zu halten weiß. Die 4 Männer schlüpfen jeder wo anders von der Bühne herunter, sie drückt jedem die Hand, verspricht sich jedem, schlüpft endlich dem Arlekin nach, wird mit diesem unsichtbar. Die 3 andern Männer kommen vorne an die Bühne geschlichen, jeder für sich. Jeder meint, ihm sei die Schäferstunde zugedacht, endlich, zu dreien entdecken sie den Betrug, ärgern sich, *Ensemble; Zerb. mit Männerquartett*

Terzett

tanzend, tanzen ab, auf später sich vertröstend. Dies
alles in größter Knappheit.
(Ende des Intermezzos.)
(Nicht zu vergessen, daß die 4 *groteske* Gestalten
sind: Arlekin ein Gauner, Brighella ein Tölpel,
Scaramuccio ein Charlatan und Truffaldin ein
grotesker Alter.)
(während ihres Abtanzens ist Gelegenheit für ein
paar Zwischenbemerkungen der Zuschauer)
[Nachträglich von Hofmannsthal mit Bleistift ein-
gefügte Zwischenbemerkungen:]
Klatsch über Bacchus Herkunft und erstes Abenteuer: Knabenhaft, Sohn einer Königstochter die
starb von Nymphen aufgezogen!
(zu dreien wie hübsch) Gespräch: Die Hauptsache
wäre etwas mager Jourdain: ich hab die Hauptsache
nicht mager gefunden.

Die Naiade, die während des vorigen verschwunden *Beginn des*
war, tritt wieder auf und meldet: *Finales, fort-*
Seit heute nacht liege ein fremdartiges Schiff in der *laufend*
Bucht vor Anker, *fremdartige Musik* ertöne von
Bord, nur einer sei gelandet, ein Herrlicher Unwi-
derstehlicher! sicherlich ein Gott, Delphine hüpfen
empor, ihn zu sehen, die Thiere des Waldes folgen
ihm bezaubert! hörst du was ich melde, Ariadne?
Das Echo: Hörst du, Ariadne!
Ariadne tritt aus der Grotte, steht in dumpfem
Hinbrüten. Bacchos' Stimme unsichtbar: lockend,
werbend.
Ariadne erschreckt und doch beglückt. Fragt sich ob
es Hermes der Götterbote sei, der komme, sie ins
ersehnte Todtenreich zu führen.
Die Stimme abermals.
Ariadne, jedesmal, solange die Stimme tönt, gelöst,
sobald die Stimme schweigt, aufs neue erstarrend.
Die Stimme schweigt.
Naiade, Dryade, Echo, leisest, äußern ihre Betrübniß
Die Stimme ertönt wieder.
Ariadne gelöst bewegt. Ariadne und die Stimme *Duett während*
zunächst mehrmals alternierend, dann auch zugleich *der hymnen-*
Zerbinetta herein. Spiel und Singscene Ariadne *artigen Musik*
des heran-

Zerbinetta ohne daß die schon anbegonnene Steige-   *schreitenden*
rung in der Hauptlinie dadurch verloren geht.   *Bacchus*
Zerbinetta ganz erregt über den schönen götterhaften
Fremdling der sich auf Schlangenpfaden, seines
Zieles aber sicher, Ariadnes Grotte nähere.
Ariadne bestürzt, ratlos, Hält daran fest: wer sie zu
suchen komme könne nur Hermes sein, der
Todtenführer
Zerbinetta, zofenhaft zudringlich, bemüht Ariadne
zu schmücken, zu putzen Ariadne läßt es geschehen,
als sei es für den Tod. Zerbinetta findet, Ariadnes
Herz klopfe höchst lebendig, ihr Auge glänze
unvergleichlich.
Triumphierendes Heranschreiten (nun in der Musik)   *Abschluß der*
Bacchos *steht da.*   *Hymne*
Zerbinetta die Naiade die Dryade ziehen sich unter
tiefen Verneigungen zurück. Echo hat sich versteckt
Ariadne und Bacchos, einander gegenüber, ganz wie
ein König und eine Prinzessin.
Zartes Liebesgespräch (noch nicht eigentliches
Duett)
[am Rand:] entfernt im Stil Marschallin-Quinquin   *Beginn des*
Sie bittet ihn, ihm die honneurs ihrer Grotte machen   *Liebesduetts*
zu dürfen. Er folgt ihr hinein. Das eigentliche
Liebesduett ertönt nun aus der Grotte.
[Am Rand, mit Bleistift:] Zerbinetta (ad spectatores)
Wie wir es sagten ist es gekommen. Naiade – Dryade
– Echo fallen ein. Desgleichen fallen allmählich
Zerbinetta und ihre 4 Anbeter in den allgemeinen
Jubel ein. Zerbinetta tanzt mit Arlekin, Brighella
mit der Naiade, Truffaldin mit der Dryade, Scara-
muccio mit Echo, sie umtanzen einmal die Bühne,
dann treten Bacchos und Ariadne aus der Höhle
hervor, er führt sie an der Hand, allgemeines
Abgehen, dem sich die Zuschauer anschließen.

[Notizen I]

[Die beiden folgenden Sätze durchgestrichen:]
Ariadne zerstückelten Sinnes verwildert wie ein scheus Thier. Sie
liegt starr an der Erde, die drei Nymphen tanzen einen sanften
traurigen Tanz um sie.
Toll, aber klug!

[Durchgestrichen:]
Als die 5 sich ihr aufdrängen: hält die beide Hände vor die Augen,
solche Fratzen ihrer verstörten Phantasie nicht zu sehen.

Die drei Nymphen mit Smeraldina eifrig bemüht, sie zu schmücken
durch Anhauch wie die homerischen Götter.
Man bringt aus der Höhle das Goldschimmernde Oberkleid.
(orientalisch, blumenbestickt, mit Agraffe. Stirnreif)
Ariadnes schreckhaftes sich entziehen wollen.
Ariadne zu Bacchus
schnell mein Herz bring es hinüber, wo es keiner Anfechtung mehr
ausgesetzt ist.

Vorspiel: siehe Mozart. Verkehr mit Sängerinnen

Ceremonie Höflichkeit
Anreden bei Shakespeare
steife Handwerksbräuche
zarteste Convention:
Haltung. Ermöglichung
mit einer Neigung unend-
lich
viel zu geben. Da
sich das Leben dem
concreten Geben versagt.
Ceremoniel der Tänzerin
Sie gibt was nur sie
geben kann.
Tanzmeister im Vorspiel

Ariadne bz. Bacchus Ton:

Gewiß ein Heiliges wohnt in dieser
Brust
verborgen und bewegt die stille Luft
daß sie ihm Zeugnis gebe –

Comus

Wie lieblich gleitet dieses auf den
Flügeln
des Schweigens durch die hochge-
wölbte Nacht
und streichelt sanft der Finsternis ihr
Federkleid
bis daß sie lächelt

So süße Bürgschaft wacher Seligkeit
vernahm ich nie zuvor. Heil fremdes
Wunder!

[*Notizen II*]

28. V. 1911

Ariadne auf Naxos
Divertissement in einem Aufzug
zu spielen nach dem ›Bürger als Edelmann‹ des Molière
von
Hugo von Hofmannsthal
Musik v. Richard Strauss

Es ist Bacchus erste Ausreise. Noch wird seine Gottheit bezweifelt.

Sein erstes Abenteuer war Circe, deren Macht an ihm versagte. Ein Grauen vor dem Verwandeltwerden hat ihm das Herz versengt. Daß er die Macht habe, zu verwandeln, zu erwecken ist eine ihm noch ungethane Erfahrung.

Sein Lied, ehe er auftritt ist Furcht vor Circe. Neue Insel, neues Leben –

Najade berichtet: von Circes Insel. Die Befreiten seine Gefährten: er entzaubert sie zum Theil*.

Echo weiß noch mehr zu erzählen: er ist es an dem Circes Kunst zu schanden geworden. Er ist sicherlich ein Gott.

Schluß: abgehen aufs Schiff. Die 4 (Arlekin etc.) jubeln voraustanzend: Auf nach *Cythere*.

* zum Teil, doch nicht sogleich. Tierhaftes bleibt an ihnen

Reproduced from Hugo von Hofmannsthal, *Gesammelte Werke in zehn Einzelbänden, Dramen V*, pp. 286–93.

Appendix C

The Playbills of the 1912 and 1916 Productions

The playbill of the 1912 production. (Both playbills are reproduced from Franz Hadamowsky's catalogue of the 1959 Hugo von Hofmannsthal exhibition. See Bibliography.)

ARIADNE AUF NAXOS

Oper in einem Aufzug · Musik von Richard Strauss

Zu spielen nach dem „Bürger als Edelmann" des Molière

Stuttgart, Königliches Hoftheater, Kleines Haus, 25. Oktober 1912

Gastspiel des Deutschen Theaters Berlin

Herr Jourdain, ein Bürger	Victor Arnold
Seine Frau	Rosa Bertens
Dorimene, eine Marquise . . .	Else Heims
Dorantes, ein Graf	Alfred Abel
Nicoline, Magd in Jourdains Haus .	Camilla Eibenschütz
Ein Musiklehrer	Jakob Tiedtke
Ein junger Komponist, dessen Schüler	Josef Dannegger
Ein Tanzmeister	Paul Biensfeldt
Ein Fechtmeister	Eckert
Ein Magister der Philosophie . .	Blümner
Ein Schneider	Ernst Matray
1. Geselle	Leo van Marken
2. Geselle	Max Schliebener
3. Geselle	Albert Burger
4. Geselle	Zimmermann
Sein 1. Gessell . . . . . }	
Ein Küchenjunge . . . . . }	Grete Wiesenthal
1. Sängerin	Marga Junker-Burchardt
2. Sängerin	Erna Ellmenreich
3. Sängerin	Lilly Hoffmann-Onegin
Der 1. Lakai	Elise Hoetzel
Der 2. Lakai	Richard Sterneck
Ein kleiner Lakai	Wenzel Mine
Ariadne	Maria Jeritza
Bacchus	Hermann Jadlowker
Najade	Marga Junker-Burchardt
Dryade	Lilly Hofmann-Onegin

Echo	Erna Ellmenreich
Zerbinetta	Margarete Siems
Harlekin	Albin Swoboda
Scaramuccio	Georg Meader
Truffaldin	Reinhold Fritz
Brighella	Franz Schwerdt
Maitre d'Hotel	Artur Anwander

Regie: Max Reinhardt

The playbill of the 1916 production

ARIADNE AUF NAXOS
(Neue Bearbeitung)

Oper in einem Aufzug nebst einem Vorspiel

Musik von Richard Strauss

Wien, K. K. Hof-Operntheater, 5 November 1916

Der Haushofmeister	August Stoll
Der Musiklehrer	Hans Duhan
Der Komponist	Lotte Lehmann
Der Tenor	Bela von Környey
Ein Offizier	Anton Arnold
Ein Tanzmeister	Georg Maikl
Ein Perückenmacher	Gerhard Stehmann
Ein Lakai	Viktor Madin
Zerbinetta	Selma Kurz
Primadonna (Ariadne)	Charlotte Dahmen
Harlekin	Gustav Neuber
Scaramuccio	Hermann Gallos
Truffaldin	Julius Betetto
Brighella	Adolf Nemeth

Personen der Oper:

Ariadne	Charlotte Dahmen
Bacchus	Bela von Környey
Najade	Berta Kiurina
Dryade	Hermine Kittel
Echo	Carola Jovanovics
Zerbinetta	Selma Kurz
Harlekin	Hans Duhan
Scaramuccio	Hermann Gallos
Truffaldin	Julius Betetto
Brighella	Georg Maikl

Spielleitung: Wilhelm v. Wymetal

Select Bibliography

Primary:

Hirsch, Rudolf, 'Auf dem Weg zu "Ariadne": Aus neugefundenen Briefen mitgeteilt', *Neue Zürcher Zeitung*, 15 Nov. 1970, p. 49.

Hofmannsthal, Hugo von, *Ariadne auf Naxos*, in *Gesammelte Werke*, Volume III, *Lustspiele III*, ed. Herbert Steiner (Frankfurt am Main, 1956), pp. 7–162.

Hofmannsthal, Hugo von, '"Ariadne auf Naxos" -Szenarium und -Notizen', *Die Neue Rundschau*, 71 (1960), pp. 91–7.

Reinhardt, Max. *Ariadne auf Naxos: Regiebuch* (Berlin, Paris, 1913).

Stern, Ernst. *Skizzenbuch von 1912: Notizen für Bühnenbild und Kostüme zu "Ariadne auf Naxos"* (Berlin, Paris, 1912).

Correspondence:

Hofmannsthal, Hugo von, 'Aus Briefen an Rudolf Pannwitz', *Mesa*, 5 (1955), pp. 20–42.

Hofmannsthal, Hugo von/Eberhard von Bodenhausen, *Briefe der Freundschaft*, ed. Dora Freifrau von Bodenhausen (Düsseldorf, 1953).

Hofmannsthal, Hugo von/Rudolf Borchardt, *Briefwechsel*, ed. Marie Luise Borchardt and Herbert Steiner (Frankfurt a.M., 1954).

Hofmannsthal, Hugo von/Rudolf Borchardt, 'Unbekannte Briefe', ed. Werner Volke, *Jahrbuch der Deutschen Schillergesellschaft*, 8 (1964), pp. 19–32.

Strauss, Richard, *Eine Welt in Briefen* (Tutzing, 1967).

Strauss, Richard/Hugo von Hofmannsthal, *Briefwechsel: Gesamtausgabe*, ed. Willi Schuh, fourth edn. (Zurich, 1970).

Strauss, Richard/Hugo von Hofmannsthal, *A Working Friendship: The Correspondence between Richard Strauss and Hugo von Hofmannsthal*, trans. Hanns Hammelmann and Ewald Osers.

Strauss, Richard/Romain Rolland, *Correspondance, Fragments de Journal*, Cahiers Romain Rolland, 3 (Paris, 1951).

Strauss, Richard/Stefan Zweig, *Briefwechsel*, ed. Willi Schuh (Frankfurt am Main, 1957).

Secondary:

Baumann, Gerhart, 'Hugo von Hofmannsthal: "Elektra"', *German-isch-Romanische Monatsschrift*, 9 (1959), pp. 157–82.

Baur-Heinhold, Margarete, *Theater des Barock: Festliches Bühnen-spiel im 17. und 18. Jahrhundert* (Munich, 1966).

Beau, Albin Eduard, 'Hofmannsthals Wendung zur Oper', *Libris et Litteris: Festschrift für Hermann Tiemann zum 60. Geburtstag*, eds. Christian Voigt and Erich Zimmermann (Hamburg, 1959), pp. 318–24.

Beecham, Sir Thomas, *A Mingled Chime: Leaves from an Autobiog-raphy* (London, 1949).

Brecht, Walter, 'Hugo von Hofmannsthals "Ad me ipsum" und seine Bedeutung', *Jahrbuch des Freien Deutschen Hochstifts*, 7 (1930), pp. 319–53.

Broch, Hermann, 'Hofmannsthal und seine Zeit' in *Hermann Broch: Kommentierte Werkausgabe*, Volume IX, Schriften zur Literatur *1: Kritik*, ed. Paul Michael Lützeler (Frankfurt am Main, 1975), pp. 111–284.

Burckhardt, Carl J., 'Erinnerungen an Hofmannsthal' in *Hugo von Hofmannsthal: Der Dichter im Spiegel der Freunde*, ed. Helmut A. Fiechtner (Bern, 1963).

Burger, Hilde, 'French Influences on Hugo von Hofmannsthal' in *Comparative Literature*, ed. Werner P. Friedrich, Proceedings of the Second Congress of the International Comparative Literature Association (Chapel Hill, 1959).

Çakmur, Belma, *Hofmannsthals Erzählung 'Die Frau ohne Schatten'*, Studien zu Werk und Innenwelt des Dichters, 85 (Ankara, 1952).

Cohn, Hilde D., 'Hofmannsthals Libretti', *German Quarterly*, 35 (1962), pp. 149–64.

Conrad, Peter, *Romantic Opera and Literary Form* (Berkeley, 1977).

Daviau, Donald G. and George J. Buelow, *The 'Ariadne auf Naxos' of Hugo von Hofmannsthal and Richard Strauss*, University of North Carolina Studies in the Germanic Languages and Literatures, 80 (North Carolina, 1975).

Del Mar, Norman, *Richard Strauss: A Critical Commentary on his Life and Works*, 3 vols. (London, 1969), II.

Diebold, Bernhard, 'Die ironische "Ariadne" und der "Bürger als Edelmann"', *Die deutsche Bühne I: Jahrbuch der Frankfurter Städtischen Bühnen* (1919), pp. 218–20.

Duchartre, Pierre-Louis, *La Commedia dell'Arte et ses Enfants* (Paris, 1915).

Einstein, Alfred, 'Strauss und Hofmannsthal', in *Von Schütz bis Hindemith* (Zürich, 1957).

Erken, Günther, 'Hofmannsthals dramatischer Stil: Untersuchungen zur Symbolik und Dramaturgie', *Hermaea*, 20 (Tübingen, 1967).

Erwin, Charlotte E., 'Richard Strauss's *Ariadne auf Naxos*; An Analysis of Musical Style based on a Study of Revisions' (unpublished doctoral dissertation, Yale University, 1976).

Fähnrich, Hermann, 'Das "Mozart-Wagner-Element" im Schaffen von Richard Strauss', *Schweizerische Musikzeitung*, 99 (1959), pp. 311–16.

Federhofer, Hellmut, 'Retrospektive Elemente in Dichtung und Musik der Oper "Ariadne auf Naxos" von Hugo von Hofmannsthal und Richard Strauss', *Musikerziehung*, 12 (1958–9), pp. 75–9.

Félibien, André, *Relation de la Feste de Versailles: Du 18. Juillet mil six cens soixante-huit* (Paris, 1679).

Fiedler, Leonard M., 'Hofmannsthal, Reinhardt und Molière' *Hofmannsthal—Forschungen*, 1 (1957), pp. 48–58.

Fiedler, Leonard M., *Hugo von Hofmannsthals Molière-Bearbeitungen: Die Erneuerung der comédie-ballet auf Max Reinhardts Bühnen* (Darmstadt, 1974).

Fiedler, Leonard M., *Max Reinhardt und Molière: Text- und Bilddokumentation* (Salzburg, 1972).

Friedmann, Lilith, 'Die Gestaltungen des Ariadne-Stoffes von der Antike bis zur Neuzeit' (unpublished doctoral dissertation, University of Vienna, 1933).

Fuhrich-Leisler, Edda, *Hugo von Hofmannsthal auf dem Theater seiner Zeit: Katalog der Ausstellung* (Salzburg, 1974).

Gilbert, Mary E., ed., *Hofmannsthal: Selected Essays* (Oxford, 1955).

Gossman, Lionel, *Men and Masks: A Study of Molière* (Baltimore, 1963).

Görlich, Gustav, 'Aus der Werkstatt des Librettisten', *Musikleben*, 6 (1953), pp. 31–4.

Gräwe, Karl Dietrich, 'Sprache, Musik und Szene in "Ariadne auf Naxos" von Hugo von Hofmannsthal und Richard Strauss' (unpublished doctoral dissertation, Ludwig-Maximilians University, Munich, 1969).

Haas, Willy, *Hugo von Hofmannsthal*, Köpfe des XX Jahrhunderts, 34 (Berlin, 1964).

Hadamowsky, Franz, *Ausstellung Hugo von Hofmannsthal: Katalog* (Salzburg, 1959).

Hamburger, Michael, *Hofmannsthal: Three Essays* (Princeton, 1972).

Hamburger, Michael, 'Hofmannsthals Bibliothek: Ein Bericht', *Euphorion*, 55 (1960), pp. 15–76.

Holländer, Hans, 'Hugo von Hofmannsthal als Opernlibrettist', *Neue Zeitschrift für Musik*, 96 (1929), pp. 551–4.

Jens, Walter, *Hofmannsthal und die Griechen* (Tübingen, 1955).

Kenkel, Konrad, 'Die Funktion der Sprache bei Hofmannsthal vor und nach der Chandos-Krise', *Texte und Kontexte*, 11 (1973), pp. 89–101.

Kennedy, Michael, *Richard Strauss*, The Master Musicians Series (London, 1976).

Kierkegaard, Sören, 'Die Stadien des Unmittelbar-Erotischen oder Das Musikalisch-Erotische', in *Entweder-Oder*, tr. Christoph Schrempf (Leipzig, 1941).

Könneker, Barbara, 'Die Funktion des Vorspiels in Hofmannsthals "Ariadne auf Naxos"', *Germanisch-Romanische Monatsschrift*, 12 (1972), pp. 124–41.

Knaus, Jakob, *Hofmannsthals Weg zur Oper: 'Die Frau ohne Schatten'* (Berlin, New York, 1971).

Krause, Ernst, *Richard Strauss: Gestalt und Werk* (Leipzig, 1955).

Krüger, Karl-Joachim, *Hugo von Hofmannsthal und Richard Strauss* (Berlin, 1935).

Leisler, Edda and Gisela Prossnitz, eds., *Max Reinhardt und die Welt der Commedia dell'arte: Text- und Bilddokumentation* (Salzburg, 1970).

Lenz, Eva-Maria, *Hugo von Hofmannsthals mythologische Oper 'Die ägyptische Helene'*, *Hermaea*, 29 (Tübingen, 1972).

Mann, William, *Richard Strauss: A Critical Study of the Operas* (London, 1964).

Marek, George R., *Richard Strauss: The Life of a Non-Hero* (London, 1967).

Mauser, Wolfram, 'Hofmannsthal und Molière', *Innsbrucker Beiträge zur Kulturwissenschaft*, 20 (Innsbruck, 1964), pp. 3–16.

Mayer, Hans, 'Hugo von Hofmannsthal und Richard Strauss', in *Ansichten zur Literatur der Zeit* (Hamburg, 1962), pp. 9–32.

Meyer-Sichting, Gerhard, 'Von Lucidor zu Arabella: Hofmannsthals Libretto-Arbeit', *Neues Forum*, 15 (1957/58), pp. 228–32.

Mic, Constant, *La Commedia dell'arte ou le Théâtre des Comédiens italiens des XVIe, XVIIe et XVIIIe Siècles* (Paris, 1915).

Miles, David H., *Hofmannsthal's Novel 'Andreas': Memory and Self* (Princeton, 1972).

Monnier, Philippe, *Venise au XVIIIe siècle* (Paris, 1907).

Mühlher, Robert, 'Hugo von Hofmannsthals Oper "Ariadne auf Naxos"', *Interpretationen zur österreichischen Literatur*, 6 (1971), pp. 63–79.

Naef, Karl J., *Hugo von Hofmannsthal: Wesen und Werk* (Zurich, 1938).

Nicoll, Allardyce, *The World of Harlequin: A Critical Study of the Commedia dell'Arte* (Cambridge, 1963).

Oswald, Victor A. Jr., 'Hofmannsthal's Collaboration with Molière', *The Germanic Review*, 29 (1954), pp. 18–30.

Panofsky, Walter, *Richard Strauss: Partitur eines Lebens* (Munich, 1965).

Pantle, Sherrill Hahn, *'Die Frau ohne Schatten' by Hugo von Hofmannsthal and Richard Strauss: An Analysis of Text, Music and their Relationship* (Berne, Frankfurt/M., Las Vegas, 1978).

Politzer, Heinz, 'Hofmannsthal und die Oper', *Forum*, 2 (1955), pp. 282–4.

Polower, Genie Edith, 'Hofmannsthal as Librettist' (unpublished doctoral dissertation, Rutgers University, 1976).

Pörnbacher, K., *Hugo von Hofmannsthal, Richard Strauss: Der Rosenkavalier: Interpretation* (Munich, 1964).

Quinault, Philippe, *Les fêtes de l'amour et de Bacchus: Pastorale de Quinault: Musique de Lully* (Paris, 1784).

Rolland, Romain, *Histoire de L'Opéra en Europe avant Lully et Scarlatti* (Paris, 1931).

Rösch, Ewald, *Die Komödien Hofmannsthals: Die Entfaltung ihrer Sinnstruktur aus dem Thema der Daseinsstufen* (Marburg, 1963).

Rosenzweig, Alfred, 'Les adaptations de Lulli et de Couperin par Richard Strauss', *La Revue Musicale*, 7 (1926), pp. 33–47.

Schaeder, Grete, *Hugo von Hofmannsthal: Die Gestalten* (Berlin, 1933).

Schaeder, Grete, *Hugo von Hofmannsthal und Goethe* (Hameln, 1947).

Schäfer, Rudolf H., *Hugo von Hofmannsthals 'Arabella'* (Bern, 1967).

Schmitz, Eugen, 'Die Neubearbeitung der Ariadne auf Naxos', *Hochland*, 15 (1918), pp. 718–20.

Schuh, Willi, *Der Rosenkavalier: Vier Studien* (Olten, 1968).

Schuh, Willi, *Hugo von Hofmannsthal und Richard Strauss: Legende und Wirklichkeit* (Munich, 1964).

Schuh, Willi, *Über Opern von Richard Strauss* (Zurich, 1947).

Schuh, Willi, 'Zu Hofmannsthals "Ariadne auf Naxos" -Szenarium und -Notizen', *Die Neue Rundschau*, 71 (1960), pp. 84–90.

Smith, Patrick J., *The Tenth Muse: A Historical Study of the Opera Libretto* (London, 1971).

Specht, Richard, *Richard Strauss und sein Werk* (Leipzig, 1921).

Steingruber, Elisabeth, *Hugo von Hofmannsthals Sophokleische Dramen* (Wintherthur, 1956).

Stenberg, Peter A., 'Ariadne auf Naxos', *Seminar*, 12 (Sept. 1976), pp. 192–3.

Stenberg, Peter A., 'Silence, Ceremony, and Song in Hofmannsthal's Libretti', *Seminar*, 11 (1975), pp. 209–24.

Stern, Ernst, *Bühnenbildner bei Max Reinhardt* (Berlin, 1955).

Stern, Martin, 'Eine heimliche Wagner-Karikatur', *Neue Zürcher Zeitung*, 29 Nov. 1959, p. 3.

Stiegele, Waltraud, 'Hugo von Hofmannsthals "Ariadne auf Naxos. Zu spielen nach dem Bürger als Edelmann des Molière": Entstehungsgeschichte und Metamorphosen' (unpublished doctoral dissertation, Ludwig-Maximilians University Munich, 1966).

Strauss, Richard, *Betrachtungen und Erinnerungen*, ed. Willi Schuh (Zurich, 1957).

Vietta, Egon, 'Die Entstehung der "Ariadne"', *Musikleben*, 7 (1954), pp. 8–11.

Volke, Werner, ed., *Hugo von Hofmannsthal: In Selbstzeugnissen und Bilddokumenten* (Hamburg, 1967).

Wachten, Edmund, 'Der einheitliche Grundzug der Strausschen Formgestaltung', *Zeitschrift für Musikwissenschaft*, 16 (1934), pp. 251–59.

Weber, Horst, *Hugo von Hofmannsthal: Bibliographie des Schrifttums 1892–1963* (Berlin, 1966).

Wellesz, Egon, 'Hofmannsthal und die Musik', in *Hugo von Hofmannsthal: Der Dichter im Spiegel der Freunde*, ed. Helmut A. Fiechtner, 2nd edn. (Bern, 1963), pp. 236–9.

Winder, Marianne, 'The Psychological Significance of Hofmannsthal's "Ariadne auf Naxos"', *German Life and Letters*, 15 (1961), pp. 100–9.

Index